A PEOPLE'S HISTORY OF CHRISTIANITY

CHRISTIAN
ORIGINS

A PEOPLE'S HISTORY OF CHRISTIANITY

Denis R. Janz
General Editor

Editorial Advisory Board

Sean Freyne, *Trinity College, Dublin*   **Elizabeth A. Clark,** *Duke University*
Susan Ashbrook Harvey, *Brown University*   **Bernard McGinn,** *University of Chicago*
Charles Lippy, *University of Tennessee, Chattanooga*   **Steven E. Ozment,** *Harvard University*
Rosemary Radford Ruether, *Pacific School of Religion*

Volume 1
CHRISTIAN ORIGINS
Richard A. Horsley, editor

Volume 2
LATE ANCIENT CHRISTIANITY
Virginia Burrus, editor

Volume 3
BYZANTINE CHRISTIANITY
Derek Krueger, editor

Volume 4
MEDIEVAL CHRISTIANITY
Daniel E. Bornstein, editor

Volume 5
REFORMATION CHRISTIANITY
Peter Matheson, editor

Volume 6
MODERN CHRISTIANITY TO 1900
Amanda Porterfield, editor

Volume 7
TWENTIETH-CENTURY GLOBAL CHRISTIANITY
Mary Farrell Bednarowski, editor

A PEOPLE'S HISTORY OF CHRISTIANITY

Volume 1

CHRISTIAN ORIGINS

RICHARD A. HORSLEY

Editor

FORTRESS PRESS

Minneapolis

CHRISTIAN ORIGINS
A People's History of Christianity, Volume 1

Cover image: The deceased Theotecnus in a tunic decorated with antelope, early Christian, fifth-century fresco. © The Art Archive / San Gennaro Catacombs, Naples, Italy / Dagli Orti (A).
Cover design: Laurie Ingram
Interior design: James Korsmo

Scripture quotations are from the New Revised Standard Version Bible, copyright © 1989 by the Division of Christian Education of the National Council of the Churches of Christ in the USA and used by permission.

Further materials on this volume and the entire series can be found online at www .peopleshistoryofchristianity.com.

Library of Congress Cataloging-in-Publication Data

Christian origins / Richard A. Horsley, editor.
    p.   cm. — (A people's history of Christianity ; v. 1)
   Includes bibliographical references and index.
   ISBN 0-8006-3411-X (alk. paper)
   1. Church history—Primitive and early church, ca 30–600. I. Horsley, Richard A. II. Series.
  BR160.C47 2005
  270.1—dc22   2005024482

Manufactured in Canada
09 08   4 5 6 7 8 9 10

CONTENTS

CONTRIBUTORS

Jorunn Jacobsen Buckley teaches in the Department of Religion, Bowdoin College. She is author of *The Mandaeans: Ancient Texts and Modern People* (Oxford, 2002) and *The Great Stem of Souls: Reconstructing Mandaean History* (Gorgias Press, 2005). Apart from Mandaean religion, her research focuses on Gnosticism and Hellenistic religions. Professor Buckley lives in West Bath, Maine.

Allen Dwight Callahan is Professor of New Testament at the Seminário Teológico Batista do Nordeste in Bahia, Brazil, and an ordained Baptist minister. He has also taught at Harvard Divinity School and Macalester College. A native of Philadelphia, Professor Callahan received his B.A. in Religion from Princeton University and M.A. and Ph.D. degrees in the study of Religion at Harvard University. He recently published *A Love Supreme: A History of the Johannine Tradition* (Fortress Press, 2005) and earlier wrote *Embassy of Onesimus: The Letter of Paul to Philemon* (TPI, 1997).

Warren Carter is Pherigo Professor of New Testament at Saint Paul School of Theology in Kansas City, Missouri. His research interests have focused on Matthew's Gospel and on ways in which the early Christian movement negotiated Roman power. He has published *Matthew and the Margins: A Socio-Political and Religious Reading* (Orbis, 2000); *Matthew and Empire: Initial Explorations* (Trinity Press International, 2001); *Pontius Pilate: Portraits of a Roman Governor* (Liturgical, 2003). Currently in press is *The New Testament and Negotiating the Roman World: An Essential Guide* (Abingdon, 2006), and *John: Storyteller, Evangelist, Interpreter* (Hendrickson, 2006). He is working on a book on John and the Roman empire.

Neil Elliott is Acquisitions Editor at Fortress Press. He holds a Ph.D. in biblical studies from Princeton Theological Seminary and has taught biblical studies and early Christian history at the College of St. Catherine, Metropolitan State University, and United Theological Seminary in the Twin Cities. He is author of *The Rhetoric of Romans: Argumentative Constraint and Strategy and Paul's "Debate with Judaism,"* JSNTSup 45 (Sheffield, 1990), and *Liberating Paul: The Justice of God and the Politics of the Apostle* (Orbis, 1994). An Episcopal priest, he is also a regular contributor to *The Witness* online.

Steven Friesen occupies the Louise Farmer Boyer Chair in Biblical Studies in the Classics Department of the University of Texas, Austin, where he moved in 2005 after teaching for many years at the University of Missouri, Columbia. He has published widely in both classics and biblical studies, and he is author of *Imperial Cults and the Apocalypse of John: Reading Revelation in the Ruins* (Oxford, 2001), and *Twice Neokoros: Ephesus, Asia, and the Cult of the Flavian Imperial Family,* Religions in the Graeco-Roman World 116 (Brill, 1993).

William R. Herzog II is the Sallie Knowles Crozer Professor of New Testament Interpretation at Colgate Rochester Crozer Divinity School. He is author of *Parables as Subversive Speech: Jesus as Pedagogue of the Oppressed* (1996), *Jesus, Justice and the Reign of God* (2000), and *Prophet and Teacher: An Introduction to the Historical Jesus* (2005), all from Westminster John Knox. Professor Herzog and his wife, Mary, live in Pittsford, New York, and have two college-age children, Dan and Catherine.

Richard A. Horsley is Distinguished Professor of Liberal Arts and the Study of Religion at the University of Massachusetts, Boston. His work has ranged widely, from ancient Galilee to contemporary religious and cultural themes. He is author of numerous influential books, including *Jesus and Empire* (Fortress Press, 2003), *The Message and the Kingdom* (with Neil Asher Silberman, Fortress Press, 2002), *Galilee: History, Politics, People* (TPI, 1995), *Jesus and the Spiral of Violence* (Fortress Press, 1992), and *Bandits, Prophets, and Messiahs* (Harper & Row, 1985).

Clarice J. Martin is Jean Picker Associate Professor of Philosophy and Religion at Colgate University in Hamilton, New York. Her teaching and research interests include the philosophies, religions, and cultures of the ancient Mediterranean world, Roman social history, and Africana women's religious history and thought. Her numerous publications include *Pentecost 2* (Fortress Press, 1996) and recently, "Polishing the Unclouded Mirror: A Womanist Reading of Revelation 18:13" in *From Every People and Nation:*

The Book of Revelation in Intercultural Perspective, David Rhoads, ed. (Fortress Press, 2005). She resides in Manlius, New York.

Carolyn Osiek is Professor of New Testament at Brite Divinity School, Fort Worth, Texas. President of the Society of Biblical Literature, and a past President of the Catholic Biblical Association, her previous books include *Shepherd of Hermas,* Hermeneia (Fortress Press, 1999), New Testament commentaries, and several influential works on family and women in early Christianity: *Families in the New Testament World: Households and House Churches* (with David L. Balch, Westminster John Knox, 1997), *Early Christian Families in Context* (edited with Balch, Eerdmans, 2003), and *A Woman's Place: House Churches in Earliest Christianity* (with Margaret Y. MacDonald and Janet H. Tulloch, Fortress Press, 2005). She is a Member of the Society of the Sacred Heart.

Raymond Pickett is Assistant Professor of New Testament at the Lutheran Seminary Program in the Southwest in Austin, Texas. He is the author of *The Cross in Corinth: The Social Significance of the Death of Jesus,* JSNTSup 145 (Sheffield, 1997). His research interests include exploring how New Testament texts shaped the identity and practice of communities of faith in the context of Greco-Roman society and in relation to early Judaism.

Barbara R. Rossing is Professor of New Testament at the Lutheran School of Theology at Chicago and an ordained pastor in the Evangelical Lutheran Church in America (ELCA). She earned her doctorate at Harvard University. Among her publications are *The Rapture Exposed: The Message of Hope in the Book of Revelation* (Westview, 2004) and *The Choice between Two Cities: Whore, Bride, and Empire in the Apocalypse,* Harvard Theological Studies (TPI, 1999). An avid environmentalist, Rossing is involved with environmental initiatives at the seminary.

Antoinette Clark Wire is Robert S. Dollar Professor of New Testament at San Francisco Theological Seminary, where she has taught since 1973. Dr. Wire is a graduate of Yale Divinity School and Claremont Graduate School. Raised in China by missionary parents, she has lived her adult life largely in California. Among her publications is *The Corinthian Women Prophets: A Reconstruction through Paul's Rhetoric* (Fortress Press, 1990), and her most recent book is *Holy lives, Holy Deaths: A Close Hearing of Early Jewish Storytellers* (Society of Biblical Literature, 2002).

ILLUSTRATIONS

Figures

FOREWORD

This seven-volume series breaks new ground by looking at Christianity's past from the vantage point of a people's history. It is church history, yes, but church history with a difference: "church," we insist, is not to be understood first and foremost as the hierarchical-institutional-bureaucratic corporation; rather, above all it is the laity, the ordinary faithful, the people. Their religious lives, their pious practices, their self-understandings as Christians, and the way all of this grew and changed over the last two millennia—*this* is the unexplored territory in which we are here setting foot.

To be sure, the undertaking known as people's history, as it is applied to secular themes, is hardly a new one among academic historians. Referred to sometimes as history from below, or grassroots history, or popular history, it was born about a century ago, in conscious opposition to the elitism of conventional (some call it Rankean) historical investigation, fixated as this was on the "great" deeds of "great" men, and little else. What had always been left out of the story, of course, was the vast majority of human beings: almost all women, obviously, but then too all those who could be counted among the socially inferior, the economically distressed, the politically marginalized, the educationally deprived, or the culturally unrefined. Had not various elites always despised "the people"? Cicero, in first-century BCE Rome, referred to them as "urban filth and dung"; Edmund Burke, in eighteenth-century London, called them "the swinish multitude"; and in between, this loathing of "the meaner sort" was almost universal among the privileged. When the discipline called "history" was professionalized in the nineteenth century, traditional gentlemen historians perpetuated this contempt if not by outright vilification, then at least by keeping the masses invisible. Thus, when people's history came on the scene, it was not only a means for uncovering an unknown dimension of the past but also in some sense an instrument for righting an injustice. Today its cumulative contribution is enormous, and its home in the academic world is assured.

Only quite recently has the discipline formerly called "church history" and now more often "the history of Christianity" begun to open itself up to this approach. Its agenda over the last two centuries has been dominated by other facets of this religion's past such as theology, dogma, institutions, and ecclesio-political relations. Each of these has in fact long since evolved into its own subdiscipline. Thus the history of theology has concentrated on the self-understandings of Christian intellectuals. Historians of dogma have examined the way in which church leaders came to formulate teachings that they then pronounced normative for all Christians. Experts on institutional history have researched the formation, growth, and functioning of leadership offices, bureaucratic structures, official decision-making processes, and so forth. And specialists in the history of church-state relations have worked to fathom the complexities of the institution's interface with its sociopolitical context, above all by studying leaders on both sides.

Collectively, these conventional kinds of church history have yielded enough specialized literature to fill a very large library, and those who read in this library will readily testify to its amazing treasures. Erudite as it is, however, the Achilles' heel of this scholarship, taken as a whole, is that it has told the history of Christianity as the story of one small segment of those who have claimed the name "Christian." What has been studied almost exclusively until now is the religion of various elites, whether spiritual elites, intellectual elites, or power elites. Without a doubt, mystics and theologians, pastors, priests, bishops, and popes are worth studying. But at best they all together constitute perhaps 5 percent of all Christians over two millennia. What about the rest? Does not a balanced history of Christianity, not to mention our sense of historical justice, require that attention be paid to them?

Around the mid-twentieth century a handful of scholars began, hesitantly and yet insistently, to press this question on the international guild of church historians. Since that time, the study of the other 95 percent has gained momentum: ever more ambitious research projects have been launched; innovative scholarly methods have been developed, critiqued, and refined; and a growing public interest has greeted the results. Academics and nonacademics alike want to know about this aspect of Christianity's past. Who were these people—the voiceless, the ordinary faithful who wrote no theological treatises, whose statues adorn no basilica, who negotiated no concordats, whose very names themselves are largely lost to historical memory? What can we know about their religious consciousness, their devotional practice, their understanding of the faith, their values, beliefs, feelings, habits, attitudes, their deepest fears, hopes, loves, hatreds, and so forth? And what about the troublemakers, the excluded, the heretics, those defined by conventional history as the losers? Can a face be put on any of them?

Today, even after half a century of study, answers are still in short supply. It must be conceded that the field is in its infancy, both methodologically and in terms of what remains to be investigated. Very often historians now find themselves no longer interrogating literary texts but rather artifacts, the remains of material culture, court records, wills, popular art, graffiti, and so forth. Many traditional assumptions about Christianity's past will have to be abandoned. When the Christian masses are made the leading protagonists of the story, we begin to glimpse a plot with dramatically new contours. In fact, a rewriting of this history is now getting under way, and this may well be the discipline's larger task for the twenty-first century.

A People's History of Christianity is our contribution to this enterprise. In it we gather up the early harvest of this new approach, showcase the current state of the discipline, and plot a trajectory into the future. Essentially, what we offer here is a preliminary attempt at a new and more adequate version of the Christian story—one that features the people. Is it comprehensive? Impossible. Definitive? Hardly. A responsible, suggestive, interesting base to build on? We are confident that it is.

Close to a hundred historians of Christianity have generously applied their various types of expertise to this project, whether as advisers or editors or contributors. They have in common no universally agreed-on methodology, nor do they even concur on how precisely to define problematic terms such as "popular religion." What they do share is a conviction that rescuing the Christian people from their historic anonymity is important, that reworking the story's plot with lay piety as the central narrative will be a contribution of lasting value, and that reversing the condescension, not to say contempt, that all too often has marred elite views of the people is long overdue. If progress is made on these fronts, we believe, the groundwork for a new history of Christianity will have been prepared.

The story begins in the first century of our era, in Galilee—a remote, impoverished, provincial backwater of the Roman Empire. Local peasants, descendants of ancient Israelites, found themselves immersed in a profound and deepening, multidimensional crisis. Perhaps in near desperation, and looking for hope or focus or meaning or inspiration or orientation for action, small numbers turned to the memory of a martyred teacher, Jesus of Nazareth. And thus were born the earliest "Jesus movements," or, if one prefers, the first communities of "Christ-believers." Volume 1, *Christian Origins,* explores the complexity of those beginnings, the movements' staying power, their variety, their proliferation into Judea, Samaria, Greece, Asia Minor, Rome, and so forth. How did these groups understand themselves, how did they begin to attract peoples of non-Israelite origin, and how did they gradually evolve and coalesce into a "religion" that came to be called Christianity? I know of no more reliable guide to these issues than Richard Horsley, the editor of this volume. At every stage, his unique combination of erudition and élan, good humor and grace, has been an inspiration to me, as I know it has been to his collaborators. He has my heartfelt gratitude for taking on this project.

Denis R. Janz, General Editor

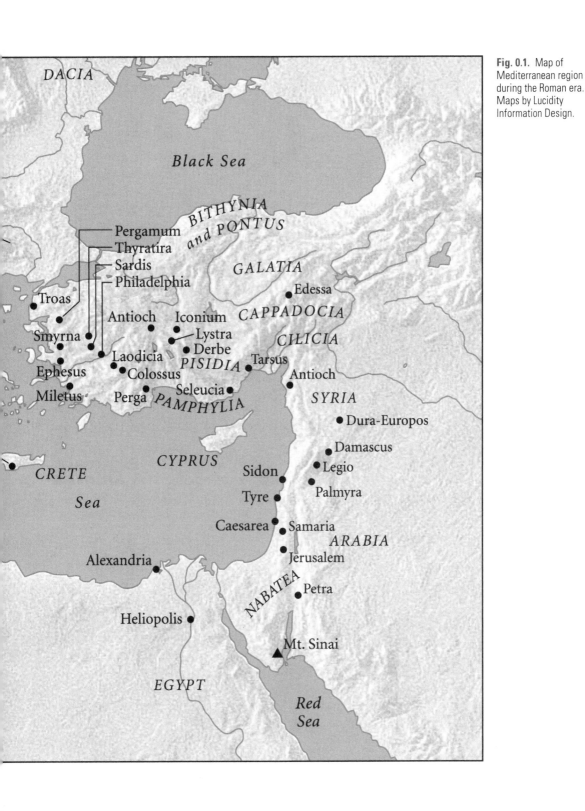

Fig. 0.1. Map of Mediterranean region during the Roman era. Maps by Lucidity Information Design.

Fig. 0.2. The Sea of Galilee (also called Lake Gennesaret or the Sea of Tiberias), seen from the Mountain of the Beatitudes near Tabgha and Bethsaida. In the first century the lake was the center of a significant fishing industry in which some of Jesus' disciples had worked. Jesus' parables reflect other spheres of economic life in Galilee in which production for export had replaced the sustenance village economy. Photo: Erich Lessing / Art Resource, NY.

UNEARTHING A PEOPLE'S HISTORY

RICHARD A. HORSLEY

Until recently a people's history of Christianity—particularly in the New Testament period—would have been considered a contradiction in terms, according to the canons of standard history. There are two reasons for this, the first having to do with the "people," and the second with "Christianity." First, until very recently, history was focused almost entirely on the ruling elites who were involved in significant events, particularly the "kings and wars," the statesmen and generals who made history. Since those who wrote history were intellectuals employed by the dominant classes, moreover, historical accounts were written in the interests of and from the perspective of the elites. The meaning of history, furthermore, turned out to be the meaning for the elites. Ordinary people simply were not a subject worthy of historical investigation, according to established historians.

Since at least the French Revolution, however, ordinary people have adamantly insisted on their own interests and rights. In fact, they were so brazen as to make history themselves in ways that could not be suppressed. In recent decades, colonized peoples, Latin American campesinos, Southeast Asian peasants, African Americans, and women's groups around the world have taken significant historical action that elites could no longer effectively suppress, much less ignore. In response, a younger generation of professional historians finally gave an ever-widening attention to the history of ordinary people.

The second reason that a people's history of Christianity would have to be considered an oxymoron is rooted in the Enlightenment origins of what is usually understood as history. The Enlightenment thinkers who determined the subject matter, methods, and criteria of what constitutes history were struggling to get out from under the authoritarian dogma of established Christianity. Accordingly, religion was defined in restrictive ways, as irrational (to be suppressed) or as a matter of individual belief (to be tolerated). As an irrational or essentially private matter, religion was excluded from history proper. History came to mean primarily the story of politics, national and international. The exclusion of religion from history was reinforced by the separation of church and state in many Western societies.

The result has been the development of smaller peripheral fields such as the history of Christianity and, for the period of the origins of Christianity, the overlapping field of New Testament studies. The modern developers of these interrelated fields, moreover, accepted both the standard focus of history on the elite and the separation of religion from history proper as focused on political affairs. This meant that the history of Christianity concentrated on the bishops, theologians, and church councils (which corresponded to "kings and wars"). And it meant that the field of New Testament focused on the origin of what was defined as a religion, as if it could be separated from the broader concrete historical context. As both a goal and a result of interpretation of the New Testament and related texts, New Testament studies focused on the origins of the Christian sacraments (baptism and the Lord's Supper), creeds, Christology, and church order. The only people who mattered were the apostles, such as Peter and Paul, and the evangelists, such as Matthew and John, and they were important primarily for their faith and theology. The principal distinction made among people was between the Jews, among whom the new religion had its background, and the Gentiles, among whom the religion flourished and expanded.

For the New Testament period in particular there is considerable irony that a people's history of Christianity would have been considered a contradiction in terms. For in the period of their origins, the communities and movements that were later called Christianity consisted of nothing but people's history. This requires a great deal of rethinking concerning some of the basic assumptions, approaches, and conceptual apparatus previously standard in the fields of New Testament and Christian origins.

Perhaps the first thing to be recognized is that Christianity did not yet exist in the New Testament period as an identifiable religion. Similar to the period of colonization of the Atlantic seaboard that preceded the origins of the United States, the New Testament period was a time of origins of parallel movements and communities, some of which later became identified as Christian. Most books of the New Testament have no reference to Christians, let alone Christianity. The people who produced and used the Gospels of Mark, Matthew, and John, for example, understood themselves as a renewal or an extension of the people of Israel. Somewhat similarly Paul seems to think of even the non-Israelite assemblies he helped catalyze in terms of an extension of Israel's blessings to other peoples in fulfillment of the promises to Abraham. Certainly there is no Christianity over against Judaism in most books of the New Testament.

This means that the people involved in these communities and move-ments were not defined by being the nonelite within Christianity. They were not the ordinary laity as distinct from the bishops, popes, theologians, and church councils. This makes the people we focus on in volume 1 of A People's History of Christianity different from the people to be focused on in the other volumes—those who were in some way Christian. They are rather very small groups from among the peoples subject to the wealthy and powerful imperial elite and their aristocracies in the provinces and cities of the Roman Empire, such as Galilee and Judea or Antioch and Corinth.

Once we recognize that the communities and movements associated with New Testament literature had not (yet) developed into what was later identified as Christianity, it should be easier not to restrict them to the cate-gory of religion. Religion as separate from politics and economics is a pecu-liar modern Western concept and phenomenon. In the ancient Roman Empire, as in most other times and places, religion was inseparable from political-economic life. The diverse communities and movements to be examined in this volume almost certainly understood themselves as more than what modern Westerners would think of as religious. Insofar as these communities and movements emerged among peoples subject to the Roman Empire, whose rulers were intensely suspicious and repressive of any disturbance of the imperial order, they often developed in conflict with the Roman imperial elite and its culture. In fact, it could be that a princi-pal reason that they developed into what can be called religion is that the Roman imperial order blocked them from continuing as more than reli-gion, in some cases as an alternative society.

Insofar as the people involved in the communities and movements of the New Testament period were acting without the leadership of a Chris-tian elite and were almost always acting in conflict with the elites who con-trolled the Roman imperial order, they were making history. Those who formed these communities took the initiatives in various ways, eventually producing the diverse wider movements that became an important histori-cal force in the late Empire.[1]

In writing the history of the Roman Empire, historians have almost always focused on the triumphs of the Roman warlords and emperors. The aristocratic ancient Judean historian Josephus focuses on the relations of the Roman imperial elite and the Herodian and high priestly rulers of Judea and Galilee. Yet one cannot read very far into his accounts without realizing that it was the popular movements, and particularly the popular protests and revolts by the Judean and Galilean peasantry, that drove events in Palestine during the time of Peter and Mary Magdalene. The rulers were repeatedly in a reactive posture, trying to respond to initiatives taken by the Judean and Galilean people. Similarly, in the Greek cities of the Empire, the aristocracies spent their time obsequiously cultivating the emperor and reliving the bygone glories of classical Greek culture.[2] Like the Galilean and Judean peasants in Roman Palestine, it was the people who formed the communities associated with New Testament and related literature who took new historical initiatives. These communities and movements, therefore, cannot be consigned to a marginalized history of religion in the ancient world but must be understood as those who made history in a more general sense, including the conflicts of power and politics.

A people's history of the New Testament period, therefore, presents a challenge to the usual understanding of history, particularly as practiced by modern Western historians. Western historians of India, for example, virtually ignored the significance of peasant movements in the anticolonial struggle because they were defined as religious. In premodern and non-Western societies, however, not only is religion inseparable from political-economic life, but adherence to traditional religion and culture can inspire historical movements. It is thus important, in response to the modern Western separation of religion from politics, to explain how religious phenomena are factors in historical movements, hence in the making of history. Established New Testament scholars, apparently embarrassed by demon possession and exorcism and people swept up in ecstatic spiritual behavior, have given such phenomena little attention, even downplayed them. Yet the spirit possession, prophecy, healings, and similar spiritual experiences may be precisely what catalyzed community solidarity and the motivation for the formation of alternative communities and resistance to the dominant order.

The historical explorations in this volume thus do not have the problem of some recent exercises in social history that have drawn criticism for having no genuine problem to figure out. The task before us is to explore the ways in which ordinary people whose lives were determined by the Roman imperial order formed communities and movements that spread and expanded into a significant historical force in late antiquity. The explorations pursue a number of interrelated factors in what were complex and varied historical developments, depending on local conditions and cultures: the interrelationship of problematic circumstances, discontented people, and distinctive leaders, messages, and organizations that resulted in movements and communities with the solidarity and staying power to survive and expand. We are striving both to discover and reconstruct significant historical communities and movements and to explain them.[3] While this often involves investigations into local conditions and cultures, it requires attention to events in the wider imperial world, since nearly all of the areas into which these movements spread were directly or indirectly subject to Rome. And since ordinary people are almost invariably subject to various layers of the wealthy and powerful, the key to understanding may often be particular relations of power.

Our soundings in people's history could thus be compared with standard history in several basic respects:[4]

	people's history	*standard history*
focus:	ordinary people	elites such as "kings and wars"
scope:	all aspects of life	mainly political events at the top
view:	from below	from above
sources:	archaeology, texts, comparative studies	written texts, archives
approach:	interdisciplinary	the discipline of history

The exploratory studies in this volume thus raise new questions about New Testament and other already familiar materials, looking again at less familiar sources, questioning old assumptions, and working critically toward new conceptual tools more appropriate to how ordinary people made history. The initiative to explore these materials in terms of people's history just happens to come at a time when recent research on various issues is forcing us to rethink assumptions about and approaches to people of the ancient Mediterranean world. Even more, our investigations of people's history lead us beyond the standard assumptions, approaches, and agenda of traditional New Testament studies in several basic respects:

	people's history	*New Testament studies*
focus:	reconstruction of people's history	interpretation of texts
scope:	all aspects of life	mainly religion and meaning
basic division:	rulers versus ruled	Judaism versus Hellenism
issues:	people's circumstances and actions	Christian theological questions
media:	oral communication in communities	writings by authors
culture:	popular tradition versus elite culture	stable Scripture
agenda:	people in their own circumstances	bridging the distance from text to today

At the risk of oversimplifying historical complexities, we can sketch some basic factors and issues involved.

INHERITING A TRADITION OF REVOLT

Certain major events and developments in the wider history of the ancient Mediterranean world helped set up the conditions in which a small number of ordinary people formed movements focused on Jesus of Nazareth.

The movements that gathered around Jesus as their martyred prophet (or messiah) originated among the peasants of Galilee and spread quickly among Judeans and Samaritans. These were all descendants of the ancient Israelites. In their Passover meal they celebrated the ancestors' escape from foreign rulers in the exodus from hard labor under the Egyptian pharaoh led by the great prophet Moses. They also cultivated the memory of resistance that the prophet Elijah led against the oppressive rule of King Ahab. Just before Jesus was born, Galilean, Samaritan, and Judean peasants lived under the rule of the military strongman Herod, who had been installed by the Roman Senate as king of the Judeans (40–4 BCE). Herod, in turn, kept intact the Jerusalem temple-state, headed by a priestly aristocracy. Herod's oppressive rule of the Judeans, Galileans, and Samaritans was a decisive stage in a long history of conflict between Israelite peoples and their rulers, one that set the stage for the Jesus movements.

The Jerusalem temple-state had been set up by the Persian Empire in the sixth century BCE. It served several purposes simultaneously: it institutionalized an indigenous people's service of their own God, it established a ruling priestly aristocracy that owed their position to the imperial regime, and it set up a Temple administration to secure revenues for the imperial court as well as itself. The Hellenistic empires established by the successors of Alexander the Great in the third century BCE imposed the Greek language and Greek political forms on much of the ancient Near East. But they left the high priesthood in control of the Temple in Jerusalem, where Judean villagers continued to deliver their tithes and offerings.

An attempt by ambitious figures in the priestly aristocracy to transform Jerusalem into a Hellenistic city-state, more integrated into the dominant imperial cultural order, evoked resistance by scribal teachers, including those who produced in the Book of Daniel the visions of future restoration of the people's independence. The imperial regime's military enforcement of the changes in the people's traditional way of life touched off a popular insurgency led by Judas "the Maccabee" ("Hammer"), from an ordinary priestly family, the Hasmoneans. After several years of guerrilla warfare, the Judean peasants and ordinary priests managed to fight the imperial armies and their war elephants to a standoff.

In the ensuing vacuum of imperial power, successive Hasmonean brothers negotiated with rival imperial rulers to take over the high priesthood in Jerusalem. Depending increasingly on mercenary troops, the Hasmonean regime in Jerusalem proceeded to expand its power over other traditional Israelite territories. After conquering Samaria and destroying the Samaritan temple on Mount Gerizim, they finally took over Galilee as well in 104 BCE and required the inhabitants to live "according to the laws of the Judeans." Galileans were thus, about a hundred years before the generation of Jesus, brought together with other Israelite people under the Temple and high priesthood. But in contrast to their Israelite cousins in Judea they would not have been accustomed to rule and taxation by the Jerusalem temple-state.

The Roman takeover of Palestine in 63 BCE and their imposition of Herod as king in 40 BCE meant that the Galilean, Samaritan, and Judean peasants were suddenly subject to three layers of rulers and their respective demands for revenues: tribute to Rome, taxes to Herod, and tithes and offerings to the Temple and priesthood. With military fortresses and highly repressive measures, Herod maintained tight control of the people. At his death, however, revolts erupted in every major district of his realm, most of them led by popular leaders whom their followers acclaimed as king, that is, in Israelite parlance, "messiah."

The Romans reconquered Galilee and Judea with typically vengeful destruction of villages, slaughter and enslavement of the inhabitants, and crucifixion of hundreds of combatants to further terrorize the populace. They installed Herod's Rome-educated son Antipas as ruler of Galilee. After ten years of ineffective rule by Archelaus, Judea and Samaria were placed under a Roman governor, who governed through the priestly aristocracy. Galileans now for the first time in their history had their ruler living in Galilee itself. In fact Herod Antipas not only rebuilt the town of Sepphoris as his fortress-capital but within twenty years built yet another capital city on the shores of the Sea of Galilee, named Tiberias after the new emperor in Rome. One can imagine that collection of the taxes necessary to fund these massive building projects was suddenly far more efficient in Galilee than under distant rulers. It may be significant to note that after only a hundred years under Jerusalem jurisdiction, Galileans were no longer under Jerusalem control during the lifetimes of Peter, Mary Magdalene, and others among the earliest participants in Jesus movements.

Both Galilee and Judea experienced increasing political-economic turmoil from around the time of Jesus' mission until widespread revolt erupted in the summer of 66 CE (as we know from the accounts of Josephus, who witnessed many of the events firsthand). The epidemic and escalating social banditry may be a good barometer of the steady disintegration of village life under the accumulating economic pressures. A series of popular prophetic movements anticipating replays of the exodus led by Moses and of the battle of Jericho led by Joshua arose in the Samaritan and Judean countryside from the 30s to the 50s. The increasingly predatory high priestly families who were building ever more luxurious mansions for themselves in Jerusalem gradually lost authority among the people and, eventually, had virtually no social control over Judean society. Eventually some of the very Pharisees and other scribal intellectuals who served the temple-state as retainers organized a terrorist group of "dagger-men" to assassinate high priestly figures who collaborated too closely in imperial rule. Repressive measures taken by the Roman governors seemed only to exacerbate the popular protests and resistance. This is precisely the historical context in which movements focused on Jesus were spreading from Galilee to Samaria and Judea and beyond to Syrian villages and towns, such as Damascus.

The historical conditions of the various areas in the wider Roman Empire in which followers of Jesus established new communities were similarly set by Roman conquest and the resulting Roman imperial order of the first century CE.

On a pretext the Romans attacked a league of Greek cities centered at Corinth and utterly destroyed the classical city in 146 BCE. A hundred years later, Julius Caesar founded a colony on the site, to which he sent some of the freed slaves and other surplus population from the city of Rome. That colony then developed into the aspiring cosmopolitan center of East-West trade in the eastern Empire, its politics typically dominated by a few extremely wealthy families and its city center rebuilt with a focus on the imperial cult. Its inhabitants would have been a mishmash of deracinated individuals cut off from any cultural roots by generations of imperial conquests, enslavement, and migration from the countryside or other cities in search of a livelihood.

In Asia Minor Roman conquest and destruction played less of a role. But the Romans did drain the area economically in the first century BCE, reinforcing the tendencies to concentrate wealth in the hands of local oligarchies. Under the Empire set up by Augustus after the battle of Actium (31 BCE), those powerful oligarchies, loyal to the imperial court that maintained them in power, controlled their cities as bastions of the imperial "peace and prosperity."

The people of Italy and Rome itself, the center of the Empire, paid a price for the imperial expansion led by the Roman warlords. While Roman and Italian peasant-soldiers were off serving in the Legions enslaving subject peoples such as Judeans and Syrians, their families fell into mounting debts. Ironically, perhaps as many as a million peasants thus gradually lost their land to the wealthy families of their warlord commanders during the first century BCE, many of them swelling the mob of the destitute in Rome itself and other cities. The wealthy patrician families, in turn, imported gangs of cheap slaves from each successive conquest to farm their burgeoning estates. Moreover, as hundreds of thousands of slaves and other displaced people flooded into Rome and Italy, the now increasingly rootless populace became ever more diverse ethnically and culturally.

POLARIZATION AND POWER

It is difficult for Americans and Europeans who live in societies of mainly middle-class people to appreciate the dramatic divide that separated the dominant elite and the ordinary people in most ancient and medieval societies.[5] The Roman Empire, under which what became Christianity developed in diverse communities, was dominated by a numerically tiny but extremely wealthy elite who owned or controlled most of the land as well as large numbers of slaves. The imperial, provincial, and city elites monopolized the civil-religious offices such as the civic and imperial priesthoods. The vast majority of people (roughly 90 percent) were peasants living at subsistence levels in villages and towns. In some areas of the Empire peasants may have retained control over their ancestral land and village communities. But many had sunk to the status of sharecroppers or landless laborers vulnerable to wealthy absentee landlords. A much smaller percentage of ordinary people eked out a subsistence living in the cities as artisans and laborers. In certain areas of the Roman Empire the estates of the wealthy were worked by smaller or larger gangs of slaves taken in various conquests of subject peoples. The large urban households and country villas of the elite were staffed by more domestic slaves, the more educated of whom served as tutors, readers, and managers. There were a very few people in between who served as agents or clients of the ruling aristocracies. But there was no middle class in either an economic or a political sense under the Roman Empire.

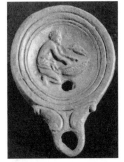

Fig. 0.3. Oil lamp decorated with fisherman and a bowl of fish, from the Herodian period. Israel. Photo: Erich Lessing / Art Resource, NY.

Given the political-economic polarization, it is not surprising that there were deep social divisions and significant cultural differences between the elite and powerful and the subordinate. Peasants were often of different ethnic and cultural heritage from their urban landlords and rulers. Villagers had little contact with the wealthy and powerful families in the cities, except for the agents sent to collect rents, taxes, and tribute. Especially where the peasantry continued on ancestral lands, villages were semi-independent communities, with their own local assemblies (called "synagogues" in the Gospels) and even distinctive local customs and rituals.

In Galilee, where the Jesus movements arose, there is little or no evidence of villagers' interaction with the new cities built by Herod Antipas, presumably in Roman style—other than tax collection and perhaps labor in the construction. The Judean historian Josephus, however, does emphasize the popular attacks on Sepphoris in 4 BCE and the regularly threatened peasant attacks on the pro-Roman elites in both Sepphoris and Tiberias during the great revolt in 66–67. In Judea villagers rendered up offerings as well as tithes to the Temple and priesthood and supposedly participated in the pilgrimage festivals centered in the Temple. The Judean peasantry, however, far from simply acquiescing to these mediating rituals, mounted periodic movements of independence from or direct attack on Jerusalem rule and found in the pilgrimage festivals occasions for protest against Roman as well as aristocratic domination. Josephus claims that the Pharisees had influence among the people (did he mean the Judean peasantry or only the Jerusalemites?). But he portrays them as agents and representatives of the Hasmonean, Herodian, and high priestly regimes. There is no evidence of the Pharisees or other scribal circles having made common cause with any peasant groups. When a "teacher" named Menahem and his scribal followers attempted to set themselves at the head of the revolt in the summer of 66, the Jerusalemites themselves attacked and killed him.

In the cities of the Roman Empire there was more contact between ordinary people and the urban elite. The free poor, like slaves and freedmen and freedwomen, often made a living by catering to the needs of the wealthy. But strict norms governed those interactions. Partly as a means of social control, the elite sponsored festivals and entertainments for the ordinary people. Imperial games funded by an urban elite in honor of Caesar might be the only occasion on which the urban poor ever tasted meat. The plebian citizens of Rome itself (but not resident aliens and other destitute people), of course, enjoyed the bread and circuses arranged by the Roman imperial aristocracy. Ordinary city folks could attend gladiatorial contests. In city centers the urban magnates erected shrines and temples to the emperor, which then constituted the very architectural environment of public life. But the riffraff would never be invited to a banquet in an aristocratic household. Some of the urban poor who made at least a subsistence living as artisans formed clubs or associations that held their own dinners, only on a relatively modest scale. Some of those clubs may have honored wealthy patrons at their dinners in return for financial support. Beyond the imperial games and city festivals, however, there was little to bridge the gulf between the extremely wealthy magnates and the mass of the poor. Recent claims that the participants in Pauline churches represented a cross section of urban society simply do not fit the sharp divide in ancient Roman urban society known from evidence outside of New Testament and other Christian sources.

POPULAR CULTURE IN INTERACTION WITH ELITE CULTURE

People's movements are usually rooted in popular culture, which is different from high culture. That should not be surprising, since peasants are often of different ethnic background from their lords and often live in semi-autonomous village communities. While culture can be diverse among the elite, even in an imperial order where the dominant culture becomes somewhat cosmopolitan, popular culture is usually far more diverse in its local variations.

Anthropologists and social historians, drawing on comparative studies of agrarian societies, have moved well beyond the problematic old two-tier model of aristocratic culture and folk culture.[6] In most situations there is an interaction between a "little tradition," the "distinctive patterns of belief and behavior... valued by the peasantry," and the corresponding "great tradition" of the elite. The popular tradition can absorb influences from the dominant culture, which is often parallel and overlapping, and the great tradition can adopt or adapt cultural materials such as stories of origin from the people, from among whom the elite may have risen to power. Yet the popular tradition can embody values and express interests sharply different from and even opposed to the great tradition. In certain circumstances the little tradition can thus become the matrix of "protest and profanation" by popular movements, even of peasant revolts.

The differences and relations between popular culture and dominant culture are particularly salient for the investigations in this volume focused on the religious-cultural dimension of people's history. The problem and our approach to it play out somewhat differently for the Jesus movements and early Gospel materials rooted in Galilee and Judea, on the one hand, and for the Pauline and other communities and movements in other areas of the Roman Empire, on the other. In both cases, very recent research on particular aspects of ancient Jewish, Greek, and Roman culture is seriously challenging standard assumptions and generalization in New Testament studies. As a result we are in a position of having to make educated projections on what the implications may be as we wait for more detailed historical investigations of particular situations and issues.

One marker of the differences between elite and people's culture and religion in the Roman Empire was literacy,[7] which was basically confined to the urban elite and some of those who served them. Most males of the aristocracy could read, although they often had slaves read to them and write letters and other documents for them. Decrees and honorific statements in honor of imperial figures or local magnates were inscribed on monuments in public places to impress the people. But literacy was not used in most social and economic interaction, certainly not among the ordinary people. Even village scribes in Egypt, who were local administrators for the central government, could barely inscribe their name on the shards given as receipts to peasants for taxes paid or on papyri lists sent to district offices.

Literacy was, if anything, more limited in Judea and Galilee than in the rest of the Roman Empire.[8] Writing was confined mainly to scribal circles and the Herodian and high priestly administrations. Oral communication dominated at all levels of the society, completely so in the villages. This makes the old depiction of the ancient Jews as generally literate and a "people of the book" highly dubious. It also calls into question the frequent assumption that early Christians were also literate and quickly also became a people of the book. This means, for example, that Judean texts from around the time of Jesus provide evidence not for what the Jews in general believed and practiced, but only for the literate circles that produced those texts.[9]

We are only beginning to realize that there was no standard and stable text of the Hebrew Bible (still often referred to inappropriately as the "Old Testament" by Christian interpreters). Close examination of the many manuscripts of the books of the Pentateuch (five books of Moses) found among the Dead Sea Scrolls discovered in 1947 indicates that different versions of these books still coexisted among the scribes and literate priests.[10] Thus no standardized scripture operated as *the* authority even in the scribal and priestly circles who controlled the Temple. It is highly unlikely, therefore, that the Hebrew scriptures were known to Judean and Galilean peasants. Scrolls, which were extremely expensive and cumbersome, were more or less confined to scribal circles.[11]

The nonliterate ordinary people could not have read them anyhow. Galilean and Judean villagers spoke a dialect of Aramaic, so they would hardly have understood Hebrew if it were read to them. The Gospel of Luke is projecting Greek urban practices onto the synagogue in Nazareth in its portrayal of Jesus opening a scroll of Isaiah and reading from it. Peasants would have known of the existence of the scripture, since it was deposited in the Temple and supposedly read (recited) on ceremonial occasions. And fragmentary knowledge of one or another version of the scripture of the Jerusalem great tradition may well have been mediated to villagers through Pharisees and other scribal representatives of the temple-state. Such mediation would have been minimal for Galilean peasants, however, since they had been brought under Jerusalem rule only about a hundred years before Jesus' birth.[12]

While only minimally and indirectly acquainted with the still-developing scriptures of the Jerusalem priestly and scribal elite, however, Judean and Galilean peasants were well-grounded in Israelite tradition—or rather their own popular Israelite tradition. Given the different regional histories of Galilee, Samaria, and Judea, there must have been local variations in the Israelite little tradition. Yet many of the most basic aspects of that tradition, such as the foundational legend of the exodus and memories of prophets of renewal such as Elijah, would have been common to all regions. Josephus mentions many incidents that indicate that Galileans were adamantly committed to the basic principles of the Mosaic covenant as the fundamental guide to socioeconomic life.[13] Josephus's hostile accounts of popular prophetic and messianic movements enable us to see this Israelite popular tradition in action, as it were. The Gospels provide what is perhaps our best access to at least a Galilean version of Israelite popular tradition.

The interrelation of high and popular culture was far more complex for the communities of Jesus-believers that emerged in the more multicultural and cosmopolitan urban contexts of Corinth and Rome and even in the smaller cities of Asia Minor. New Testament interpreters have tended to work with a highly synthetic construction of Hellenistic culture and religion, to which they then compare Pauline letters and other New Testament literature. But cities had their own distinctive cultural features. An indigenous Thracian or Macedonian culture, for example, apparently survived in Thessalonica under the veneer of official assimilation of Roman culture under Augustus and his successors. Because it was a hub of shipping, Corinth became a cultural melting pot after its colonization by Roman veterans and freedpersons, who presumably spoke Latin. Rome would have been the most culturally diverse city of all—underneath the revival of traditional Roman culture spearheaded by Augustus as official policy.

As suggested by some of these distinctively local cultural variations, there seems little reason to imagine that ordinary people in cities of the Empire were assimilated to and identified with the high culture known in Greek and Latin literature, philosophy, inscriptions, and monuments. For example, scholars have recently rediscovered how Paul's arguments resemble the standard patterns of Greek rhetoric. This may well suggest that he shared cultural forms that had become common coin of oral communication in Greek-speaking cities. Yet Paul gives no indication that he knew classical Greek literature. It appears unlikely, therefore, that this diaspora Judean from the Greek-speaking city of Tarsus, who played a key role in the formation of communities of Christ-believers, helped to mediate Greek high culture. It is surmised that most of the urban poor in Greek cities participated in the imperial festivals sponsored by the urban magnates as a means to maintain social order and consolidate their own power.[14] While they were undoubtedly influenced by the festivals and monuments sponsored by the city elites, however, it would be unwarranted simply to assume that they merely acquiesced.[15]

A major aspect of popular culture in relation to elite culture that had not been a factor for the Galileans, Samaritans, and Judeans among whom the Jesus movement originated arose for the non-Israelite peoples who joined communities of Jesus-believers. For those of Israelite heritage, the Jesus movements developed on the basis of their own popular tradition. Indeed, the Jesus movements for which we have documentation appear to understand themselves as fulfillments of Israelite historical and prophetic tradition. The non-Israelite peoples who joined the nascent communities of Christ-believers, however, were, to a greater or lesser extent, identifying with and assimilating another people's cultural tradition. Envoys of Christ from the Judean diaspora such as Paul, Barnabas, and Prisca and Aquila were presenting a message and movement identified with and developing out of Israelite popular tradition. The Gentile peoples among whom they worked were thus put in a position of identifying in some way with Israelite tradition. On the one hand, this meant a rejection or dis-identification with the dominant Greek urban and Roman imperial culture. On the other hand, it meant identifying with another subject people's tradition, in some relationship with whatever culture they brought with them into the new community. The resulting new social-cultural identity would almost certainly have been a hybrid.

THE PROBLEM OF SOURCES

As suggested by the lack of sources for popular culture, investigation of people's history with a view from below faces a serious problem with regard to sources. Investigators of the history of kings and wars, bishops and councils, can easily find written sources in books and archives. Ordinary people in previous eras, however, have seldom left written sources as evidence of their own stories, hopes, and actions. Writers of the literate elite in antiquity, moreover, rarely mention ordinary people, and most modern scholars who interpret ancient sources generally work from a culturally dominant perspective. The people make the papers only when they make trouble for their rulers, who then condemn their irrational and unjustifiable "riots" and "banditry." Complaints by writers from the elite thus provide at least some indirect evidence, but we must obviously discount the hostility of such accounts.

Some of the Judean literature produced by the scribal elite of an imperially subjected people took stands against the imperial order. Occasionally some of the various Judean scribal circles who served as retainers of the Herodian and high priestly aristocracy protested when their patrons collaborated too closely with their own imperial patrons. The apocalyptic and hymnic literature they produced (for example, the Book of Daniel, the Psalms of Solomon), however, does not necessarily represent the views and expectations of Judean and Galilean peasants.[16]

With regard to elite written sources, but perhaps particularly with regard to hostile witnesses such as Josephus or the Roman historian Tacitus, it is up to the critical investigator, in effect, to force the issue. Historians must critically pose appropriate questions in order to elicit evidence from such elite sources.[17] Read as a source for an essentialist Judaism subdivided into four sects, Josephus's histories yielded information about the "Zealots," along with the Sadducees, Pharisees, and Essenes. Once we recognized the Zealots as a synthetic modern scholarly construct, suddenly Josephus became a source for a variety of popular protests and movements of resistance and renewal that took distinctively Israelite forms.[18] Various birth narratives were just further examples of a vague myth of the birth of a hero until historians asked sufficiently precise questions that led to different social locations of the various stories.[19]

Indeed, sufficient critical source-analysis has been done to provide some useful guidelines for critically cutting through the rhetoric and interests of elite sources, and additional principles will surely emerge. For example, since the authors of written texts, who were almost always male, tended to write women out of history, modern historians must take every clue to discern the presence and often the prominence of women, as feminist scholars have insisted.[20]

Some of the people investigated in this volume, however, are highly unusual, almost unique among ordinary people in antiquity, for having left texts that survive in writing. Insofar as the communities and movements that they represent or address had not yet developed a hierarchy that stood in power over the membership, most New Testament and related texts, in contrast with Josephus's histories or Pliny's letters, provide more or less direct sources for these people's movements. In the case of the Gospels, the contents are stories and speeches that are not only about peasants but stem from a peasant movement and, in the cases of Mark and Q, even represent a popular viewpoint. As sources from and for popular movements among peoples subject to imperial and local rulers, the Gospel of Mark and Q, and even the Gospels of John and Matthew, appear all the more striking in comparison with literature from the Judean scribal elite, such as the Psalms of Solomon or 1 Maccabees. These Gospel sources must be used critically, of course. They have distinctive viewpoints and interests. But they are some of those rare historical cases of literature that represents the view from below. Of non-Gospel literature, the Revelation to John, *The Teachings of the Twelve Apostles (Didache)*, and the Epistle of James (Jacob) also appear to be such sources.

We must be far more suspicious of some other New Testament and related documents. While the Gospel of Luke includes materials of popular provenance, its viewpoint is no longer that of the peasants from whom they originated. Insofar as Luke's Gospel is addressing later communities in a different cultural ethos from the one in which his Gospel materials originated, it is in a mediating position with regard to earlier Jesus movements. As for the Book of Acts, insofar as Luke has written the history of Paul's mission from a very distinctive point of view, we must seriously discount his presentation of Paul's activities and words in various mission sites, his sketches of leading figures in the assemblies Paul supposedly founded there, and his representation of the attitude of Roman authorities toward the developing movement and the hostile response of the Jews. The deutero-Pauline letters such as Colossians and Ephesians and particularly the Pastoral letters still represent communities of ordinary people. Insofar as they insist that their people pattern their family and community life after the dominant social order, however, they appear to be blunting the ways in which those communities might have been striving toward alternatives rooted in popular interests.

In addition to literary sources we have at least some evidence from very recent archaeology. Archaeologists are finally exploring sites of ordinary people's lives, and not just the monumental sites for which it is easier to obtain funding. An increasing supply of inscriptions from antiquity provides additional evidence. Extreme caution must be used, however, in extrapolating from inscriptions left by the (semi)literate to the views of ordinary people. Crude graffiti, for example, cannot be taken as evidence for literacy.

LEADERS AND COMMUNITIES, PEOPLE AND TEXTS

The relationship between leaders and followers in the communities and movements of the New Testament period is closely related to the question of nonelite sources, since some of the latter were produced by some of those leaders. While leaders of popular movements occasionally come from higher social ranks, they usually emerge from among the people themselves.

In the movements and communities of the New Testament period, most of the leaders, such as the apostles and prophets, emerged from among the ordinary people. As fishermen, Peter and Andrew, James and John, and others of the Twelve were hardly businessmen but more like sharecroppers who "farmed" the Sea of Galilee (had they lost their ancestral land in Galilean villages?). Diaspora Judeans from various cities of the Roman Empire were prominent in the early leadership. Prisca and Aquila, among those expelled from Rome in the 40s, were poor artisans (were they descendants of slaves or freed slaves?). Leaders such as Mary of Magdala and Phoebe of Cenchreae (Rom. 16:1-2), neither of whom is identified by her husband and embedded in a patriarchal family, had apparently become independent women, perhaps by force of difficult circumstances.

Some of the leaders in the communities and movements were also the composers of letters or Gospels. Those texts, moreover, not only constitute our principal or in some cases our only sources for communities but were key factors in their life and development as well. There is thus necessarily a close relationship, for example, between the Gospel of Matthew and the communities in which it arose and was used, or between Paul's letters to the Corinthians and the Corinthian community, or between the Revelation to John and the seven assemblies to which it is addressed. Our purpose is to explore primarily the history of the people involved, not the texts as texts (the principal goal of New Testament studies). It is necessary, therefore, to clarify critically the relation of such leaders and texts to the communities they addressed.

Fig. 0.4. Lone fisherman in a small boat, relief on a funeral stele, found on L'Isle Saint Jacques, France. First or second century CE. Evidence indicates the fishing industry in Roman Galilee generally involved much larger boats worked by crews. Photo: Erich Lessing / Art Resource, NY.

Paul has proved an especially puzzling case for recent interpreters. Many of the arguments in his letters appear similar to the standard forms of Greco-Roman rhetoric. But that does not mean that he had received a formal rhetorical education (handbooks of the time represented a systematization of long-standing practice in public culture). Certainly his letters give no sense that he had any knowledge of Greek literature. We must doubt the claim in the Book of Acts that he was a Roman citizen. His comment that with regard to the Law he was a Pharisee (Phil. 3:5) does not mean that he received a scribal education in Jerusalem at the feet of Gamaliel (Acts 22:3) and became a protégé of the leading Pharisees. As an enforcer of a program of ethnic-cultural discipline and solidarity (*ioudaismos*, Gal. 1:13-14) among Judeans, Saul in effect operated as a mediator of the imperial order. As a diaspora Judean who had become caught up in an apocalyptic perspective while in Jerusalem, Saul certainly did become downwardly mobile by joining a popular movement led by Galilean peasants such as Peter and James. Thereafter he became as fanatically dedicated to spreading the new movement of "God's assembly" as he had been of persecuting the movement previously.

More important, we have recently become more critically aware that we cannot read the history of a Pauline Christianity directly off the pages of Paul's letters.[21] In the course of his mission, he came into cities as an outsider who worked, initially with other outsiders, to catalyze new communities among residents there. His letters are ad hoc communications aimed at maintaining cohesion and discipline of the local community and loyalty to his own leadership. Most of his letters give evidence of serious conflict among the members of the local assembly or between some in the assembly and himself. Far from Paul's argument being direct evidence for Pauline Christianity, however, they are rather sources for various voices that can be heard, however faintly, through Paul's arguments aimed at persuading them to agree with his own point of view. Thus Paul's letters provide windows (however cloudy) onto the struggles in which the communities addressed were engaged.

There appears to be less tension between other texts and the communities they address. Nevertheless, we cannot reconstruct the beliefs and behavior of communities directly off instructions in the *Didache* or the discourses in Matthew or the revelations to John.

AGENDA, ASSUMPTIONS, APPROACHES

In distinction from the standard agenda of New Testament studies, the explorations of people's history in this volume do not focus primarily on interpretation of New Testament and related texts. Those texts may provide our principal sources. But our studies focus rather on communities or movements in key locations such as Galilee, Judea, Antioch, Corinth, and Rome; on basic social forms and factors such as family, slavery, and poverty; and on modes of communication and leadership such as storytelling and prophecy.

Correspondingly, our investigations do not depend heavily on the standard assumptions, approaches, and interpretive accounts of New Testament studies, which have been heavily determined by Christian theology. Rather, the exploration of new materials, new questions, and different questions addressed to familiar texts requires us to work critically toward the new assumptions and approaches that seem appropriate to the focus on the people and their communities, social forms, and distinctive modes of communication. Different approaches may be appropriate for different explorations.

We focus on the religious aspects in these case studies. This is only appropriate in a people's history of Christianity and exploits the professional training and experience of the authors of these chapters in the interpretation of the symbolizing practices of texts, stories, symbols, and rituals. Yet insofar as religion is inseparable from the political-economic aspects of ancient life, religious motives and expressions can be understood only in the political-economic context in which they are embedded.

Aware that studies of popular culture in the Reformation and early modern Europe have been criticized for neglecting material conditions,[22] we include analysis of political-economic structures and power relations. We are interested in the dynamics of those power relations, however, not in the structures for their own sake. Hence we attempt to move beyond recent applications of functionalist sociological models to biblical texts and history, which may obscure the fundamental divide between the powerful elite and the mass of ordinary people in the Roman Empire.[23] The rise and expansion of new social movements may be interrelated more with the historical shifts and changes in fundamental structures and challenges to basic social forms than to the structures themselves. Moreover, we are now exploring these ancient social movements in a newfound awareness that power operates not only through political-economic structures but through religious symbols, rituals, and movements as well. The formation of communities whose loyalty (faith) focused on Jesus Christ as their Savior and refused loyalty to Caesar as the Savior who had supposedly brought them peace and security had implications for imperial power relations, however limited at the outset.[24]

Another concern of our explorations is to use information, where available, on local conditions in particular areas of the Roman Empire in which Jesus movements and Christ-centered communities developed. In this regard recent investigations of archaeological and textual evidence enable us to move underneath older synthetic generalizations about the Hellenistic world to distinctive political-economic patterns and cultural features of key areas.[25] Rarely is it possible to construct much of a "thick description" (anthropologist Clifford Geertz's term for a detailed, multi-level analysis) because of the relative lack of evidence from antiquity. Yet with more precise localized information in a few cases it may be possible to investigate indigenous social forms and the particular cultural traditions of communal life in the context of the political-economic-religious pressures impinging on local subsistence communities.

Together with archaeological and historical information and analysis, we seek cultural information for particular areas and communities. To focus on one key example, it is helpful and significant to know that people in Galilee were poor. It is even more useful and significant to know that they were being further impoverished by increasing taxation or rents. To understand the origins and concerns of a new popular movement, however, it would be much more useful and significant to understand the particular cultural meaning and social implications of their impoverishment. To understand and explain the people's movements, stories, and prophecies we are exploring, the key questions might well be the cultural meaning of their desire for dignity and the political-economic-religious mechanisms by which dignity is denied them. Information on that cultural meaning and those mechanisms might also be the clues to why a particular leader, message, or ritual could become an originating catalyst or a continuing cultivator of a movement or community.

Our investigations help clarify the ways and extent to which the communities and movements of the New Testament period formed and expanded in resistance to the dominant social-religious as well as political-economic order in the Roman Empire. Yet the people involved in these communities, as mostly subsistence peasants and artisans and even slaves, were embedded in that dominant order in various connections. They could not help adjusting and accommodating in various ways. And there were inevitably internal politics in these communities and movements, whether struggles between rival leaders or between local factions or between leaders and followers. All of those conflicts can be discerned even in the same community, as in the case of the Corinthian assembly behind 1 and 2 Corinthians. We thus attend closely to the internal politics of these movements and communities. It is impossible, however, to treat separately the movements' resistance to the dominant order and their assimilation and reinscription of aspects of that order. The latter is inevitably entailed in the interaction with the dominant order by communities of resistance, which were *in,* if not *of,* the dominant order.

Since our purpose is to explore the development of particular communities or movements, as well as key social forms and factors and modes of communication involved in most of them, we do not emphasize particular methods or models. Our approaches are eclectically multidisciplinary and self-consciously critical when adapting a given method for a particular purpose.

EARLY JESUS
MOVEMENTS

Part 1

Fig. 1.1. Map of Palestine in the first century CE.

JESUS MOVEMENTS AND THE RENEWAL OF ISRAEL

RICHARD A. HORSLEY

The Middle Eastern peasants who formed the first movement that focused on Yeshua bar Yosef (whom we know as Jesus) eked out a living farming and fishing in a remote region of the Roman Empire. At the outset their movement was similar in form and circumstances to many others that arose among people of Israelite heritage. Their families and village communities were steadily disintegrating under the increasing pressures of offerings to the Jerusalem Temple, taxes to Herodian kings, and tribute to their Roman conquerors. Large numbers of Galilean, Samaritan, and Judean peasants eagerly responded to the pronouncements of peasant prophets that God was again about to liberate them from their oppressive rulers and restore cooperative community life under the traditional divine principles of justice. The other movements ended abruptly when the Roman governors sent out the military and slaughtered them. The movements that formed around Yeshua bar Yosef, however, survived the Roman crucifixion of their leader as a rebel "king." In fact, his martyrdom became a powerful impetus for the expansion and diversification of his movements.

To understand the earliest Jesus movements in genuinely historical terms requires some serious rethinking of standard assumptions and approaches in conventional New Testament studies, which developed as a foundation for Christian theology. Standard interpretation of the Gospels in particular focuses on Jesus as an individual figure or on the Christology of one of the Gospels. It is simply assumed that the Gospels and other scriptural books are religious and that Jesus and the Gospels were pivotal in the origin of the new, universal, and truly spiritual religion, "Christianity," from the old, parochial, and overly political religion, "Judaism." In the ancient world in which the Gospels originated, however, religion was not separated from political-economic life. In fact, at the time of Jesus there was no such thing yet as a religion called Judaism, judging from our sources such as the Gospels, the Dead Sea Scrolls, or the contemporary Judean historian

Josephus. Similarly, something that could intelligibly be called Christianity had not developed until late antiquity, well after the time when the books that were later included in the New Testament and related literature were composed by leaders associated with the movements focused on Jesus.

It makes sense to begin from the broader historical conditions of life under the Roman Empire that constituted the historical context of Jesus' mission and to focus first on the many other Judean, Samaritan, and Galilean movements that illuminate the form of the earliest Jesus movements.

POPULAR RESISTANCE AND RENEWAL UNDER ROMAN IMPERIAL RULE

The ancient world was divided fundamentally between rulers and ruled, in culture as well as in political-economic structure. A tiny percentage of wealthy and powerful families lived comfortably in the cities from the tithes, taxes, tribute, and interest that they extracted from the vast majority of people, who lived in villages and worked the land. We must thus first examine the historical dynamics of that fundamental societal division in order to understand the circumstances in which the early Jesus movements formed and expanded.

Fig. 1.2. Judean silver shekel, from the time of the first Jewish revolt against the Romans (66–70 CE). Obverse shows a chalice and the Hebrew inscription "year 2," "shekel of Israel"; reverse shows pomegranates and the inscription "Jerusalem the Holy." The minting of coins was itself an act of rebellion against Rome. Israel Museum, Jerusalem; photo: Erich Lessing / Art Resource, NY.

At the time of Jesus, the people of Israelite heritage who lived in the southeast corner of the Mediterranean world, Judea in the south, Galilee in the north, and Samaria in between, lived under the rule of Rome. A Roman army had conquered the area about sixty years before Jesus' birth. The Romans installed the military strongman Herod as their client king to control the area. He in turn kept in place the Temple and high priesthood. The temple-state and its high priestly aristocracy had been set up by the Persian imperial regime centuries earlier as an instrument of their rule in Judea, the district around the city of Jerusalem. Subsequent imperial regimes retained this political-economic-religious arrangement for the control of the area and collection of revenues. With the decline of Hellenistic imperial power, the Hasmonean high priests extended Jerusalem's rule over Idumea to the south and Samaria and Galilee to the north, little more than a century before the birth of Jesus. After the Roman conquest, however, the high priestly aristocracy at the head of the temple-state in Jerusalem was again dependent on the favor of the imperial regime. Dependent, in turn, on the favor of the high priesthood were the professional scribal groups (such as the Pharisees) that worked for the priestly aristocracy as administrators of the temple-state and custodians of the cultural traditions, traditional laws, and religious rituals in which its legitimacy was articulated.

The old construct of a monolithic Judaism glosses over the fundamental division and multiple conflicts that persisted for centuries in Judean and Galilean history. Conflicts between rival factions in the priestly aristocracy, who competed for imperial favor, and the corresponding factions among scribal circles came to a head in the Maccabean Revolt of the 160s BCE. Further conflict developed as the Maccabean military strongmen consolidated their power as the new high priestly regime. The groups known as the Pharisees, Sadducees, and Essenes, whom we now understand to have been closely related to the Qumran community that left the Dead Sea Scrolls, cannot be understood in early modern terms as sects of Judaism. They were rather rival scribal factions or parties who competed for influence on the high priestly regimes or, in the case of the Essenes, withdrew into the wilderness when they lost out.

The history of Judea and Galilee in the two centuries preceding and the century immediately after Jesus' mission, however, was driven by the persistent conflict between the peasantry and their local and imperial rulers. In fact, according to our principal sources for these centuries—such as the books of the Maccabees, the *Jewish War* and the *Antiquities of the Jews* by the Judean historian Josephus, and later rabbinic literature—it was actions by Judean and Galilean peasants that drove most of the major historical events. The period of history around the time of Jesus was framed by four major peasant revolts: the Maccabean revolt in the 160s BCE, the revolt at the death of Herod in 4 BCE, the great revolt against Roman rule from 66 to 70 CE, and the Bar Kokhba revolt in 132–35 CE. In the immediate period of Jesus' mission and the first generation of Jesus movements, furthermore, peasants and ordinary people in Jerusalem mounted numerous protests and formed a number of renewal and resistance movements, most of which the Romans suppressed with brutal military action. Almost all of these revolts, protests, and movements were directed both against the foreign imperial rule of the Romans and against the Herodian and high priestly rulers in Jerusalem.[1]

Such popular revolts are rare in most areas of the world and periods of history. In response to their perpetual subjection to exploitative practices of the elite, peasants regularly engage in hidden forms of resistance, such as sequestering portions of their crops before the tax collectors arrive. Peasants generally do not mount serious revolts, unless their backs are against the wall or they are utterly outraged at their treatment by their rulers. They do, however, organize vocal protests against their conditions and treatment.

We can see the remarkable level of organization and discipline that popular protests were capable of generating in the strike against the emperor

Caligula mounted by Galilean peasants a few years after Jesus' mission there (Josephus, *Ant.* 18.269–84). Gaius Caligula, incensed that diaspora Jews refused to render him divine honors, ordered his statue installed in the Jerusalem Temple by military force. As the military expedition prepared to march through Galilee, large numbers of peasants organized a strike, refusing to plant the crops. The Roman Legate of Syria as well as the Herodian officers in control of Galilee knew well that they faced the prospect of a "harvest of banditry" instead of the crops on which their expropriation of tribute depended. Gaius's timely death prevented an escalation of the conflict. Clearly, Galilean and Judean people were capable of mounting serious widespread protests and other movements of resistance.

As the Galilean peasant strike illustrates, most of the widespread peasant revolts, urban protests, and popular renewal-resistance movements were rooted in and inspired by Israelite tradition. The central social memories of the origin and formation of Israel as an independent people focused on their liberation from foreign rule of the pharaoh in Egypt and on their Covenant on Sinai with their true, divine king (God), to the exclusion of oppressive human rulers ("no gods other than me"; "no images"). Judeans' and Galileans' loyalty to these formative traditions shaped their very identity as a people and led them to oppose foreign and Jerusalem rulers who conquered them and interfered with their community life directly under the covenantal rule of God.

Perhaps the most vivid example is the Passover celebration of the exodus from foreign oppression in Egypt. Jerusalem rulers had long since centralized this celebration in Jerusalem so that it would associate the formative memory and identity of Israel as a people with the Temple and its priesthood. Celebration of the exodus by pilgrims to Jerusalem, however, became a time of heightened awareness of their own subjection by the Romans and intense yearning to be independent again, in accordance with God's will and previous deliverance. In response to regular outbreaks of protest at festival time, the Roman governors made a habit of posting Roman soldiers on the porticoes of the Temple courtyard to intimidate the Passover crowds. But that merely exacerbated the intensity of popular feeling. Under the governor Cumanus at mid-first century, the crowds burst into a massive riot, provoked by a lewd gesture by a Roman soldier—and were slaughtered by the troops (*War* 2.223–26; *Ant.* 20.105–12).[2]

Most distinctive and widespread resistance and renewal efforts among the Galilean, Samaritan, and Judean people were the popular messianic movements and the popular prophetic movements. The many movements that took one or the other of these two distinctively Israelite forms are surely most important in understanding why the Galilean and Judean peoples, more than all others subjected by the Romans, persisted in mounting repeated resistance against Roman rule. These movements are most important for understanding the social forms taken by the Jesus movements. Both the popular prophetic movements and the popular messianic movements were following distinctively Israelite "scripts" based on memories of God's original acts of deliverance led by the great prophets Moses and Joshua or by the young David as the people's "messiah." Memories of these founding events were still alive in villager communities, ready to inform the people's collective action in circumstances of social crisis.[3]

When Herod finally died in 4 BCE, after a long and intensely oppressive rule over the people he had conquered with the aid of Roman troops, widespread revolts erupted in nearly every district of his realm (*War* 2.56–75; *Ant.* 17.271–85). In Galilee, Perea across the Jordan River, and Judea itself, these revolts were led by figures whose followers acclaimed them king, according to Josephus. They attacked the royal fortresses and storehouses, "taking back" the goods that had been seized and stored there, and they raided Roman baggage trains. In Galilee the movement led by Judas, son of the famous brigand-chief Hezekias, was suppressed within a few months, with great slaughter and destruction in the general area around Nazareth—shortly before Jesus came to live and grow up there. In Judea the movement led by the strapping shepherd Athronges and his brothers managed to maintain the people's independence in the Judean hill country for three years. Roman troops were finally able to ferret it out, again with much slaughter and the crucifixion of thousands as a means of terrorizing the people into submission.

Again in the middle of the great revolt of 66–70 CE, Judean peasants acclaimed Simon bar Giora as king (*War* 2.652–53; 4.503–34, 574–78; 7.29–36, 153–55). The Romans having been temporarily driven out, he moved around the countryside in the area of Hebron, where the young David had gotten his start. He liberated (debt-)slaves, restored people's property, and in general effected justice for the people. Having amassed a peasant army of thousands, he entered Jerusalem, joining other forces from other areas of the countryside that had taken refuge in the fortresslike city to resist the inevitable Roman reconquest. After being captured in the Roman reconquest of the city, Simon was taken in chains to Rome. There he was formally executed as the vanquished enemy general (the "king of the Judeans") by the emperor Vespasian and his son Titus in the lavish celebration of their glorious triumph.

All of these movements appear to have been patterned after the messianic movement led centuries earlier by the young David. As the Philistines continued their attacks against the Israelite peasantry, the people acclaimed David as their messiah-king (2 Sam. 2:1-4; 5:1-4) to lead them against the oppressive foreign rulers and to reestablish justice among the people. In his accounts of the movements in 4 BCE and 66–70 CE, Josephus does not use the term "messiah" ("anointed"), probably because he was writing for a Greek-speaking audience. But if we translate his accounts back into the Hebrew-Aramaic culture of Judea and Galilee, these movements must be understood as messianic movements patterned after the liberating revolts led by David and other popularly acclaimed messiah-kings in formative Israelite tradition.

That several such messianic movements emerged a generation before and a generation after the time of Jesus' mission is significant when we recognize that literature produced by the Judean scribal elite rarely mentions a messiah. This is in sharp contrast to previous Christian understanding, according to which the Jews were eagerly expecting *the* Messiah to lead them against foreign rule. But as scholars finally began to recognize about forty years ago, there was no such job description just waiting for Jesus to fulfill (in his own way). The Judean elite, of course, would not have been interested, since their positions of power and privilege depended on the Romans, who appointed oppressive kings such as Herod. Perhaps it was against just such an illegitimate king set in power by the Romans that the memory of the popularly acclaimed messiah-king David and other popular kings was revived among the Judean and Galilean peasantry and came to life in numerous movements for the independence and renewal of Israel right around the time of Jesus.

After the revolt led by Judas, son of Hezekias (4 BCE), this Israelite cultural "script" of a popular messianic movement would certainly have been alive in the area around Nazareth, the very area in which Jesus supposedly grew up. And its brutal suppression by the Romans would have left a collective social trauma of villages pillaged and burned and family members slaughtered and enslaved by the Romans. Such historical events and cultural memories cannot have been without their effect on popular life in Nazareth and other Galilean and Judean villages.

In another distinctively Israelite form, a number of popular movements led by prophets in anticipation of new acts of deliverance by God appeared in mid-first century. According to the ever hostile Josephus, "Impostors and demagogues, under the guise of divine inspiration, provoked revolutionary actions and impelled the masses to act like madmen. They led them out into the wilderness so that there God would show them signs of imminent liberation" (*War* 2.259), and "For they said that they would display unmistakable signs and wonders done according to God's plan" (*Ant.* 20.168).

The first of these movements led by prophets was among the Samaritans (circa 36 CE). A prophet led a crowd up to Mount Gerizim, the most sacred mountain, promising that they would recover the holy vessels from the tabernacle of the formative exodus-wilderness experience of Israel, buried at the spot where Moses had put them. But the Roman governor, Pontius Pilate, dispatched cavalry as well as infantry, killed some, took many prisoner, and executed the leaders (*Ant.* 18.85–87).

Perhaps the most famous prophetic movement was led about a decade later (circa 45 CE) by Theudas, who "persuaded most of the common people to take their possessions and follow him to the Jordan River. He said he was a prophet, and that at his command the river would be divided and allow them an easy crossing.... A cavalry unit killed many in a surprise attack [and] having captured Theudas, cut off his head and carried it up to Jerusalem" (*Ant.* 20.97–98; also mentioned in the Book of Acts 5:36). About another decade later (56 CE), just prior to Paul's visit to Jerusalem after

his mission in Corinth, Ephesus, and Macedonia, a Jewish prophet from Egypt rallied many thousands in the countryside. He led them up to the Mount of Olives, opposite Jerusalem, declaring that the walls of the city would fall down and the Roman garrison would be overpowered, giving them entry into the city. The Roman governor Felix, with heavily armed cavalry and infantry, killed hundreds of them, before the prophet himself and the others escaped (*Ant.* 20.169–71; *War* 2.261–63).

As with the messianic movements, so these prophetic movements were peasant movements clearly patterned

Fig. 1.3. The hill of Gamla, in Israel. Fortified by Josephus during the First Jewish revolt, the town finally fell to Vespasian's troops in 67 CE. Photo: Erich Lessing / Art Resource, NY.

after formative events in Israelite tradition. In the general characterization by Josephus (who called those who performed signs of liberation in the wilderness "prophets") and in the case of Theudas, who told his followers to take their goods along and expected the waters to be divided, these figures stepped into the role of a new Moses (or Joshua), leading a new exodus (or entry into the land, which had been more or less collapsed with the exodus in popular memory). The Judean prophet from Egypt patterned his role and the anticipated divine act of deliverance after Joshua's leadership of Israel in taking over their land from oppressive kings in their fortified cities, particularly the battle of Jericho. Judging from the terms used in Josephus's hostile accounts, these prophets and their followers were acting under inspiration.

The most noteworthy aspect of these movements to the ruling elite, of course, was the threat they posed to the imperial order. Josephus says that they were out to make "revolutionary changes." The Israelite traditions they were imitating, the exodus led by Moses and the entry into their own land led by Joshua, moreover, suggest that these movements anticipated a restoration of the people as well as a liberation from alien rule. Given our limited sources, of course, we have no indication of how they imagined the future of an Israel again living in independence of foreign domination. Although Josephus claims that the Samaritans were armed, his accounts of the others suggest that, unarmed, they were acting in anticipation of God's action to deliver them. The Roman governors, however, saw them as serious threats to the imperial order and sent out the troops to crush them and kill their prophetic leaders.

In all of these protests and movements the ordinary people of Galilee, Samaria, and Judea were taking bold action, often involving considerable organization and discipline, in making history. The people, facing acute economic distress and a disintegrating political order, took control of their own lives, under the leadership of popular kings (messiahs) like Judas ben Hezekias or popular prophets such as Theudas. These movements of social renewal and political resistance put the Roman and Jerusalem rulers on the defensive. The peasants were challenging the Roman imperial order! In response, the Roman governors, along with the Jerusalem high priesthood in some cases, took brutal, sometimes massive military action, often symbolically decapitating or ceremonially executing the prophetic or messianic leader.

Most striking is how, with the exception of epidemic banditry, these protests and movements took distinctively Israelite social forms. The protests were driven by outrage at the violation of traditional Mosaic covenantal principles. Both the messianic movements and the prophetic movements were decisively informed by (or patterned after) social memories deeply embedded in Israelite tradition. That there were so many of these movements that took one or another of two basic social forms strongly suggests that these distinctive cultural memories, these "scripts" for movements of renewal and resistance, were very much alive in the village communities of the peoples of Israelite heritage in Palestine around the time of Yeshua bar Yosef.

THE EARLIEST JESUS MOVEMENTS

It is in precisely this context of persistent conflict between the Judean and Galilean peasantry and their Jerusalem and Roman rulers that we must understand the origins and development of the earliest Jesus movements. Given how prominent the popular prophetic and messianic movements were in the immediate historical context, moreover, we might expect that the earliest movements that formed in response to Jesus' mission would exhibit some similar features and patterns.

Several closely interrelated factors in the traditional Christian theological scheme of Christian origins, however, have worked to isolate Jesus from his historical context, even to keep Jesus from having any direct relation to Jesus movements. First, since he was supposedly a unique person and revealer, Jesus is treated as separate from the social roles and political-economic relationships in which historical figures are usually engaged. Second, rather than being read as complete stories, the Gospels have been taken merely as containers in which to find individual sayings. Jesus' sayings are then understood as artifacts that have meaning in themselves, rather than as genuine communication with other people in historical social contexts. Third, Jesus is viewed as a revealer, separated from the formation of a movement in the context of the village communities in which people lived. Not Jesus himself but the disciples were supposedly the ones who established a community—in Jerusalem after the outpouring of the Holy Spirit at Pentecost, from which they then founded "churches" in Judea and beyond.

The net effect of these interrelated factors of theologically determined New Testament interpretation is a combination of assumptions and procedures that would be unacceptable in the regular investigation of history. When historians investigate popular movements and their leaders (for example, the civil rights movement and its leaders such as Martin Luther King Jr.), they consider multiple contextual and relational factors.[4] Since there are no leaders without followers and no movements without leadership, *leader-follower interaction* is central. Leader and movement would not emerge in the first place, moreover, unless there were a *problematic historical situation*. Yet we do not understand why the leader and followers who form a movement find their situation intolerable unless we know something of the previous *historical developments* that led to the problems. And we cannot understand why they found the situation intolerable unless we have a sense of their cultural values. Indeed, we cannot understand how and why the leader's message and program resonate with followers such that they form a movement without a sense of the *cultural traditions and values* that provide the media in which they communicate.

To investigate the earliest Jesus movements, including possible similarities with contemporary Galilean and Judean movements, we will follow just such a relational and contextual approach—simply bypassing the problematic assumptions, approaches, and concepts of previous New Testament interpretation. We will focus mainly on what are by consensus the earliest Gospel sources, the Gospel of Mark and the sequence of Jesus speeches that appear in closely parallel versions in Matthew and Luke but not in Mark, and known as Q (for *Quelle*, the German word for "source").[5]

The Agenda

Both of the earliest Gospel texts, Mark and Q, represent Jesus and followers as a prophet-led movement engaged in the renewal of Israel that condemns and is condemned by the Jerusalem (and Roman) rulers.[6]

The people who produced and used the sequence of Jesus speeches that is called Q understand Jesus as—and themselves as the beneficiaries of—the figure whose activities fulfilled their yearnings for a prophet who would heal and bind up the people and preach good news to the poor (Q/Luke 7: 18-35). They even see his exorcisms as manifestation of a new exodus, done "by the finger of God," a clear allusion to Moses' divinely empowered performances in the exodus (Q 11:14-20). In the longest speech of Q (6:20-49), moreover, Jesus speaks as the new Moses, enacting a renewal of the covenant as the guiding principles for cooperation and solidarity in community relations. Jesus' speech sending envoys out into villages indicates that the movement of renewal of Israel is expanding by sending delegates to more and more village communities. In speeches that take the distinctively Israelite form of prophetic woes and oracles, Jesus pronounces divine condemnation of the Jerusalem rulers and their representatives. He pronounces a series of woes against the scribes and Pharisees and prophetic oracles of lament over the aristocracy who presume on their lineage, the Jerusalem ruling house (Q 11:39-52; 13:28-29, 34-35). The speeches heard by the Q people thus represent Jesus as the latest in the long line of Israelite prophets to be killed by the oppressive rulers.

The people who produced and used Mark's Gospel had an even more vivid sense of Jesus, his disciples, and themselves as engaged in a renewal of Israel against, and under attack by, the Jerusalem and Roman rulers. Jesus called and commissioned the Twelve as the representative heads of the twelve tribes of Israel as well as disciples who extend his mission of renewing Israel in village communities. The hearers of Mark's story resonated to the clear allusions to the origins of Israel under Moses and the renewal of Israel led by Elijah in the sequences of sea-crossings, exorcisms, healings, and wilderness feedings in the middle of the Gospel (3:35—8:29). That a renewal of Israel is under way is confirmed by the disciples' vision of Jesus with Moses and Elijah on the mountain. And in a series of dialogues (Mark 10:2-45) Jesus presents Torah-like instruction to the communities of his followers, teaching that constitutes a renewed Mosaic covenant, indicated by the recitation of the covenantal commandments. After he marched up into Jerusalem with his entourage, he had condemned the Temple itself in a forcible demonstration reminiscent of Jeremiah's famous pronouncement that God would destroy the Temple because of the rulers' oppressive practices (Mark 11; Jeremiah 7 and 26). Finally, just before he was arrested, tried, and executed by the Romans, Jesus celebrated the Passover at the "last supper," a meal that renewed the Mosaic covenant with the Twelve representatives of Israel, and announced that the cup was "my blood of the covenant" (an allusion to the original covenant meal (Exodus 24).

Mark and Q are different in overall literary form, the one a complex story in a sequence of episodes, the other a series of speeches on different issues. They appear, moreover, to have been produced and used by different communities or movements. Yet they both represent Jesus as a Moses- and Elijah-like prophet engaged in the renewal of Israel in its village communities and pronouncing prophetic condemnations of the Jerusalem Temple, its high priestly rulers, and its Pharisaic representatives. That the two earliest Gospel sources, so different from one another in form, share this portrayal of Jesus as leader of a movement suggests the same role and relationship with followers at the origin of the respective communities or movements. Within the overall agenda shared by both texts, we will focus our investigation on a few key aspects of both movements: the sending of workers on the mission of building and expanding the movement, covenant renewal, and persecution by hostile authorities.

Before moving to those key aspects, however, we may note some distinctive features of Mark and Q that seem to distinguish their communities from other movements of Jesus followers. Mark appears to be setting its movement's identity off against the Jerusalem community headed by Peter and others of the Twelve. The story portrays the disciples as increasingly misunderstanding Jesus' mission and, in the crisis in Jerusalem, betraying, denying, and abandoning him. Mark represents Jesus' role as in a sense patterned after a messianic role in addition to his dominant prophetic role. Yet the narrative qualifies and criticizes the messianic role in decisive ways. Mark also downplays Jesus' resurrection so seriously that it is merely instrumental to calling the hearers of the story back up to Galilee to continue the movement that Jesus had started. The Q speeches indicate no knowledge of a resurrection at all. Jesus' death is understood as the climax of the long line of prophets killed by the rulers. And Q's Jesus demonstrates virtually no messianic traits in his dominantly prophetic agenda.

In these ways and more Mark's story and the Q speeches appear to address movements that originated in Galilee and spread into the bilingual villages of nearby areas (Aramaic and Greek). They are both different from other communities or movements of Jesus loyalists, such as the Jerusalem community known from Acts and the assemblies that Paul addresses in his letters. Before we explore these earliest sources and Jesus movements, however, it makes sense to have a more precise sense of the historical conditions in which the Jesus movements developed.

Conditions in Galilee[7]

Galileans were people of Israelite heritage. They shared with their more southerly cousins in Judea and Samaria the formative traditions of Israel. Most basic were stories of the exodus led by the prophet Moses, celebrated annually in the Passover, and of Israel's covenant with its divine king mediated through Moses on Sinai. Memories of northern Israelite prophets such as Elijah and Elisha would also presumably have been particularly prominent in Galilee.

Galilee, however, had recently come under Jerusalem rule, about a hundred years before Jesus' birth, after being under separate imperial jurisdiction for hundreds of years. During the lifetime of Jesus, Galilee was again placed under separate imperial jurisdiction, no longer under rule by the Jerusalem temple-state. Galileans thus may well have been ambivalent about Jerusalem rule. On the one hand, they were again reunited with others of Israelite heritage, which could well have generated a revival of Israelite traditions. On the other hand, they may not have been overly eager to pay tithes and offerings to the Temple in addition to the taxes demanded by King Herod and the tribute taken by Rome.

Moreover, in Galilee more than in Judea there would have been a discrepancy between the Judean-Israelite "great tradition" cultivated by scribal circles in Jerusalem, partly embodied in the scrolls of the Pentateuch, and the "little" or popular Israelite tradition cultivated in village communities.[8] When the Jerusalem high priesthood took over Galilee, they imposed "the laws of the Judeans" (presumably including the Pentateuch) on the inhabitants. It is difficult to imagine that a century of Jerusalem rule provided sufficient time for Galilean peasants, who lived largely in semi-independent village communities, to assimilate much from the official "laws of the Judeans"—even if they were being pushed on the people by scribal and Pharisaic representatives of the temple-state. The only close contemporary evidence we have, Josephus's accounts of the great revolt in 66–67, indicates that collective actions by Galileans were motivated by their adherence to the basic principles of the Mosaic covenant, and these accounts give no evidence for Galilean acquaintance with laws in the Pentateuch.[9]

The Galilean people eagerly asserted their independence of both Jerusalem and Roman rule at every opportunity. After the Romans imposed Herod as "king of the Judeans" in 40 BCE, Galileans repeatedly resisted his attempts to control their territory (*War* 1.304–16, 326; *Ant.* 14.415–33, 450). When Herod died in 4 BCE, peasants in the area around Nazareth, having acclaimed Judas ben Hezekiah their king, attacked the royal fortress in Sepphoris (*War* 2.56; *Ant.* 17.271). Seventy years later, at the beginning of the great revolt, the peasants quickly asserted their independence of their rulers. In western Galilee they periodically attacked the city of Sepphoris, which remained loyal to the Romans. In eastern Galilee they repeatedly resisted attempts to bring them under control, whether by the Herodian officers in Tiberias or by Josephus, who had been delegated by the provisional high priestly regime in Jerusalem (Josephus recounts these events in his *Life*).

The Roman imposition of Herod Antipas following the revolt in 4 BCE meant that for the first time the ruler of Galilee was located in Galilee itself and not at a considerable distance. The location of the administration within view of nearly every village meant greater efficiency in tax collection. That efficiency and Antipas's need for extraordinary revenues to underwrite the huge expense of building two capital cities, Tiberias as well as Sepphoris, must have exacerbated the economic burden on the peasant producers. Both cities, built in Roman style by a ruler who had been educated in Rome, must have seemed like alien urban society set down into the previously Israelite rural landscape remote from the dominant high culture.

With peasant families forced into escalating debt in order to pay taxes and still support themselves, village communities were threatened with disintegration. There is simply no solid evidence to support the romantic notion of the last generation that Jesus attracted primarily the marginalized members of society, such as "sinners" and prostitutes or rootless individuals who had abandoned their lands and families. Evidence for economic conditions and land tenure in Palestine at the time of Jesus suggests that peasants in the hill country of western Judea had indeed been losing their lands to wealthy Herodian landlords. By contrast, that Herodian officers in Galilee had their estates on the east side of the Jordan River suggests that villagers in Galilee were still on their ancestral lands.[10] Mark and Q themselves, moreover, represent Jesus as engaging the poor peasantry in general. The frequent attention to debts and their cancellation point to an audience still on the land but unable to make ends meet, given the demands for taxes and tribute. The people available for hire as day laborers in some of Jesus' parables were previously assumed to be landless laborers. But those looking for work in a society such as Galilee were more likely villagers who needed to supplement the dwindling subsistence living they were still eking out on their land or peasants working off debts. And as studies of peasant revolts have found, it is villagers in just such circumstances who tend to become involved in popular movements and revolts. On the other hand, those who have already lost their land become heavily dependent on wealthy elite families or their agents and hence are less free to join movements.

Mission

Our earliest Gospel sources offer a number of indications that a movement developed and expanded in Galilee and areas beyond, catalyzed by and focused on Jesus. These indicators come into focus once we cut through previous assumptions regarding Judaism and Christianity that turn out to be historically unfounded.

In contrast to the portrayal of Paul in Acts as founding a new *ekklesia* ("assembly") as a counterpart to the Jewish *synagoge* ("assembly"), in Galilean, Judean, or Syrian villages it was not necessary to form new communities. As in most agrarian societies, the fundamental form of societal life in Galilee and Syria was the village community, comprised of a larger or smaller number of households. The latter were the basic productive and reproductive unit, while village communities had mechanisms for mutual cooperation and aid to help maintain each household as a viable multigenerational unit in the community.

The speeches in both Q and Mark's story portray Jesus and his disciples as developing a movement based in village communities. In Q, the covenant renewal discourse (6:20-49), which addresses local social-economic relations, makes sense only in the context of local communities. The Lord's prayer, with its mutual cancellation of debts, and the discourse on anxiety (11:2-4, 9-13; 12:22-31) also presuppose village communities. Mark's story, moreover, has Jesus repeatedly teaching and healing in villages or "towns" and "places." Most significant, surely, is how Mark's story, almost in passing (as if it would be obvious), has Jesus and his envoys carrying out their teaching and healing in the village *assemblies*. The Greek term *synagoge*, like the Hebrew and Aramaic *knesset* in rabbinic texts, meant "assembly." In the Gospels and in most references in contemporary Judean texts it refers to the local village assembly. According to later rabbinic texts, these village assemblies met twice a week (compare the community fasts mentioned in the *Didache* 8:1). As the religious-political form of local cooperation and self-governance of the semi-independent village communities, the assemblies dealt with common concerns such as the water supply and held community prayers and discussions.[11]

Independently, Mark (6:6-13) and Q (10:2-16) both have Jesus deliver a speech that commissions workers to assist in the program of extending the movement (of renewing Israel) to other village communities.[12] That these "discourses" exhibit the same basic structure, with different wording, suggests that such sending of Jesus envoys was a standard practice in the earliest phases of the Jesus movements. In both versions of the commissioning, the workers are sent out in pairs to other villages where they were to stay with, and accept subsistence support from, a household in the community. Given the small houses and crowded conditions known from archaeological excavations (several houses of two rooms roughly six feet by nine feet off central courtyards), we can assume they were not working with individual families, but wider village communities. Charged to expand Jesus' own mission of preaching and healing, these workers were apparently also, in effect, carrying out what might be called community organizing. The expectation, surely based on experience, was that a whole village might be receptive or hostile. In the former case it apparently became associated with the wider movement. In the latter, curses might be called down upon it for its rejection of the opportunity offered: "Woe to you Chorazin! Woe to you Bethsaida!"[13]

Fig. 1.4. "Peter's House," ruins of a modest first- or early-second-century house in Capernaum, Israel. Capernaum was one of several densely populated towns surrounding Lake Genessaret (the Sea of Galilee) and figures prominently in the accounts of Jesus and his disciples in the Gospels. Photo: Erich Lessing / Art Resource, NY.

In this connection we should follow up the few clues Mark gives about how the most prominent leaders of the movement—Peter, James, and John—may have come from a somewhat different personal and familial situation from the villagers among whom they built the movement. Their fishing enterprise involved the collaborative effort of several men.[14] Herod Antipas, needing to expand his revenues in order to fund his ambitious city-building, developed fishing into an industry. Working through brokers as intermediaries, the king supplied the equipment, especially the costly large (twenty-six-foot) boats that required a crew of five or six (compare the size of boat required in Jesus' sea-crossings in Mark). Collaborative crews evidently contracted to deliver a certain percentage or amount of their catch to the processing depots in return for keeping the rest (somewhat like sharecroppers). The principal processing center for the fish was the burgeoning boomtown of Magdala, "tower of fish" in Aramaic, where people cut loose from their ancestral lands and village communities found work. We might speculate also that the Mary known as "from Magdala," evidently an independent woman (not identified by her attachment to either father or husband), may have been such a destitute person cut loose from her family of origin.

Cross-cultural studies suggest that it is precisely such people with experience beyond a village and contact with outsiders who tend to become leaders in movements of renewal or resistance. Some of the principal leaders of the Jesus movements were apparently "downwardly mobile" people with direct experience of indebtedness to the very power holders who were oppressing the people with heavy taxation and interest on loans prohibited by Israelite covenantal law. These leaders would have had an unusually poignant sense of how the Israelite ideal of a life of cooperation and justice in semi-independent, self-sustaining communities was disintegrating. Such

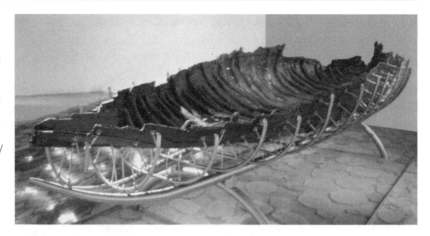

Fig. 1.5. This Roman-era boat was recovered from the Sea of Galilee in 1986. The remains are 8.2 meters long and 2.3 meters wide. Numerous repairs, made with different types of lumber, show the boat had a long working life. Yigal Allon Center, Ginosaur, Israel. Photo: Erich Lessing / Art Resource, NY.

people would have responded eagerly to a message of God's imminent restoration of Israel. Having already been cut loose from the land, moreover, they would have been free to move about from village to village on speaking-healing-organizing missions, in contrast to villagers who needed to remain in place in order to work the fields.

The earliest Gospel sources portray the Jesus movements as having developed initially in Galilee. Mark represents Jesus as having his base of operations in Capernaum, a village on the northern shore of the Sea of Galilee—an account that is generally accepted as historically credible. That also fits the idea of Peter and Andrew and James and John's having been fishermen. In the mission speech in Q, Jesus utters curses on Capernaum, the nearby village of Chorazin, along with Bethsaida, a town across the border in Herod Philip's territory. Such curses presuppose that the mission was active in those communities but that they later backed away or rejected the mission.

Fig. 1.6. Modern reconstruction of a Roman fishing boat based on the archaeological remains of a boat from first-century Galilee. The size of the craft indicates the scale of the Roman fishing industry, requiring a hired crew much larger than a family operation. Photo: Richard A. Horsley.

Mark then also has Jesus and his disciples extend their mission beyond Galilee into the villages of Tyre to the northwest, those of Caesarea Philippi to the north, and those of the Decapolis to the east and south of the Sea of Galilee. This may well reflect the movement's extension by the time Mark's story was composed and being performed in the constituent communities a few decades after Jesus' own mission. It should not be surprising that movements of local renewal and resistance to rulers among one people would become appealing to others and extend over the frontiers. The Syro-Phoenician-woman episode in Mark's story indicates that the inclusion of a women specifically known as from the dominant Hellenic culture was a serious issue for the Jesus movements. Yet the rapid expan-

Fig. 1.7. Ruins of the synagogue of Chorazim, situated above Lake Genessaret (the Sea of Galilee). Hellenistic architectural style. Photo: Erich Lessing / Art Resource, NY.

sion of the Jesus movements beyond the primarily Aramaic-speaking Galilee into Syrian villages, including some Greek-speaking communities, suggests that villagers of previously non-Israelite culture fairly easily identified with Israelite tradition. This is indicated by the very existence of Mark and Q in Greek as texts performed in communities of a movement.

Covenant Renewal

Closely coupled with the exodus, in the formative traditions of Israel, was the covenant with God made on Mount Sinai. The Mosaic covenant and its fundamental principles of political-economic relations (the Ten Commandments) played a crucial role in the people's repeated resistance to oppressive rulers and struggles to restore just social relations. According to Josephus's accounts of the social turmoil of the great revolt, roughly a generation after Jesus' mission in Galilee, violations of covenantal principles by the elite were what mobilized Galilean peasants to collective action. Clearly, the covenantal principles still provided the operative foundation for social-economic relations in village communities and for their political-economic relations with their rulers.[15]

Ostensibly, of course, covenantal principles and mechanisms were still observed by the temple-state as well as the peasantry. There was society-wide observance, for example, of the seventh-year rest for fields and the seventh-year cancellation of debts, traditional covenantal mechanisms designed to keep subsistence peasant households viable on their land. Hillel, the distinguished elder of the Pharisees, had promulgated the famous *prosbul* as a bypass of the sabbatical cancellation of debts, ostensibly to "ease credit" for already indebted peasants. The covenant was thus clearly still well-known among scribal groups such as the Pharisees, who strove to adapt or vitiate covenantal principles in order to allow the consolidation of power in the Jerusalem temple-state. As we know now from the Dead Sea Scrolls, the dissident scribal and priestly community that withdrew to the wilderness at Qumran used the Mosaic covenant as the basic model for their utopian attempt at the renewal of Israel.

It should not be surprising therefore that in both Mark's story and the Q speeches, in which the main theme is the renewal of Israel over against its rulers, covenant renewal should figure prominently. In Mark the covenant theme runs throughout the narrative, with a covenant discourse and a covenant meal at crucial points in the story. In Q the longest and most substantive speech is a renewal of the covenant. The prominence of covenant renewal in the earliest Gospel sources suggests that it was prominent in the Jesus movements that produced and used them.

The basic components of the Mosaic covenant even provide the structure of the longest speech in Q (6:20-49).[16] In the original pattern, a declaration of God's deliverance (focused on the exodus) as a basis of obligation prefaced the principles of social relations that constituted the core demands of the covenant, which were then sanctioned by blessings and curses. These components can be observed at many conspicuous points in the books of the Hebrew Bible: in covenant making, covenantal laws, and covenantal teachings. They are also prominent in key texts of the Qumran community found among the Dead Sea Scrolls.

Most significant for the covenant speech in Q is how the pattern of components is creatively transformed in the initiation ceremony for those entering the renewed covenantal community in the Qumran Community Rule (1QS). The covenant speech in Q exhibits a similar adaptation of the basic components. In both the blessings and curses components, a previously sanctioning motivation has been transformed into a new declaration of God's deliverance, only now in the present and future ("Blessed are the poor, for yours is the kingdom of God"). Other materials now provide the sanction (double parable of building houses on the rock or sand). Still central, of course, are the covenantal principles (laws, teachings, focal instances) that allude to and adapt traditional covenant principles, as guidance for community social and economic interaction.

The covenantal discourse in Q, moreover, is couched in performative speech, that is, speech that makes something happen (for example, "I now pronounce you husband and wife"). The speech enacts a renewal of the Mosaic covenant in the assembled community. The blessings pronounced on the poor, hungry, and mourning announce God's new deliverance happening in the mission of Jesus and the formation and life of the movement, with the corresponding pronouncement of woes on the wealthy. The declaration of covenantal principles (the "love your enemies" set of sayings) gives focal instances of ways in which community members are to quit their local quarrels, insults, and conflicts and return to the covenant ideals of cooperation and mutual support. They are to "love your enemies, do good, and lend." The thrust is to restore the mutuality and solidarity of village community life. That presumably would strengthen the village community with regard to the pressures that are contributing to its disintegration, most obviously the heavy taxation resulting in indebtedness to the cursed wealthy, which exacerbates their poverty and hunger.

Closely associated with the covenant commandments in Israelite tradition were the time-honored mechanisms of prohibition of interest on debts and sabbatical cancellation of debts and release of debt-slaves. Debts were the bane of peasant life and could become a downward spiral from which a family could never recover. That is why Israelites and most other peasantries developed mechanisms of what has been called a "moral economy," mechanisms that could keep each constituent multigenerational family economically viable.[17] The "Lord's Prayer" in Q, also performative speech, is thus also a covenantal economic as well as religious prayer. The "third petition" is a combination of a plea to God for cancellation of debts and the corresponding commitment to cancel whatever debts were owed by fellow villagers. As expressed in the parallel petitions of the prayer, cancellation of debts along with the provision of subsistence food ("daily bread') is what the kingdom of God means.

Parallel to the covenantal speech in Q, Mark presents a covenantal discourse in a series of dialogues (Mark 10) that deal successively with marriage, status in the community, economic relations, and leadership. These dialogues feature a number of covenantal law–like pronouncements ("What God has joined together, let no one separate!" 10:9) as well as recitation of the covenant commandments (10:19). Like the original covenant principles, the principles enunciated in this series of dialogues (like the focal instances in Q 6:27-39) govern particular facets of local social-economic relations, that is, prohibition of divorce protecting marriage at the core of the family unit (no adultery), sanction against the desire for surplus goods (wealth; no coveting, no stealing of others' goods), and a declaration that leaders must be servants, not aspire to power (one of the purposes of the covenant as a whole).

Besides this covenantal renewal discourse directed to social-economic-political relations within the community of the movement, Mark includes other dialogues with covenantal themes. The most pointed is his charge against the scribes and Pharisees from Jerusalem who urge peasants to "devote" *(korban)* their property to the Temple. He declares that such demands violate the basic covenant commandments. He gives the example of "honoring father and mother" to illustrate that the goods and produce of peasant families are needed for local subsistence, as in supporting the elders who can no longer labor productively (Mark 7:1-13). This appeal to the original covenantal "commandment of God" in order to condemn the predatory devices of the representatives of the Temple reinforces peasant families' and village communities' attempts to resist the oppressive demands of their rulers. Similarly, Jesus declares that the scribes based in the Temple "devour widows' houses" (household or possessions). He then illustrates how this happens in the widow's donation of the last copper coin of her "living" to the Temple, again reinforcing the popular resistance to Temple demands. Mark's story thus has Jesus use covenantal references both as principles of community welfare and cooperation and as principles of resistance to the ruling institutions and their representatives.

The covenant renewal discourses and other covenantal teaching in the two earliest Gospel sources offer further indications that the Jesus movements that used these texts were based in local communities that they were attempting to restore to the ideals of mutuality and cooperation of Israelite tradition. Other peasant peoples usually had traditional principles and mechanisms that corresponded to Israelite covenantal commandments and sabbatical cancellation of debts. Thus the (renewed) Israelite covenant that forms a central aspect of Jesus movements would have been easily adapted by village communities across the frontier in Syria.

Persecution and Repression

Ancient and medieval rulers seldom kept their peasants under surveillance. The Judean historian Josephus makes it sound highly out of the ordinary even when Herod arranged for informers on the residents of Jerusalem. About the only time that rulers paid any heed to the semiautonomous village communities over which they "ruled" was at harvesttime, when they sent officers to the threshing floors to appropriate taxes. The Roman approach to "pacification" was to terrorize the populace by brutal slaughter and enslavement of villagers and gruesome public crucifixion of insurgents. As noted above, the Roman governors and their clients in Jerusalem and Galilee seem to have been regularly taken by surprise by protests, prophetic movements, and rebellions. Only after disruptions arose did they send out massive military force to destroy them.

It may be all the more telling, therefore, that Q and Mark contain so many references to persecution of movement members: the likelihood of being arrested, brought to trial, even crucified (Mark 13:8-9; Q 12:2-3; 14:

26). In fact, one of the standard speeches shared, in different versions, by Mark and Q is an exhortation about remaining steadfast when brought to trial and faced with the threat of execution (Mark 8:34-38; Q 12:2-12). The people who heard Q apparently understood themselves to be in the long line of prophets who had been persecuted and killed (11:47-51; 13:34-35; compare 6:22-23). All of these references and passages suggest that the movements had come to the attention of the rulers of Galilee and other territories, who periodically took repressive action to check the growth of the movement. This parallels the experience of other movements of Jesus-followers: periodic attacks by the high priestly or Herodian rulers on the leaders of the Jerusalem community as portrayed in Acts and Paul's arrest and imprisonment as mentioned in his letters. The gist of the warnings and exhortations about repression in both Mark and Q is that it is only to be expected. The people are not to worry about it, however, but to be ready to face martyrdom, as had Jesus, in the trust that they would receive divine inspiration in the hour of testing and would be vindicated in the divine judgment.

WHAT HAPPENED TO THESE JESUS MOVEMENTS?

There is no obvious reason to imagine much continuity between any of the early Jesus movements or Christ-believers and what later became established Christianity, since the latter was shaped by later generations of "bishops and councils." It was later church councils, for example, that canonized the four Gospels. By the time of those fourth- or fifth-century councils, however, Mark was being read differently from the way it was understood in the early communities for which it was produced. The principal way in which Mark and the Q speeches found minimal continuity with later developments was through their absorption and transformation into the Gospels of Matthew and Luke. As the first Gospel in the canon, Matthew became the most widely influential in the next several centuries. The initial absorption of Mark and Q into the composition of Matthew's Gospel, however, did not dramatically alter the identity and agenda of the movements addressed in Mark and Q. Like its sources, Matthew's Gospel and its community still understood themselves as a renewal of Israel, not a new religion.

We simply do not know what the outcome of the Jesus movements in Galilee and southern Syria may have been, how long their influence lasted in the village communities in which they took root. It must be due to the rapid spread and dramatic impact of Jesus' mission in the first generation that we have records of such popular movements in the first place. Peasant movements generally leave no records. Galilean villages in which the movement took root may have been among those decimated in the Roman reconquest in the summer of 67. Villages further north and east in Syria were probably much less affected.

It would be unwarranted to conclude that these movements represented by Mark and Q simply died out and left no trace after a generation or two and that the diverse branches of later Christianity developed only on the basis of the urban communities established by Paul and others. The letters of Pliny provide evidence that the movements of Jesus-followers or Christ-believers continued to spread into village communities as well as cities as far away as northern Asia Minor into the second century. It is tempting to imagine that the teachings included in the movement manual or handbook known as "The Teaching of the Twelve Apostles" (Didache) may have been directed to Greek-speaking village communities of a movement in Syria similar to the one addressed in the Q speeches. The issues addressed and the teachings given appear as a likely later stage in the development of a movement parallel to the one addressed in the Q speeches. For example, the covenant discourse that opens "The Teaching" is expanded with traditional Israelite covenantal teachings, but lacks the performative power involved in the Q speech's transformation of the covenantal components. And the workers ("prophets") sent out in the mission discourses in Q and Mark have now become a problematic drain on the economic resources of subsistence communities when they want to prolong their prophetic "mission." The communities to which the Didache is addressed do not appear to be the same as those addressed in Q or Mark. The instructions for the eucharist assume that Jesus stands in continuity with "the Holy Vine of David," that is, the popular messianic tradition, not the popular prophetic tradition of Moses and Elijah, and baptism is done with a full-blown trinitarian formula. The communities addressed in the Didache, however, are a network of village and small-town assemblies that parallel those addressed in Q and Mark.

THE RENEWAL OF ISRAEL

The earliest Jesus movements, known from the earliest Gospel sources Mark and Q, did not comprise a new religion. Rather, they were movements whose agenda was the renewal of Israel in resistance to the imperial rulers of the people. These movements did not form new communities but set about renewing the social-economic relations of already-existing Galilean village communities according to the basic principles of the

Mosaic covenant. They quickly spread to villages across the frontier under the jurisdiction of other Roman client rulers. But they continued to cultivate the Israelite tradition and covenantal principles, as adapted and transformed in Jesus' teaching and practice. And they continued their distinctively Israelite identity even after they took root in Greek-speaking communities and performed the story and speeches of Jesus in Greek.

In their origins the earliest Jesus movements are part of the history of the Galileans, Judeans, and Samaritans under the rule or continuing authority of the high priestly rulers in Jerusalem. Jesus and the movements that formed in response to his mission are closely parallel in basic ways to other popular movements at the time among the Judeans and Samaritans as well as the Galileans. All of these popular movements formed in resistance to the Jerusalem as well as the Roman rulers, consistent with the general division in ancient societies between rulers and ruled. In social form these Jesus movements parallel the popular prophetic movements insofar as both Mark and Q, with numerous allusions to Israelite tradition, represent Jesus as a Moses- and Elijah-like prophet leading a renewal of Israel. Mark complicates this somewhat with some messianic motifs, yet cautiously and critically so.

Whereas the other popular prophets called their followers away from their village communities into the wilderness, however, the Jesus movements focused on renewal of village communities themselves. And that may explain why the rulers of Galilee and nearby areas did not destroy the Jesus movements in the same way that the Roman governors simply eliminated the Samaritan and Judean prophetic movements. The imperial authorities, however, after executing Jesus as a rebel leader, did carry out periodic repression of his movements. In so doing they perhaps sensed that these movements aimed to strengthen village independence, mutual support, and solidarity in resistance to the imperial order and its disintegrative effects on the subject peoples.

FOR FURTHER READING

Fiensy, David. *The Social History of Palestine in the Herodian Period.* Lewiston, N.Y.: Mellen, 1991.

Horsley, Richard A. *Hearing the Whole Story: The Politics of Plot in Mark's Gospel.* Louisville: Westminster John Knox, 2001.

———. *Jesus and Empire: The Kingdom of God and the New World Disorder.* Minneapolis: Fortress, 2003.

———. *Jesus and the Spiral of Violence: Popular Jewish Resistance in Roman Palestine.* Minneapolis: Fortress, 1993 [1987].

————, with John S. Hanson. *Bandits, Prophets, and Messiahs: Popular Movements in the Time of Jesus.* Harrisburg, Pa.: Trinity Press International, 1999 [1985].

————, and Neil Asher Silberman. *The Message and the Kingdom: How Jesus and Paul Ignited a Revolution and Transformed the Ancient World.* Minneapolis: Fortress, 2002 [1997].

Scott, James C. *The Moral Economy of the Peasant: Rebellion and Subsistence in Southeast Asia.* New Haven: Yale University Press, 1976.

WHY PEASANTS RESPONDED TO JESUS

WILLIAM R. HERZOG II

The first century in Palestine witnessed the rise and fall of many popular movements, none of which survived the death of their founders.
The Jesus movement was a notable exception to the rule. Why was this the
case? As an exercise in doing history "from below,"[1] or doing a people's history, this chapter will explore one aspect of Jesus' teaching by proposing
that his use of parables reflects the work of a prophetic pedagogue of the
oppressed who enabled peasants to articulate the increasing stress they
were experiencing, explore the reasons for that distress, and identify possible responses to it. His memorable oral stories struck a sympathetic chord
with his hearers and raised their awareness of the reasons for the situation
of the villagers by posing problems to be solved and action to be taken. As
a result, Jesus' parables raised the consciousness of the peasants who heard
him and coalesced in a movement that perdured long after his death and
perpetuated the memory of his activities and the generative themes found
in his teaching.

How did this happen? What motivated peasants to form a movement
with enough staying power to survive the crucifixion of its leader? What
attracted the peasants of Judea and Galilee to join and spread the Jesus
movement? Answering these questions will clarify how a people's history
differs from the standard view of these events. The standard view assumes
that the movement began after Jesus' death as a result of Pentecost. The
view developed here suggests that the Jesus movement began in the villages of Galilee during Jesus' life. The standard view assumes that the Jesus
movement arose as a consequence of the resurrection, and it was the proclamation of this message that attracted people to the Jesus movement. This
view proposes that the Jesus movement arose as a consequence of Jesus'
prophetic activity and teaching in Galilee as a response to the oppressive
conditions affecting the peasants and other rural poor folks.

It will be necessary to complete three tasks to provide even a partial answer to the questions already noted. First, we need to conduct a brief overview of how the Romans and their client rulers brought increasing economic and social pressures on village life in Galilee and Judea. Second, since ruling elites and their retainers controlled public communication and held a virtual monopoly on literacy, we must explore how it is possible to hear the voices of villagers who are immersed in "a culture of silence." Third, we will use the life and work of Paulo Freire to sketch a political and cultural analogy for understanding the type of figure Jesus was. Since both figures generated movements that adopted their methods and teachings, understanding Freire and his movement may help to bridge the gap from founder to movement, from Jesus to the Jesus movement.

JUDEAN AND GALILEAN SOCIETY: A GREAT DIVIDE

Rulers and Ruled

It is somewhat ironic that we begin our efforts to unearth a people's history by examining the activity of their rulers, but the rulers, to a large extent, created the conditions to which the poor were compelled to respond. Jesus and his followers lived and worked in a society marked by a great divide. The great divide was based on the rulers' control of the ruled. For all intents and purposes, Rome ruled Galilee and its environs through the client king Herod Antipas, to whom they gave control of Galilee after the death of his father Herod the Great. Similarly, the Romans placed Judea under the client rule of the priestly aristocracy in Jerusalem, after making it a Roman province in 6 CE. They were accountable to a Roman prefect, who was, in turn, accountable to the legate of Syria. Pontius Pilate, perhaps the best-known prefect, ruled from 26 to 36 CE, his term of office largely overlapping the high priesthood of Caiaphas, who held that position from 18 to 36 CE. All of this means that Palestine was an "imperial situation" governed by a "politics of violence."[2]

The power of the high priestly aristocracy in Jerusalem was based in their control of the Temple and its sacrificial system, which posed its own distinctive problems. The high priestly rulers in Jerusalem still expected Galileans to pay their tithes and offerings to the Temple and priesthood, despite the fact that they had been placed under the political-economic jurisdiction of Herod Antipas. The result would have been an ambiguity among Galilean peasants faced with multiple demands for tribute to Rome, taxes to Herod Antipas, tithes and offerings to the Temple. To complicate matters further, the high priests were conflicted and compromised in their role as keepers of the temple. Their dilemma surfaced with special inten-

Fig. 2.1. Scale model of Jerusalem and the Second Temple at the time of King Herod the Great, ca. 20 BCE. Herod's decades-long project to expand and beautify the monumental Temple complex impressed his Roman patrons—and others as well (Mk 13:1; *Sukkot* 51:2). Photo: Erich Lessing / Art Resource, NY.

sity during the pilgrimage festivals that celebrated the liberating power of God to redeem a people from bondage to empires. Yet the priests who presided over these festivals were little more than quislings collaborating with Rome to perpetuate their own power and privilege. In fact there is evidence that the high priestly families became ever more exploitative of the people. A well-known lament from the Talmud captures a popular view of these collaborating high priestly houses.

> Woe is me because of the house of Boethus,
> woe is me because of their staves.
> Woe is me because of the house of [Annas],
> woe is me because of their whisperings.
> Woe is me because of the house of Kathros,
> woe is me because of their pens.
> Woe is me because of the house of Ishmael ben Phiabi,
> woe is me because of their fists.
> For they are high priests, and their sons are treasurers, and their
>   sons-in-law are temple overseers, and their servants beat the
>   people with clubs.
>
> <div align="right">(<i>b. Pesahim</i> 57a; <i>t. Menahot</i> 13:21)[3]</div>

If this lament reflects the historical dynamics and circumstances of the first century, then it witnesses to the use of violence (staves, clubs, and fists), debt records and "great tradition" texts (pens), control of temple offices and functions (high priests, treasurers, and overseers), and rumors and backbiting (whisperings) to maintain their control of the province in the service of their Roman overlords. Not surprisingly, when Roman policy or actions clashed with the local culture of the peasant villagers, the local power brokers almost always sided with the Romans at the expense of the peasants of the land, a habit that only increased the people's mistrust of client kings and high priests. The political situation was volatile, and the tensions between the rulers and the ruled were pervasive. The parable of the wicked tenants (Mark 12:1-12) provides a glimpse "from below" of how the peasants viewed their leaders as part of the problem.

Rich and Poor in City and Countryside

An integrally related aspect of the great divide in Palestine was geographical as well as political-economic: the concentration of the rich in the cities and the poor in the countryside, a chasm such as the one that separates the rich man from Lazarus (Luke 16:19-31). The relationship between city and village was essentially predatory and exploitative, primarily in the form of taxes and tribute. While the extent of tribute and taxation is debated, most estimates run between 25 and 30 percent of a peasant's harvest.[4] By any measure it was oppressive, especially in light of the multiple demands on Galilean peasants for Roman tribute, Herodian taxes, and temple tithes. Taking tribute was a form of domination. Rulers extracted the lion's share of the harvest (the so-called surplus) from those who had produced it for their own political ends and economic purposes. Any resistance to paying taxes and tribute was met with violent retaliation.

Early in his rule in Galilee, Antipas rebuilt the city of Sepphoris and founded a new city on the Sea of Galilee, named Tiberius in honor of his patron, the Roman emperor Tiberius. These cities were strategically placed so that every village in Galilee was no more than a day's walk from one of the capital cities. Antipas's city-building had a serious impact on villagers, particularly economically. Taxes were no doubt increased to support these building projects. And the close proximity of the ruling class to the villages meant that peasants would have been subjected to an ever more efficient and intrusive collection of rents and indirect taxation. The peasants of Galilee thus came under increasing economic stress. Many were forced to borrow to plant their crops, a move that set them on a path that often led to the loss of land through the use of debt instruments.

This cycle of debt and loss led to the formation of popular movements amid other forms of unrest. The contemporary Judean historian Josephus provides a glimpse of these movements. During Pilate's time as prefect of

Judea (26–36 CE), an unnamed Samaritan gathered a following and attempted to lead them to the top of Mount Gerizim, where he promised to unearth the "sacred vessels" buried where "Moses had deposited them" (*Ant.* 18.85–87). Pilate dispatched troops who killed some, dispersed others, and executed its leaders. About a decade later, a figure named Theudas led a band of followers to the Jordan River, where he promised to part the waters. Before he could perform his mighty act, Roman forces killed many, took many prisoner, and decapitated him to deter others from pursuing his course of action (*Ant.* 20.97–98). A few years later a prophet "from Egypt" led thousands of common people around through the wilderness to the Mount of Olives, where he promised that the walls of Jerusalem would fall at his command. Then they could enter Jerusalem where he would rule the citizen-body (*War* 2.261–63; *Ant.* 20.169–72).

Clearly, these popular figures tapped into a deep well of discontent. After all, the promise of deliverance implies oppression and misery, just as the promise to reveal the sacred vessels suggests discontent with the Temple in Jerusalem and its polluted vessels. The efforts to repeat the mighty salvific acts of the past imply a people held in bondage as surely as the people of Israel were slaves in Egypt before their redemption. These popular movements indicate that the people were looking for leaders, but they were not looking to the house of Herod or the high priestly houses in Jerusalem to find that leadership.

This activity also provides an indirect indicator of what was happening socially and economically in Galilee and Judea. Peasants usually do not challenge authority in direct ways unless they are threatened with the loss of their subsistence or some other set of equally important securities. Normally, peasants will endure exploitation as long as their subsistence is assured. This enables them to maintain their honorable standing as a member of a village community. These smallholders occupy the top of the rural hierarchy on the poor side of the great divide. After peasants have lost their land, usually through debt instruments, the best they can hope for is to become tenants living in a contractual relationship with a member of the ruling class, much like the tenants in the parable of the wicked tenants (Mark 12:1-12). They have lost the safety net of village and kinship groups, but they still have a tie to the land. If they lose their status as tenants, then they become day laborers like the workers in the parable of the laborers in the vineyard (Matt. 20:1-16). They are landless and vulnerable.

In the hierarchy of rural life, then, there are two thresholds at which peasants may lose their previous status, and it is at these moments that they will resist their decline most fiercely. As James C. Scott observes, "downwardly mobile peasants may resist most bitterly at those thresholds where they risk losing much of their previous security."[5] The first threshold occurs when peasants lose their land. When threatened with the loss of their land and the security of their village, they will form movements and perhaps even rebel. The same is true when peasants reach the second, more desperate threshold, "when the subsistence guarantees *within* dependency collapse," and the relative stability of tenancy gives way to the perilous life of a day laborer.

Fig. 2.2. The scale of this stone oil press (Herodian, first century BCE) points to Roman consolidation of the olive oil industry, following economic pressures that drove many families off their ancestral lands. Fields and orchards fell into the hands of absentee landlords who profited from the labor of sharecroppers or day laborers, dynamics that appear in Jesus' parables. Photo: Erich Lessing / Art Resource, NY.

The popular movements, focused as they were on the liberation from bondage and the entrance into the land of promise, suggest that peasants were losing their land as well as their hold on the promise embodied in the land. This was a situation that would force peasants into mass movements like the ones mentioned by Josephus. It would also counsel peasants to use "the (less risky) weapons of the weak" at their disposal in order to continue "the prosaic but constant struggle between the peasantry and those who would extract labor, food, taxes, rents and interest from them."[6] The peasants of Galilee and Judea were thus in crisis, as many of Jesus' parables attest.

Traditions and Transcripts

Yet another key aspect of the great divide in advanced agrarian societies is between what anthropologists call the "great tradition" and the "little tradition," which also usually corresponds to the divide between literacy and orality. In societies like first-century Galilee and Judea,[7] where the few have almost everything and the many have almost nothing, these dramatic and drastic inequalities require legitimation and some degree of mystification. For these reasons, no system of domination is complete until the rulers have imposed their ideological worldview on the peasants and artisans whom they control.

The primary means for attempting to achieve this goal is the formation and propagation of a "great tradition," or history as seen "from above." Formulated in urban areas, it is produced in written form since, in an oral, illiterate culture like first-century Palestine, written texts carry an aura of power and authority. The great tradition in its varied forms attracts guardians who limit access to it, control its parameters, and determine both its interpretation and its application. In the case of Galilee and Judea, the sacral elites in the Jerusalem Temple and their scribal retainers, as well as political factions like the Pharisees, performed these tasks. Given these dynamics, it is clear that the great tradition, even when it appeared as a reading of Torah, could neither support the lives of peasant villagers nor serve their interests. Since this is the case, it makes sense that the farther down the scale of social stratification one moves (from elites to retainers to artisans and peasants), the less binding the great tradition becomes, and the more likely that countertraditions will emerge in the form of a little tradition.

The little tradition, in its local variations, is centered in the villages, towns, and hamlets of agrarian societies, at the other end of the social hierarchy from the rulers. This cultural and geographical distance provides space for the little tradition to take root and grow. It expresses, as Scott notes, "the distinctive patterns of belief and behavior which are valued by the peasantry of an agrarian society."[8] In addition, it incorporates the peasants' selective appropriation of the great tradition in a manner that supports their life and sustains their culture. The little tradition captures a view of history seen from below. In addition to providing a repository for the collective wisdom of the village, the little tradition provides a resource for resisting the imposition of any great tradition by ruling elites, for the simple truth is that, in spite of their most determined efforts, ruling classes usually fail to impose their view of the world on the peasantry. Peasants find ways to achieve what Scott calls a "negotiated subordination." Yet, even a negotiated subordination indicates that the hegemony of the rulers and the ruling class is not complete. Hegemony is a goal, not a fact.

Although it might seem, at first glance, that the little tradition and the great tradition occupy parallel universes and never intersect, nothing could be further from the truth. The two traditions often do deal with the same materials, though from very different points of view. The Jerusalem high priests embraced Abraham as their eponymous ancestor while popular Israelite tradition rejected the use of Abraham as a legitimating figure (Luke/Q 3:9). The parable of the rich man and Lazarus portrays Abraham as the redeemer of the destitute. In similar fashion, the two traditions developed their conflicting views of the Mosaic covenant, sabbatical traditions, the meaning of the exodus and the Passover, the temple and tithes, and the high priestly families who controlled Jerusalem. The two traditions contested common ground, crafted their own distinctive emphases, and provided a framework for the theological and ideological conflicts in Galilee and Judea.

It might appear that the great tradition of the elites and the little tradition of the people of the land are equally accessible, but in a situation in which power relations favor the rulers over the ruled, this could not be the case. Indeed, it will take "eyes to see" the outlines of and "ears to hear" the echoes of the little tradition of oppressed groups. The situation is even more complicated. In a political setting where the few dominate the many, one could expect to find three different kinds of political discourse. The first is a "public transcript"[9] of events and arrangements seen through the eyes of the ruler and the ruling class, a "shorthand way of describing the open interaction between subordinates and those who dominate," or, in other words, "the *self*-portrait of dominant elites as they would have themselves seen." One can see an example of this self-portrait in the landowner's closing speech in the parable of the laborers in the vineyard (Matt. 20:1-16). The public transcript controlled by the rulers will include the great tradition as their way of interpreting and justifying the current political order while legitimating their right to rule. When forced to assume a role onstage in the political theater scripted by the elites, the powerless will feign compliance with the public transcript of the rulers.

The second kind of discourse we could expect to find in this situation is a "hidden transcript" that captures what the oppressed say to each other when they are offstage, out of earshot of their masters and their agents or retainers. The hidden transcript distills what peasants really believe but are too intimidated and cowed to express openly. The consequences would be too dire to contemplate, since most elites countenance no open opposition and tolerate no subversive speech. The hidden transcript will reflect many of the themes of the little tradition, whose characteristic themes include "a struggle over the appropriation of symbols, a struggle over how the past and the present shall be understood and labeled, a struggle to identify causes and assess blame, and a contentious effort to give partisan meaning to local history."[10]

It is evident that these themes cannot be explored in open discourse but remain embedded in the "alternative moral universe" and hidden in the "latent normative subculture" of the peasant village, where it may assume the form of "millennial dreams, popular theater, folk tales, folk sayings, myths, poetry, jokes and songs," to which we would add parables.[11]

If the little tradition with its hidden transcripts remains offstage and oral, then how can anyone gain access to it or identify its themes? The task would be impossible were it not for a third kind of political discourse found among the oppressed classes and expressed inadvertently through the public transcript of the elites or indirectly when a peasant is forced into a role onstage under the direct gaze of the ruling elites. Scott describes this third form of political discourse as "a politics of disguise and anonymity

Fig. 2.3. Bronze coin showing ears of grain, from the period of Herod Agrippa I, King of Judea (42 CE). Coins struck by Jewish leaders bore images of grain (symbolizing prosperity) or religious symbols (symbolizing piety); images of rulers, as on Roman coins, were considered idolatrous and offensive. From the Reifenberg Collection, Israel. Photo: Erich Lessing / Art Resource, NY.

that takes place in public view but is designed to have a double meaning or to shield the identity of the actors." This means, in effect, that "a partly sanitized, ambiguous and coded version of the hidden transcript is always present in the public discourse of subordinate groups."[12]

This chapter proposes that Jesus engaged villagers with a little-tradition version of the themes of justice and judgment found in the Israelite version of the covenant at Sinai and codified in portions of Torah. As he did, he entered the scene in a contentious effort to give a different partisan meaning to history. The work of Paulo Freire clarifies such a process.

PAULO FREIRE ON TEACHING PEASANTS

One way to approach Jesus' parables is to examine how they might have contributed to "a struggle over the appropriation of symbols, a struggle over how the past and the present shall be understood, a struggle to identify causes and assess blame, a contentious effort to give partisan meaning to local history," in short, to examine how Jesus' parables contributed to a first-century "pedagogy of the oppressed."[13] The work of Brazilian educator Paulo Freire can provide some vital clues for discerning the function and purpose of Jesus' parables as part of a larger political and theological program, that is, as they contributed to the foundation of a movement or the formation of a political faction.[14]

Freire's unorthodox educational work began when he left a traditional teaching position to work with illiterate peasants, who, he was convinced, could be taught to read. In spite of his conviction that peasants could acquire literacy, Freire has acknowledged that his initial efforts were naive because they failed to account for the political dimension of education. He discovered this oversight when he began to work in earnest with peasant villagers.

To his surprise, Freire learned that their rulers had already imbued them with a form of "banking education" that deposited the elites' view of the world in the hearts and minds of peasant villagers. To use terms already introduced into this discussion, this deposit is very much like a form of the great tradition informed by the public transcripts of the elites. Freire's peasant students had already been inculcated with a view of the world that justified the rulers' wealth and explained their poverty. The present political, economic, and social arrangements reflected God's design, and peasants were taught that their responsibility was to adjust to the role God had assigned to them. There was no hope of change; the future was as fixed as the present. It was clear to Freire that, as long as peasants were confined in this ideological prison, they had neither a history to call their own nor a key able to unlock their role in creating history. They were effectively submerged in a culture of silence born of the violence and intimidation they had suffered in those rare moments when they had shown enough courage or temerity to speak.

In spite of this unpromising beginning, Freire continued to develop a four-stage pedagogy, three stages of which are germane to this discussion.[15] First, believing that his educational project should begin with the peasants' context, he sent teams of participant-observers to live in peasant villages until they could learn to see the world through peasant eyes. They studied the peasants' language and speech patterns and discovered a peculiar beauty and wisdom in their speech. Out of this immersion experience, the teams began to assemble "generative words" that could be used as building blocks to construct the peasants' "thematic universe," which differed in significant ways from the deposit of the great tradition. In other words, the teams had begun to discover forms and, in some cases, vestiges of a latent, buried little tradition of the peasant villagers enhanced by the villagers' hidden transcripts.

Second, building on these generative words and themes, Freire prepared what he called "codifications," visual pictures that posed a problem and objectified some aspect of peasants' lives. Freire would present these codifications to a group of peasant villagers in what he called a "culture circle." The codification was a stimulant intended to generate conversation; it was open-ended, not an end in itself. Stimulated by the codification and problem-posing questions, the peasants would begin the process of learning to interpret their world and discover how it works, why it works the way it does, and who benefits at whose expense. The conversation was, therefore, political, economic, social, and religious all at once.

As they examined these codifications, peasants became interpreters of their world and began to discover that social, political, and economic realities were not so much unchangeable givens as they are human constructions subject to revision. These codifications generated an increasingly analytical conversation that encouraged peasants to move from surface features to explore more submerged and less obvious issues. They began to realize, for example, how their poverty was a consequence of the wealth accumulated by the elites. This led to the discovery that their poverty was neither an immutable necessity nor a divine punishment but a changeable human contingency. Social description moved into social analysis. While the villagers were learning to read specific codifications that posed particular problems, they were also learning how to continue learning in this manner. They were developing insights and skills that were transferable, and they were becoming adept at interpreting their world without the physical presence of Freire and his participant-observers.

The third phase of the pedagogy involved decoding, problematizing, and recodifying what the codifications had revealed. The process of problematizing takes what were previously thought to be fixities and re-presents them as problems to be solved. This process led to decoding what was previously believed to be true, and, as it did, it revealed that the world was a series of problems susceptible to a variety of solutions. In other words, the peasants were "decoding" (deconstructing) the great tradition of their rulers. As they worked collectively on these newly defined problems, the villagers were empowered to make their own history, while becoming subjects in that history. In essence, they were "recodifying" the world by appropriating their little tradition. Freire called this entire process "conscientization," the development of a critical consciousness able to break the culture of silence, decode its hold over the villagers, and recodify a vision of a transformed world.

Fig. 2.4. Plowing and sowing. As the Roman empire expanded and incorporated the agricultural economies of conquered lands, nostalgic depictions of farming became favorite themes in domestic art among the Roman elite. Roman mosaic from a series depicting agricultural labor (see Color Plates D and E), from Saint Romain-en-Gal, first half of the third century CE. Musée des Antiquités Nationales, Saint-Germain-en-Laye, France. Photo: Erich Lessing / Art Resource, NY.

If learning should lead to doing, it was not enough simply to decode, problematize, and recodify problems. Freire needed to encourage his students to codify "limit situations," those moments when peasants could challenge their rulers, and "limit acts," the means by which the challenge would be made. This whole cycle embodied the meaning of *praxis*, which describes a dialectical process, "reflection and action upon the world in order to transform it." This pedagogy produced two major outcomes. First, the participant-observers discovered that a little tradition was already present in the peasant villages. Second, they were able to teach the oppressed how to develop the fuller potential of that tradition in the service of resistance and identity formation.

Freire's pedagogy of the oppressed became a movement in the last third of the twentieth century, and, because his methods were transferable, they were introduced wherever despotic regimes dominated peasant populations. His work was useful in a variety of contexts because it identified a set of key components needed to empower peasants living under authoritarian regimes. Its transferability contributed to its success. Freire's pedagogy succeeded because it was not dependent on him but relied for its success on the ability of peasants to learn how to read and interpret their world. In doing this, they had learned more than a particular interpretation of their world or a new ideology; they had learned how to learn and so could transfer their skills to other contexts and issues, a necessary skill if the pedagogy was to contribute to the emergence of a movement. A leader like Freire or Jesus might initiate the process, but it was inherently a communal or village-based activity that could be conducted in the leader's absence. This would be a precondition for the shift from pedagogue to pedagogy; in other words, the pedagogy outlasted the pedagogue and took the form of a movement.

JESUS AS TEACHER OF GALILEAN PEASANTS IN CRISIS

Jesus' parables functioned in just that way: as verbal codifications in dialogue with the peasants of his day. Just as Freire used visual codifications, so Jesus used verbal codifications we call parables. Modern interpreters treat parables as conveying self-contained messages that can be decoded and communicated to others. Jesus' parables served a different purpose in a different style of learning based in peasant villages. Interpretation was a communal activity. Freire gathered villagers in "culture circles," but Jesus used the regular village assemblies as occasions for speaking in parables. The parable was the starting point, not the end of the process. Unlike the modern Western separation of religion from political and economic matters, the parable and discussion would have included the full spectrum of concerns shared by peasant villagers at their regular gatherings (synagogues were not yet buildings but community gatherings to discuss matters of interest and concern to the village). If the parables worked in this fashion, the task of telling parables became part of a larger learning process that encouraged and enabled peasants to interpret their world. As the parables crystallized the peasants' insights into how their rulers' practices were affecting their village life, they also galvanized the formation of the Jesus movement.

The Great Divide as Violation of Torah and Covenant

Jesus' parable of the rich man and Lazarus objectifies the great divide between a wealthy and powerful elite and an impoverished peasantry whose situation is steadily deteriorating. It juxtaposes the fate of a destitute beggar and the fortune of a wealthy elite, both in this age and in the age to come. The unexpected turnabout in the age to come re-presents the disparity as a problem-posing (problematizing) opportunity that decodes the typical meaning of rich and poor and recodifies the relation between them. The parable (Luke 16:19-31) can be divided into two scenes:

16:19-22 Scene 1: rich and poor, the order of things
16:23-31 Scene 2: rich and poor, the disorder of things

The first scene contrasts the life of the rich, who live in extravagance, with the life of the destitute, who live in abject poverty. As a skilled storyteller and codifier, Jesus uses a few deft verbal brush-strokes to sketch the picture. The rich man is "dressed in purple" (the most expensive color, which only the highest elites or royalty could afford) and "fine linen" (imported cloth from Egypt), "feasted sumptuously every day" (not just on festive occasions), and lives a life protected from contact with the poor (the great gate that sealed him from the beggars on the streets near his house). The poor beggar is covered with sores (consequence of malnutrition), perpetually hungry (desires to be fed with what falls from the table), and desperate enough to fight the street curs for the table scraps and garbage thrown out of the rich man's house (getting "licked" by the dogs in the process). The end of scene 1 implies that, as the crown of a virtuous life, the rich man is buried honorably, while Lazarus's corpse is gathered up from the street and thrown into a garbage dump for the indigent.

So far, all has proceeded according to expectation. The shock comes when the hearers learn that Lazarus, whose name means somewhat ironically "God helps," is reclining on Abraham's bosom, like an honored guest at a banquet, while the rich man is in the flames in Hades. It is important not to read Hades as equivalent to the Christian notion of "hell." It is rather the place that the dead go to await resurrection as well as a place for learning lessons neglected in life. Thus the second and longest scene of the parable could be called "the pedagogy of the oppressor." The very presence of Lazarus on Abraham's bosom is, within the narrative structure of the parable, a

There was a rich man who was dressed in purple and fine linen and who feasted sumptuously every day. And at his gate lay a poor man named Lazarus, covered with sores, who longed to satisfy his hunger with what fell from the rich man's table; even the dogs would come and lick his sores. The poor man died and was carried away by the angels to be with Abraham. The rich man also died and was buried. In Hades, where he was being tormented, he looked up and saw Abraham far away with Lazarus by his side. He called out, "Father Abraham, have mercy on me, and send Lazarus to dip the tip of his finger in water and cool my tongue; for I am in agony in these flames." But Abraham said, "Child, remember that during your lifetime you received your good things, and Lazarus in like manner evil things; but now he is comforted here, and you are in agony. Besides all this, between you and us a great chasm has been fixed, so that those who might want to pass from here to you cannot do so, and no one can cross from there to us." He said, "Then, father, I beg you to send him to my father's house—for I have five brothers—that he may warn them, so that they will not also come into this place of torment." Abraham replied, "They have Moses and the prophets; they should listen to them." He said, "No, father Abraham; but if someone goes to them from the dead, they will repent." He said to him, "If they do not listen to Moses and the prophets, neither will they be convinced even if someone rises from the dead."

—Luke 16:19-31

codification for the rich man to decode. Abraham tries to teach the rich man, but the rich man keeps refusing to learn what Abraham offers while insisting on his own agenda. Send Lazarus with water! Send Lazarus to my five brothers! He sees Lazarus as a servant or a subservient messenger, assuming that Lazarus cannot be with Abraham for any other purpose, certainly not as a guest at a banquet. But Abraham refuses either to provide relief or to accede to any of the rich man's requests. His strategy seems to be: turn up the heat, and see if he responds.

Throughout his pedagogy of the oppressor, Abraham is trying to elicit from the rich man the recognition that Lazarus is a child of Abraham every bit as much as he is. Notice that Abraham uses kinship language when addressing the rich man (*teknon,* child), while the rich man calls Abraham "father" *(pater).* Of course, if Lazarus is a child of Abraham, and the rich man is a child of Abraham, then the rich man and Lazarus are brothers, but this is what the rich man fails to comprehend. He is concerned only about his father and five brothers; that is, his notion of kinship is based on class solidarity and self-interest. If the rich man realized that Lazarus was his brother, then the first scene of the parable would be shameful, unthinkable, and inconceivable.

This is, of course, what the Torah taught. Even the great tradition produced in Jerusalem had incorporated the early Israelite covenantal traditions that the land was a gift of Yahweh (Lev. 25:23), and the yield of the land was not to be hoarded but shared so that everyone would have enough (Leviticus 25; Deut. 15:1-18).[16] But the rich man and his class have been hoarding the wealth of the land while reducing the Lazaruses of the world to utter ruin, all the while claiming to be the children of Abraham, their eponymous ancestor. What makes the name Lazarus so ironic is that it may well represent Abraham's steward, Eliezar, who was sent among the people of Israel to see how well they were fulfilling their obligation to show hospitality,[17] the virtue for which Abraham, the ancestor, was renowned. This is why Abraham appeals to Moses and the prophets. Moses had taught the principles of the covenant, according to which Israelites were not to take advantage of their brothers and become oppressive rulers, but, when they did, the prophets condemned kings and royal officials for their exploitation of the poor. (See, for example, Isa. 1:16-17; 5:7; Jer. 5:23-29; 21:11-14; Amos 2:6-11; 5:10-24; Micah 3:1-3, 9-12.) But Abraham's appeal falls on deaf ears and what looks like a hardened heart. Hades may not be hell, but it is rapidly becoming so in light of the rich man's refusal or inability to repent and accept Lazarus as his brother.

Read in this fashion, the parable codifies the two-tiered society that existed in Herod Antipas's Galilee and the high priests' Judea and Jerusalem. Only by the most blatant violation of the Mosaic covenantal prin-

ciples, such as taking interest on loans and demanding exorbitant taxation, had such a great chasm developed between rich and poor under the
Roman client rulers. Iniquity produced inequity. Jesus' parable codifies the
cause of injustice and inequities and poses them as a problem to be solved.
In this case, an important hint is found in the conversation between Abraham and the rich man. The restoration of social relations based on a broad
understanding of kinship needs to replace the class structure that has
usurped it and created a ruling class no longer obedient to the Torah but
dedicated to ruthlessly exploiting the peasants of Galilee and seizing their
land through oppressive debt instruments. The loss of kinship ties (either
fictive or real) leads to destitution and ruin for figures like Lazarus, and the
cultivation of the great chasm separates rich from poor. The common
ground they share as the people of God has been lost. If the symptom in
the codification is a desperate beggar, he also becomes a symbol of the
social disease that afflicts Galilee and Judea. The parable has problematized the great divide and recodified its meaning. It does not point to the
normal order of things ("the poor you will always have with you") but to
the failure to take the covenant seriously. The rich are not blessed by God,
nor is poverty a judgment from God. The common rationalizations that
justify the order of things come unraveled when faced with the disorder of
things in the banquet hall of Abraham, where Lazarus reclines as an honored
guest. But how can street garbage like Lazarus become a guest of honor?
Either something is wrong with the afterlife, or something is terribly wrong
here in this life. If explored with enough tenacity, the parable could reveal
the relationship between wealth and poverty, eventually disclosing the systems that maintain the great divide by turning the Lazaruses of the world
into disposable street beggars so the ruling elites can add to their already
massive wealth. Lazarus is typical of the people who were excluded from
kinship networks and village life, exiled to a social death as part of the collateral damage of the system.

If Jesus told this parable as a pedagogue of the oppressed and used the
parable to stimulate a problem-posing conversation in a peasant village,
the villagers would begin to decode the social scene presented to them and
problematize the presence of a beggar who was "thrown down" (a passive
verb, perhaps indicating the purposive activity of God) at the rich man's
gate. As he does in so many of his parables, Jesus includes the superrich
and the desperate poor in the same story, a situation that happened very
rarely in his world, in order to show how the two are related and imply
each other. It is impossible to have great concentrations of wealth at the
top of a social system without massive misery at the bottom. The reversal
of fortunes and the subsequent pedagogy of the oppressor encourage listeners to decode the rich man's attitudes and to grasp how Abraham is

recodifying the world to accord with the word of Moses and the way of the prophets, in short to restore an understanding of kinship and hospitality adequate to speak to the struggles of the peasant villagers.

As the parable illustrates, the figure of Abraham carried significant symbolic importance. Was he the honorable ancestor of the rich man's class, the prototypical eponymous ancestor whose identity legitimated the rulers of Israel (Luke/Q 3:7-9), or was he, along with his steward Eliezar, the friend of the Lazaruses of the world and the host of the banquet that would welcome them home, restoring the hospitality denied to them in life? It was no accident that Abraham is depicted as the host of a banquet with Lazarus as guest of honor (Luke/Q 13:28-29).

Paying the Price on Payday

The parable of the laborers in the vineyard (Matt. 20:1-16) draws on the image of the vineyard in order to problematize the relationship between rich and poor. The parable juxtaposes a member of the ruling class with destitute day laborers who have nothing left to sell but their labor. The most desperate day laborers would have lost any safety nets that village and kin might have been able to provide. They were often the second or third son born into a peasant household. When they began to consume more than they could produce, they were turned out of their village and home and left to fend for themselves. Once day laborers lost their support network, their situation was critical, and they fell into a group in agrarian societies called the "expendables,"[18] who work intermittently until they die from the complications of malnutrition or disease. Day laborers work when recruited, and, especially if they had lost their land, they begged when they could not work. Theirs was literally a dead-end life. To make life more difficult, these desperate day laborers competed with other peasants who still owned their land but worked as day laborers to supplement their subsistence living.

The parable depicts the owner of the vineyard going to the marketplace to hire day laborers, presumably to assist in harvesting his crop of grapes. In order for grapes to yield good wine, they must be harvested within a short time span, so day laborers are needed. The owner's subsequent trips to hire more laborers implies that he has large vineyards and a bumper crop of grapes. Is this an echo of the great harvest in the parable of the rich fool (Luke 12:16-21)?

It is unlikely that an elite landholder himself would hire day laborers. It is much more likely that his steward, who appears later in the parable, would have done this task. But, like a good political cartoon, the parable codification makes the landowner a major player in the scene it has codified, so it can prepare the hearers for the final confrontation. In this way, Jesus makes the normally invisible elites visible.

The owner does not really bargain with the day laborers, as his successive trips to the marketplace reveal. He agrees with the day laborers for a *denarius* (the standard wage for a laborer), and, on his second trip to the *agora*, he sends others into his vineyard with the promise to pay them what is "right" *(dikaios)*. At the eleventh hour, he simply orders the workers, "you go into the vineyard," without any promise of pay. All of this indicates that the "owner of the vineyard," as he is described, calls the shots and determines the wages of the day laborers. Their numbers reduce their bargaining power. Even at the end of the day, some laborers are still waiting in the *agora*, hoping to be hired even for an hour.

The parable unfolds in three scenes:

20:1-7	Scene 1: hiring day laborers
20:8-10	Scene 2: paying day laborers
20:11-16	Scene 3: clashing with day laborers

Just as the first scene of the parable was set in motion by the actions of the owner of the vineyard, so the second scene is set in motion by his instructions to his steward, "give them their pay, beginning with the last and then going to the first" (20:8). The normal order would be to pay the first hired first and the last hired last, but the owner reverses the order so that the first hired will know that the last hired have received a *denarius*, rather than a partial wage in proportion to the time they worked and the contribution they made to the hard labor of harvesting ("the burden of the day and the scorching heat," 20:12). From the protest of the first-hired workers, it is clear that they believe their labor has been shamed.

The payment schedule sends them a message that the owner values their hard day's work no more than an hour of work from the last hired. It is a sharp and calculated insult. Normally, day laborers would keep silent (culture of silence) and express their reaction to the

> For the kingdom of heaven is like a landowner who went out early in the morning to hire laborers for his vineyard. After agreeing with the laborers for the usual daily wage, he sent them into his vineyard. When he went out about nine o'clock, he saw others standing idle in the marketplace; and he said to them, "You also go into the vineyard, and I will pay you whatever is right." So they went. When he went out again about noon and about three o'clock, he did the same. And about five o'clock he went out and found others standing around; and he said to them, "Why are you standing here idle all day?" They said to him, "Because no one has hired us." He said to them, "You also go into the vineyard." When evening came, the owner of the vineyard said to his manager, "Call the laborers and give them their pay, beginning with the last and then going to the first." When those hired about five o'clock came, each of them received the usual daily wage. Now when the first came, they thought they would receive more; but each of them also received the usual daily wage. And when they received it, they grumbled against the landowner, saying, "These last worked only one hour, and you have made them equal to us who have borne the burden of the day and the scorching heat." But he replied to one of them, "Friend, I am doing you no wrong; did you not agree with me for the usual daily wage? Take what belongs to you and go; I choose to give to this last the same as I give to you. Am I not allowed to do what I choose with what belongs to me? Or are you envious because I am generous?" So the last will be first, and the first will be last.
>
> —Matt. 20:1-16

insult with grumbling offstage, where the rulers could not hear them. But this insult is so shameful and devastating that they have to respond, even if it means confronting an elite onstage. If they do not, then they would be consenting to their own degradation because they would be agreeing with the owner about the relative worth of their labor. If they do not respond, their daily wage will fall below a *denarius* and plunge them even deeper into poverty and destitution.

Uncharacteristically and quite unexpectedly, the third scene is initiated by the day laborers, who respond to the shaming of their labor. The owner's response is swift and sharp. First, he singles out one laborer to make an example of him: "he replied to one of them." Second, he appeals to the supposed negotiation for a *denarius*, "I am doing you no wrong; did you not agree with me for a denarius?" This gives the impression that the two parties negotiated a mutually agreeable wage, when the truth is that the owner most likely offered a *denarius* and took whoever would accept the wage. Third, he expels the laborer from his vineyard: "take what belongs to you and get." This is called blackballing or shunning; the laborer will not work for him again.

The culminating response is the most important because the owner justifies his actions by mystifying them, portraying them as an act of generosity: "I choose to give to this last the same as I give to you." Notice that the issue is no longer a wage but a gift, solely determined by the owner. His rhetorical question, "Am I not allowed to do what I choose with what belongs to me?" assumes that everyone would assent to his claim. If so, then the day laborers must be complaining about his generosity. The Greek form of the question is much more pointed than its translation would suggest. The owner asks, "Or is your eye evil because I am good?" (my translation). This accusation declares that what the day laborers have complained about reveals their evil while underscoring the goodness of the owner.

If the parable ends with this question, as a codification might, a peasant audience would have a great deal to decode, problematize, and recodify. They would need to decode the owner's claim that the land belongs to him and his class, for the Torah declares that the land belongs to Yahweh, who distributes it as a gift to the people of the land. If the covenant is true, then the ruling class is exposed and judged as arrogating the prerogatives of Yahweh for themselves and their class, but this requires "eyes to see." This being the case, the owner in the parable has attempted to dismiss this insight by calling it the product of an "evil eye" (false consciousness). As the parable problematizes the stormy outrage of the laborers against the calm claims of the owner, they will have to decode his arrogant claims and recodify what stems from an "evil eye" and what comes from having "eyes to see" (critical consciousness; see Q/Luke 10:24; Mark 8:17-18).

Seen through this perspective, the owner's conviction that he is giving generously must be measured against the extension principle of the Torah, which requires that the haves distribute the wealth of the land to the have-nots and not hoard it for themselves. By contrast, the owner pays or gives nothing more than a malnutrition wage, a mockery of the extension principle of the Torah. The owner's generosity is a figment of his imagination, and his exploitation of day laborers contributes to the great chasm that separates the rich from the poor. He does not embody the rectitude he presumes, but he and his class represent a major obstacle to the establishment of justice based on Torah. In the hands of a pedagogue of the oppressed, the parable stimulates an effort "to identify causes and assess blame" in a very local version of history like a vineyard on payday when the goods of the land are redistributed. It argues that the owner practices a form of blaming the victim in order to justify a system that condemns the many to poverty in order to support the few. Confronted with a raw display of power to shame them, the day laborers speak the truth to the face of power, and one of them pays the price. The saying attached to the parable in 20:16 (the last will be first and the first last) may express the reflection of the early church on the parable, or it may reflect Jesus' closing provocation to stir his listeners to break the spell woven by the owner in his address to the workers.

This parable could have served well as a codification to stimulate peasant reflection on the mystification contained in the parable and expressed through the owner's final riposte. The owner has mystified greed as generosity and distorted the meaning of the Torah to claim that his land belongs to him. He has dismissed the protest challenge of the day laborers as products of an "evil eye" when the day laborers have actually revealed that they have "eyes to see." Exploration of the dynamics in the parable could lead to identifying causes of poverty and assessing blame for the poverty in the land. It is a contentious parable in which the public transcript and official version of events is expressed by the householder (oikodespotes), while the day laborers subtly force him to condemn himself by exposing his arrogance and abrogation of Torah. As peasants explored the parable, they would distinguish the false consciousness of the "lord of the vineyard" from the critical consciousness of the day laborers. Although they hardly speak, they elicit the false consciousness of the landowner as he tried to silence their protest and stigmatize them as having an evil eye.

Whose Vineyard Is It, Anyway?

The parable of the wicked tenants (Mark 12:1-12 // Matt. 21:33-46; Luke 20:9-19) opens with an allusion to Isa. 5:1-7. The imagery at the beginning of Jesus' parable clearly echoes Isa. 5:1-2, the first of three distinct sections found in this prophetic text: (1) 5:1-2, a love song; (2) 5:3-4, a judicial parable and plea; and (3) 5:5-7, a judgment oracle. What begins as a love song ends in judgment, an indictment on the house of Israel and the people of Judah:

> [Yahweh] expected justice,
>   but saw bloodshed;
> righteousness,
>   but heard a cry! (5:7)

The issue in Isaiah is that the vineyard failed to produce a proper crop, "[Yahweh] expected it to yield grapes, but it yielded wild grapes" (5:2b). The issue in Jesus' vineyard parable is the character of the tenants who were called to care for it.

The parable depicts an absentee landowner who plants a vineyard, leases it to tenants, and then sends servants to receive his share of the harvest. To understand the characters in the parable, it might help to know that there was a three-tiered structure of rural stratification. First, at the top of the hierarchy, were freeholders living in villages. They had not only a kinship network to rely on but the safety net of the village itself. Second, if a peasant lost his land or was forced to leave the village for other economic reasons, his next best hope was to become a tenant in a contractual relationship with a landowner, like the tenants in the parable. Since they were responsible to prune and care for the vineyard until it began to produce grapes, they had probably received a three- to four-year contract, a relatively secure position for a tenant. They were still in an extremely vulnerable situation because they had lost the safety net provided by their village and kinship ties, and they were directly dependent on a member of the landowning class, not an enviable position, to be sure. Tenants had lost the status of being a freeholder with a moral claim on village and kinship systems of support, and they were liable to be caught in a downward spiral because their tenancy was so fragile and uncertain. Finally, at the bottom of

---

Then he began to speak to them in parables. "A man planted a vineyard, put a fence around it, dug a pit for the wine press, and built a watchtower; then he leased it to tenants and went to another country. When the season came, he sent a slave to the tenants to collect from them his share of the produce of the vineyard. But they seized him, and beat him, and sent him away empty-handed. And again he sent another slave to them; this one they beat over the head and insulted. Then he sent another, and that one they killed. And so it was with many others; some they beat, and others they killed. He had still one other, a beloved son. Finally he sent him to them, saying, 'They will respect my son.' But those tenants said to one another, 'This is the heir; come, let us kill him, and the inheritance will be ours.' So they seized him, killed him, and threw him out of the vineyard. What then will the owner of the vineyard do? He will come and destroy the tenants and give the vineyard to others. Have you not read this scripture:

'The stone that the builders rejected
    has become the cornerstone;
  this was the Lord's doing,
    and it is amazing in our eyes'?"

When they realized that he had told this parable against them, they wanted to arrest him, but they feared the crowd. So they left him and went away.

—Mark 12:1-12

the rural social hierarchy were day laborers, who could not even count on a contract with an elite but worked a day at a time as needed and often not at all, in which case they were reduced to begging.

Assuming that the vineyard is intended as a symbol of Israel, the situation described in the parable depicts Yahweh as an absentee landowner who has hired tenants to care for his vineyard. They are to act as his proxies and to be dependent upon him. If the vineyard is the "house of Israel" and "the people of Judah" (Isa. 5:7), then who are the tenants? How do we understand their character and behavior? By using the parable to comment on the political conditions of Galilee and Judea, Jesus has problematized the situation in the vineyard of the people of Israel under the reign of Herod Antipas and the high priests.

From a prophetic perspective, the tenant is an appropriate figure to represent the ruling classes of "the house of Israel and the people of Judah." The Torah makes it clear that the land belongs to Yahweh (Leviticus 25; Deut. 15:1-18), who contracts with the rulers of Israel as an absentee landlord would contract with tenants. The tenants do not rule the vineyard but serve at Yahweh's behest. But this view clashes with the conviction of the Herodian ruling house in Galilee and the high priestly houses in Jerusalem, who assume that they are the rulers of the vineyard on behalf of their colonial masters.

Clearly, this view of the land as belonging to Yahweh also conflicts with the belief of the Roman overlords, who see it as an asset to be exploited for the immediate benefit of their clients' ruling houses in Galilee and Judea and ultimately for themselves. At one level, the parable codifies the conflict between a view of the vineyard as Yahweh's possession or as the possession of rulers operating with a "proprietary theory of the state," the notion that the ruler owns all the land under his control and can dispose of it as he chooses. This ideology certainly guided Rome's attitude toward the land and the practices of the Herodian kings.

In the parable, however, the tenants reject the role that Yahweh gives them by refusing to return a portion of the harvest to the owner. The very client rulers who, in Jesus' day, were zealous in the collection of tribute, tolls, and taxes refuse to offer to Yahweh what he requires of them. Rather than uphold their covenant (contract), which requires them to distribute the wealth of the land to those in need, they boldly attempt to seize the inheritance for themselves, thereby eliminating Yahweh from the vineyard and eradicating his claims. Along the way, Yahweh sends "servants," most likely intended to represent the prophets who reminded the tenants of their proper role (Amos 3:3). The escalating violence directed first at the servants and then at the son reflects the determination of the tenants to maintain order and deny all claims except those that come from Rome.

To portray urban elites as tenants in Yahweh's vineyard is decidedly a peasant's-eye view of the status and prestige of the ruling houses in Galilee and Jerusalem. For the villagers who gathered to hear, the parable decodes the claims made by the rulers in Jerusalem and problematizes the political situation in which the so-called caretakers of the vineyard are attempting a hostile takeover of Yahweh's land. In a similar vein, Jesus speaks of a tradition in which the rejection of the prophets by the rulers is a major theme (see Matt. 23:29-35). The critique of Israel's rulers has a long history in the prophetic literature (Jer. 10:21; 12:10; 23:1-4; Ezek. 34:1-24; Zech. 13:7-9). Isaiah contains one of the sharpest critiques in the prophetic literature, which could serve as a commentary on Jesus' parable: "The Lord enters into judgment with the elders and princes of his people: It is you who have devoured the vineyard; the spoil of the poor is in your houses. What do you mean by crushing my people, by grinding the face of the poor? says the Lord God of hosts" (3:14-15). Jesus' parable stands in this tradition.

On one level the parable discloses a reading of history according to the little tradition and assigns blame to the rulers, who have failed to serve as tenants and caretakers of the vineyard. Rather than honoring their contract (translate as "covenant") with Yahweh, they have attempted to seize the vineyard for themselves and wrest control from Yahweh. This is nothing if not a "contentious effort to give partisan meaning to local history," the history of Galilee under client kings and Jerusalem under the high priestly houses. The problem of the vineyard is with the tenants, who have lost all perspective on their role. "This is the heir; come, let us kill him and the inheritance will be ours" (12:7). Having problematized the political situation, the parable opens the way to recodifying the high priestly rulers and Herodians as tenants who have usurped their role and abandoned their covenant responsibility.

RETURNING TO THE QUESTIONS

This inquiry began by asking a series of questions about why peasants were motivated to join a group and generate a movement that survived the crucifixion of its founder. What attracted peasants to Jesus and the Jesus movement? Why did it survive?

According to the Gospel accounts, Jesus recruited a small group of itinerant followers on the way to forming a movement. Small-group formation occurs in recognizable circumstances. "Group formation is always rooted in the solution to some problem. It is a truism in small-group research that small groups emerge because some person becomes aware of a need for change."[19]

As the discussion of Herodian Galilee and the high priests' Judea has indicated, exploitation and oppression generated enough problems to encourage group formation. Jesus' prophetic pedagogy would have increased the peasants' consciousness of these problems and the search for ways to address them. Since his manner of teaching engaged the peasant villagers of Galilee around matters of importance to them, he would have shared common ground with the members of the movement. It was easier to join the Jesus movement than the factions led by charismatic leaders like the Samaritan, the Egyptian, and Theudas. They recruited people to travel with them. But Jesus' movement was village-based and built on the premise that peasants could pose and solve problems within the patterns of village life. Any villagers who met to discuss current issues were already participating in the movement.

But what was the relationship of Jesus to his group and then to the movement that emerged from it? The standard view sees Jesus as a charismatic leader standing apart from the people, calling them to follow him or gather in large crowds to learn from him. Jesus is an authoritative teacher with all the answers. His goal is to lead his followers away from Judaism to form a new Christian religion. His charisma would be reflected in the church's Christology.

Given the circumstances sketched here, it is more likely that Jesus was a "reputational leader" who attracted peasants to his movement because he embodied their values. He himself was a product of village life, a village artisan in Nazareth, so there was a fit between the leader and the movement. Reputational leaders gain public attention because they are able to question and even dislodge important norms and values shared by the larger society. They have authority but in a way different from the authority of a charismatic leader. "This authority derives from the successful criticism and dislocation of the higher-order norms which legitimate the authority prevailing in a given society."[20] The three parables studied here have criticized the Jerusalem leaders as tenants who have lost their way, dislodged the landowner's claim to be generous while he pays a poor wage, and undermined the rich man's assumption that his wealth marks him as a favored son of Abraham.

As he conducted his pedagogy of the oppressed, Jesus drew on the resources of the Galilean little tradition and the Israelite traditions he learned in the assemblies of his hometown. He drew upon the traditions that he shared with other Galileans, and when he left a village, his method of teaching remained in the hearts and minds of the villagers who continued the project. Jesus galvanized a movement because he enabled peasant villagers to draw on their own experiences to analyze their world and to become subjects of their own history. The Jesus movement was a people's movement whose strength not only grew from its leader but developed a people's pedagogy that empowered the exploited and oppressed to claim their own history and their role in creating it. For the peasants of Galilee, it must have seemed as if the reign of heaven was at hand.

FOR FURTHER READING

Freire, Paulo. *Pedagogy of the Oppressed.* Trans. Myra Bergman Ramos. New York: Seabury, 1973.

Herzog, William R. II. *Parables as Subversive Speech: Jesus as Pedagogue of the Oppressed.* Louisville: Westminster/John Knox, 1994.

———. *Prophet and Teacher: An Introduction to the Historical Jesus.* Louisville: Westminster/John Knox, 2005.

Lenski, Gerhard. *Power and Privilege: A Theory of Social Stratification.* New York: McGraw-Hill, 1966.

Scott, James C. *Domination and the Arts of Resistance: Hidden Transcripts.* New Haven: Yale University Press, 1990.

———. *Weapons of the Weak: Everyday Forms of Peasant Resistance.* New Haven: Yale University Press, 1985.

Stegemann, Ekkehard W., and Wolfgang Stegemann. *The Jesus Movement: A Social History of Its First Century.* Trans. O.C. Dean Jr. Minneapolis: Fortress, 1999.

Stegemann, Wolfgang, Bruce J. Malina, and Gerd Theissen, eds. *The Social Setting of Jesus and the Gospels.* Minneapolis: Fortress, 2002.

WOMEN'S HISTORY FROM BIRTH-PROPHECY STORIES

ANTOINETTE CLARK WIRE

CHAPTER THREE

> He has thrown down the mighty from their thrones,
> and he has exalted the humble.
> The hungry he has filled with good things,
> and the rich he has sent away empty! (Luke 1:52-53)

Those lines are part of Mary's song that Luke includes in the prologue to his Gospel. But Mary's song of birth prophecy does not stand alone. It is part of a long tradition of birth-prophecy telling in ancient Israel, extending from several centuries before Jesus into the centuries after. Mary's song, in fact, draws on this tradition, specifically from the song of Hannah sung at the birth of the prophet Samuel many centuries before (1 Sam. 2:1-10). Near Jesus' time, it was transposed into Aramaic for recitation in the synagogues to those who no longer understood the archaic Hebrew (*Tg. Neb.* 1 Sam. 2:1-6):[1]

> *And Hannah bowed* in a spirit of prophecy *and she said*
> "My son Samuel is already destined to be a prophet over Israel.
> In his days they will be released from the hand of the Philistines
> and by his hands they will have done for them wonders and great acts.
> So *my heart* is great with the portion the Lord has given to me.
> And even Haman, the son of Joel, the son of my son who is destined to
>   rise up—
> he and his fourteen sons will be speaking in song with their brothers the
>   Levites
> to make praise with harps and lutes in the house of the sanctuary.
> So *my horn is exalted* with the gift that *the Lord* has assigned to me...."
>
> Concerning the sons of Haman she prophesied and said
> "Those who were satiated with bread
> and were swelling in plenty
> and were spreading out in wealth
> have become poor.

> They went back to hiring themselves out for bread—
> food for the hole.
> Mordecai and Esther who were thin
> became rich and forgot their poverty.
> They went back to being free people.
> So Jerusalem who was like a *sterile wife*
> is destined to be filled with her people of exile.
> And Rome which was filled with great numbers of people—
> its military camps will be gone
> and it will be captured
> and it will be burned.
> All these are the great acts *of the Lord*
> who has control over the world. . . ." (*Tg. Neb.* 1 Sam. 2:1-6)[2]

Clearly, the song mentioned in 1 Samuel 2 has been updated here for recitation in a new context.

What is the historical value of such prophetic songs and stories and the oral tradition in which they were embedded? Can a culture's songs and stories be significant sources for people's history? Clearly, they do not give reliable data concerning the persons they tell about, nor do they provide measurable statistics about common people. What they do offer, if they are indeed popular traditions, is an inside view of the assumptions, perspectives, and values of the people who tell them, showing how they portray the conflicts of their time and which side they are on. But what could be more important for people's history?

Yet songs and stories are seldom used, not only because historians prefer "hard facts," but also because stories from ancient times are available only through written texts, by which they have become the mouthpiece of the literate few. In the present critical environment dominated by literary analysis, any questions about the oral history of stories we find in texts are dismissed as romantic. A circle has been drawn around the literate (at most 15 percent) of the Greco-Roman world, outside of which is written, "Here be dragons." But most of the people were here, and we know they told stories that, if they survive in good number and receive a careful hearing, could tune us in to their perspectives. These perspectives, in turn, are needed to build the broad framework for reconstructing a people's history.

IDENTIFYING ORAL-DERIVED STORIES

Twentieth-century study of oral literature has sharply shifted our understanding of the way oral stories are shaped and transmitted.[3] Research has shown that, rather than stories being composed once, at the time of an originating event, and handed down with predictable losses until they are preserved in writing, oral storytellers compose stories afresh each time they tell them. They are guided not by a word-for-word memory but by certain sequences of events and verbal formulas that become traditional as listeners come to expect "the story of..." This story may be told in minutes or hours depending on the attention of the audience and the immediate interests of the teller. Even the written story is not an exception to this process but an instance of it—a vitiated instance because its writing for readers is cut loose from its eventual reading for listeners, and this breaks the communication circuit. If oral telling is a creative, two-way communication, our locating popular ancient stories is not a process of tracing a literary story back to its original shape and setting; instead, it becomes a more intricate process of hearing vestiges of multiple oral tellings in a written version that survives. Where enough traces cohere, we can speak of performance settings that helped to shape the story, the tellers who were active there, and perspectives they were promoting.

Fig. 3.1. Biblical texts give only occasional information about the religious experience of women, let alone their exercising leadership roles. Here scenes from the Book of Samuel—including Hannah presenting Samuel to Eli, Samuel before Eli, God appearing to the sleeping Samuel, Hannah at the altar and before Eli, Saul before Eli, and Samuel anointing Saul—are depicted in a twelfth-century Bible manuscript. MS M619, recto, from the Cathedral Priory of St. Swithin, Winchester, England. Photo: The Pierpont Morgan Library, NY / Art Resource, NY.

When such vestiges have more to do with form than content, they provide us a gauge for identifying oral tradition. From his study of speech in traditional societies Richard Bauman has identified certain characteristics of what is called oral literature: archaic speech; figurative language; parallelism or other repetition; beginning and ending formulas; unusual pitch, stress, or rhythm; and reference to speaking traditionally. Others have added to this list direct discourse, back-channeling (audience participation), and economy of speech.[4] One form of economy of speech strings clauses together with "and" rather than subordinating most clauses. Economy also leads to telling stories with the commonest nouns and verbs and few adverbs or adjectives. A final, more general sign of oral transmission is that common patterns of telling are favored so that many stories are found with a similar format.

As a test case in using a culture's common stories to construct people's history, I take up the pattern that developed when birth-prophecy stories were being told in ancient Judea and Galilee and diaspora communities of Judeans. Groups of Jesus-followers were developing in this world, and their early stories were a part of the same Israelite tradition. This tradition was in turn functioning within the Greco-Roman world and heavily shaped by it, to the point that many of the relevant stories are found in Greek.

THE BIRTH-PROPHECY STORY

I will focus here on twenty-six birth-prophecy stories that appear to come from the centuries just before and after Jesus' birth. Because the stories outside Matthew and Luke are not widely known, I will quote selections. The stories are of two kinds: those telling for the first time or in new ways the birth of past biblical figures, and those telling the birth of contemporary leaders. I take up first the new stories about biblical figures because they show us that not only recent events but Israel's whole oral tradition is being reconfigured. Yet patterns of speech are never completely new, and birth prophecies appear already in the Hebrew Bible (Gen. 5:29; 17:19; 18: 10; 1 Sam. 1:17; 2 Kings 4:16). However, it is in Roman times that the telling of birth prophecy seems to flower.

First, new stories are told about archaic figures that dramatize the earth's corruption and God's plan to save one special child through a flood. In *1 Enoch* Noah's grandfather goes "to the ends of the earth" to report Noah's birth to his great-grandfather Enoch:

> Just now a child has been born to Lamech my son
> and his form and his image are [not like human beings
> and his color is] whiter than snow
> and redder than a rose
> and the hair of his head is whiter than white wool
> and his eyes are different—like the rays of the sun!
> And he stood up from the midwife's hands
> and opening his mouth he blessed the Lord of the age!
> And my son Lamech was alarmed
> and he fled to me
> and he does not believe that it is his son
> but that [it is] from the angels....
>
> Then I [Enoch] answered saying,
> "The Lord will renew order on the earth....
> And this child that was born will be left to survive

and his three children will be saved when those on earth have died.
And he will wean the earth of the corruption that is in it.
And now say to Lamech,
'The child is yours rightly and purely.
Call his name Noah
for he will be your survivor on whom you can rest,
[he] and his sons from the earth's corruption
and all the sinners and all things fulfilled on the earth.'"
(Greek text of 1 En. 106.10-13, 18)

Other Roman-period birth-prophecy stories tell new events about Israel's founders. In Biblical Antiquities Abraham's great-great-grandmother Melcha prophesies at her son Serug's birth:

> From this one will be born in the fourth generation
> the one who will make a home above the heights,
> and he will be called perfect and spotless
> and he will be the father of nations
> and his covenant will not be dissolved
> and his seed will be multiplied forever. (L.A.B. 4.11)

About Moses one can even speak of a competition concerning who receives the prophetic dream. In one story the Judean historian Josephus attributes it to an Egyptian priest and in another to Amarames, Moses' father (Ant. 205–6, 210–18). In Biblical Antiquities it is his sister Miriam who has the dream, then later the Pharaoh's daughter dreams as well (L.A.B. 9.10, 15–16). But each dream is quite different to suit the person who receives it and to prefigure Moses' work in a new way. Of Miriam it is said:

> And the spirit of God fell on Miriam at night
> And she saw a dream
> and she recounted it to her parents that morning saying
> "I saw [a dream] this night
> and look! a man was standing there in linen clothing.
> And he said to me
> 'Go and say to your parents
> "Look! What is born from you will be thrown out in the water.
> In the same way water will be dried up through him.
> And I will do signs by him
> and I will save my people
> and he himself holds leadership always.'"
> And when Miriam recounted her dream
> her parents did not believe her. (L.A.B. 9.10)

Another group of stories retell the times of the judges and prophets. Samson and Samuel are born to barren mothers in much-elaborated stories, while Elijah and Elisha, whose births are not told at all in scripture, are born with prodigies that point to their work.

> Elisha was from Abel Meholah of the land of Reuben.
> And about this one a sign happened
> that at the time he was born in Gilgal
> the golden calf bellowed out [so] sharply
> that it was heard in Jerusalem.
> And the priest said through the Urim
> "A prophet is born to Israel
> who will destroy their carved and molten objects!"
> And when he died he was buried in Samaria. (*Liv. Pro.* 22)[5]

Fewer stories prophesying contemporary births survive, perhaps because figures who brought hope to Israel in this time were few and far between, perhaps because stories of their deaths were many and could serve some of the same functions when told with accounts of vindication.[6] Or was it dangerous in a Roman province to tell stories of present deliverers? One contemporary story is told as a flashback when a Gentile prince converts to Israel's ways. Here Josephus's literary pretensions do not allow anything like a recovery of oral lines of speech.

> At this time Helena, Queen of the Adiabenes, and her son Izates changed their life to take on the customs of the Judeans for this reason. Monobazus, King of Adiabene . . . , succumbing to desire for his sister Helena, was carried away by the relation into marriage and made her pregnant. And once when he was lying with her and resting his hand on his wife's stomach when she had fallen asleep, he thought he heard some voice commanding him to take his hand from her womb and not to constrict the baby in it, who by God's providence would experience both a fortunate beginning and a like ending. Shaken by the voice, he immediately woke up his wife and told her these things, and he named the son Izates (genius). (*Ant.* 20.17–19)

At other points surviving texts give only a hint of a mother's birth-prophecy story, as when Paul defends his call to proclaim Christ to the Gentiles by referring back to the time "when he . . . set me apart from my mother's womb and called me through his grace" (Gal. 1:15). Yet several very full stories have survived concerning John the Baptist and multiple stories about Jesus of Nazareth, in addition to one about Rabbi Ishmael the High Priest. All these, with the new and retold biblical stories, allow us to ask three key questions: First, who told the stories, and when, where, and how; that is, what vestiges of oral performance context can be found in the written stories? Second, why were the stories told; that is, what can we learn about the assumptions, values, and perspectives of the stories' tellers and listeners? Third, how do these findings make a contribution to a people's history of Jesus movements in Judea and Galilee?

WHO TOLD THE STORIES: ORAL PERFORMANCE CONTEXTS

An oral performance is a specific event in which a story is told in a certain way to a certain group at a certain time. To study this would seem to be a limited inquiry that could be quickly accomplished at whatever level the information allowed. However, an event of storytelling encompasses not only its teller, the story itself, and the audience, but also their interaction in the performance context, including its sights and sounds, its allusions to the past, and its projections into the future. This makes an adequate investigation highly complex. What is more, traditional stories found in written texts can be assumed to have had multiple—to us countless—previous performances. It is no wonder that scholars limit themselves to studying a story's single written text.

Yet once a traditional story is recognized not to be a fixed entity in a literary text with a frail past and future but to be a flexible yet hardy narrative that carries the meanings of a culture through multiple performances, then everything possible must be done to track a story's performance history. Ideally, one can observe a certain story actually being told in a variety of indigenous contexts or, barring that, find various renditions of a story that survive in textual, epigraphic, artistic, and ritual forms. But in the absence of such evidence, it is not insignificant to have a number of stories from a particular culture and period that share significant similarities in form and content and may therefore be taken as a kind of class whose performances can be expected also to bear similarities. It is with such an approach that I am considering this specific group of birth-prophecy stories, looking for signs of performance contexts in which they have come to take the shape that we find.

Some of these birth-prophecy stories show signs of being told to confirm existing authority structures, institutions, and dynasties. So the story cited above about the voice of Israel's God speaking in a Gentile king's bed is told by Josephus to show that powerful Gentiles come to respect and even join the people of Israel. It suggests as well a previous telling at the time of King Monobazos's death, when Queen Helena remembers or constructs the event in support of her son's claims to the throne against the claims of his older brothers.

There are also birth-prophecy stories that show signs of being told to celebrate some great memory, often in song or in ritual. So a prophecy of Moses' birth in the Talmud is remembered when his sister Miriam sings to celebrate its fulfillment after crossing the sea. Here we also see confirmation of the existing authority of scripture by answering questions it leaves open, that is, why Miriam stands at a distance to watch Pharaoh's daughter take Moses from the Nile, and why after Israel's crossing of the sea she is said to dance as the sister of Aaron rather than of Moses—namely, to observe the initiation and fulfillment of her prophecy made before Moses was born:

> *"And Miriam the woman prophet, the sister of Aaron,*
> *took [a tambourine in her hand*
> *and all the women went out after her*
> *with tambourines and with dance]."*
> The sister of Aaron and not the sister of Moses?
> Rabbi Amram said Rab said
> but some said that Rabbi Nachman said Rab said
> "It teaches that she prophesied
> when she was [only] the sister of Aaron
> and she said
> 'It is destined for my mother to bear a son
> who will be the savior of Israel.'
>
> And on the day that she bore Moses
> the whole house was filled with light.
> Her father stood up
> and he kissed her on her head.
> He said to her
> 'My daughter, your prophecy is established!'
>
> And on the day they threw him into the river
> her father stood up
> and he slapped her on her head.
> He said to her
> 'My daughter, where is your prophecy?'"
>
> It is this that is written
> *"And his sister placed herself at a distance*
> *to know what would be done with him"*
> to know what would be the outcome of her prophecy.
>   (*b. Sotah* 12b–13a; Exod. 15:20; 2:4)

In addition to signs that birth-prophecy stories were performed when people were celebrating memories and when they were confirming traditions—the latter interest found especially among story writers such as these talmudic biblical interpreters—a third context that shaped these stories is the circle of women around birth. It appears that these stories were told either when waiting for a birth or when announcing a birth in order to assert this event as the turning point for Israel. Assertion is different from celebration in that we celebrate in a familiar festival or cultic setting, where everyone joins the song or the ritual. We assert where something is contested, most often where alternate stories dominate, and what we assert makes a claim against the obvious. This performance context of assertion at the time of birth will be the focus of the present investigation. The point is not to deny other purposes for telling such as the celebration and confirmation mentioned above, but to clarify in particular one storytelling context that left its mark on how these birth prophecies were told.

Fig. 3.2. Women's experience in patriarchal cultures, like first-century Roman society, was generally circumscribed by narrow roles and expectations; recovering that experience requires reading "against the grain." Biblical scenes (Ruth gives birth to Obed, grandfather of David; Naomi fondles the child and is congratulated by neighbors, Ruth 4:13-17; Elkanah and his wives, Hannah and Perinnah, go up to worship in Shiloh) are depicted in a thirteenth-century Bible manuscript. MS M638, folio f19, France (probably Paris). Photo: The Pierpoint Morgan Library / Art Resource, NY.

That birth is a women's world in this culture and in traditional societies today hardly needs defending. But who configured that context in the storytelling is an open question. The child Noah "stood up from the midwife's hands and he opened his mouth and praised the Lord" (*1 En.* 106.6). So in this case one potential storyteller is the midwife, who would have a raft of accounts and might choose the most hopeful in a harsh world. Miriam, who prophesies about her mother's impending birth of Moses, represents the close female relatives present at birth, and Abraham's great-grandmother "Melcha, the daughter of Ruth," represents earlier generations of women, some yet at hand with stories to tell (*L.A.B.* 9.10; 4.11). Most vividly, Mary and Elizabeth in Luke's story dramatize the importance of women in the family when Mary comes and stays with her great-aunt until she delivers in her old age (Luke 1:39-56). But stock female characters would also appear in men's stories about birth, so a cast of women does not prove women tellers, nor does it show a consistent assertion under denial.

More significant are the remarkable number of references in these stories to women's physical experiences in the process of birth, experiences that a man would know about only from a woman with whom he was intimate, and then only if she had chosen to tell—which is not to be taken for granted in a traditional society in which roles are highly gendered. To review these experiences in the order they come in childbirth, first we hear the repeated anguish of finding that one has again not become pregnant (*L.A.B.* 42.1–7; 50.1–8; *Midr. Ele Ezkera* 15.10–18;[7] Luke 1:25). Second we hear of the choice of a man at some time not to sleep with his wife, itself a deprival for a woman who wants a lover or a child or both, but worse when it is taken as proof that a child conceived is from another man. This appears in the story of Melchizedek's birth (see below), but is also an innuendo in the stories of Noah's birth, of Samson's birth in Josephus, and of Jesus' birth as Matthew tells it (*2 En.* 71; *1 En.* 106.5–12; Josephus, *Ant.* 5.276–85; Matt. 1:18-25). Third is the fear of threats against the child's life (*Life of Adam and Eve* [*L.A.E.*] 21; Josephus, *Ant.* 2.215–18; 20.22; Luke 2: 34-35, 51). Fourth is the leaping of the child in its mother's womb (Luke 1: 41-44). Fifth is the interminable delays in childbirth (*L.A.E.* 21). Sixth is the intensity of the labor pains: a woman dressed in the sun cries out in torment to give birth; Moses' mother, Jochabele, "passed the vigil without noticing because the labor was gentle, and when the birth pains came they did her no violence" (Rev. 12:2; Josephus, *Ant.* 2.218). Labor pain may also be linked to the assumption that a mother at birth is prone to be beside herself and hence may speak prophetically in ways not her own, though this link is not made explicit in the stories. Seventh is the exaltation of seeing the child for the first time, most often expressed in these stories in terms of the luminous child who lights up the house (*L.A.E.* 21; *1 En.* 106.2, 5, 10; *2 En.* 71; *b. Sotah* 12b–13a; *Liv. Pro.* 21; *Midr. Ele Ezkera* 15.10, 18). Eighth is the dripping breasts and constant nursing of the child—"And Hannah sat and nursed the baby until he was two years old" (*L.A.B.* 51.1–3)—as well as the challenges of what the child can and cannot eat (*L.A.B.* 42.3; Luke 1:15). Finally, there are the practices of ritual purity through bathing and sacrifices (*Midr. Ele Ezkera* 15.13–15; Luke 2:22-24). Men would know about some of these elements, but the stories' constant expressions of the physical aspects of birth as a woman's experience must be marks that women tellers have left on these stories.

Perhaps most indicative of women's storytelling is the key roles women play in these stories. The few stories where women have been marginalized and the focus set on male issues of the child's paternity and protection— as in Noah's story above, or Jesus' story in Matthew—only highlight in contrast the overriding focus on women. In the first place, most of the early Jewish birth-prophecy stories I could find attribute the vision or prophecy to the mother or another female relative or prophet. Less than a quarter of the stories tell the father's experience, and in these he usually receives the vision with the mother or wakes her immediately to tell it to her. A smaller fraction attribute the prophecy to a male relative or male prophet.[8] This distribution may reflect an assumption in the culture that mothers at birth are prone to visions and revelations. But most stories go beyond seeing her as a channel of information and depict her as the protagonist of the story.

The mother faces many obstacles and must overcome them in order for the child to prosper. In some stories she is simply not believed when recounting the prophecy, as in the above two accounts about Miriam at Moses' birth, and she must persevere until time proves her right (*L.A.B.* 9.10; *b. Sotah* 12b–13a). In several stories she is implicated in some sin and must struggle to prove herself innocent. So Eve, in spite of her initial sin, gives birth to Cain with the aid of the angel Michael; Samson's mother asks the angel to return and confirm to her husband that the child is his; and Mary is declared innocent by an angel in Joseph's dream (*L.A.E.* 18–21; Josephus, *Ant.* 5.275–84; Matt. 1:18-25). In Luke's story of Mary it may be the stigma of sin from bearing a child outside marriage that makes Mary pause, but she then accepts the angel's announcement and praises God for exalting the humble (Luke 1:26-56). The struggle is most dramatized in the story of Sophonim, the mother of Melchizedek. *Second Enoch* tells how Melchizedek is protected from the flood and preserves the priestly line due to his mother's virtue. The story begins after his father Nir's long service in the sanctuary. Nir finds his wife, Sophonim, pregnant and sends her away in anger:

> And Sophonim answered her husband saying,
> "Look! my lord! it is the time of my old age
> and there is no youth in me
> and I don't know how my womb's indecency has been conceived."
> And Nir did not believe her.
> And Nir said to her a second time
> "Go away from me
> lest I hurt you and sin before the face of the Lord!"
> And it happened when Nir was speaking to his wife,
> Sophonim also fell at Nir's feet and died.
>
> And Nir was in great turmoil
> and he said in his heart
> "Did this happen to her from my word?
> And now the Lord is merciful and eternal
> because my hand was not upon her."
> The archangel Gabriel appeared to Nir and said
> "Don't think that your wife Sophonim died on account of guilt.
> For the child that is born from her is righteous fruit

and I will take him to paradise
so you will not be the father of God's gift."

Nir and his brother Noah then go out and dig a secret grave to "cover our disgrace."

Fig. 3.3. Noah and the dove. Early Christian fresco, catacomb of SS. Marcellino e Pietro, Rome. Photo: Scala / Art Resource, NY.

And Noah and Nir went in to bury Sophonim
and they discovered the youth sitting next to the dead
    woman.
And there were clothes on him.
and Noah and Nir were terrified
for the youth was fully developed.
He was speaking with his mouth
and he was praising the Lord.
Noah and Nir looked intently at him
and they said, "This thing is from the Lord, my
    brother."
And look, the seal of priesthood was on his chest
and it was glorious to see. . . .
And they called his name Melchizedek.

And Noah and Nir took the body of Sophonim
and they took off her black garments.
They washed her body
and they put on bright and splendid garments
and they made her a grave
and Noah and Nir and Melchizedek went
and they buried her honorably in public. (*2 En.* 71)[9]

The most prominent struggle women undergo in these stories concerns accusations that they are barren. So *Biblical Antiquities* adds to the Bible's story not only the name of Eluma, the mother of Samson, but also a dramatic argument:

Every day her husband Manoah would say to her
"Look! God has closed your womb so that you not bear children.
And now let me go so that I can take another wife
and not die without fruit!"
And that woman would say
"Not me did God close up, so that I not bear children,
but you, so that I not have fruit!" (*L.A.B.* 42.1–2)

The story continues with her midnight prayer on the roof begging to know which one of them—or both—is sterile. When an angel finally comes at morning to say that she is sterile but God has now opened her womb, she tells Manoah, but he does not believe her. Instead he prays on the roof for an angel to come inform him. Yet the angel comes to her out in the field, and when she runs and fetches Manoah, the angel only tells him:

> "Go in to your wife
> and do all these words!"
> And he said, "I am going,
> but see, Lord, that *your word be done* concerning your child!"
> And the angel said, "It will be done." (*L.A.B.* 42.7)

This narrative is built around the biblical story that appears in Judges 13, but it is told from the very different perspective of a woman's struggle for a child.

The classical story of barrenness about Hannah in 1 Samuel 1–2 is also retold in *Biblical Antiquities*. Her husband's other wife is now given voice, berating Hannah:

> "What advantage is there for you
> that your husband Elkanah loves you
> since you are just a dry stick?
> And I know that he will love me,
> entranced at the sight of my sons
> established around him like an olive orchard!"

Hannah is unable to make a sound when praying, and Eli the priest thinks she is drunk, but when she receives the child, she praises God loud and long. It is she who challenges her husband to join her, and they lead the people, dancing and singing, to Shiloh.

> Come to my voice, all nations
> and lean toward my address, all kingdoms
> because my mouth has been opened for me to speak
> and my lips have been ordained to praise the Lord!
> Drip, my breasts, and tell your testimony
> because it is ordained for you to nurse!
> For he who is nursed by you will be established
> and the people will be illumined by his words
> and he will make known to the nations their limits
> and his *horn will be* greatly *exalted.*
>
> Speak, speak, Hannah, and refuse to be silent!
> Sing praises, daughter of Batuel
> for your miracles that God has done with you.
> Who is Hannah that a prophet comes from her?
> And who is the daughter of Batuel that she has
>   borne a light for the peoples?

> *Rise up,* you too Elkanah, and *gird your loins!*
> Sing praises at the signs of the Lord....
> Look! the word has been fulfilled
> and the prophecy has come to be! ...
>
> *And they departed* from there
> and they gained ground with delight
> rejoicing and exulting in heart
> at all the glory God had done with them.
> But the people went down in unison to Shiloh
> with tympanies and dances
> lutes and lyres
> and they came to Eli the priest, offering him Samuel.
> They stood him before the sight of the Lord,
> they anointed him and they said,
> "A prophet lives among the people
> and will be a light to this nation for a long time!"
> (*L.A.B.* 50:1; 51:3–6)

The story of Elizabeth, mother of John the Baptist, again takes up the theme of barrenness. Here the vision concerning a child is attributed to the father, Zechariah, in the temple, yet when he does not believe and is made mute, it is the mother Elizabeth who becomes the protagonist. She receives Mary, prophesies about her child, and finally insists against opposition on naming her own son John as the angel said. Only when the father agrees by writing the name on a tablet does he receive his voice again and praise God, prophesying his son's work (Luke 1:1-25, 39-80).

The high point of stories about a woman's persistence in seeking a child may come in the account of Rabbi Ishmael the High Priest, a somewhat later story about a figure living when there were high priests:

> They said about Rabbi Ishmael the High Priest
> that he was one of the seven most beautiful people
> who were in the world
> and his face was the image of an angel of the Lord of Hosts.
> When most of the days of Rabbi Yose his father were spent
> his wife had said to him
> "My lord, my man
> what is this that I see?
> Many people succeed in their progeny
> but we have not succeeded in having children
> since we have no heir, son or daughter."
> Rabbi Yose said
> "This happens for them because they guard themselves
> when they leave the bathhouse.

If something should meet them that is not fitting
they go back to the bath and they bathe a second time
and because of this they succeed in their progeny."
And she said to him
"If this is the thing that obstructs
look! I will take on being strict in these very things."

And when she went to the bath
and she left the bath house
a single dog met her.
She went back and bathed a second time.
(A camel) met her.
She went back and bathed
until [she went back and bathed] eighty times.
The Holy One Blessed Be He said to Gabriel
"The righteous woman takes great pains.
Go and appear to her in the image of her husband."
Immediately Gabriel left
and he went and sat at the entrance of the bath house
and he appeared to her in the image of Rabbi Yose her husband
and he grasped her and carried her to her house.
And the same night she became pregnant with Rabbi Ishmael.
And he was made beautiful in countenance
and beautiful in appearance
in the image of Gabriel. (*Midr. Ele Ezkera* 15.10–18)

Here physical aspects around a woman's giving birth and the drama of a woman's persistence come together in a way that makes significant women's telling of these stories hard to deny.

WHY THE STORIES WERE TOLD: TELLERS' AND HEARERS' PERSPECTIVES

Not all the threads dangling from these birth-prophecy stories can be pulled at this time. One could collect and catalog what the storytellers assume about their life and environment—for example, that family members will argue openly and that angels visit women directly but approach most men in dreams. One could also investigate if there is any sequence in the different contexts that leave their mark on these stories, that is, whether stories tend to first be asserted in birth settings, then be celebrated in women's songs that become known at festivals or pilgrimages, and finally be told to confirm patterns of conduct and institutions, as they often function in writing. The dialogue portions of each story could form the basis of a study on the perspectives of tellers and listeners. By enacting each role vocally, tellers draw from their listeners sympathy for one figure or disdain for another and thereby intensify the power of the story to provoke a particular stance toward mothers like this one. Key images could also be traced across these stories. Has storytelling so much associated Moses with water, Elijah with fire, and Elisha with life that these images have found their way into their birth stories? So of Elijah:

> When he was about to be born
> his mother Sochaba saw that bright shining men were greeting him
> and that they were wrapping him in bands of fire
> and were giving him flames of fire to eat.
> And his father Asom came and reported in Jerusalem
> and the oracle said to him
> "Don't be afraid
> for his dwelling will be light
> and his word a verdict
> and he will judge Israel with sword and with fire."
> This is Elijah
> who brought fire down from heaven three times
> and held rain in his own tongue
> and raised the dead
> and was taken up into heaven in a whirlwind of fire. (*Liv. Pro.* 21)

This favorite image of light or glory in the newborn's face cuts across many stories. Did it, with variants such as beauty and wisdom, become characteristic of this kind of story, indicating what the birth of a son signifies among people who have no leader?

I will focus here on the prophecy itself, whether spoken by a parent figure or by an angel to him or her, and specifically I ask what the prophecy says that the child will do. This would seem to reveal in the most explicit way the interests of the tellers and listeners who cultivate these stories. As with the images mentioned above, some biblical figures are already associated with certain feats. But it is when a specific expectation appears in many stories that we should be able to see why this kind of storytelling flourished.

A number of stories include prophecies that the child will overcome the corruption of the world and reestablish good order, righteousness, and peace. In the case of the births of Noah and Melchizedek, the corruption is understood to have come from angels who have forced themselves on human women to breed a race that is lawless, provoking God to plan a flood (*1 En.* 106.6–18; *2 En.* 71; compare Gen. 6:1-6; *1 En.* 1–19). In stories about later figures, Israel has fallen into sin, and Samuel is born to be "a light to this nation," Elijah to "judge Israel with sword and with fire," Elisha to "destroy their carved and molten objects," and Jesus "to save his people from their sins" (*L.A.B.* 51:6; *Liv. Pro.* 21 and 22; Matt. 1:21). This saving from corruption and sin is understood on the one hand to be an internal transformation, so Noah "will wean the earth of the corruption that is in it," and John the Baptist will "turn the hearts of fathers to their children and the disobedient to the mind-set of the righteous" (*1 En.* 106.18; Luke 1:17). But this follows a change of external circumstances, so Enoch announces to Noah's grandfather, "The Lord will renew order on the earth.... There will be a great wrath on the earth and an inundation, and there will be a great destruction for one year" (*1 En.* 106.13–15). And Zechariah praises God:

> He has raised up a horn of salvation for us...
> salvation from our enemies
> and from the hand of all those that hate us.
> (Luke 1:69, 71)

It is this prophecy of deliverance from enemies and establishment of a kingdom that recurs in so many of the stories from this period. Isaac will "be a kingdom and a priesthood and a holy people"; Moses "will be the savior of Israel" and "will free the Hebrew people from the oppression of the Egyptians"; Samson "will free Israel from the hand of the Philistines"; in Samuel's days "they will be released from the hand of the Philistines"; and God will give Jesus "the throne of his father David and he will rule over the house of Jacob forever" (*Jub.* 16:18; *b. Sotah* 12b; Josephus, *Ant.* 2.215; *Tg. Neb.* 1 Sam. 2:1; Luke 1:32-33).

This is not understood to be a palace coup that will substitute one ruler with another until a third arrives. Permanent change is stressed: Abraham's covenant "will not be dissolved," Moses "holds leadership always," Aaron "will hold my priesthood forever," Samuel "will be a light to this nation for a long time," and John the Baptist will cause the people to serve "in holiness and righteousness before Him all the days of our life" (*L.A.B.* 4.11, 9.10; Josephus, *Ant.* 2.216; *L.A.B.* 51.7; Luke 1:74-75).

As well as introducing a permanent and secure life, this liberation from enemies is seen as a return of the people to God and to a life of justice and peace.

> "Blessed is the Lord God of Israel
> because he has come to look after his people and achieved their release!...
> As a dawn from on high he will come to look after us
> to shine on those seated in darkness and death's shadow
> to make our feet go straight into the way of peace." (Luke 1:68, 78-79)[10]

The justice and peace are often characterized by reversals of status. Mary praises God because

"He has thrown down the mighty from their thrones
and has exalted the humble." (Luke 1:52)

Hannah prophesies the ultimate reversal:

> Jerusalem who was like a *sterile wife*
> is destined to be filled with her people of exile.
> And Rome which was filled with great numbers of people—
> its military camps will be gone
> and it will be captured
> and it will be burned.
> All these are the great acts *of the Lord*
> who has control over the world.
> *He makes dead, and he speaks to make alive. . . .*
> *He stands the poor up from the dirt*
> *and from the dump he raises up the emaciated*
> to live with the righteous, the *great* of the world!
> And the *seats of honor* he has held for them.
> Look! before the Lord the work of human beings is revealed!
> Below he has prepared Gehenna for the evil
> but for the righteous doing his will he has adorned the earth.
>   (*Tg. Neb.* 1 Sam. 2:5-6, 8)

One does not have to look closely to see the meaning of these prophecies in the late Second Temple period. Though there were a few Judeans from prominent families in cities of the Roman East—such as Josephus, Paul, and Philo—who had resources for education and opportunities for community leadership, most did not. The great majority of Israel's heirs lived in rural Palestine ruled by rapacious appointees of an empire organized for exploitation. Far from protecting them, the rulers exacerbated the people's hunger, illness, and constant fear of expropriation and violence. It was in this setting, described in some other articles in this volume, that birth-prophecy telling came into its season. Tall foreign men had come and plundered like angels, and stories about antediluvian times made new sense. Corruption seeped into the people of Israel as its Herodian rulers—half-Judean but educated in and for Rome—built new cities for themselves and seduced their brothers' wives. Prophets predicted the destruction of Jerusalem (Mark 13:2; Josephus, *War* 6.300–309).

But there were also voices that prophesied hope. Storytellers told about God's promises at past births that had been fulfilled in each stage of the people's history, freeing them from their enemies, meeting their physical needs, and bringing their hearts back to God. And they told of new births in their own time. They told the birth of the Gentile prince Izates, who with his mother would support Jerusalem in a famine, and the birth of the prophet John, who spoke the truth to Herod Antipas (Josephus, *Ant.* 20.49–53; Luke 1:57-80, 9:7-9).

Yet these birth stories did not tell the feats of Izates and John nor the healings of Jesus nor the martyrdom of Rabbi Ishmael the High Priest. They considered it sufficient to tell the day of these individuals' births and the prophecies made at those times as the turning point for the people. Paul speaks of having been set apart and called when he was in his mother's womb (Gal. 1:15). Why then? Perhaps because those who shaped the stories experienced it that way. They saw the possibilities of the people as a whole determined by who was born and what that one would do to save the people as God had revealed it to them. Not that they were unaware of the difficulties of raising the child and the challenge it would be to fulfill the prophecy, but they understood and communicated that the turning point had been passed and the people now had prospects.

At the same time these storytellers told their own struggles and triumphs as women. They faced many and various challenges, including the struggle to bear a child at all, to be recognized as its true and righteous mother, to tell the prophecy and be believed or—if not believed—to keep watch until the prophecy was fulfilled, and finally to keep telling this and other birth-prophecy stories so that the people would know what God was doing.

BIRTH-PROPHECY STORIES AS WOMEN'S HISTORY

In what sense can we speak of these stories as women's history and take them as a contribution to a people's history of Jesus-followers and other Judean and Galilean communities? The approach applied above could be compared to what some call micro-history, in which a certain trove of court records or a diary gives us detailed access to a specific long-past incident that can illuminate the period.[11] But here we have tales, not records, and they are scattered across centuries. My approach may be closer to what literary studies calls the "new historicism," in which a marginal bit of literary evidence may expose an odd but pervasive aspect of social history to give a fresh slant on that time and text.[12] Closer yet may be the approach of social memory studies, which looks for all evidences—material, textual, oral, ritual—of how a culture constructs its identity through remembering its past, thereby shaping its future.[13] But in the context of this volume it will be most useful to compare my approach to people's history as defined by Peter Burke.[14] My study meets his definition of people's history very closely in its reaching through literary texts to oral sources and its use of interdisciplinary methods such as folklore analysis. Also, my effort has been to seek out social perspectives rather than objective facts, and specifically the perspectives of ordinary people, not the small literate class. Although the stories each tell about particular events in the lives of individual people, the result of studying them has not been to learn more about the pregnancy of Hannah or the birth of Jesus. Rather, the point has been to learn about a collective movement among women and others around them to cultivate patterns of storytelling that promote confidence in their people's future.

The one characteristic of people's history according to Burke that does not seem to fit is that it should focus not on politics, but on every human activity. What we have found is that this people's perspective is highly political. They do not imagine justice and peace in the abstract or in the world to come, but they expect them in their own time and place, and specifically through being saved from their enemies or, as the opening story of Hannah in the targum puts it, through the renewal of Jerusalem and the destruction of Rome. Burke may not mean to exclude political perspectives from people's history, except as politics is the purview of kings. And it is true that the stories do not assume that political change will transform their world apart from social and religious renewal. Yet this observation about how much depends on politics, on who rules, provokes several important questions: Is a political reading of the stories too extreme, perhaps caused by setting Mary's and Hannah's praise at the head? And why would women who have generated so many of the turns in these stories be interested in politics? Should it rather be seen as an overlay by other storytellers, such as those who wrote our texts?

To begin with the last question, the writers of texts in this period can hardly be charged with anti-imperial programs. With the exception of Revelation 12, in which a woman's giving birth provokes a war in heaven and the prophecy of Satan's last struggle on earth, followed later by the vision of Rome's destruction (Rev. 17:1—18:24), writers largely assume the imperial context in which they have the opportunity to write. Certainly, the targumist who tells Hannah's story is no radical. But the stories that the writers include typically do tell prophecies of the end of Israel's oppression by another nation. And, integral to that, the stories decry the violence and oppression that has come with the invaders, angelic or human, and with the people learning their rapacious ways. It is also unlikely that these liberation themes derive strictly from their use in song and ritual, since celebrative use assumes an already-existing agreement on what is celebrated. In fact, the choice to retell or construct birth stories for ancient figures who liberated and renewed the people must come from where the stories are being asserted, and their extensive birth images, themes, and narratives suggest for this a birth-related context.

But what have women to do with politics? Occupied and postcolonial regions today make clear that, no matter how traditional the culture, women are far from oblivious to invasion and exploitation. In fact, they are the most vulnerable to sexual attack and cultural enslavement, as the motif of the colonized woman in colonial literature shows.[15] And if they survive they bear on their bodies the long-term results of war's violence. So there is nothing anomalous about women's stories asserting political reversal that makes space for communal healing.

Finally, have I overplayed the political and social aspect of these particular stories? Not at all. When cataloging their themes I made the surprising discovery that no story mentions the major threat to the mother's life that birth represented. Between infancy and old age this is without doubt her most dangerous moment. Yet the stories are so much centered on what the child means for the destiny of the people that the mother's survival does not get attention, even when her physical experience is mirrored and her struggle is magnified. Nor can it be said that the stories are more theological than political. The stories do not promote a specific theology in the conceptual sense. Instead they praise the God who hears prayer, opens wombs, and overpowers oppressors with the birth of a child and the imparting of a prophecy. God is the one who acts to save the people, and the birth being told demonstrates that action. Though there must surely have been mothers, sisters, and fathers whose prophecies did not come to fruit and liberators who were not prophesied at birth, this kind of storytelling appears where it is said that the prophecy is indeed fulfilled. As Hannah sings in her lyrical hymn in *Biblical Antiquities,*

> Look! the word has been fulfilled
> and the prophecy has come to be! (*L.A.B.* 51)

Lest the focus on the people's salvation rather than on the mother's survival be taken as a sign that these storytellers are modest or self-effacing, we need only remember Mary's praise of God:

> Look! from now on all generations will call me blessed
> since the powerful one has done great things for me!
> And holy is his name
> and his mercy is for generations and generations of those who fear him!
> (Luke 1:48-50)[16]

or Hannah in the targum, "*My horn is exalted* with the gift that *the Lord has assigned to me!*" (*Tg. Neb.* 1 Sam. 2:1). These mothers assert their giving birth as the turning point for Israel. They praise God in a kind of rapture that is at once communal and individual, theological and political.

And how is this "history"? What we have from these stories is a certain perspective on the past, present, and future that appears to have been cultivated by nonliterate women to assert their crucial role in history. History is not only about them, but they made it, or they claim that God made it through them and to their glory as well as God's. At least some of these stories were sung into praises that communities used at circumcisions, festivals, or pilgrimages to celebrate what God had already done and could do again. In addition, writers of apocalypses, histories, retellings of scripture, talmudic teachings, lists of prophets' lives and deaths, Gospels, letters, and midrashim all drew on this tradition to foster some aspect of its power. It is traditions like this that stretch across a culture and indicate strong perspectives that can provide historians a broad framework to integrate their bits and pieces of data in reconstructing a people's history.

When we speak of the role of certain of these stories in emerging Christian history, it is this context we should be investigating. The issue for people's history is not, finally, where Jesus was really born and what visitors he received there, let alone what Luke meant with the shepherds and Matthew with the wise men in the telling of Jesus' birth. Rather, it is the more difficult question of who told these stories and what they were asserting, that is, what side of their people's struggle they were on. From finding the stories of John and Jesus embedded in the narratives of the Israelite tradition we can make certain claims about incipient Christian history to test with other kinds of evidence or other methods of analysis.

It appears that John the Baptist and Jesus were born into an exploitative political context in which women and other family members would contest their people's fate by prophesying that a newborn child would liberate the people from Roman rule and restore justice and peace. In this context women also told the birth prophecies of major figures in their past who had rescued Israel and established it. All this was taken to be God's work. Not only did these stories assert prophecies from God and women's struggles to promote them, but many stories became praises of God that were sung and sometimes enacted in celebrations. Finally, the stories we read became texts to confirm the message of writers. It probably cannot be determined whether John and Jesus were prophesied at birth or whether they were given stories to honor the liberation and renewal they brought about. Both are likely. But the significance of women as birth-prophecy storytellers is clear: women had a leading voice in the shaping of emerging Christian history.

FOR FURTHER READING

Ben-Amos, Dan, and Kenneth S. Goldstein, eds. *Folklore: Performance and Communication.* The Hague: Mouton, 1975.

Brown, Raymond E. *The Birth of the Messiah: A Commentary on the Infancy Narratives in the Gospels of Matthew and Luke.* New York: Doubleday, 1993 [1977].

Charlesworth, James H., ed. *The Old Testament Pseudepigrapha.* 2 volumes. Garden City, N.Y.: Doubleday, 1985.

Foley, John Miles. *The Singer of Tales in Performance.* Voices in Performance and Text. Bloomington: Indiana University Press, 1995.

Hearon, Holly E. "Storytelling in the World of Antiquity." In *The Mary Magdalene Tradition: Witness and Counter-Witness in Early Christian Communities,* 19–42. Collegeville, Minn.: Liturgical, 2004.

Horsley, Richard A. *The Liberation of Christmas: The Infancy Narratives in Social Context.* New York: Crossroad, 1989.

Schaberg, Jane. *The Illegitimacy of Jesus: A Feminist Theological Interpretation of the Infancy Narratives.* San Francisco: Harper & Row, 1987.

Sutter Rehmann, Luzia. *"Geh, frage die Gebärerin!" Feministisch-befreiungstheologische Untersuchung des Gebärmotivs in der Apokalyptik.* Gütersloh: Gütersloher, 1995.

Wire, Antoinette Clark. *Holy Lives, Holy Deaths: A Close Hearing of Early Jewish Storytellers.* Studies in Biblical Literature 1. Atlanta: Society of Biblical Literature, 2002.

TURNING THE TABLES ON JESUS: THE MANDAEAN VIEW

JORUNN JACOBSEN BUCKLEY

CHAPTER FOUR

The social history of early Christians comes more clearly into view when one considers people and groups directly descended from early followers of Jesus. But where are they? Of all the groups connected in some way with the origins of Christianity, the only one that still survives is the Mandaeans, the "knowers" or Gnostics (from Aramaic *manda:* knowledge). They do not seem to fit the traditional rubrics of Judaism or Christianity. John the Baptist, not Jesus, is their prophet. At some point in late antiquity they sharply rejected Jesus as understood by some nascent Christian groups and abandoned Jewish institutions and doctrines as well. They survived for centuries under the rule of Eastern empires and Islamic caliphates. Today there remain about a hundred thousand Mandaeans living mainly in Iran and Iraq, where they continue to survive under increasing political pressure. Their story and ways are instructive for seeing how all the elements of a social context figure in the social shape of their religious life and history.

Mandaeans are a people with their own spoken language (called *ratna*) and a religion with distinctive ritual practices and complex cultural traditions transmitted in an elaborate literature. Throughout the centuries Mandaean priests have copied this literature in their ancient scribal language (the origin of *ratna*), which belongs to the eastern Aramaic language group.

The best-known Mandaean ritual is baptism, a baptism by immersion (done by a priest) in "living" or flowing water. This ritual is performed as a regular rite of purification and of connection with the heavenly world, called the Light-World. Thus Mandaean baptism is not an initiation ritual. Other, smaller forms of washing rituals do not require priests. The Mandaeans also perform complex rituals for the dead, with the aim to rescue the soul and spirit from the deceased body into the Light-World. Priest initiations secure the continuity of the Mandaean communities, and the Mandaeans also have their own marriage liturgy.

Fig. 4.1. Mandaean baptism of a bridal couple in the Karun River, Ahwaz, Iran, April 1996. One priest is reading the liturgy standing behind the crouching bridegroom; another is praying behind the first priest; and a third is in the water, showing the bride her place to be baptized. Photo by the author.

Mandaean cosmology includes a great many creation stories, most of them recognizable as Gnostic revisions of Hebrew Bible traditions, with a supreme divine being in the Light-World, an imperfect creator, and a substantial number of benevolent angels or spirits. Evil principles in Mandaean mythologies are a result of imperfection stemming from the primordial Light-World, or evil exists independently as an eternal entity along with its opposite, the Light. Mandaean rituals aim at controlling and overcoming evil, and therefore, the Mandaeans have a more optimistic worldview than some of their ancient Gnostic neighbors. Their myths and rituals exist in a mutually supporting relationship.

The Mandaeans tend to think that faithful adherence to their rituals has saved them from extinction. A talent for hiding under rubrics that offered a chance at sheer survival, a resolute pacifism, esotericism, historical invisibility, and a lack of worldly power have obviously also enabled the continued existence of the Mandaeans. Their traditional occupation as goldsmiths and silversmiths has made the Mandaeans famous in their home countries and abroad. Today many Mandaeans have become more visible in the world as professionals: engineers, doctors, and intellectuals.

ORIGINS AND LINGUISTICS

Significant bits of evidence suggest that the Mandaeans may have originated in Palestine as early as the time of John the Baptist and Jesus. In many of their prominent traditions the Mandaeans understand themselves as former Judeans, centered in Jerusalem. Their voluminous texts display extensive knowledge of biblical traditions and Israelite cultural traditions, including key figures and divine names that they sharply reject or denigrate. Most significant may be linguistic evidence and the historical legends in some of their texts.

The Mandaic language appears to be the prototype for the development of the later Elymaic and Characene scripts centered in southwest Iran. Characene coins with Aramaic-Mandaic inscriptions dating as early as circa 180 CE are found in Media. Other coins relevant to the Mandaic alphabet derive from Pusht e-Kuh, fairly close to the upper reaches of the river Karka. Yet other coins have been found in Taq e-Bustan, situated very near Kuh e-Parou/Paran. This is only a short distance from the famous rock of Behistun, on a vital stretch of the trade route belonging to the Silk Road connecting the Near East and China.

Mandaic underlies the second- and third-century alphabets of the Tang e-Sarvak rock inscriptions (east of Ahwaz). Those scripts are mainly Mandaic, and the Mandaeans may have had their own script by the time they migrated to southern Babylonia from the west. Their alphabet existed in the second century—at the latest—in southern Mesopotamia. Middle-Iranian script systems were dependent on Aramaic, the language group to which not only Mandaic but also Babylonian Hebrew belongs. Aramaic predominated in Syria and Mesopotamia during the Persian Empire and after the centuries of Greek as the official language under the Seleucids. It was again popular under the Parthia Empire, which was replaced by the Sasanid Empire in 224 CE. While in recent centuries the Iranian Mandaeans have been concentrated in southwestern Iran, in Khuzistan, early evidence locates them in Media, north and east of present-day Luristan and Khuzistan. Thus, it seems that in earlier centuries Mandaeans were more spread out in Iran than they are today.

Despite their location in the East, European scholars of early Christianity and Gnosticism became interested in the Mandaeans not primarily because of linguistics, but because of their possible contacts with early Christian movements. The 1920s and 1930s saw the translations of some central Mandaean texts into German. The idea that the Mandaeans might

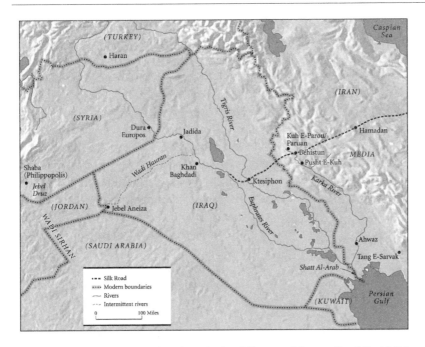

Fig. 4.2. Map of the Mandaean territories (Syria, Iran, Iraq, Saudi Arabia, Turkey). Map by Lucidity Information Design from a drawing by the author.

somehow be related to early Christianity fell out of favor after World War II. I wish to revive the idea, however, drawing on established and neglected scholarship and on my own recent research.

I also deal with Mandaean sources that few scholars have taken seriously as containing historically valuable material. In addition, I focus on the Mandaean traditions about John the Baptist, which are far more extensive than anything we find in other ancient sources. We should also give attention to Mandaeism's Israelite or Judean origins and its connection to Jesus traditions—indeed, the Mandaeans' possible brief flirtation with what later on became Christianity. Whether they arose in Babylonia (as a few scholars hold) or in Palestine, Mandaeans had early-first-century roots, in my view. Careful, detailed reading of maps has steered parts of my argument. All of this is intended to break open the Mandaean question again by combining old questions with new ones. Polemics will loom large, for, while struggling for self-preservation, the Mandaeans engaged in zesty and often humorous fights against their "others."

HARAN GAWAITA AND KING ARDBAN

As my point of departure I take the Mandaean emigration tradition found in the Mandaean text *Haran Gawaita*[1] and its evidence regarding the putative "rescuer of the Mandaeans": Ardban, the Arsacid king of Persia. *Haran Gawaita* is a collection of Mandaean mythological and historical traditions.

While a relatively poorly preserved text (the text's beginning is broken off), it contains a version of the legend of an emigration of the Mandaeans from Jerusalem (see sidebar).

There are many problems with this text, which nonetheless contains clues to history. The very title of the text, *Haran Gawaita*, means "inner Haran." "Inner" (versus "outer") in Mandaeism is a frequent expression for "mystical" or "hidden." Haran Gawaita would then be a symbolic, legendary, or mythologized place. However, the majority of scholars have taken the term to indicate a real, geographical location: Haran, the once-famous town in present-day southern Turkey. I have grave doubts about this solution, for, as baptizers, the Mandaeans would hardly have considered the arid Haran a likely spot. They would have sought flowing water. I also question why they would have wandered as far north as Haran before turning south toward the Euphrates.

> Haran Gawaita received him, that city in which there were Nasoraeans[2] [that is, learned Mandaeans], because there was no road for the Jewish rulers. Over them [that is, the Mandaeans] was King Ardban. And sixty thousand Nasoraeans abandoned the Sign of the Seven and entered the Median hills, a place where they were free from domination by all other races. And they built their cult huts *(bimandia)* and abode in the Call of the Life and in the strength of the high King of Light until they came to their end. And they loved the Lord, that is, Adonai, until in the House of Israel there was created something which was not placed in the womb of Mary [Miriai], a daughter of Moses. It was hidden in her womb for nine months and bewitched her until the nine months were fulfilled and she was in labor and brought forth a messiah. (3)
>
> — *Haran Gawaita*

Among the many other places named Haran/Hauran are an area east of Damascus, a locale west of Jebel Hauran, and the larger area of Bashan/Aurantis. But "inner Hauran" may refer to a much more likely place. With rivers in mind, I suggest a new possibility for *Haran Gawaita*'s Hauran: the long Wadi Hauran, a seasonal river beginning east of Jebel Aneiza (3,068 feet) near the present-day borders of Jordan, Saudi Arabia, and Iraq. From the mountain range Jebel Hauran (Jebel Druze), northwest of Philippopolis, to where Wadi Hauran starts is about 155 miles due east. From Judea and Bashan the Mandaeans might have followed another *wadi* (river), Wadi Sirhan, southeastwards for a while, before turning northeast toward Wadi Hauran. Wadi Hauran flows into the Euphrates between Jadida and Khan Baghdadi.

I propose that *Haran Gawaita*'s "Inner Hauran" may be a mythologized Wadi Hauran. The puzzling phrase "Haran Gawaita received him" (or "it") may be a reference to the *wadi* receiving someone into safety from the city where the Mandaeans formerly lived. So, I suggest, in a preliminary way, that Hauran is not a city but a river and that "him/it" may refer to a group of fleeing people.

Focusing on rivers, we find that a river named Hauran is indeed present in the Mandaean liturgies, in the baptism hymn prayer 28.[3] Prayer 49 has "Hauraran and Karkawan-Ziwa" (*Canonical Prayerbook* 43), and in prayer 379 a blessing is pronounced, "in the Jordan and in the land of Hauraran" (*Canonical Prayerbook* 298). (An extra syllable—such as *ra-* in "Hauraran"—is not unusual in Mandaean place-names and in names of figures belonging to the Light-World.) "Hauraran" also appears in the *Ginza*: in *Right Ginza* 15, 2 and in *Left Ginza* 3, 60 (302, line 28, and 593, line 23). In both instances, it looks like a mythologized Light-World place. In the section "Abatur's Complaint" in *The Book of John,* we find "Hauraran the Great" (232, line 17). In regards to the second term, "Karkawan-Ziwa," ("Karkawan, the Radiance"), it is a mythologized Karka, the river in Khuzistan, Iran, that is, prime Mandaean territory.

According to the *Haran Gawaita* quotation above, the Mandaeans are clearly persecuted by a faction of the Jews (*iahuṭaiia,* a pun on the word for "miscarriage": *iahta,* and the verb root "to sin": HṬA). They find refuge in the far-western area of Iran called Media. But they still belong to the "Sign of the Seven," which denotes planet worship, though the Mandaeans equate the term with Jewish traditions. When the bewitching fetus, the Messiah (*mšiha,* "anointed one," meaning Jesus), makes his mark on the mother-to-be, it is a bad omen for the Mandaeans (who have their own *positive* traditions about Miriai, Jesus' mother!).[4] Only with the birth of "the anointed one" do the Mandaeans break with the Jewish god Adonai.

Historical nuggets are present in *Haran Gawaita*'s cryptic tale. Obviously, one must ask: who is Ardban? He is identified as protector of the Mandaeans in *Haran Gawaita* as well as in other Mandaean texts. Scholars have usually counted five kings named Ardban/Artabanos, belonging to the Persian dynasty of the Arsacids. These kings ruled an area roughly equivalent to present-day Iran, but also parts of eastern Iraq and western parts of what is now Afghanistan. The entire question of Mandaean origins and emigration routes has for years focused on *which* Ardban *Haran Gawaita* means. According to more recent interpretations made on the basis of numismatics, four Ardbans occur in the Arsacid list of kings, not five.[5]

Ardban II (formerly designated as Ardban III, when scholars still assumed the existence of five Ardbans), ruled circa 11–38 CE. This is the king who is most plausible as rescuer of the Mandaeans, despite the scholarly hesitation to accept the existence of Mandaeans as early as the 30s. One can eliminate the other kings named Ardban for simple reasons: Ardban I is too ancient, ruling for the very few years 128–124 BCE. We have no reason to put the Mandaeans that early, and any references to Jesus, John the Baptist, and their mothers would in that case be anachronistic.

Reigning only from 79 to 81, Ardban III can of course be associated with the aftermath of the destruction of the Temple in Jerusalem and the Roman devastation of Judea. But historically, this king is unlikely to have had a role in a Mandaean exodus. Any Judean rulers persecuting Mandaeans at such a late date are out of the question, for the oppressors then would have been Roman ones, whom the Mandaean sources never evince. Some Mandaean traditions do mention the destruction of the Temple, but this information is not tied to their own emigration legend. Finally, Ardban IV (213–224) is too late.

Ardban II rules just at the time when a group loyal to John the Baptist might have fled from Palestine. In 35—when his power was increasing— Ardban II threatened to retake Mesopotamian territory that then belonged to the Romans. The relationship between Ardban and the emperor Tiberius was marked by conflicts. We know something about Ardban's ruling policies from Roman historians. At times, Ardban seems to have favored the Greek aristocracy in Babylonia, but he also had a tendency to side with Jews. The Semitic masses in Middle Babylonia were difficult to suppress, and the Greek rule became increasingly a token one. On the western flank Ardban had to deal with the Romans and their supporters and, on the other, Indian rulers whose territory extended far into eastern Iran.[6] It was not until the second century that the Romans again began major campaigns in Mesopotamia.

With respect to *Haran Gawaita,* it is important to realize that, historically, Ardban had no jurisdiction in Palestine and therefore could not have helped the Mandaeans flee from Judea. But he could have supported them once they were in his territory, helping them cross the Tigris, near Seleukia. However briefly, therefore, the Mandaeans were seen as a part of the Jewish population in Babylonia. A few scholars still maintain that the Mandaeans were indigenous to Babylonia and therefore naturally established residents there. I hold a different view, proposing that they had migrated from the west.

Haran Gawaita seems to imply that a certain number of Mandaeans severed their ties with their original religion, while another group remained Judean. If the separation happened in Babylonia rather than Palestine, perhaps we can tie the text's information to the Jewish divisions and the Greek versus Syrian revolts in Seleukia in the mid- to late 30s, toward the end of Ardban's reign (he died in 38). *Haran Gawaita* says that the Mandaeans stayed in Media until "they came to their end." More reasonably, the translation should be changed to "they were completed."[7]

The text lists seven Mandaean leaders installed in their respective territories. Among these (named) men, we find one appointed by the waters near the mountain range of Parwan. This may well be Kuh e-Parou (spelled Kuh e-Paran/Paruan on some maps), near rivers and close to Behistun, Iran. Geographically—as far as the places of the Mandaean leaders are identifiable—we are in Mandaean territory: the mountains of southeast Media. And we have archaeological evidence from this area, as noted above.

JOHN

Even before entering Media, according to *Haran Gawaita*, the Mandaeans abandoned Adonai because of the birth of the messiah. How exactly one should interpret this is difficult to determine. Did the Mandaeans hear about Jesus only once they were in Babylonia? Had they mulled over the impact of the budding Jesus movement before or while they fled? Or had the Mandaeans even witnessed interactions between John the Baptist and Jesus in Palestine?

John often appears under the compound Arabic-Aramaic name Yahia-Yuhana, but sometimes he is called only by his Aramaic name, Yuhana. A reformer within the Mandaean religion, John is not a founder of the religion (one notes the parallels to the claims in the Gospels of Mark and Matthew regarding Jesus as reformer). Traditions about John are found in *The Book of John, Haran Gawaita*, the *Ginza*,[8] and a few other texts. Mandaeans may well have had a direct connection with John the Baptist. They see John (whom they do not refer to as "the Baptist") as a relative of the Mandaean apostate Jesus. The Mandaeans know of the traditions about John and Jesus as found in the Gospel of Luke, but, as will become evident, they have an entirely different idea of the interactions between Jesus and John at Jesus' baptism.

According to *Haran Gawaita*, a pure seed from the Jordan was sown into Enišbai (Elizabeth) in order to produce a prophet who would destroy Adonai and his works (5). This is a striking contrast to the witchcraft responsible for the pregnancy of the messiah's mother, as told in *Haran Gawaita*. To protect the babe, the prominent Mandaean spirit and messenger Anuš-ʿutra places him on the white mountain of Parwan, where a female spirit, a lilith named Ṣufnai, sets John under a nourishing tree. Then, at seven years of age, John learns the alphabet by heavenly means, and at twenty-two John is sufficiently instructed in Mandaean wisdom to enter human society and commence his role as prophet in Jerusalem (7). *The Book of John* has precisely the same age of maturity for John, as we will see.

In the *Ginza*, we find several traditions. First, in *Right Ginza* 2, 1, Jesus is said to turn the Jews into "God fearers" as he appears in the "house of the people" (50). *Bit ama* ("house of the people") is a term for the assembly house of the Jews (the expression occurs in *The Book of John* too). This may be a reflection of Jewish factions in competing diaspora synagogues.

According to the Babylonian Talmud, Sabbath Babli, the "people of the earth" *(am ha-arets),* will die because of two sins, and one of them is to call the synagogue *bit am* (76, note 1). Were the Mandaeans included in this derogatory category, as being ignoramuses regarding rabbinic law?

Also in *Right Ginza* 2,1, Jesus (identified with Nbu or Mars) is criticized for other sins, such as turning people into hermits and celibates. He pretends to be the Mandaean messenger Anuš. Even before Jesus appears, John (Yuhana) has already been baptizing for forty-two years. Jesus is presented here as a sincere disciple of John. Only later does Jesus turn deceptive and become an apostate Mandaean. The text predicts that Manda d-Hiia ("Knowledge-of-Life," the primary Mandaean Light-World messenger) will turn up when John's earthly life is at its end. In the guise of a child aged three years and one day old, the messenger Manda d-Hiia will come to John, speak to him about baptism, and instruct John's friends. But the child's chief role is to tell John that his earthly life is over.

Second, in *Right Ginza* 5, 4, which uses John's Aramaic name, Yuhana, throughout, the interaction between John and Manda d-Hiia is a bit different. The messenger Manda d-Hiia demands baptism (at the start, nothing is said of his childlike appearance), but John is hungry and tired and wants to wait until the next day. Manda d-Hiia prays, asking the twenty-four hours of the night and day to compress themselves so that he can be baptized immediately. This magical manipulation is successful, and John wakes up thinking he has had sufficient rest. A conversation ensues between the two figures. At this point, John calls Manda d-Hiia "little boy," and his age is, indeed, stated as three years and a day.

The savior-child then asks John various questions about baptism: what type is it, what names are spoken over the baptized person. John's disciples are present, and, deeply impressed by the knowledgeable child, they advise their master to pay close attention to this particular baptism candidate. Indeed, as the child enters the water, the Jordan becomes so excited that it flows excessively, and John nearly loses his balance and worries about being swept away. Then the Light-World radiance of Manda d-Hiia causes the Jordan to dry up, and John, perturbed, asks: What am I going to baptize you in now?

After additional miracles, John realizes that the baptism candidate is the very one in whose name John performs his baptism. It becomes clear that these events spell John's death sentence. John leaves his body, sees it lying on the riverbank, and feels sorry for it. Manda d-Hiia wonders why John is sad about the empty body and offers to put him back into it, if he wishes! Oh no, says John, who expresses worry about the pupils he has to leave behind, not about his own release from the body. Manda d-Hiia picks up sand to cover the corpse: this is the origin of burial.

Third, Yuhana is mentioned in several other *Ginza* contexts, such as *Right Ginza* 7, which contains a collection of wisdom sayings attributed to John (this is the only place in the *Ginza* that the Arabic form of John's name is used). Toward the end, *Right Ginza* 7 states, "This is the speech about the wise ones, which Yahia, the son of Zakria—in Jerusalem, the city of the Jews—taught and revealed" (219, lines 33–36).

The most expansive, baffling, and humorous Mandaean story of John is told in *The Book of John* (tractate 6, chapters 18–33). In terms of sheer volume it exceeds anything known of John from late antiquity. While Mandaeans hold *The Book of John* in high esteem, most scholars have summarily dismissed it as too late to be of real interest historically, mainly because the codex is seen as post-Islamic. That the book in its present form was edited in early Islamic times is not an argument against its value. Many of its traditions are ancient (certainly pre-Islamic), show considerable familiarity with Jewish culture, and may well contain strains of history. At times, the contents are somewhat jumbled, but in order to create a sense of sequence I have rearranged some of the segments of the text.

The birth of John, a heavenly child, is foretold in Jerusalem via dreams and omens. Fire appears at the *bit ama,* smoke emanates from the temple, and shakings rattle the *makarbta* (the heavenly throne-chariot known from the traditions about the prophet Ezekiel, which is prominent in later Jewish mystical texts). The Jewish priests are distressed, and, among them, Elizar remains cynical, at first, as he berates several of the others. But he is told to consult the dream-interpreter Liljuk, who is drowsing on his bed. The priest Tab-Yomin is chosen to seek out Liljuk and tell him about the upsetting events. Liljuk—sleepy but professional—consults his book of dream interpretation and understands that bad trouble is in store for the priests, the rabbis, and the "great Torah." He says that Enišbai will have a child in Jerusalem, and two signs will appear: a star over Enišbai and a fire over the future father, Aba Saba Zakria (Zechariah).

Liljuk writes this down in a letter, and when Tab-Yomin returns with the letter to his fellow priests, the men are in mourning already. After Elizar and Aba Saba Zakria silently exchange the letter, the former asks Aba Saba Zakria to leave Judea *(iahud)* in order to prevent fights from erupting in Jerusalem (78). At this, Aba Saba Zakria becomes angry, strikes Elizar on his head, and rains colorful curses on him. The other priests calm him down, as they realize that John is fated to arrive, be a Mandaean baptizer, and become a prophet in Jerusalem. As Elizar and Aba Saba Zakria leave the presence of the other priests, two lamps follow them. Neither of the two men knows what this means. But the other priests realize that it is a sign of John's imminent power.

The Book of John presents a long lineage of Aba Saba Zakria's named priestly ancestors (almost all of them are named in pairs, not singly). None of them are recognizable to me as "historical" persons. The priests stress that none of these ancestors had wives or sons until a very old age, when, indeed, the offspring became prophets in Jerusalem. This, the priests say, is precisely what will happen to Aba Saba Zakria: the set pattern will continue.

As in the Gospel of Luke (1:59-63), after John is born, the priests ask what name John shall have, and the mother, Enišbai, decides the matter. The Light-World figure Anuš-'utra snatches away the newborn baby to the mountain Parwan, where he is fed *mambuha* (the water drunk in Mandaean baptisms). He remains on that mountain, learning his wisdom, until he turns twenty-two (compare *Haran Gawaita* as cited above). Then John is placed on a cloud that travels and descends to Jerusalem, where a woman named Battai announces the arrival of the man who was spirited away when still a baby. Enišbai becomes so rattled at Battai's utterance that she runs out of her house without a cloak, which upsets Aba Saba Zakria enough to demand a divorce from his wife. The Jerusalem priests tell him to calm down, and he relents. John greets his mother and kisses her, but the text does not dwell on how he reacts to his father.

As John starts preaching, the priests ask him to leave, saying, "By your voice, the *bit ama* shakes, by the sound of your sermons, the temple *(bit mqadšia)* shakes, and by the sounds of your speeches, the vault[9] of the Judean priests *(qumba d̠-kahnia)* shakes." John challenges them to kill him, burn him, and cut him to pieces. Perhaps sadly, the priests respond that they know that fire will not burn John, neither will swords cut him. John's audience includes Miriai (Jesus' mother), his own mother Enišbai, and also the men Jaqif (Jacob) and Beni-Amin.[10] His teaching focuses on Mandaean ethics and rituals, with, among other surprises, a clear—and positive—reference to the mountain Carmel. The competition between Elijah and the priests of Baal in 1 Kings 18 may be reflected here. (*Right Ginza* contains references to Carmel as a site of evil forces, but John is absent in these traditions.)

In *The Book of John* we also find a "theology of the garment" (known from early Christian texts such as *The Recognitions* and *The Pseudo-Clementine Homilies*), that is, the notion that the heavenly powers bestow a "garment" onto a succession of prophets. Here, too, is an echo of the Elijah traditions, but especially of the connection between Elijah and Elisha. The names in the book's list of garment receivers are not of prophets, but of the leaders belonging to the four world ages according to Mandaean chronology. John claims that *he* has received the garment, and this is a bit odd, because John is not usually added as a fifth to the four world-age leaders *(rišia d̠-dara)*. We may detect a mixture of leader ideologies here.

In *The Book of John* 30, Jesus—cšu mšiha ("Jesus, the anointed" or

"Jesus the Messiah")—son of Miriam, appears at the river and demands baptism. John criticizes him for betraying the Judeans, introducing sexual abstinence, abolishing the Sabbath—which Moses (Miša) had made binding—and spreading the use of musical instruments: horns and the shofar (104). A discussion follows, sounding suspiciously like a rabbinic debate, with challenges and retorts. John does not want to baptize Jesus, but a letter from the Light-World judge tells John to perform the ritual. Evil omens immediately occur: Ruha (the evil Holy Spirit) appears, and a cross shows up over the Jordan, which turns into a sewer. This is quintessential Mandaean anti-Jewish and anti-Christian polemics.

Further on in *The Book of John*, John acquires a family, in accordance with the pattern mentioned above: that the priests became husbands and fathers late in life. Anhar is John's wife, and the couple has eight children: two sets of twins and one set of quadruplets. The five girls and three boys all have Mandaean *malwašia* (that is, astrologically determined names, in use among the Mandaeans even today). John tells Anhar to instruct her daughters; he will take care of teaching his sons.

Anhar expresses anxiety at the prospect of John's death, but John objects, using the opportunity to emphasize the Mandaean prohibition against mourning for the dead and to revile Jewish mourning customs. When John is told to ascend to the Light-World, he will not return, he says. His father was ninety-nine years old when John was born, and his mother was eighty-eight, and Judean customs were not followed at John's birth. So why, John asks rhetorically, should such rules be in force now? (John's death is described in *Right Ginza* 7, summarized above.)

One may notice among the many striking details, from a comparative perspective, that baby John is hunted by Herod but escapes to safety, like baby Jesus in the Gospel of Matthew. Both John and Jesus are renewers of long-standing traditions, not founders of new religions. Both men are prophets, but John also belongs in a lineage of priests, and he is literate. Human agency is stressed in the killing of Jesus, but not of John. In fact, the priests in *The Book of John* know that John cannot be killed by human beings or by fire. One wonders if the Mandaeans denied what the Gospels and the Judean historian Josephus relate about John's death.

John marks much less of a break in a set pattern of heaven-designated prophets than Jesus does in the Gospels, despite the combined priestly and prophetic features in the portrayal of John, especially in *The Book of John*. John's mother belongs to the tribe of Aaron (compare Epiphanius, *Heresies* 310, 13:6), and his father has Moses among his ancestors. This certainly gives John a weighty heritage. But of course the Gospel traditions in Q/Luke 7:24-28 and the *Gospel of Thomas* 46 have Jesus declare that John was greatest of those born by women.

Fig. 4.3. Mandaean wedding scene with three priests praying in front of the wedding canopy: from left to right, Sheikh Salah Choheili, Sheikh Najah Choheili, Sheikh Taleb Dorragi. Ahwaz, Iran, 1996. Photo by the author.

Both in the Gospels and in the Mandaean traditions John has the same parents, carries a prophetic role, practices baptism in the river Jordan, has Jesus as a follower wishing to be baptized, and evokes hostility from the Judean rulers. In short, the Jesus movement and the Mandaeans look to the same prophetic figure, John. It is likely, therefore, that the Mandaeans originated in an environment of prophetic activity, as the Jesus movement did. But they remained loyal to John. As for Jesus, the Mandaeans consider him to have turned against *both* Judaic or Jewish traditions *and* his own native religion, which is the Mandaean one. Thus, we find a double critique of Jesus.

CONTEXTS AND POLEMICS

Mandaean literature demonstrates historical, thematic, and linguistic continuity. It remained unknown by other groups in late antiquity, except for the Manichaeans (who borrowed parts of Mandaean poetry as early as the third century). Despite some editing in the early Islamic era, the bulk of Mandaean literature derived from a time long before Islam.

The relations between the Mandaeans and other groups in the early Christian centuries can be discerned in polemics. It is striking that in texts such as *Right Ginza* 2, 1, we find the accusation that the Jews do not agree among themselves; they "do not stand in one word" is the recurrent expression. Moreover, the Jews have distorted, abandoned, and forgotten their own traditions, their law, and the works of Abraham (*Right Ginza* 2, 1, 43). It is not, of course, the case that the Mandaeans approve of Adonai, Moses, Abraham, and Adonai's female counterpart Ruha. But the thrust of the polemics is: abandonment of traditions. This would be parallel to the Jewish–Christian argument against Gentile Christianity, and the polemics indicate Judaic traditions as the Mandaean "original home." Surely, the Mandaeans were not the first group to challenge the Jerusalem-centered Judean rulers, nor were they the first ones to flee eastward for that reason (compare the Dead Sea community and the traditions associated with the disciple Thomas).

The Mandaeans focus on John, and their attempts to come to grips with the Jesus traditions with which they were familiar fit into the context of internal Christian discussions about John's status. These discussions take place in the diaspora, where the quarrel concentrates on water versus spirit baptism.[11] As John-adherents, Mandaeans took part in these debates, whether in Babylonia or further west. Of course, if they were Christians early on (as one scholar suggests), they would certainly have been part of internal Christian deliberations.

Haran Gawaita's story of John pursued by Herod, sheltered on a white mountain, and fed first by fruits from a tree and then by the lilith Ṣufat (6) shows affinities with the apocryphal *Gospel of James* (or *Protevangelium Jacobi*), which is dated after about 150 CE. In the latter, John's mother, Elizabeth, with her babe in arms, is protected by a magical mountain, which "made a light to gleam for her."[12]

In *Right Ginza* 1, 1, and 2, 1, Pilate is called "Paltus malka ḏ-alma" ("Pilate, king of the world").[13] With regards to "Jesus-as-Paul," in *The Book of John* 31 we encounter the compound "Mšiha Paulis" ("Paul, the Anointed/Messiah"). This expression is used no fewer than five times in the formula in which the reviled "Holy Spirit" Ruha, during John's baptism of Jesus, turns the tables and changes the Mandaean ritual into the reviled Christian one (*The Book of John* 108). To give Paul the negative epithet "messiah" hints at a conjoined Mandaean and Judean-Christian opposition to Gentile Christianity.

This particular Mandaean tradition attacks a Pauline view of Jesus and his followers, and it might date to late-first-century CE arguments over the legitimate heritage of the missions of Jesus and John. In *Right Ginza* 2, 1 we do not find "Mšiha Paulis"—as attested in *The Book of John* 31—but "Mšiha rumaia" (*Right Ginza* 49:14). *Rumaia* can mean "Roman," that is, Byzantine, but also "deceiver," even "paralysis" or "pain." If one disregards the many-layered meaning of the term *rumaia*, this expression may be later evidence of an anti-Pauline stance, from a time when the Byzantine church had gained hegemony. Or it may simply indicate that Jesus' healings were seen as ineffective.

IMPLICATIONS

We can now venture an outline of the probable origins of the Mandaeans—as one of several diverse movements involved in the origins of Christianity. The Mandaean movement, however, rejected the line of development that became orthodox in the West. The implications of my probes into the Mandaeans' mythological-historical traditions about "inner Hauran," their focus on and loyalty to John, and their anti-Jewish and anti-Christian polemics all point in the same direction.

The most likely possibility for the location of "inner Hauran" by which they escaped from Palestine is Wadi Hauran. Only that location provides the water essential for their central rite of baptism. Similarly, only Ardban II, in the late 30s CE, fits appropriately as the Persian king who aided them. The Mandaeans' retrojection of Ardban as their rescuer all the way to Palestine is hardly feasible historically. But coming from Palestine the Mandaeans, moving through Wadi Sirhan toward the territory ruled by Ardban, could have been protected by the Nabataeans, who controlled the area to the northeast of Palestine.[14] This is made all the more historically plausible when we recall that in the late 30s the Nabataeans were at war with Herod Antipas, the Roman client ruler of Galilee and Perea, who had been sharply condemned by the prophet John.[15] The Nabataeans may well have been positively disposed toward a group loyal to John. From the Nabataean territory, the Mandaeans went to Babylonia and Ardban's protection.

It is abundantly clear from the rich lore about John in Mandaean texts that the early Mandaeans were focused on and loyal to him as a prophetic reformer of Mandaean/Israelite tradition. The hypothesis that the Mandaeans originated in the second or third century among Jews or Semitic people living in Mesopotamia allows plenty of time for traditions about John to have moved east from Palestine. But I have suggested a different view: that the earliest Mandaeans, having originated in Palestine and hurrying along from there, brought John's baptism to Mesopotamia. Such a scenario of course allows for a very short time span regarding the eastward spread of John's traditions. A direct historical connection between the Mandaeans and John the Baptist is thus possible.[16] The Mandaean story of Jesus as an apostate Mandaean seeking baptism from John can be explained as a mythologized elaboration on a historical core, a core confirmed by Gospel accounts of John as the "forerunner" and baptizer of Jesus.

Assuming a Mandaean origin in Palestine around 30 CE, I hold it probable that the Mandaeans would have witnessed a relationship and rivalry between John and Jesus and their respective disciples. Being uninterested in the tradition that Herod killed John, however, the Mandaeans emphasized that their prophet was "called to the Light-World." The old question of why the Jewish historian Josephus never mentions the Mandaeans can easily be answered. By the time Josephus wrote his histories, in the 70s and after, the Mandaeans were long since settled in Media. And Josephus is interested in John only as a prophetic critic of Herod Antipas.

The Mandaeans thus present a John-centered glimpse into a part of the very earliest development toward what became Christianity. Their arguments against Judaean traditions constitute a parallel to the activity of Jesus, who also contested the Israelite heritage. The Mandaeans understand Jesus as having been a Mandaean. He even tried to save his soul by seeking John's baptism. In the Mandaean view, however, Jesus' baptism backfired. He wanted to create his own religion and thus left both Israelite and Mandaean ancestral traditions behind, and the central symbols in Mandaean baptism transmogrified into Christian ones.

It is hardly the case that the Mandaeans were Gnostics already in the early 30s. In their origins they would have constituted a small group loyal to John. But rejecting both Adonai and (Jesus as) the messiah, the Mandaeans may well have become the inventors of—or at least contributors to the development of—Gnosticism. Once located in Media, on the major trade route tying Babylonia to Iran and Central Asia, the Mandaeans drew on various religious traditions, and they produced the most voluminous Gnostic literature we know, in *one* language. Like the traditions associated with Thomas in east Syria that also developed in a Gnostic direction, they influenced the development of Gnostic and other religious groups in late antiquity. In the second century, for example, Valentinian Gnostics (in Rome and Alexandria) adopted a Mandaean baptismal formula. And in the third century the Manichaean Coptic *Psalms of Thomas* show their dependence on Mandaean poetry.

FOR FURTHER READING

Buckley, Jorunn Jacobsen. *The Great Stem of Souls: Reconstructing Mandaean History.* Piscataway, N.J.: Gorgias, 2005.

———. *The Mandaeans: Ancient Texts and Modern People.* AAR Religions. New York: Oxford University Press, 2002.

Drower, E. S. *The Mandaeans of Iraq and Iran.* Piscataway, N.J.: Gorgias, 2002 [1962].

Fourouzandeh, Massoud, Alain Brunet, and Abbas Tahvildar. *Baptists of Iran: Les Baptistes d'Iran.* Tehran: Key, 2001.

Mandaean Union. Online: http://www. mandaeanunion.org.

CITIES AND TEXTS

Part 2

Christian Origins

CONFLICTS
AT CORINTH

RAY PICKETT

W omen abstaining from sexual relations with their husbands. People claiming "we all possess knowledge" and "all things are lawful for me" going to city temples to eat "meat offered to idols." Some overindulging and others going hungry at celebrations of the Lord's Supper. Ecstatic prophecy in the middle of worship. "Super-apostles" performing signs and wonders. These are some of the practices and behavior among the Corinthians in the first couple of years after Paul and his coworkers carried out their mission in Corinth—to hear Paul tell about it. Affairs in the earliest community of Christ-believers in Corinth were evidently more complex and conflictual than the idealized portrayal of the earliest community in Jerusalem, who were shown "breaking bread together . . . with glad and generous hearts," in Acts 2:43-46. In the two decades following the mission of Jesus in Galilee and his crucifixion in Jerusalem as a rebel against the Roman imperial order, communities of his followers sprang up around the eastern Mediterranean. At the center was the assembly in Jerusalem, headed by the disciple Peter and later by Jesus' brother James. Communities and movements took root in the villages and towns of Palestine and Syria, such as Damascus. The large city of Antioch, at the northeast corner of the Mediterranean Sea, became another center of Christ-believers. And from the assembly of Antioch eager envoys of the movement branched out to Cyprus and across Asia Minor into the cities of Greece to catalyze yet additional communities. The apostle Paul and his coworkers established communities of Christ-believers in the province of Galatia, the Macedonian towns of Philippi and Thessalonica, and the Greek cities of Corinth and Ephesus. Although it is Paul's letters and legacy that survived and became authoritative in the formation of Christianity, other apostles and interpretations of the gospel competed for the attention and loyalty of the earliest believers.

The only one of these assemblies in which we can trace much of the early history is that in Corinth, and that is because so much conflict developed

Fig. 5.1. Map of the
Eastern Mediterranean in
the first century CE.

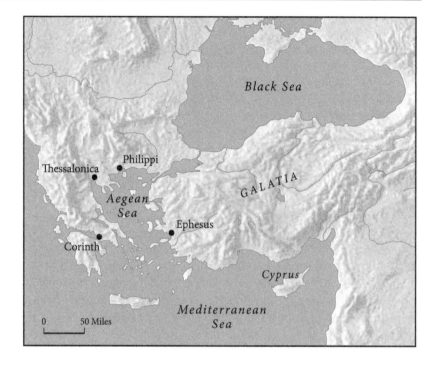

within the community and between its members and Paul. The Corinthian letters tell the story of Paul's arduous attempts to shape the attitudes and practices of believers who not only diverged from and disagreed with his teaching on occasion, but who also questioned his credibility because, as they put it, "his bodily presence is weak, and his speech contemptible" (2 Cor. 10:10). Their perception of Paul was a far cry from the idealized Paul of later generations, who became the prototypical theologian of salvation by faith. The canonical status of Paul's letters created the impression that the members of the churches he founded immediately accepted everything he wrote as the basis of their faith, worldview, and community life. Hence his letters are simply assumed to provide windows directly into what somehow immediately sprang into existence as Pauline Christianity. However, a critical reading of the Corinthian correspondence betrays a community born of struggle and conflict in which assembly members pursued a variety of views and practices.

This people's history of the assembly of Christ in Corinth shifts the focus from Paul to the beliefs and practices of the Corinthians. We are no longer interested primarily in Paul himself, much less primarily in his theology. Rather, we are interested in the people he interacted with in particular cities, what they believed, how they interacted with and responded to the mission of Paul and his many coworkers, and how they struggled to form

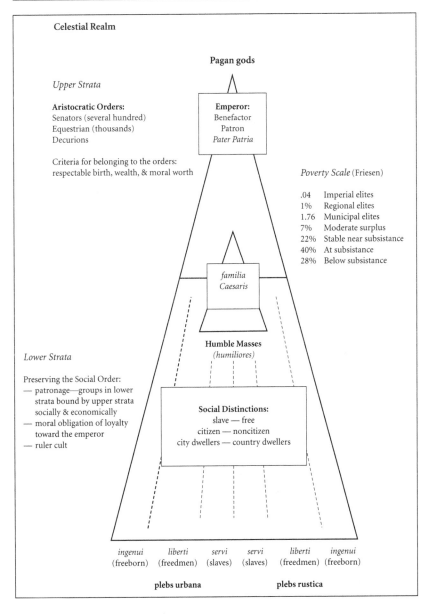

Fig. 5.2. Diagram of Roman social order.

Celestial Realm

Pagan gods

Upper Strata

Aristocratic Orders:
Senators (several hundred)
Equestrian (thousands)
Decurions

Criteria for belonging to the orders:
respectable birth, wealth, & moral worth

Emperor:
Benefactor
Patron
Pater Patria

Poverty Scale (Friesen)

.04 Imperial elites
1% Regional elites
1.76 Municipal elites
7% Moderate surplus
22% Stable near subsistance
40% At subsistance
28% Below subsistance

familia Caesaris

Humble Masses
(humiliores)

Lower Strata

Preserving the Social Order:
— patronage—groups in lower
strata bound by upper strata
socially & economically
— moral obligation of loyalty
toward the emperor
— ruler cult

Social Distinctions:
slave — free
citizen — noncitizen
city dwellers — country dwellers

ingenui (freeborn)   *liberti* (freedmen)   *servi* (slaves)   *servi* (slaves)   *liberti* (freedmen)   *ingenui* (freeborn)

plebs urbana   **plebs rustica**

supportive communities, often in hostile political circumstances. Historically, Paul's letters have been used primarily as a basis for reconstructing his own theology, which has entailed interpreting his rhetoric in terms of anachronistic theological concepts. Paul's letters have had such a profound influence on the history of Christianity that it is difficult not to privilege his voice and his perspective when reading them. But in this study we are interested in what his letters to the Corinthians can tell us about the beliefs and practices of members of the assembly that he and others helped start in first-century Roman Corinth.

READING BETWEEN THE LINES

Our primary sources of information about the origins and early years of the assembly are 1 and 2 Corinthians. In these letters Paul responds to reports about particular developments after he left Corinth, including conflicts that arose within the assembly and between some of its members and Paul himself. In the formulation of his arguments, Paul provides a great deal of information regarding their views and practices. The key terms, concepts, and themes in these letters are distinctively different from those in Paul's other letters. We do not know how the Corinthian believers themselves actually responded to the reading of Paul's letters in the gathered assembly, but it is evident that certain views and practices in the community were at variance with Paul's expectations. Since Paul's rhetoric both provides the source of our knowledge about the Corinthians and shapes our perceptions of them, we must read critically "between the lines" and "against the grain."

The "Corinthian correspondence" in fact consists of several letters in an ongoing exchange between Paul and the believers in Corinth. Paul had written a previous letter to the assembly (1 Cor. 5:9), so the letter we know as 1 Corinthians was his second letter to them. Second Corinthians is believed to include two or more letters that Paul wrote subsequently. The various arguments in 1 Corinthians and the sections of 2 Corinthians can be used to reconstruct both internal developments in the *ekklesia* and Paul's relationship with its members, which became quite strained.

The text of 1 Cor. 1:10—4:21 refers to a report that came from people of Chloe's household about divisions in the assembly. One cause of the discord may be personal or household attachments to Apollos and Paul (1 Cor. 1:12). First Corinthians 5 addresses the assembly's apparent tolerance of a man living with his father's former wife; 6:1-12 tackles the question of taking internal community conflicts to the civil courts. It is clear from 1 Cor. 7:1 that Paul is replying to a letter from the Corinthians about abstinence from sexual relations in marriage. That he begins several more arguments in the rest of the letter with the phrase "now concerning" (7:1; 7:25; 8:1; 12:1; 16:1) suggests that he was repeatedly responding to questions posed in their letter. The text of 1 Cor. 8:1—11:1 focuses on "meat offered to idols," chapters 12–14 on "spiritual gifts," 16:1-4 on the collection for the saints in Jerusalem, and 16:12 on Apollos. In 11:17-34 Paul objects to how the Corinthians are observing the Lord's Supper, and in chapter 15 he responds to the denial of the resurrection by some.

Some new issues crop up in 2 Corinthians. A "painful visit" is mentioned in 2 Cor. 2:1-3 that resulted in further acrimony between members of the community and Paul. Some rival apostles enter the situation, whom Paul refers to as "super-apostles," and he offers an agonizing defense of his own apostleship in 2 Corinthians 10–13 and mentions a "letter of tears" in 2 Cor. 2:4. Second Corinthians 1–7 indicates that some sort of reconciliation occurred between Paul and the Corinthians, presumably necessary before plans for completion of the collection for Jerusalem attested in 2 Corinthians 8–9.

Information on life in the city of Corinth, the context in which the assembly developed, can be gleaned from archaeological explorations as well as Greek and Latin texts. And the letter known as 1 Clement provides at least a glimpse of further conflicts in the Corinthian assembly toward the end of the first century, two generations after its origin.

ROMAN CORINTH

The ancient Greek city of Corinth was destroyed by Roman forces in 146 BCE, and then refounded as a Roman colony by Julius Caesar in 44 BCE. Although some connections with the historic Greek city were preserved in the design of the new city, the organization of the colony was thoroughly Roman—including its architecture, political structures, and social institutions. Temples from the Greek era were rededicated to the same divinities, but there were some distinctly Roman cults as well. All of the overlapping kinship, tribal, and civic networks that held society together in the Greco-Roman world were grounded in and renewed by periodic sacrifices in temples and elsewhere.

After Julius Caesar's adopted son Octavian defeated his rival, Mark Antony, in the nearby battle of Actium, the Roman imperial cult became increasingly central in Corinth as in other cities of the Roman Empire. The wealthy magnates who controlled affairs in the cities of Greece competed to bestow lavish honors on Augustus (as Octavian was now called), with statues of him alongside those of Greek gods in their temples, shrines prominently located in public places, and elaborate games in honor of Caesar. Urban elites who sponsored these honors even redesigned their city squares, the center of public life, to focus attention on temples to the emperor. Temples dominated the public square during the time of Paul's mission in Corinth and served as religious-political centers of the city. The

Fig. 5.3. Through mass-produced images and civic ritual, provincials represented to themselves both Roman power and Roman piety. This statue of the emperor Augustus (erected in Corinth probably between 12 BCE and 14 CE) depicts him with his toga pulled over his head in the gesture of sacrifice; embodying *pietas,* he exemplified the proper attitude expected of any loyal Roman male citizen. Paul protests the veiling of men at prayer in 1 Corinthians 11. Corinth Museum. Photo: *Cities of Paul* © 2004 The President and Fellows of Harvard College.

building, maintenance, and sacrifices conducted in the imperial cult as well as the older city temples were sponsored by the wealthy elite, who also functioned as the priests. Their purpose was to foster a sense of cohesion across class lines and a sense of belonging to the Roman imperial order by involving people of every social stratum in citywide sacrificial rituals and festivals. It has been surmised that the only time many people ever tasted meat was at the annual festival in honor of Caesar. Since nonliterate ordinary people left no written records, however, we really do not know what their attitudes may have been.[1]

A factor that decisively influenced the development of the ethos of the rebuilt city of Corinth was its location. Situated on the narrow isthmus between the Aegean Sea to the east and the Adriatic Sea and the imperial metropolis of Rome to the west, Corinth rapidly became a burgeoning center of seaborne commerce and the gate to the east for the imperial business. The growing city soon became the capital of the province of Achaia and the center of Greece generally. A considerable quantity of commerce thus passed through Corinth along with many travelers. The flow of outsiders into and through the city, moreover, would only have compounded the multicultural atmosphere resulting from Roman colonization: a mixture of languages, principally Latin and Greek, and the juxtaposition of Roman political forms and Greek cultural and religious forms.

The political-economic structure in Corinth would have been consistent with that of the Roman Empire as a whole. Roman social historians find that Roman imperial society involved a gaping gulf between the tiny percentage of ruling elites and the rest of the population. An extremely wealthy minority of less than 3 percent, who lived in luxury in the cities, owned most of the productive land, which provided the basis of their wealth and power. Merchants, traders, special artisans, and some veterans, comprising another 7 percent of the population, may have had a moderate surplus of resources. The remaining 90 percent of the population lived at or below subsistence level. Thus most people in the Roman Empire were poor, living just above, just at, or just below the subsistence level.[2]

Framed by the broad political-economic division between the very rich and the poor, the other main divisions in the social order were between citizen and noncitizen, freeborn and freedpersons, and freeborn and slave.

Fig. 5.4. Temple E, approximately 50 meters to the west of the Forum of Roman Corinth. In antiquity the entire podium on which the column bases stand was hidden by a marble revetment. Photo: *Cities of Paul* © 2004 The President and Fellows of Harvard College.

That Corinth had been rebuilt as a Roman colony and had grown rapidly as a commercial center in the early Roman Empire made the distinction between citizen and noncitizen relatively unimportant. Under Roman rule the assemblies of free citizens had gradually lost their influence in city affairs, as power was consolidated by city councils of wealthy elites whom the Romans entrusted with maintaining the imperial order. In new and expanding Roman Corinth, however, the populace consisted of newcomers to the city rather than native Corinthians with roots in indigenous cultural tradition. Many thousands of people uprooted from the social circumstances of their origins found their way to Corinth in search of a living. The presence of these people of various ethnic and cultural origins would have contributed to an ethos of social rootlessness and lack of traditional cultural orientation among the people of the city.

The division between freeborn and slave, on the other hand, would have been very important in the social ethos of Corinth, both directly and indirectly. The Roman Empire was a slave society. Slaves were so inexpensive that slave ownership went far down the social scale. It is estimated that in imperial society slaves made up as much as one-third of the population, and another third were people who had been manumitted from slavery. Slaves were "animate tools," nonpersons, with no legal rights and permanently stigmatized as dishonorable. Invoking the image of the slave market, 1 Cor. 7:23 (see also 6:19-20) alludes to the absolute subjection of slaves: "you are not your own; you were bought with a price." While some slaves were better off than others, all slaves were marginal, having experienced what Orlando Patterson calls "social death" in relation to the family, society, and cultural identity of their origins.[3] Besides being socially dishonored, moreover, slaves were routinely subjected to physical and sexual abuse. We have no way of estimating the number of slaves in Corinth. We do know of a direct link between Corinth and Galilee created by the Roman enslavement of subject peoples a decade or so after Paul and other envoys of Christ carried out their mission. Vespasian, the Roman general and future emperor who led the brutal Roman reconquest after the great revolt of Judeans and Galileans in 66–67 CE, sent thousands of Galileans as slaves to Corinth to work on Nero's project of cutting a canal across the isthmus.

Slavery also made a deep impact on the social ethos of Corinth indirectly through the large number of ex-slaves and descendants of slaves in the populace of Corinth. In Roman society freedmen and freedwomen continued to be tainted by their servile backgrounds. Descendants of slaves were still dishonorable people. At the founding of Corinth in 44 BCE, Julius Caesar had peopled the colony largely with ex-slaves, along with other surplus population from Rome and army veterans. Thus a large segment of the Corinthian population would have been descendants of freedmen and freedwomen. In a town such as Thessalonica much of the populace would likely have been of the same ethnic background, with live memory of common culture, customs, and religious rites. Even in a large metropolis such as Rome or Antioch, where large numbers of people with the same ethnic and cultural background had settled, ethnic groups such as Judeans, Syrians, and others would have shared common culture and customs with each other. By contrast, the descendants of slaves in Roman Corinth, who had been systematically deracinated, stripped of their previous identity by social death, lacked a common ethnicity and culture.

Fig. 5.5. This may have been the base of a great bronze statue of Athena erected in the middle of the Corinthian Forum. It bears a partial inscription that twice mentions "Augustales," associations of wealthier freedmen who wished to gain status by showing benevolence to their city. The Augustales were officially constituted as religious groups devoted to the local expression of imperial cult; as such they functioned as one component in a comprehensive attempt to humor the emperor into all aspects of life in the empire. Photo: *Cities of Paul* © 2004 The President and Fellows of Harvard College.

Moreover, with so much of the population of Corinth being the descendants of slaves, a desire for social status was likely a prominent part of the social ethos. One indicator of the quest for social acceptability in Corinth may be the numerous inscriptions found at Corinth that mention a society of freedmen called the *Augustales*. The latter were freed men and women dedicated to the cultivation of the imperial cult. They collectively purchased public monuments as means of obtaining a measure of civic status as well as the promise of imperial favor for demonstrating their loyalty to the emperor. In Corinth they erected a huge blue marble step with a statue of Augustus and an inscription to his ancestral spirits.

ORIGINS AND ORGANIZATION

Two images have dominated the standard impression of the early Christian mission. One is of Paul, as the prototypical missionary, preaching the gospel on street corners or in the marketplaces of Greek cities, leading some in the audience to become converts to the new religion of Christianity. The other is the scheme by which Luke, the author of the Book of Acts, organizes his presentation of Paul's mission: when he came to a new city, Paul went first to preach in the Jewish synagogue, until some of the Jews reacted in anger, whereupon he and his converts formed a new congregation. Paul's own letters, surely a more reliable source, along with supplementary information from Acts, present a very different picture: a collaborative team worked in a town for months, even years, engaged in sustained teaching located in the households of those who joined the fledgling communities. The members of these teams appear to have been of three sorts or to have had three kinds of relationships with each other. As we shall see below, they also developed various kinds of relationships with the expanding membership of the assemblies whose formation they were trying to catalyze.

In Corinth several coworkers collaborated during the first year or so, as the assembly was established. After their collaboration in Thessalonica, Timothy joined Paul in Corinth and thereafter visited more frequently (1 Cor. 4:17; 16:10; 2 Cor. 1:19). Later, Titus was instrumental in helping overcome the hard feelings that had developed between Paul and the Corinthians (2 Cor. 2:13; 7:6, 13-14; 8:6, 16, 23; 12:18). During the roughly eighteen months he was in Corinth, Paul and his partners also worked closely with Prisca (Priscilla) and Aquila, a Judean couple who came to Corinth after the emperor Claudius expelled Judeans from Rome around 49 CE (Acts 18:2). Like Paul and many other such apostles and coworkers, they were thus diaspora Judeans. They also shared the same trade as tentmakers (Acts 18:3). Having apparently established a good working relationship for over a year in Corinth, they continued their collaboration for several years in Ephesus. Prisca and Aquila were already Christ-believers before coming to work in Corinth, or at least that is the impression given by Acts (18:26), which also means that a community of Christ-believers had already sprung up in Rome. Others whose role as apostles paralleled (and rivaled) that of Paul, worked in Corinth after he left: first Apollos (1 Cor. 3:5-6; 4:6; 16:12) and later the "super-apostles" (2 Corinthians 10–13). The mission in Corinth as elsewhere was thus a collaborative, and at times competitive, effort sustained over several years.

Ekklesia was the term used for the local community in places such as Corinth as well as for the movement as a whole, comprised of several local *ekklesiai.* Its usual translation "church" does not convey the connotation of the word. In ancient Greek cities the *ekklesia* was a political term, referring to the governing assembly of free citizens in the *polis* ("city"). In the imperial context of the first century CE it was used by a variety of groups to represent a gathered assembly. In the Greek translation of Israel's scriptures, it referred to the local village assembly (also called *synagogue*), or the overall assembly of all Israelites. The latter usage helps explain how the "assembly" could refer to both the local community and the overall movement it comprised, especially for Paul and Prisca and others of Judean heritage. Corinthians would have understood its connotations as a parallel to if not replacement of the assembly of the *polis,* whose former power had been siphoned off into the aristocratic city council under Roman rule.

Several "house assemblies" emerged as the basic components of the overall assembly (1 Cor. 11:18; 14:23; 16:19). The patriarchal household, which included any domestic slaves as well as family members, was the basic unit of Greco-Roman society. And households lived in close proximity, since most people in Corinth as in other cities lived in tenement housing, called *insulae,* or shared houses—or slept in the street.[4] Before long there must have been such household assemblies in several neighborhoods not only in the city of Corinth itself but in the larger region of Achaia, judging from the references in the correspondence (2 Cor. 1:1; 9:2; 11:10). Not surprisingly, the heads of those households in which the house assemblies were centered emerged as key players in the overall assembly. Specifically named are Gaius, Crispus, and Stephanas (1 Cor. 1:14; 16:15-17; Rom. 16:23; Acts 18:8). Was Chloe, from whose household came "Chloe's people" in 1 Cor. 1:11, also one of those key heads of household? The household of one or more of the coworkers such as Gaius may also have hosted a house assembly, as that of Prisca and Aquila did later in Ephesus (Rom. 16: 23; 1 Cor. 16:19). But other leaders, including women, emerged as well, such as Phoebe, leader of the assembly in the town of Cenchraeae on the Aegean coast just to the east of Corinth. This also indicates that the assembly in Corinth was part (perhaps the center) of a movement that quickly expanded into the surrounding area of Achaia.

As might be expected, some of these emerging local leaders became in effect liaisons and representatives of apostles such as Paul after the latter left Corinth. Stephanas and his household members appear to have been messengers of Paul and perhaps the ones who carried 1 Corinthians to the assembly in Corinth. Phoebe is later commended to the assembly in Rome by Paul as the "patroness" as well as "minister" *(diakonos)* of the assembly at Cenchraeae and of himself, where she is apparently now playing a role in the westward expansion of the mission.

While the coworkers must have carried out their teaching in the smaller house assemblies, the *ekklesia* as a whole gathered regularly for celebration of the Lord's Supper and accompanying prayers, discussion of common concerns, and socializing. Baptisms were evidently conducted in the name of Christ, and Paul's allusion to the standard inclusive baptismal formula known from Gal. 3:28 ("no longer Jew or Gentile,...slave or free,...male and female") indicates that they were familiar with that—although later Paul claims in a defensive tone that he baptized only Crispus, Gaius, and the household of Stephanas (1 Cor. 1:13-16). At several points in 1 Corinthians Paul appeals to the basic "traditions" of the new movement as he has received them from other apostles or from the Lord (11:2, 23-26; 15:3-5), and he repeatedly appeals to the basic preaching or teaching he had done while among the Corinthians. Thus, besides the fundamental rites of baptism and the Lord's Supper, the Corinthians had apparently repeatedly heard the gospel focused on the crucifixion and resurrection of Jesus Christ. But it is apparent from the letters that the Corinthians did not necessarily comprehend or appropriate those traditions, rituals, and teachings in accordance with Paul's own understanding. Their initial hearing of Paul's preaching of "the word of the cross" was attended by a "demonstration of Spirit and power" (1 Cor. 1:18-25; 2:4), and manifestations of the Spirit in the form of spiritual wisdom, prophecy, speaking in tongues, and other spiritual phenomena continued to be an important aspect of how many Corinthian believers expressed their identity in Christ.

MEMBERSHIP AND IDENTITY

Who were the people that joined the new assembly in Corinth? Reacting against an earlier view that the early Christians were largely from among the poor, scholars interested in the social world of Paul formed a "new consensus": Based on a literal understanding of 1 Cor. 1:26-30 ("not many of you were rich,...wise,...of noble birth"), they argued that therefore "some" were indeed rich and nobly born. Further estimating that particular individuals who joined the Corinthian assembly were well-off or rich because they were heads of households, they claimed that the social composition of the churches in Corinth and elsewhere was a cross section of Roman urban society as a whole.[5] We should not assume, however, that even those who had a modicum of surplus were reasonably well-off, nor that being a head of household meant that a person was well-off or wealthy. Moreover, Paul's arguments are often not susceptible to literal understanding. In contrast to modern industrial societies, which have a substantial middle class, there really was no middle class—no mid-range economic group of any importance—in the cities of the Roman Empire. More recent critical analysis finds no indication that any of the members of the

Corinthian assembly were especially well-off. That is, just like the populace of the Roman Empire generally (except for the very wealthy elite), they lived just above, just at, or just below the subsistence level.[6]

We may understand the dynamics of what developed in the Corinthian assembly a bit better, however, by considering indications in our sources of the kinds of people resident in Corinth who joined the assembly in the context of the particular social ethos of the city. Almost certainly many were descendants of freedmen and freedwomen, and some were or had been slaves. There is a prima facie case for this simply in the fact that so many of those brought to the colony in Corinth had been freedpersons and in the fact that so many in the Empire generally were slaves. Two members of the assembly in Corinth had Latin names typical of slaves' nicknames: "Lucky" (Fortunatus) and "the Greek" (Achaicus). As members of the household of Stephanas, they would have been slaves or recently manumitted slaves.

That at least some members of the assembly were slaves and others were freedpersons is assumed at a particular step in one of Paul's arguments, in 1 Cor. 7:17-24. Ironically, significant versions of the Bible, including the New Revised Standard Version (NRSV), offer translations of this passage that say the virtual opposite of how the Greek text reads in 7:21. In attempting to persuade some people not to withdraw from sexual relations with their spouses, Paul repeats his "rule in all the assemblies," that people remain in the life circumstances in which they were called. He takes as his examples the three pairs of opposites in social status that were mentioned in the standard baptismal formula used in the initiation of members into the assembly: circumcised and uncircumcised ("Jew and Gentile") should remain as they were, and married and unmarried ("male and female") should remain as they were. When he comes to "slave and free," however, realizing that to instruct slaves to remain in their position would in fact be counter to the intention of the baptismal formula, he insists on an exception to his rule: "Were you a slave when called? Never mind. But if you can gain your freedom, avail yourself of the opportunity. For he who was called in the Lord as a slave is a freedman of the Lord. Likewise he who was free when called is a slave of Christ. You were bought with a price; do not become slaves of men" (1 Cor. 7:21-23; my translation). Some of those he was addressing must have been slaves ("if you can gain your freedom . . . you were bought with a price"). And others must have been freedpersons and yet others freeborn—or the play on the relative statuses of slave and freedperson would have made no sense.

Slaves would presumably have found attractive a community whose baptismal principle was to erase the distinction between slave and free. The admonition that slaves should by all means avail themselves of an opportunity to obtain their freedom (1 Cor. 7:21) is suggestive in this connection. Just what would that opportunity have been? They would have had no say about whether their masters emancipated them. The opportunity must have been one that the master did not initiate but that would be attractive enough to the master that he would relinquish ownership. The opportunity referred to must have been something coming from the assembly. Several later sources indicate that assemblies in the old Pauline mission area would buy members out of slavery from the community fund they collected (for example, Ignatius, *Letter to Polycarp* 4:3).[7] It is conceivable that the opportunity for the slaves mentioned in 1 Cor. 7:21 may have been an early example of a community's ability to buy people out of slavery. The economic situation and social circumstances of those who joined the assembly in Corinth—slaves desiring freedom, freedpeople who could not attain social respectability, recent arrivals in the city also now cut off from their ethnic and social roots—undoubtedly made a considerable difference in the dynamics of how the community developed.

Preoccupation with Paul's own conception of his gospel and mission has eclipsed important questions about what it was like for those first converts as they negotiated a new identity and new way of life. The people who responded to the mission of Paul and others in Corinth were making a conscious decision to redefine themselves: they joined a community presumably convinced that the God of Israel vindicated a Judean from Galilee who had been executed in Jerusalem as an enemy of the Roman order. The sovereignty of the God of Israel, who was also the one God of all peoples, was now being mediated through Jesus Christ as Lord. But what did it mean for non-Israelites living in one of the principal cities of the Roman Empire, amid temples and shrines devoted to Caesar as Lord and Savior, to shift their loyalty, their faith, to Christ as their Lord and Savior. What did those first believers in Corinth find compelling about Paul's gospel or about the teachings of Prisca and Aquila? What simply did not register? How did they respond to other apostles who came to Corinth after Paul left? And what clues do we have about the assembly of Corinthians two or three generations later?

In antiquity even more than today people were defined by their place in the social order and by the social groups to which they belonged. Most people were shaped by the ethnic and religious heritage into which they were born. As sociologists of knowledge have explained, conversion and the development of new life in a new community is often a complex process. The people who joined the new "assembly of saints" in Corinth already had an existing cultural identity that was primary, one into which they had been socialized by their upbringing. Conversion and development of a new social-religious movement would have involved a process of "secondary socialization" or "re-socialization."[8] Their new identity-in-formation emerging from their conversion and participation in the new community was overlaid on a preexisting social identity that included certain obligations and was circumscribed by a rigidly stratified system of rank and status. Even as believers adopted new personae in the community of Christ, they also continued to function in public and domestic domains in accordance with prescribed social roles. They thus had to continually negotiate the roles and responsibilities into which they had been socialized as they also attempted to fashion a new life. Thus it should not be surprising that there were serious conflicts within the developing new assembly in Corinth as well as among some of the Corinthians.

DIVISIONS IN THE ASSEMBLY

Several house assemblies and the assembly as a whole appear to have been meeting regularly by the time Paul left for Ephesus. In addition to the Lord's Supper, such meetings involved sharing of psalms, teachings, prophecies, revelations, and interpretations (see 1 Cor. 14:26). In contrast to the assemblies of saints in Thessalonica and Philippi, who were harassed by the authorities or other outsiders (see 1 Thess. 1:6-7; 4:10-1; Phil. 1:27-30; 3:17-21), the Corinthians apparently experienced little to no conflict with outsiders. However, conflicts emerged within the Corinthian assembly and between some Corinthians and Paul. At some point after Apollos had been teaching in Corinth, the Corinthian assembly wrote Paul a letter inquiring about several matters that had arisen. As the opening of his subsequent responses to those questions indicates (1 Cor. 7:1; 8:1; 12:1; 16:1, 10), their questions related to ascetic withdrawal from conjugal relations, whether it was right to eat meat offered to idols, spiritual gifts, and the collection for the assembly in Jerusalem. Paul had also heard from Chloe's people that there were divisions in the assembly, and he heard that a man was living with his father's former wife and that some were denying the resurrection of the dead and others were practicing a baptism for the dead. These are the issues to which Paul responds in 1 Corinthians, and we can reconstruct some of what was happening by a critical "reading between the lines" of his respective arguments.[9]

Wisdom, Spiritual People, and Spiritual Gifts

The divisions addressed in 1 Cor. 1:10—4:21 were directly connected with the attachment of some Corinthians to particular apostles, especially Apollos and Paul himself (1 Cor. 1:10-12). They were also closely related to excitement about an esoteric "wisdom" *(sophia)*, judging from Paul's sharp

Plate A. In order to recover the experience of ordinary people, a people's history must often read "against the grain" of elite literary sources and "gentlemen's history." Portrait of the baker Paquio Proculo and his wife, Roman fresco, Pompeii. Museo Archaeologico Nazionale, Naples. Photo: Scala / Art Resource, NY.

Plate B. Contemporary Mandaeans in Iran. Mandaeans, living today in Iran and Iraq, trace their heritage to the first followers of John the Baptist. Photo: unknown photographer.

Plate C. A people's history is interested in the popular devotion of a period. Here a barefaced Christ is depicted as Good Shepherd. Fresco, Catacombs of Saint Priscilla, Rome. Photo: Erich Lessing / Art Resource, NY.

Plate D. (left) People at work: picking grapes. Roman mosaic from a series depicting agricultural work throughout the year (see Fig. 2.4, and Color Plate E). First half of the third century CE. From Saint Romain-en-Gal, France. Photo: Erich Lessing / Art Resource, NY.

Plate E. (right) People at work: treading grapes. Roman mosaic from a series (see also Fig. 2.4, and Color Plate D). Photo: Erich Lessing / Art Resource, NY.

Plate F. Working people at leisure: tavern scene with two guests at a table. Incised drawing, Roman, second century CE. Museo Ostiense, Ostia, Italy. Photo: Erich Lessing / Art Resource, NY.

Plate G. Though Rome had destroyed Corinth and enslaved its population in 146 BCE, in Paul's day the new Corinth, a Roman colony, celebrated Rome's power over other peoples. Mourning women and children, bound men, and battlefield trophies are standard motifs of Roman triumphal architecture. The Façade of Captives, from the north side of the Corinthian agora, was probably erected to commemorate an imperial campaign, perhaps the Parthian victories of Septimius Severus (ca. 200 CE). Corinth Museum (No. 175). Photo: *Cities of Paul* © 2004 The President and Fellows of Harvard College.

Plate H. Elite depictions of the good life routinely depicted the service of slaves. Pompeiian ladies with their slave hairdresser, wall-painting from Herculaneum, Italy. Museo Archeologico Nazionale, Naples. Photo: Erich Lessing / Art Resource, NY.

Plate I. Slaves were stock characters of abuse and contempt in Roman comedy. Scene from Atellan farce: man wearing a slave's mask and two women. Fresco. Pompeii. Photo: Scala / Art Resource, NY.

Plate J. Scene depicting two women adherents of a mystery cult. Fresco from the Villa of Publius Fannius Sinistor, Boscoreale, about 50 CE. Museo Archeologico Nazionale, Naples. Photo: Erich Lessing / Art Resource, NY.

Plate K. A people's history finds ample evidence of the leadership of women in early Jewish and Christian communities. Orante (praying figure). Scenes from the life of a deceased woman in the Chamber of the Velatio. Fresco, second half of the third century CE. Catacomb of Priscilla, Rome. Photo: Scala / Art Resource, NY.

attack on it (1:17-25). Based on this wisdom some Corinthians claimed not only eloquence of speech but also an exalted spiritual status as "wise, powerful nobly-born, rich, honored, strong, and kingly" (1:26; 4:8-10). Such terminology originally expressed the self-image of the aristocracy, but had long since been spiritualized in philosophy and mystical theology, as evident in the Wisdom of Solomon 6–10 and the scriptural interpretation of the Alexandrian Judean Philo. It is not surprising that the exalted spiritual status articulated in such spiritualized aristocratic terms would be attractive to some of the Corinthians. As perpetually dishonored freedmen and freedwomen, they would presumably have yearned for respectable status in their regular social lives. Whatever their social status outside the community, they had now attained high spiritual status through the wisdom taught in the assembly.[10]

These Corinthians' exalted spiritual status was also connected to their experience of the Spirit. Paul's insistence that true wisdom is to be found in the cross of Christ (1 Cor. 1:24-25) appears to be an attempt to counter a Corinthian preoccupation with "interpreting spiritual things to those who are spiritual" (1 Cor. 2:13). Judging from Paul's sharp qualification of the same terms in other arguments of 1 Corinthians, this appears to be the self-understanding of the people he is addressing in these passages: they think of themselves as "spirituals" (*pneumatikoi*, 2:13, 15; 15:44) who possessed "spiritual things/gifts" (*pneumatika*, 10:1-4; 12:1; 14:1).

The experience of the Spirit and the spiritual status and spiritual gifts it supplied was evidently also closely connected with the experience of baptism, as indicated by Paul's direct linking of baptism with the personal attachment to apostles and divisions in the assembly in 1 Cor. 1:12-16. In the mission led by Paul and others, the Spirit was always understood as spiritual power received by the individuals undergoing the baptismal rite of initiation into the community. This is the general understanding that Paul appeals to when trying to make the manifestations of the Spirit "edifying" for the community as a whole (1 Cor. 12:4-13). The "spiritual" Corinthians, however, must have experienced baptism more as a personal endowment with spiritual power and wisdom, judging from Paul's sudden defensiveness about having baptized any of the Corinthians (1:12-16). And that experience of baptism as individual spiritual endowment fits well with the practice of "baptism for the dead," presumably the vicarious endowment of the souls of the deceased by the Spirit with immortality, which some Corinthians were evidently practicing (1 Cor. 15:29).

Spiritual wisdom and the exalted status associated with it may have been connected with personal attachment to one of the apostles, judging from the slogans of various Corinthians mocked by Paul (1 Cor. 1:10-12 and 3:21-23). "I belong to Paul." "I belong to Apollos." "I belong to Cephas."

"I belong to Christ." We may surmise that Paul had added the last two in rhetorical mockery. There is no evidence that Cephas (Peter) had ever visited Corinth. And Paul may be trying to indicate that it as inappropriate to treat the apostles as gurus as it would be to treat Christ as such. Nevertheless, it is possible that these Corinthians were focused on heavenly wisdom in such a way that Christ was understood rather as a wisdom teacher or revealer parallel to his apostles, who were now envoys of the new revelation of wisdom. Paul's mention of Apollos in the context of his rejection of esoteric wisdom (1 Corinthians 2–3) suggests that he may well have stirred up the excitement about wisdom and exalted spiritual status in Corinth. According to Acts, Apollos was an eloquent Judean from Alexandria, well versed in Israelite scripture (understood as wisdom in Alexandrian circles) and fervent in the Spirit (Acts 18:24-26). The fact that Apollos, who knew only the baptism of John and was instructed more fully in "the way of God" by Prisca and Aquila, introduced the Corinthians to an alternative interpretation of Christ indicates that Paul was not the only apostle who had preached and taught in Corinth. At least some Corinthians may well have resonated more with his gospel of heavenly wisdom than they did with a gospel that emphasized "Christ crucified."

The "spiritual gifts" discussed in 1 Cor. 12–14 should almost certainly be understood as closely related to the "spiritual things" spoken by and to "spiritual" people addressed in 1 Corinthians 1–4. Both the "spirituals" in Corinth and Paul understand these "spiritual things" as given by the Spirit (12:4-11), the same Spirit operative in baptism (12:13). Prophecy and speaking in tongues appear to be the two gifts most desired in Corinth. Whereas Paul regarded prophecy as the preeminent spiritual gift because it is intelligible to all and therefore builds up the whole community (1 Cor. 12:1-5), the most popular spiritual gift in Corinth appears to have been speaking in tongues, which was unintelligible speech. Speaking in tongues may have been similar to revelatory prophecy in Hellenistic religions and seems to have had similarities to what Philo describes as ecstatic prophecy. Usually during prophecy the person remained self-possessed (1 Cor. 14:32), but glossolalia or ecstatic prophecy apparently involved a trancelike possession by the Spirit (see Philo, *Life of Moses* 1:175). That seems to fit the characteristics that Paul objects to in the "tongues" experienced among the Corinthian spirituals.

In the text chosen for translation in standard English editions of the New Testament, Paul declares bluntly that "women should be silent in the assemblies," that is, they should not prophesy at all (1 Cor. 14:34-35). There are dislocations in the Greek manuscripts of this passage and further doubts about whether Paul actually wrote the paragraph in 1 Cor. 11:3-16, which mentions women prophesying (11:5). If Paul did write these words, then they also happen to provide evidence that women were particularly active among the Corinthians caught up in the "spiritual gifts" of prophecy and tongues. This would fit with texts from the ancient Mediterranean world in general, which portray women more often than men as ecstatics. Such activity was often seen as subversive. Cross-cultural studies of spirit possession indicate that such ecstatic experiences function as a release valve for internalized oppression. Moreover, these experiences can empower groups that were otherwise marginal in society and enable them functionally to destabilize a given authority structure. For women in the *ekklesia,* as well as slaves and others of marginal social status, the wisdom and power that came with being imbued with the Spirit allowed them to transcend traditional sexual and religious norms that were a means of control in imperial society.[11]

There is an obvious tension between Paul's gospel focused on the crucifixion and resurrection of Christ and his emphasis on the community of Christ and the Corinthian personal transcendence and spiritual gifts empowered by the Spirit. Paul's conceptions of the gospel and the community of Christ were shaped by Israelite religious-political tradition and its focus on God's fulfillment of the promise to Abraham, in which other peoples along with Israel would receive blessings of a new life in the kingdom of God. His proclamation of Jesus as Lord on a universal horizon trumps the authority of all principalities and powers, including the emperor, and the assemblies of Christ he organized throughout the Empire were part of an international and alternative society to the imperial social order.[12]

For the Corinthian spirituals the challenge to the ideology of imperial society expressed in Paul's gospel may have been much less important than the opportunity to reinvent themselves by spiritual empowerment and personal transcendence. Possession by the Spirit endowed them with wisdom and spiritual gifts, and this served to enhance their status. In a society in which most everyone was consumed with surviving the struggles of daily life, they experienced this as liberation from whatever oppression they endured living under imperial hegemony. Through the spiritual transcendence enacted in baptism, they experienced a transition from a state of dishonor and humiliation to an exalted spiritual status. The meetings of a house assembly or the gatherings of the assembly as a whole provided a communal environment in which social pressures and constraints were relaxed so that believers could reinforce and consolidate their new identity. Such meetings may well have provided a countercultural social space where socially marginal folks were energized to speak and act in ways not afforded them in the public domain by the official city and imperial institutions. On the other hand, the Corinthian spirituals construed the manifestations of Spirit, power, and glory associated with baptism and reception of the

Spirit as symbols of elite spiritual status (1 Cor. 1:26; 2:13; 4:8-10), a spiritualized version of status-consciousness in the dominant culture, and used them to distinguish themselves in the community. And this spiritual competitiveness would likely have contributed to the discord in the *ekklesia*.

Freedom

The elevated spiritual status and consciousness that resulted from being imbued with the Spirit was experienced by at least some Corinthian as "freedom." That was a key symbol for them, as was the closely related slogan "all things are lawful/possible for me" that Paul quotes twice and qualifies, sharply, at 6:12 and 10:23. "Where the Spirit of the Lord is, there is freedom" (2 Cor. 3:17) might well have been a favorite maxim of the believers in Corinth. The slogan "all things are lawful" was a phrase spoken by people of rank asserting their independence from those who would impinge upon their freedom (see Dio Chrysostom *Diss.* 62.3; 3:10). It is not difficult to imagine how attractive this would be to those who had spent a lifetime as low-status freedpeople or immigrant laborers.

Different members of the assembly in Corinth, however, used their newfound freedom in different ways that appear to reflect two contrary dispositions toward "the world." One of these appears to be an early example of the sexual asceticism that became such a prominent feature of subsequent Christian life. On the principle that "it is good for a man not to touch a woman" (7:1), some of the Corinthians were withdrawing from conjugal relations, presumably for spiritual reasons ("fasting and prayer," 7:5). These must have been mainly women. The "rhetoric of equality" Paul uses in 1 Cor. 7:2-6, addressing women as well as men, which was unusual in ancient writings, makes sense only if he is trying to persuade women in particular to abstain from sexual relations only temporarily.

Although spiritually inspired, their asceticism also had a political dimension. In patriarchal Greco-Roman society a woman's identity was more or less embedded in that of the males to whom she was subordinate and dependent. Women typically married young, bore many children, and were mostly confined to the domestic domain of their husband, or master's household. The women in the Corinthian congregation who refrained from sexual relations were similar to other religious ascetics in the ancient world who renounced bodily and worldly indulgences to devote their lives to contemplation and vision of the divine. In its connection with esoteric wisdom and ecstatic prophecy the Corinthian women's sexual asceticism is strikingly similar to that of the Therapeutridae portrayed by Philo. The latter were previously married women who had become virgins again in their exclusive devotion to heavenly *Sophia* (Wisdom). The Corinthian women's asceticism was an enactment of freedom in the Spirit or Wisdom, which evoked a singular commitment to the divine that was very much alive in and among them through the various manifestations of the Spirit. The women who thus abstained from sexual relations were contravening Greco-Roman cultural conventions regarding gender. Insofar as the whole imperial order was founded on the patriarchal family, with marital relations and productivity having been strongly advocated by the emperors themselves since Augustus, they were also challenging the imperial order that devalued them and sought to control their behavior.

The case of a man living with his father's former wife seems to be the antithesis of the Corinthian women's asceticism, almost an expression of sexual license. While Paul thinks this behavior a dire threat to the community's integrity, nothing suggests that the Corinthian believers were concerned, and some were evidently delighted (1 Cor. 5:6). The liberties being taken by the man and his (presumably former) stepmother, however, could also have been an expression of the newfound freedom in which some of the Corinthians were now living. As noted just above, whereas men tended to marry late, and marry women half their age, women were married in their mid-teens. The man and the woman in this case could easily have been roughly the same age. And some of their friends in the assembly were insisting, in their wisdom and high spiritual status, that "all things are lawful/possible for me."

The expression of freedom that bothers Paul the most, if we judge from the care, subtlety, and vehemence with which he crafts his response, is the liberty that some Corinthians took in "eating meat offered to idols" (1 Cor. 8:1—11:1). This freedom was rooted in their possession of "knowledge." They claimed, in inclusive fashion, that "we all possess knowledge" (8:1). The *gnosis* that they possessed was rooted in a philosophical interpretation of Israelite biblical tradition that "there is no God but the One" and "an idol (false god) has no existence in the world" (8:4). On the basis of this *gnosis* they thus assumed that since the gods supposedly honored in sacrifices did not really exist, it was alright to "eat food offered to idols" and even to attend feasts in the local temples (1 Cor. 8:7-13; 10:20-22). The Greco-Roman social order at every level was founded upon and reinforced through sacrifices, whether in public temples or extended families.[13] Such cultic meals involved a *koinonia,* or communion with deities. Paul regarded this as incompatible with the *koinonia* believers shared in the Lord's Supper (10:20-21) and, in effect, as idolatry. Some of the Corinthians evidently considered it an expression of the newfound "authority" or "liberty" (*exousia*) with regard to established social-religious practices.

CHANGING RELATIONS WITH PAUL

When the assembly in Corinth heard Paul's long letter (1 Corinthians) read to them, they heard arguments that downplayed, even rejected, their excitement over wisdom, spiritual status and gifts, and freedom. If the Corinthians' relationship with Paul was strained before they received 1 Corinthians, it quickly deteriorated afterwards. Far from being persuaded by his arguments, at least some in the assembly became all the more critical of him. One person in particular seems to have taken the lead in opposing and insulting Paul (2 Cor. 1:23—2:11). Receiving news of the situation, perhaps through Timothy (1 Cor. 16:12), Paul came to Corinth. His (second) visit, which he later termed a "painful visit," however, only exacerbated the conflict between apostle and assembly (2 Cor. 2:1-3; 12:21; 13:2). At some point thereafter the Corinthian community received yet another communication from Paul, often called the "letter of tears" (2 Cor. 2:4, 9; 7:8, 12), a desperate defense of his role as an apostle, a letter that many think we have in 2 Corinthians 10–13.

If we judge from his self-defense in this letter, it seems that the Corinthians who were so critical of him were offended by his refusal to accept support from them and his insistence on supporting himself by manual labor (11:7-11; 12:13-18). This had been a bone of contention before. Adamantly sticking to his idiosyncratic principle, he had presented his refusal to accept the support due all apostles as an example of not using one's freedom, thus specifically addressing the Corinthians so enamored of freedom (1 Corinthians 9). It may well have been a matter of (wounded) pride for some Corinthians, living in an ethos of anxiety about social status. They felt demeaned that Paul refused to let them support him, as other assemblies supported apostles and as the assembly of Philippians helped finance his mission (1 Cor. 9:4-6, 12; see also 2 Cor. 8:1-2). Those excited about their newfound exalted spiritual status as "wealthy," "kings," and "nobly-born" may well have found it troublesome that one of their apostles engaged in demeaning manual labor.

It is conceivable that the way support was offered in Corinth seemed to Paul too close to the pattern of patronage in Roman imperial society. It was standard practice for wealthy elites to receive enhanced prestige by supporting economically impoverished clients, who became dependent on the support of their patron. Perhaps, in status-conscious Corinth, offer of support from one or another head of household in the assembly placed Paul perilously close to a demeaning dependency, like that of a "house philosopher." The Corinthians apparently inferred from Paul's refusal of support that they "were made inferior to the rest of the churches" (2 Cor. 12: 13). Paul's financial self-sufficiency dishonored them. And given his repeated self-denigration as "the scum of the earth" (for example, in 1 Cor. 4:8-10), they became increasingly disenchanted with Paul because he did not exhibit the marks of a powerful apostle, with eloquence, wisdom, revelations, and other wonders. "His bodily presence is weak, and his speech contemptible" (2 Cor. 10:10). Indeed, he kept calling them to imitate his own self-debasement, hardly a route attractive to those whose previous life had been nothing but the dishonorable status of slaves, freedpersons, and dislocated immigrants to the city.

Some Corinthians even rejected Paul's authority in favor of rival apostles who better fit their idea of what an apostle should be. Judging from Paul's defense of his own role, other apostles had come to the Corinthian assembly after his "painful visit." They emphasized their credentials as "Hebrews, Israelites, descendants of Abraham, and ministers of Christ" (2 Cor. 11:22-23)—a further indication that the movement of which the assembly in Corinth was a part was an extension of the heritage of Israel and a fulfillment of the promises to Abraham. They also performed or claimed to have performed the "signs of a true apostle, . . . signs and wonders and mighty works," and this is presumably why Paul mocks them as "super-apostles" (2 Cor. 12:11-12). Their message and program were different enough from Paul's that he could charge that they had brought "another Jesus, . . . a different spirit, . . . a different gospel" (11:4-5; 4:2). And they had no problem with accepting financial support from the Corinthians, along with letters of commendation to other assemblies—which leads to Paul's dig at them in a later letter as "peddlers of God's word" (2 Cor. 2:17; 3:1; see also 11:7-11; 12:14-18).

Throughout its prolonged conflict with Paul, the Corinthian assembly had received visits from one of Paul's right-hand men, first Timothy and later Titus (1 Cor. 4:17; 16:12; 2 Cor. 12:18; 7:13-14). Through the mediation of Titus, the Corinthians were gradually persuaded to be reconciled with the apostle who had led the initial mission in Corinth and had been desperately struggling to regain their favor (2 Cor. 12:18; 2:13; 7:6-7; 13-14; 8:16). Somehow the majority of the assembly turned against the ringleader of the opposition (2:5-8; 7:12). In regret and grief, says Paul, they repented, and Paul extended his forgiveness. He also encouraged them to extend the forgiveness to the troublemaker whom they were now punishing (2:5-10; 7:9-12).

The Corinthians' reconciliation with Paul cleared the way for the completion of the collection "for the poor among the saints in Jerusalem" that had begun much earlier. The collection had grown out of an agreement with Peter, James, and John that Paul and Barnabas could expand the movement among non-Israelite peoples from their base in the Antioch assembly, but that they should "remember the poor." The idea was that since the

Fig. 5.6. With the rise of Roman power, cities in the Greek East offered various forms of worship as a way of representing the new reality. Outright worship of the emperor would not have been accepted in a Roman colony, but honors were paid to the emperor's family. On his visit to Corinth in the second century CE, Pausanias saw a temple of Octavia, Augustus' sister, above the Forum. Though he makes no other mention of the imperial cult in Corinth, there is abundant archaeological evidence that the city was greatly influenced by imperial propaganda. This bronze coin from the reign of Tiberius depicts Livia, wife of Augustus; on the reverse, a temple with a cult statue and the inscription *"GENT IULI"* (*"Gentis Iuliae,"* "Of the Julian Family"). Photo: *Cities of Paul* © 2004 The President and Fellows of Harvard College.

other peoples had come to share in Israel's spiritual blessings, they should be of service in terms of material goods to the assembly in Jerusalem. The collection became the economic embodiment of the international movement that Paul, other apostles, and their coworkers such as Prisca and Aquila were building in various cities and towns around the Mediterranean. Despite their own poverty, the assemblies in Macedonia and Achaia were engaged in saving and sending what they could muster to Jerusalem (2 Cor. 8:1-6; 9:1-5). Practically, the procedure was for each member of the local assemblies to "put aside and save" whatever extra they earned. What was collected was then to be taken by delegates of the various assemblies to "[the poor among] the saints in Jerusalem" (1 Cor. 16:1-4; 2 Cor. 8:8-15; Rom. 15:26-27).

Arrangements for the completion of the collection indicate that it became an occasion for local leaders to become involved along with the apostles and their coworkers in the cooperation among the assemblies. For example, a "brother famous among all the assemblies for his proclaiming the good news," was designated by the assemblies themselves to travel with Paul and Titus in administering the collection (2 Cor. 8:18-19, 22; 9:4-5). This collection in which the Corinthians and other assemblies participated offers a striking contrast with the Roman imperial order in which they all lived. In the midst of an imperial political-economic-religious order in which goods flowed vertically upwards to the imperial metropolis, whether in the form of trade or of tribute, subject peoples such as the Corinthians and other assemblies were sending goods horizontally to aid another people subject to the Empire.

AFTER PAUL

We lose track of what happened in the Corinthian *ekklesia* for nearly two generations following the turbulent years of its formation. At some point, probably during that time, the letters of Paul were combined in a collection and circulated among the assemblies in Greece and Asia Minor, perhaps even more widely. The effect would have been to press his authority onto the common life of those communities, presumably including the Corinthian assembly. Disciples of Paul also wrote letters to the Colossians and to the Ephesians and later yet the Pastoral Epistles, 1 and 2 Timothy and Titus. These letters represent a conservative tendency to conform social relations within the assemblies to the patterns that formed the basis of the Roman imperial order and its constituent cites. They insist that in the patriarchal slaveholding family that is now to form the basis of the assemblies of Christ as well as the hierarchical imperial order, wives were to obey their husbands and slaves their masters. Women such as those in the Corinthian community may well have been who the deutero-Pauline letters were trying to bring under control. It is evident during these generations that men were gradually displacing women in most leadership positions.

There was also a far less conservative line of development from Paul. Its traces can be found in noncanonical literature such as *The Acts of Paul and Thecla*. Whether or not there was any connection with women in the first generation of the Corinthian assembly, the figure of Thecla attests a more active role for women in the assemblies of Christ, continuing the role of Prisca and Phoebe and the Corinthian women prophets.

Another possible connection between issues evident in the earliest community in Corinth and later assemblies of Christ elsewhere is what has been called the practice of "ecclesial manumission." Emerging Christian literature includes admonitions "to minister to widows, to look after orphans and the destitute, and to redeem from distress the servants of God," and "instead of lands, to purchase afflicted souls" (Hermas, *Mandates* 8:10 and *Similitudes* 1:8). Those to be redeemed from distress probably included the imprisoned as well as slaves. Some communities, at least, had a practice of buying enslaved members out of slavery using the common fund. This practice is attested, ironically, in the efforts of emerging authorities of the assemblies to control it. Ignatius, the bishop of Antioch early in the second century, himself about to be martyred by the Romans, instructs his fellow bishop Polycarp to "let [slaves] endure slavery to the glory of God, that they may obtain a better freedom from God. Let them not desire to be made free from the common fund, that they not be found the slaves of desire" (*Letter to Polycarp* 4:3).

Redemption of members from slavery by assemblies of Christ, an early version of which may be alluded to in 1 Cor. 7:21 as the "opportunity" that some slaves in the early Corinthian assembly might have had, was still being practiced in the early second century. It persisted despite the efforts of bishops such as Ignatius to accommodate to the standard patterns of the imperial order—the line of development that led to what became established Christianity in the later Roman Empire.

We catch sight of yet another conflict in the Corinthian *ekklesia* toward the end of the first century through the letter called *1 Clement*, sent from its counterpart in Rome.[14] The letter is focused entirely on "the detestable and unholy sedition (or insurrection)... which a few reckless and arrogant persons have kindled"; that is, a few upstarts are rebelling against the well-established "elders" (presbyters) of the assembly, who are supposedly blameless (*1 Clem.* 1:1; 47:6). That the upstarts are characterized as "the honorless" rising up against "the honorable," "the disreputable" against "the reputable," and "the foolish" against "the prudent" may mean that the

elders of the Corinthian assembly had gained in respectability. But it may simply reflect the values and orientation of the officers of the Roman assembly who wrote the letter. It is evident that the elders are not simply the heads of households but the officers or ministers of the assembly, who have been removed from their positions. The assemblies that had been led by informal charismatic leadership of apostles, prophets, and teachers had been developing standardized offices such as "overseers" and "ministers" (bishops and deacons), who were understood to have derived their authority from Christ by way of appointment by the apostles (*1 Clem.* 44:2-5).

The officers of the Roman assembly who sent the letter warn the assembly in Corinth that they were "creating danger" for themselves (of intervention by Roman or local authorities) insofar as reports of their rebellion had reached outsiders, as well as other assemblies of Christ (*1 Clem.* 47:7). They insist on submission to the imperial order and indeed pray for obedience to their rulers and governors (60:4). Of course, Paul had also counseled obedience to rulers, as the expedient stance toward the Roman imperial order. But he had also insisted to the Corinthians that the Empire was imminently to be eliminated as God brought it under subjection to Christ, the true emperor (1 Cor. 2:6-8; 15:24-28).

Along with obedience to the imperial order, the Roman letter to the Corinthians pressed them to conform their community and family life to the dominant social order. The very intervention of the Roman *ekklesia* in the affairs of Corinth is modeled on the actions of the Roman senate and the emperor. Correspondingly, the letter advocated obedience to the officers of the assembly and subordination to the socially dominant, patterned after the hierarchy of state and society (for example, *1 Clem.* 21:6; 63:1). "Peace and concord" meant submission, in contrast to the unity in diversity that Paul had advocated in 1 Corinthians 12–14. Paradigmatic is the subordination of women being presented as the ideal, only without the reciprocal responsibilities of husbands and fathers found in the deutero-Pauline Pastoral Epistles.

We have no idea, of course, exactly how the Corinthians responded to the admonishment by the officers of the Roman assembly. Seventy years later, Dionysus of Corinth wrote to the assembly in Rome that their letter *(1 Clement)* was read aloud regularly for the instruction of the congregation. Under such pressures the Corinthians were presumably adjusting to their positions in the Roman imperial order. But we do not know that for sure. After all, the Corinthians had a heritage of independent spirit, challenging outside authority figures, and contention. And it is because people do not always obey those in authority that the authorities write letters calling for obedience.

FOR FURTHER READING

Judge, E. A. *The Social Pattern of the Christian Groups in the First Century: Some Prolegomena to the Study of New Testament Ideas of Social Obligation.* Christ and Culture Collection. London: Tyndale, 1960.

Meeks, Wayne A. *The First Urban Christians: The Social World of the Apostle Paul.* New Haven: Yale University Press, 1983.

Pickett, Raymond. *The Cross at Corinth: The Social Significance of the Death of Jesus.* Sheffield: Sheffield Academic, 1997.

Wire, Antoinette Clark. *The Corinthian Women Prophets: A Reconstruction through Paul's Rhetoric.* Minneapolis: Fortress, 1990.

MATTHEW'S PEOPLE

WARREN CARTER

CHAPTER SIX

Most of those who listened to Matthew's Gospel in the late first century experienced tough living conditions. Regular food shortages,
squalid conditions, hard work, sickness, and poverty marked the life of
these followers of Jesus in one of the largest cities of the Roman Empire.
After outlining some features of Matthew's people, describing a people's
history approach, and sketching some contours of the Roman imperial
world, I will discuss ways in which Matthew's Gospel shapes his people's
negotiation of Rome's world as followers of Jesus. The Gospel offers a frequently contestive vision and alternative identity and way of life, even
while enmeshed in and imitating imperial values and practices.

Matthew's Gospel was probably written in the 80s CE. The community
for which it was produced is usually located in Antioch, on the Orontes
River. The city's population was approximately 150,000 to 200,000, and it
was the capital of the Roman province of Syria.[1]

Antioch was strategically located on the Empire's eastern frontier. Buildings, governing and military personnel, coins, taxes, and festivals displayed
Roman control in the city. Especially prominent were its three or four
Roman legions. Several times they had been sent to subdue revolts in
Galilee and Judea. In 66 CE, for example, the general Vespasian had mar-
shaled his troops at Antioch and levied extra supplies for them before
marching south.

Conflicts in Galilee and Judea to the south strained relations with
Judeans within Antioch. Matthew's people, comprising one or more assemblies and focused on the prophet-messiah Jesus as their Lord, had not yet
distinguished themselves as "Christian." They had not yet separated from
the people and heritage of Israel but still identified themselves as part of
the large Judean population resident within Antioch. Previously, Herod,
the Roman client king of Judea, had endowed construction of an elaborate
colonnade on the main street in Antioch partly to cultivate an atmosphere

favorable to the Judeans there. But after the revolt in Galilee and Judea broke out in 66, hostilities against Judeans increased in Antioch. Titus, the son of Emperor Vespasian and the general who was victorious over Jerusalem in 70, had to intervene to protect their rights in the city. Nevertheless, Rome issued *Judea Capta* coins that celebrated Rome's defeat of Jerusalem in 70 CE. These coins contributed to an ongoing atmosphere of hostility by presenting Judeans as a conquered people.

Followers of Jesus had existed in Antioch since the 30s or 40s. Matthew's people had developed from one of the more expansive "assemblies" *(ekklesiai)* that emerged beyond Palestine in the decade or so after Jesus' death. They perhaps originated with Jesus-followers forced out of Jerusalem (Acts 11:19-24; 15; Gal. 2:1-14). They maintained active communication with the assembly in Jerusalem headed by Peter and later James, brother of Jesus. And from the assembly in Antioch envoys such as Barnabas and Paul spread out into the eastern Mediterranean and Asia Minor to begin to catalyze other communities.

Matthew's people, while mainly Judean, were diverse in gender and cultural location. They included Judean and non-Judean, urban and rural, poor and poorer folks. The size of the community is unknown, but it would have comprised a tiny fraction of the population of that large city. The people knew oral and written traditions about Jesus and his mission. Those traditions probably included a form of the Gospel of Mark and a series of sayings of Jesus we know as "Q." They emphasized that the prophet-messiah Jesus had challenged Roman rule in Judea and Galilee by enacting a vision of societal life shaped by God's rule. As a consequence he had been crucified around 30 CE.

Fig. 6.1. Terracotta brick with the name "Leg(io) X (Fretensis)," the Roman Tenth Legion, which destroyed Jerusalem in 70 CE. The Roman defeat of the Jewish revolt had repercussions throughout Jewish life and literature—including the Gospels in the New Testament. Photo: Erich Lessing / Art Resource, NY.

Matthew's people understood themselves as belonging to the tradition of Israel and Israel's God. Central to Israelite traditions were confrontations with imperial rulers such as the Pharaoh of Egypt, king of Assyria, Babylonia, and Persia, and the Hellenistically inspired Seleucid king Antiochus Epiphanes. Also crucial were confrontations within Israel between, on the one hand, kings and high priests in the Jerusalem temple and, on the other, prophets such as Elijah and Jeremiah who declared God's judgment against unjust rulers and institutions. As a group within Judaism they followed Israel's traditions and practices as interpreted by Jesus (1:21-23; 5:17-48).

After Rome's destruction of Jerusalem and its Temple in 70 CE, Matthew's people were in conflict with other Judean communities over the shape of post-70 Judaism and the role of Jesus. Foundational to their community identity was their conviction that in the mission, crucifixion, and resurrection of Jesus, God's just and life-giving purposes were being revealed and established as a judgment on and alternative to the Roman imperial order.

THE CHALLENGE OF PEOPLE'S HISTORY

Fig. 6.2. Bronze Roman coin struck to commemorate the Roman defeat of Jerusalem. The obverse depicts the emperor Vespasian (who as general had laid siege to Jerusalem) and on the reverse the Roman god of victory stands over a disconsolate woman, "Judaea Capta" ("vanquished Judea"). Photo: Erich Lessing / Art Resource, NY.

People's history is one of several new historical approaches (including history "from below" or history of popular culture) that challenge the "traditional paradigm" of "Rankean history."[2] Peter Burke, one of its leading practitioners, identifies seven distinguishing characteristics:

Traditional History	*New Histories/People's History*
1. Focus on politics	1. Focus on Every Human Activity
2. Analysis of Events	2. Analysis of Structures
3. Viewed from Above: The Great Men	3. Viewed from Below: The People
4. Written Sources	4. Any/Other Sources
5. Focus on Individual Acts	5. Focus on Collective Movements
6. Objective/Facts (How It Happened)	6. Perspectival; Socially Located; Multivocal
7. The Discipline of History	7. Interdisciplinary

In this perspective, a history of Matthew's people would examine (1) the everyday life of Matthew's people in Antioch, (2) in their imperial context, (3) keeping *the people* at the center, (4) using all sources (5) to understand them as participants in a collective movement. Such work would be (6) perspectival, influenced by the societal locations of scholars, as well as (7) interdisciplinary, employing methods and models from historical and literary analysis, classical studies, and anthropology. The indefinite article "*a*" used with "people's history" encapsulates these emphases.

Yet a people's history approach to Matthew faces significant obstacles. One problem involves limited space. The scope of the inquiry is far too extensive for one chapter. This discussion is partial and initial at best.

A second problem concerns definition. As much as a small group of followers of Jesus is our focus, they belong (mostly) among the nonelite, forming one subculture or part-culture among other subcultures or part-cultures that exist in some relationship with the elite. How do we describe these diverse interactions?

A third problem concerns sources. The Gospel provides the only written source specifically related to Matthew's people. While it includes numerous hints and reflections of daily imperial life, there are difficulties in treating a text as a window on the world behind it when we do not know if the text exists in prescriptive, descriptive, affirmative, or hortatory relationship (or combinations thereof) to its context. Sources often employed in people's histories (diaries, personal letters, oral histories) are absent. The only remnants of Antioch's material culture originate from the wealthy and powerful and mediate their values, perspectives, and practices.[3]

The lack of sources and the limits of the Gospel's content prevent us from pursuing various dimensions of the lived experience of Matthew's late-first-century people. For instance, did Matthew's people participate in or attend various entertainments in Antioch at the hippodrome and amphitheater? Did any of them belong to the three or four legions stationed in Antioch? Were any of Matthew's people members of religious groups as patron or participant? What did they do when a trade or artisan guild invoked and sacrificed to a god, or when a neighborhood street feast, sponsored by a wealthy patron, honored the emperor? The Gospel offers no clarification about such situations.

Fourth are problems of explanation and synthesis. The analysis of "any human activity" (rather than specific religious issues), of structures (rather than individuals), and of collective movements (rather than particular events and key figures) moves biblical scholars to the sometimes unfamiliar domains of classical studies and social-scientific models of societal interaction and structure.

Yet the task of peeling back layers of time to focus on ordinary people's lives remains tantalizing. These lives participate in what Robert Scribner describes as popular culture, "a system of shared meanings, attitudes and values, and the symbolic forms (performances, artifacts) in which they are expressed and embodied." Popular culture exists within a larger, ever-changing, and stratified culture. It is shaped by basic modes of production and life experiences into "part-cultures" (such as peasants, urban artisans, or Matthew's people).

Dominant groups, Scribner argues, use their power to impose values and practices on subordinate groups. Subordinate groups respond variously with acquiescence, cooperation, co-optation, or silent acceptance along with skepticism, resistance, rejection, or complex combinations thereof. In turn, the dominant culture may ignore, tolerate, encourage, exploit, oppose, or (attempt to) eradicate subgroups. That is, dominant groups attempt to establish social organization and cultural understandings in which subgroups are distinguished from and subordinated to the dominant group. Popular culture exists within a triangle of processes comprising the cultural formation exerted by dominant groups, the differentiation of subgroups, and their subordination to the dominant group. Popular culture is often a subordinate culture marked by deference. But it is also an alternative or counterculture opposed to the dominant forces.

This framework provides guidelines for a people's history of Matthew's community. First, concern with the larger cultural context involves more than the synagogue and post-70 Judaisms with which Matthean scholars have been preoccupied. Second, the focus falls not on the "great men" of the elite, but ordinary people. Third, the distribution and exercise of power are center stage along with the complex negotiated interactions between dominant and subordinate groups (spanning acquiescence to resistance). Fourth, subordinated communities comprise alternative or countercultural groups that both adapt to and contest dominant values and practices. Fifth, the use of anthropological models to analyze the larger cultural system and their attempts to subordinate and differentiate subgroups allow us to connect some dots, thereby compensating to some extent the lack of sources and data.

Such an approach to a people's history of Matthew contrasts in significant ways with standard histories of Matthew's community.[4] Standard approaches have focused on key events, dates, and major figures specific to the Matthean community such as relations with Jerusalem, mission, conflicts, and the roles of putatively important figures such as James, Peter, Barnabas, and Paul. A people's history approach, by contrast, centers on the common folks and their everyday living conditions in the context of the events and structures of the wider imperial world. Standard approaches have highlighted ethnicity, especially struggles between Judeans and non-Judeans over identity markers and between Matthew's community and the wider Judean community. A people's history approach attends to dynamics of power, gender, social status, and ethnicity as constructed by imperial dynamics. Standard approaches focus almost exclusively on religious matters such as the (non)observance of key Judean practices like table fellowship and circumcision, while a people's history approach attends to everyday societal matters such as Torah's prescriptions for justice, socioeconomic conditions, and gender relationships. Whereas New Testament sources, notably parts of Acts and Galatians as well as Matthew itself, have formed the core for standard approaches, people's history also employs social-scientific analysis and historical and classical studies of the conditions of life in the Roman Empire.

Shaped by these perspectives, I will discuss aspects of the interaction between Matthew's people and the powerful political, economic, societal, and religious forces of the Roman Empire. In negotiating Rome's world, Matthew's people exist as a subordinated group. But the Gospel also shapes it to be an alternative or countercultural group that contests aspects of the surrounding society. Because of space limitations I have chosen to give minimal attention to likely conflict with a synagogue and to internal dynamics among Matthew's people, such as opponents, community structures, discipline, leadership, and the role of women.

Further, I will move between analysis of the realities of the first-century world and Matthew's prescriptive vision for his people. In telling its hearers how to live, the Gospel can function variously to confirm, encourage, remind, recover, contest, and correct the actual circumstances of his people. It is difficult to identify specific instances when Matthew is affirming or when he is trying to change ways of living. The Gospel's frequent repetitions and "bullying" tone might suggest much correction, or they might indicate great efforts to support an existing way of life. Either way, the Gospel encourages, renews, and sustains the distinctive way of life of followers of Jesus. It strongly counters pressures to cultural conformity and imitation in difficult and at times overwhelming circumstances. Matthew's Gospel provides us a sense of how Matthew's people, distinguishing themselves from the dominant Judean community in Antioch, navigated between a local synagogue and the ruling powers of the Roman imperial order.

POWER AND POVERTY IN THE ROMAN IMPERIAL ORDER

How do Matthew's people negotiate the interplay of subordination and differentiation in Roman-dominated, late-first-century Antioch? Studies of the Roman Empire, peasant societies, and forms of resistance enable us to sketch some of the ways in which power was exercised, encountered, and negotiated by Matthew's people.[5]

The Roman imperial world effected cultural formation and subordination through interrelated political-economic and cultural-religious means. The imperial order comprised vast societal inequalities, economic exploitation, and political oppression. A Roman and provincial ruling elite of 2 to 3 percent of the population controlled political, religious, and legal institutions, the military, economic production and distribution, and the consumption of resources. Land, predominantly in elite control, was the basic source of wealth. Military conquests effected subordination and added land and wealth from tribute and forced labor, from taxes and rents (often paid in kind; Pliny, *Ep.* 10.8.5), and from peasant

> *Calgacus, a British chief, rallies his troops to fight the Romans*
>
> Robbers of the world, now that earth fails their all-devastating hands, they probe even the sea; if their enemy have wealth, they have greed; if he be poor, they are ambitious; East nor West has glutted them; alone of humankind they covet with the same passion want as much as wealth. To plunder, butcher, steal, these things they misname empire; they make a desolation and they call it peace . . . our goods and chattels go for tribute; our lands and harvests in requisitions of grain; life and limb themselves are worn out in making roads through marsh and forest to the accompaniment of gibes and blows. . . .
>
> —Tacitus, Agricola 30–31 (selections)

Fig. 6.3. As a "tributary economy" the Roman empire depended upon exactions from the provinces it controlled, through taxes and tolls. This relief on a Roman funerary stele depicts a tax-collection scene, apparently depicting the occupation of the deceased. Second or third century CE. Rheinisches Landesmuseum, Trier, Germany. Photo: Erich Lessing / Art Resource, NY.

farmers defaulting on loans, rents, or taxes (Philo, *On the Special Laws* 3.159–63). Taxes and rents typically claimed between 30 and 70 percent of productivity. From 3 to 4 percent of the population consumed over 50 percent of agrarian production, while most people lived at subsistence levels.

The writer Tacitus notes that during the emperor Tiberius's rule, "the provinces, too, of Syria and Judea, exhausted by their burdens, were pressing for a diminution of the tribute" (*Annals* 2.42). When people in Jerusalem rose in revolt against their Roman and high priestly rulers in 66 CE, they burned the building that stored debt records. The poor in Antioch mounted a similar protest, burning land registers and debt records in 70 CE (Josephus, *War* 7.55, 61).

The societal power of this ruling 2 to 3 percent involved control over the rural and urban economic spheres. Cities like Antioch were not only "consumer" cities that siphoned off the productivity of surrounding territory through rents and taxes.[6] The ruling group also controlled urban production, intercity trade and commerce, and urban–rural and urban-urban interactions involving investment, trade, commerce, and banking.[7] Elite households needed abundant and accessible cash from land, loans, investment in trade, dowries, inheritances, and rents from houses, apartments, shops, and warehouses, to maintain and enhance their sociopolitical status and power. They displayed power, status, and wealth through expensive buildings, housing, clothing, food, acts of patronage, and so forth. Elites secured their advantage at the expense of the poor and poorer.

Religious institutions and personnel were an integral part of these dominant socioeconomic and political structures, further effecting cultural formation and subordination. Imperial theology, proclaimed by elite personnel, buildings, coins, rituals, festivals, inscriptions, and literary works announced that the gods had chosen Rome to rule and sanctioned its vertical sociopolitical order.[8] Members of the ruling elite served as priests and priestesses for various cults, which included honoring the emperor and imperial family. They financed civic celebrations and temples and secured honor and influence for themselves. Synagogue leaders, with whom Matthew's people stood in conflict in Antioch, probably exercised power, wealth, and status as members of the local elite.[9]

A huge socioeconomic gap separated the wealthy and powerful from skilled and unskilled urban workers, from rural peasants working small landholdings, from day laborers, and from slaves. Workers provided cheap labor and, often, economic skills to increase elite wealth. While Cato the Younger, by one estimate, enjoyed revenues of 550 to 600 *sesterces* a day from property valued at 4 million *sesterces,* an unskilled laborer earned 1 to 3 *sesterces* (Matt. 20:2). Very limited opportunities existed for social improvement. Numerous tensions marked this stratified society: rich and poor (and poorer), Roman and provincial, propertied and non-propertied, male and female, rural and urban. Generally, the former were honored and the latter despised. C. R. Whittaker observes, for example, that the "term 'poor,' in Roman status terms, usually meant anyone not of the ruling orders,"[10] and disdained by them (Cicero, *On Duty* 1.150; 2.52–56; *Letters to Atticus* 1.16; Juvenal, *Satires* 3.147–53; Tacitus, *Histories* 1.4).

Fig. 6.4. The majority of individuals in the early Christian assemblies would have been independent low-income laborers and artisans. Sign for a Roman blacksmith, first century CE. Vatican Museums, the Vatican. Photo: Alinari / Art Resource, NY.

While most were poor, gradations of poverty did exist. Estimates of preindustrial cities identify 4 to 8 percent as incapable of earning a living, 20 percent in permanent crisis, and 30 to 40 percent (artisans, shopkeepers, officials) who temporarily fall below subsistence levels. Falling below subsistence levels—whether permanently or temporarily—depended on work availability, harvest yields, disease, weather, high prices, profiteering, short supply, low wages, and so on. Rare indeed were "successful" freedmen such as Trimalchio, ridiculed by Petronius, who managed to gain moderate income and some reserves with which to survive times of shortage. Very few gained a higher living standard through trade, through skilled business or artisan service of value to a wealthy patron or former owner, or through inheritance or legacy. At the lowest end, many could not find work to provide housing or food and lived as beggars (Martial, *Epig.* 10.5).

Most inhabitants of Antioch lived in atrocious and cramped conditions marked by noise, filth, squalor, garbage, human excrement, animals, disease, fire risk, crime, social and ethnic conflicts, malnutrition, natural disasters (especially flooding), and unstable dwellings (Seneca, *Ep.* 56; Martial, *Epig.* 12.57). Fear and despair were pervasive. The life expectancy for nonelites was low: for men twenty-five to forty years, less for women. Infant mortality was high: about 28 percent born alive in Rome died within a year; 50 percent did not survive a decade.[11] The poor comprised Matthew's people.

Provincials negotiated Rome's power in diverse ways. These included alliances or power sharing between Roman and provincial elites (Aristides, *Roman Oration* 64; Plutarch, *Precepts of Statecraft* 814C; Dio Cassius 52.19.2-3), submission, collaboration, accommodation, dissent, and resistance. Resistance could be overt and violent. Bandit groups, and pirates at sea, attacked the personnel and property of the wealthy and powerful. But more frequently, peasants and artisans chose covert, self-protective, and nonviolent protests mixed with self-benefiting accommodation and survival. Some groups envisioned the end of Rome's world and organized alternative social relationships and experiences. Visionary writings from philosophers, prophets, and apocalyptic seers imagined alternative identities and societal interactions.[12]

GOD'S EMPIRE VERSUS ROME'S

What strategies does the Gospel offer Matthew's people for negotiating the sociopolitical, economic, and religious structures and power of Rome's world, and how are these followers of Jesus who manifested God's empire to live in relation to imperial expressions in Antioch? In sum, the Gospel exposes the Empire's strategies and structures of control and evaluates them negatively in relation to God's purposes. It advocates alternative practices that embody God's purposes and shapes Matthew's people into a community marked by an alternative social experience. Matthew's people are to live in this way until the eschatological establishment of God's empire.

The Gospel wants Matthew's people to understand Rome's Empire theologically as devilish and under God's judgment. The story of the devil's temptation of Jesus reveals to Matthew's people that Satan, the opponent of God's purposes, is the power behind the Roman Empire. In the third temptation, the devil offers Jesus dominion over "all the empires/kingdoms of the world and their glory" (4:8-9). The term "kingdoms" or "empires" is explicitly political, denoting empires (1 Macc. 1:6, 16), including Rome's (*Sibylline Oracles* 3.47; Josephus, *War* 5.409; Appian, *Civil Wars* 2.86). The scene presents the devil as controlling the world's empires and the "super-power" Rome as operating under Satan's direction and power. It allies Satan with Rome's sanctioning divinities like Jupiter, who had elected Rome, and like *Nike/Victoria, Pax,* or *Aeternitas,* who were claimed to be active in Rome's actions. Jesus refuses to give the devil *proskynesis* (4:9), an act of political submission and allegiance in prostration, because his loyalty as "son" (3:17) is to God, "Lord of heaven and earth" (11:25). This cosmic analysis frames the Gospel's resistance to Rome's "devilish" or satanic power. It creates for Matthew's people cosmic and societal differentiation from the Empire. It offers them a paradigm for rejecting Roman imperial rule and for refusing allegiance to it.

But the Gospel assures Matthew's people that Satan's power is not supreme. Through the Gospel, Jesus confronts Satan's power in people possessed by demons (4:24; 8:16, 28, 33; 9:32; 12:22; 15:22). Demoniacs embody and personalize Rome's demonic and destructive rule. In casting out the demons, however, Jesus overcomes Satan's power and frees people from its grip. In 8:26-34, for example, Jesus casts a demon out of two men living in a graveyard into a herd of pigs who destroy themselves in the sea (8:28-34). Significantly, the pig was the mascot of the Roman Tenth *Fretensis* Legion stationed in Syria, which had fought against Jerusalem in the 66–70 war. The scene depicts the demon-possessed nature of the present, Jesus' liberating power, and the people's desire for Jesus to assert God's authority in destroying Rome. Jesus' exorcisms directly confront the "power behind the throne," subvert Roman rule, and assert God's empire (12:28).

Demonic possession frequently occurs in contexts of oppression.[13] Frantz Fanon's study of the impact of imperial power in French-dominated Algeria, for example, argues that oppressed persons frequently understand conflicts with the ruling powers in terms of traditional cosmic myths and evil spirits. Contexts of oppression create an internally conflicted identity among the oppressed such as Matthew's people. They despise exploitative power yet must cooperate with it to survive. In seeking to be free from it and have power over it, they acknowledge its desirability. Jesus' exorcisms express such desires.

Moreover, Fanon's study links psychosomatic illnesses with the same context of oppression. He describes the physical impact of colonial power on terrified locals: "his glance ... shrivels me up ... freezes me, and his voice ... turns me into stone." Fanon describes symptoms of pains, menstruation disorders, and muscular rigidity and paralysis. Reporting on Serbian imperialism in Kosovo in 1999, Deborah Amos observed extensive paralysis and muteness in response to the trauma and violence, phenomena well attested in research on trauma effects. These responses attest subduing power, but they are also coping mechanisms, even self-protective protest against imperial power, through inactivity and noncompliance. In Matthew, the paralyzed (4:24; 8:6; 9:2, 6), shriveled up (12:10), and mute or deaf (9:32-33; 11:5; 12:22; 15:30-31) frequent the Gospel, embodying and protesting the traumatic impact of Roman power. It is possible that such strategies are evident among Matthew's people.

Chapters 2–4 provide them with further analysis of imperial power at work. Chapter 2's story of King Herod exposes and condemns Rome's client kings, allies, and agents. King Herod, Rome's "king of the Jews" (Josephus, *Ant.* 16.311), unsuccessfully uses conventional imperial tactics—alliances with local elites (2:3), spies (2:5-6), subterfuge and espionage (2:8), military violence (2:16)—against Jesus. Three references to Herod's death (2:15, 19, 20) reveal God thwarting Herod. This scene makes Matthew's people aware of imperial strategies, offers the magi's actions as an example of noncooperation with the Empire's rulers, and reassures them of God's thwarting power.

Herod's son Archelaus continues Roman power, causing Joseph to relocate to Galilee (2:22-23). But all is not well in "Galilee under the Gentiles." A citation from Isa. 9:1-2 describes Galilee as a place of imperial darkness and death that needs God's light or saving presence and reign, as in the time of Assyria's threat (4:14-16).[14] God intervenes through Jesus, who manifests God's empire and begins to counter Rome's disastrous rule with teaching, community formation, and healing (4:17-25). Galilee's ruler, Herod's son Antipas, continues his father's murderous opposition to God's agents. He beheads the prophet John, who challenges his power and announces God's rule (14:1-12). Resisting Rome by following Jesus is dangerous for Matthew's people.

Matthew underlines Rome's pervasive opposition to God's purposes and agents in the depiction of another representative of Rome's power, the governor Pontius Pilate (27:11-17). The "trial" narrative emphasizes Pilate's role in representing Rome's exploitative imperial order. The governor has life-and-death power over Jesus.[15] The opening exchange identifies Jesus' crime to be his treasonous identity as "king of the Jews" (27:11-14), a title bestowed only by Rome and only to those who represent, not challenge, its interests (Josephus, *War* 2.60–62, assigned to Athrongaeus; 2.434, assigned to Menahem; 4.510; 7.29 assigned to Simon bar Giora). The scene exposes Pilate enacting Roman justice to protect elite interests. He and his Jerusalem allies work together to manipulate the crowd into doing the rulers' will (27:20) and taking responsibility for it (27:25). The scene thereby shows

Pilate's attempt to wash his hands of any responsibility to be callous and futile (27:24). Pilate sentences Jesus to be crucified (27:26), a sentence that reflects Jesus' status as much as his crime. Crucifixion was reserved for rebellious foreigners and provincials who contested Roman control (Josephus, *War* 2.306, 308; 5.449–53; Philo, *Against Flaccus* 72, 84).

While exposing Rome's strategies and the risks of dissent, the Gospel also encourages Matthew's people. Jesus' resurrection reveals God's greater power and reveals the limits of Pilate's and Rome's power (chapter 28). Despite exercising the ultimate power in putting Jesus to death, they cannot keep him dead. The Gospel warns Jesus' followers that they too should expect appearances before governors (10:18-25).

The Gospel also exposes and condemns the Jerusalem rulers, Rome's allies,[16] for shaping a society that fails to enact God's just purposes. The chief priests, appointed by the Romans, ruled Judea as local agents of Roman power (Josephus, *Ant.* 20.249-51). The "most notable Pharisees" allied with "powerful citizens" cooperated with Rome (*War* 2.330–32; 2.410–18). Matthew introduces the chief priests and scribes as Herod's allies (2:4-6). From 12:14 the Pharisees plot Jesus' death and work with the chief priests to arrest Jesus (21:45-46; 26:4, 47). Chief priests, scribes, and elders (26:57-68) work with Pilate to execute Jesus (27: 1-2). These rulers with soldiers of the Roman governor formulate a story to counter God's raising of Jesus (28:11-15).

Fig. 6.5. In addition to economic exactions, the Roman empire controlled vast populations through the use of violence and terror. Rome crucified thousands of Judeans during the years leading up to the Jewish revolt. Here an iron nail has been driven through the ankle bones of a twenty-five-year-old man, Yehohanan, found in a Jewish grave from the Herodian period, Givat ha-Mivtar, northeast of Jerusalem. Israel Museum, Jerusalem. Photo: Erich Lessing / Art Resource, NY.

Matthew's Jesus questions the legitimacy of these Jerusalem-based, Roman client rulers in 9:36. He describes the people as sheep without "shepherds," a common metaphor for rulers (Suetonius, *Tiberius* 32) who care only for their own interests. They fail, unlike God (Psalm 23) and Jesus (Matt. 2:5), to represent God's just rule. In Ezekiel 34, such shepherds/ leaders rule with "force and harshness" (34:4, 17-19), depriving the people of food, clothing, and care for the sick, injured, and weak. Matthew's people are to understand that leaders allied with Rome, such as the Jerusalem rulers, enforce a society contrary to God's purposes.

This point is emphasized in the numerous scenes that present Jesus in conflict with these rulers over their respective visions of society. Jesus conflicts with them over doing mercy on the Sabbath (12:1-14), his authority (12:22-45), and their unjustly depriving the elderly of material support (15:1-20). The interpretation of scripture is often central to these disputes. Its interpretation was a political act since it involved the control and shape of society. Matthew's Jesus declares that their leadership and the (unjust) social order that they oversee are contrary to God's purposes; God will "uproot" them (15:13), an image of judgment and condemnation (Jer. 1:10; 12:17).

Jesus enacts this condemnation symbolically against Jerusalem's Temple, the center of their power. As an instrument of shaping society, the Temple secured the elite's sociopolitical, economic, and religious domination through taxes, buying and selling sacrifices and supplies for Temple ritual, administering landed estates, receiving and storing gifts (compare Matt. 15:5), and controlling ritual.[17] The Temple, like others in Rome's world, was part slaughterhouse, worship center, and bank (Josephus, *War* 2.293; *Ant.* 18.60).

Jesus condemns the Temple order and practices of changing money and selling sacrifices (21:12-13). Jesus quotes Isa. 56:7 ("a house of prayer") to contrast Isaiah's inclusionary vision with the elite's exclusionary practices. Jesus enacts this inclusionary vision by healing in the Temple the blind and lame who were usually excluded from it (Matt. 21:14; compare Lev. 21:16-24; 2 Sam. 5:8). He names their Temple a "den for robbers/bandits" (Jer. 7:11). The phrase evokes Jeremiah's condemnation of the powerful who seek the Temple's protection but contravene God's will with exploitative and oppressive social and economic actions: acting unjustly; oppressing the alien, orphan, and widow; shedding innocent blood; and pursuing other gods (Jer. 7:5-6, also 7:9). Their actions meant judgment in 587 BCE. It is likewise for Jerusalem's first-century Temple. Matthew's people understand the Temple's destruction by Rome in 70 CE to be God's judgment (Matt. 22:7).

Jesus elaborates the condemnation of the rulers in parables (21:28—22:14), foretelling their demise (21:41; 22:7). The curses of chapter 23 identify the leaders' failures. Jesus curses them for neglecting "the weightier matters of the law, justice, mercy and faithfulness" (23:23). The Gospel describes them as "evil" (9:4; 12:34) and "tempting" Jesus (16:1-4), applying to them features of the devil (4:1, 3; 13:38-39) and presenting them as the devil's allies and agents. Matthew's Gospel resists their way of organizing society by depicting it as devilish and contrary to God's purposes. This condemnation defines Matthew's people as a distinctive and alternative community committed to God's purposes manifested in Jesus and in opposition to imperial ways of organizing society.

The Gospel also reframes imperial practices and offers ways in which Matthew's people can negotiate imperial demands while maintaining their allegiance to God's purposes manifested in Jesus. Two scenes engage taxation, a fundamental means whereby elites effected subordination. The first scene, 17:24-27, recognizes the normal practice that rulers take "tolls or tribute."[18] The first term denotes taxes on "public purchases and sales"

(*Ant.* 17.204), agricultural products (*Ant.* 18.90), tribute to Rome (*War* 2.118, 404), and other taxes (*Ant.* 19.25). The second term denotes taxes on personal wealth assessed in a census (BAGD, 430). This scene specifically concerns a third tax, the two-drachma tax that Rome levied on Jews after the defeat of Jerusalem in 70 CE (Josephus, *War* 7.218; Dio Cassius, 65.7.2). The tax identified Jews as a conquered people required to honor the victorious power. It insulted their monotheism and allegiance by co-opting a tax previously paid to the Jerusalem Temple to maintain the temple of Jupiter Capitolinus, patron god of victorious Rome and of the Flavian emperors.

Should Matthew's people pay this tax that expresses loyalty and submission to Rome? Not to pay would invite harsh retaliation. Jesus advocates payment (17:27) as a pragmatic strategy to avoid punishment for the rebellion of nonpayment (Josephus, *War* 2.403–4; *Ant.* 12.158–59; Tacitus, *Annals* 3.40–41; 4.72–73; 6.41; *Histories* 4.73–74). But studies show that submissiveness coerced from peasants is often qualified by self-protective acts of defiance that contest the public transcript and assert dignity and independence. Accordingly, while Jesus requires payment, he recasts the tax's significance.

His instruction to procure the coin from a fish's mouth evokes previous scenes in which God displays compassion and sovereignty over fish (7:10; 14:13-21; 15:32-39). This display of sovereignty counters Rome's control of the fishing industry as part of its proprietary economy whereby the emperor was "ruler of lands and seas and nations" (Juvenal, *Satires* 4.83–84) and "every rare and beautiful thing in the wide ocean . . . belongs to the imperial treasury" (*Satires* 4.51–55). Jesus' assertion of authority over fish locates the tax within God's sovereign purposes. For Matthew's people, paying the tax no longer expresses submission to Rome's sovereignty but self-protectively contests Rome's claims, subversively expresses God's sovereignty, and anticipates the establishment of God's just empire over the nations.

The Gospel provides them with further guidance for negotiating taxation. The taxing question appears again in 22:15-22: Pharisees and Herodians, Rome's allies, question Jesus about "taxes to the emperor."[19] Jesus' answer expresses the double pose of subordinated groups that James Scott identifies, namely, feigned and self-protective public obedience, with a hidden and coded transcript of dissent. Jesus focuses on the *denarius* that paid the tribute. This handheld billboard represents the appropriation of peasant production. It announces the emperor's status and his role as agent of the gods; the image of Tiberius's mother, Livia, enthroned as Pax, the heavenly counterpart of Pax Romana, symbolized Rome's divinely sanctioned gift of "peace." Jesus' demand for the coin turns the tables of power (compare 5:38-42), seizing the initiative and requiring obedience to his demand (22:19). His instruction to "pay back" to Caesar and to God poses the question of the relationship between the two clauses. Does the second annul, endorse, or contextualize the first? Does Jesus advocate public revolt, accommodation, or disguised (nonviolent) dissent? Since God is "Lord of Heaven and Earth" (11:25), all things belong to God. But Rome's coin bearing the emperor's image and representing imperial claims violates God's order and is under God's judgment (22:20-21; compare Exod. 20:1-6; Deut. 8:5). Hence Matthew's people are to pay the tribute with a hidden transcript. They give back what represents not Rome's eternal order blessed by the gods, but Rome's violation of God's order and certain judgment. Their action is one of disguised nonviolent dissent.

In these critiques of rulers, Temple, and taxation, the Gospel recalls for Matthew's people traditions from the Hebrew Bible that condemn imperial structures and point to God's alternative purposes. Twice in chapters 1–4,[20] for example, Matthew evokes Isaiah 7–9 (1:23; 4:15-16) and the struggle of King Ahaz of Judah with Kings Pekah of Israel and Rezin of Syria, under Assyrian threat. Isaiah depicts three perspectives on the latter's imperial power: God opposes it, uses it, and (imitating it) destroys it to establish God's reign. These perspectives interpret the events of 70 CE, in which Rome is understood to have enacted God's punishment on Jerusalem (22:7). They provide Matthew's people with perspectives on Rome's power. It is temporary and under God's judgment.

The Gospel also fosters Matthew's people's anticipation of the eschatological establishment of God's purposes. This final repudiation of Rome's cultural formation involves an eschatological scenario in which God destroys Rome's world and establishes God's heaven and earth (19:28; 24:35). In 24: 27-31, Matthew presents Jesus' return as the end of all empires, especially Rome's.[21] Verse 28 describes the final battle in which Rome's army, represented by the eagle, is destroyed. Verse 29 denotes judgment on the cosmic deities that Rome claimed sanctioned its power. The Son of Man establishes God's "everlasting dominion . . . and kingship that will never be destroyed" (see Dan. 7:13-14). Interestingly, in depicting God's empire in terms of overwhelming power, destroyed opponents, and the imposition of universal rule, this scene imitates imperial power and reflects the Gospel's embeddedness in imperial culture.

This final judgment culminates Jesus' manifestation of God's reign/empire throughout his ministry (4:17). Jesus manifests God's claim and reign as "Lord of heaven and earth" (11:25) in words (for example, chapter 13) and in actions (12:28) that challenge and transform the status quo. The imperial language for God's action draws on Israel's traditions involving the king (compare Psalm 72) but also reflects the Gospel's embeddedness in and accommodation to its imperial world. Homi Bhabha has discussed the dynamic of mimicry that operates in colonial situations among oppressed groups who imitate their oppressors, sometimes to ally with them, but often to mock and menace them.[22] For Matthew's people, God's empire outmuscles and counter-masters Rome's Empire.

Matthew's people are presented as an embodiment of Jesus' manifestation of God's rule or empire. Jesus' ministry creates a countercultural community committed to God and Jesus. It is to embody God's reign as an alternative to the Empire's societal reality. While Matthew's people are subordinated to Roman rule, they also distinguish themselves with an alternative societal experience.

Among Matthew's people, the exercise of power and patterns of societal interaction are to contrast with the hierarchical and tyrannical norms of the Empire. Jesus identifies the domination pattern of the "rulers of the Gentiles" and

> But Jesus called them to him and said, "You know that the rulers of the Gentiles lord it over them, and their great ones are tyrants over them. It will not be so among you; but whoever wishes to be great among you must be your servant."
>
> —Matt. 20:25-26

"their great men" who "lord it over" and "rule" others (20:25). He forbids his followers from imitating the behaviors and structures of the Empire's rulers. Instead, Matthew's people are to embrace the marginality and humility of the Empire's lowest members, slaves. They are not to dominate but to seek the other's good, in imitation of Jesus (20:26-28; compare 23:11-12).

Matthew's people are also to adopt household structures that challenge conventional household patterns. Since Aristotle's time, elite households, like the Empire, were to be androcentric, patriarchal, and hierarchical. The head male ruled over wife, children, and slaves and secured wealth. Matthew 19–20 challenges this pattern with more mutual relationships. Husbands and wives participate in "one flesh" relationships (19:3-12). Households include children, in that all disciples are deemed to share the marginal cultural location of children (19:13-15). Following Jesus, not gaining wealth (status and power), defines discipleship (19:16-30). All disciples are slaves like Jesus (20:17-34). This structure reflects that *God* is father (23:9; 5:16, 45; 6:9) not the emperor *(pater patriae)*, that Jesus is the only master (23:10), and that all disciples bear a marginal and vulnerable identity as God's children (5:9, 45). The chapters, if followed, set Matthew's people at odds with elite domestic and societal structures.

Matthew's people are not to invest themselves in the exploitative quest for wealth and status. Jesus encounters a "rich man" (19:23, 24), a member of the economically powerful elite (19:16-30). This man is deeply invested in his great wealth (19:22). He asks Jesus about "eternal life" (19:16) and how to "enter the empire/rule of the heavens" (19:23, 24) and find salvation (19:25). Jesus rehearses four commandments from the Decalogue concerning societal interactions (Exod. 20:12-16) and cites Lev. 19:18, requiring love for neighbor and self (19:18-19). The rich man claims compliance (19:20). His response, though, reveals his blindness to the ways in which his economic activity and system contradict God's purposes for human interaction. His claims not to have stolen and to have loved his neighbor are exposed by his abundant wealth (19:24). He has more because he has misused and exploited the poor (so Isa. 10:1-3; Ezek. 22:6-31; 34: 1-22; Amos 5:10-12; Sir. 13:2-7, 17-19). The "rich man" provides Matthew's people with a negative paradigm for community economic relations.

Contrary to Rome's exploitative economics, Jesus forms an alternative economic system and community based in repentance and care for the poor. He requires the rich man to divest and redistribute wealth among the poor (19:21). This act of restitution and justice sets right inequalities and transforms unjust structures, relationships, and practices. This act of "release," like the year of Jubilee in Leviticus 25, restores what belongs to the poor and counters the elite's excessive accumulation. Jesus' advocacy of such actions to benefit the poor (most of society) contradicts the elite's practices that, motivated by love of status *(philodoxia)*, sought their own advantage and ignored or despised the unworthy poor (for example, Seneca, *Blessed Life* 24). Jesus' (counter)cultural formation involves a changed identity, societal orientation, and economic activity. This different economic system differentiates the man—and Jesus' followers, Matthew's people— from the practices of the dominant order.

The rich man chooses against Jesus' way and for the status quo. He prefers to serve mammon, not God. Wealth rules his heart (6:24). He represents "the nations," who seek possessions rather than God's reign and justice (6:33-34). His "delight in riches" has choked (13:22) "the word of the empire" (13:19), that is, God's empire. He has preferred corrupting pieces of silver that are instruments of injustice rather than God's empire and its messenger (26:15-16; 27:3-10).

Not surprisingly, the Gospel claims that God's blessing and empire, encountered by Matthew's people, especially embrace the poor (5:3). Citing Psalm 37, the third beatitude reverses the imperial economic order by promising the earth, the basis of wealth, to the meek (5:5). Psalm 37 (37:3, 9, 11, 22, 29, 34) depicts the meek as the poor who are endlessly oppressed by the rich. The powerful rich are the "enemies of the Lord" (37:20) who "carry out evil devices" (37:7), "plot against the righteous" (37:12), and "bring down" and kill the poor and needy (37:14, 32). The psalm promises that God will destroy the wicked wealthy (37:9, 13, 20), giving the poor access to adequate resources (the land) previously denied them. Matthew's people are involved in this transformation already, and it will be completed in the final, future, eschatological act of differentiation (24:27-31).

The Gospel continues its countercultural formation of Matthew's people by having Jesus outline economic practices based on God's purposes of mercy and justice, not exploitative self-interest. In 5:41 Jesus requires compliance with *angaria*, compulsory service, whereby Rome requisitioned labor, transport (animals, ships), and lodging from subject people. But he instructs followers to subvert imperial authority by carrying the soldier's pack twice the distance, putting the soldier in danger of being disciplined for overly harsh conduct.[23] In 6:1-18 Jesus' warning against doing acts of justice (prayer, almsgiving, fasting) for public applause rejects the elite emphasis on gaining status. Elite patronage for deserving poor involved "self-regarding" displays concerned with enhancing elite status, reciprocity, creating dependents/clients, love of honor *(philotimia)*, and reputation *(philodoxa)*.

By contrast, Jesus urges not the hoarding, consuming, and displaying of wealth but its distribution to benefit others. He assumes almsgiving (6:2), a word that at its root concerns mercy, a fundamental quality of God's empire that God wants exhibited in human interactions (5:7; citing Hos. 6:6 in 9:13 and 12:7). Acts of mercy (6:2-4) involve giving to beggars and lending where reciprocity is unlikely (5:42). He requires nonviolent subversive responses that attempt to throw the exploitative imperial power off balance (5:41). He urges prayer for daily bread, often answered in the merciful actions of those who pray (6:11). He advocates fasting (6:16-18), since to fast is to live justly and with mercy in sharing food, housing the homeless, clothing the naked, and comforting the afflicted (compare Isa. 58:6-14; Matt. 25:31-46). He commands preaching God's empire, healing the sick, raising the dead, cleansing lepers, casting out demons without payment (10:7-8). This differentiated way of life for disciples is without anxiety for material goods (food, drink, clothing), since God's justice and reign will ensure enough (6:19-34). Love for one's neighbor as for oneself summarizes this way of life (22:39; compare 7:12).

This contestive way of life that the Gospel urges for Matthew's people does not include violent attacks on or withdrawal from Roman imperial society. Fight (5:38-48; 26:52) and flight (28:18-20) are forbidden to Matthew's people as they negotiate the power differential that pervades everyday interaction. While some disciples abandon economic activity and social structures to follow Jesus (4:18-22; 9:9; 19:16-30), there is no general call for Matthew's people to detach themselves from all family, material, and societal ties. Instead they are to practice nonviolent resistance (5:38-48) typical of the calculated and self-protective practices of peasants identified by James Scott. Jesus' first scenario (5:39) offers a nonviolent response to the superior's slap. Instead of cowering submission or violent retaliation, offering the other cheek deflects the intended intimidation and demeaning treatment. Moreover, disciples are to love enemies (5:44), imitating God's ways (5:45-48). As an inclusive community committed to justice (6:34), Matthew's people contrast with and resist the hierarchies of Rome's world.

This commitment to justice from Matthew's people, in the midst of Rome's injustice, is shaped, as we have noted, by Israel's traditions. Matthew's people are to observe Torah practices (Sabbath, purity, tithes, oaths, and so forth) as interpreted by Jesus (5:17-48; 22:37-39). These practices enact justice, mercy, and faithfulness (23:23), basic to the alternative societal order that Jesus reveals as God's reign and purpose.

The Gospel, then, offers Matthew's people various strategies for negotiating the elite-dominated, sociopolitical, Roman imperial order. They are to understand the imperial system as devilish and under God's imminent judgment and destruction. Within it, God's transforming empire is at work, creating and calling Jesus' disciples—Matthew's people—to a challenging countercultural societal experience that embodies God's reign in alternative practices. Until its future triumph, violent (human) opposition is forbidden. Accommodation, submission, and nonviolent resistance are necessary.

POVERTY, FOOD, AND HEALTH

Matthew's people encounter Rome's power every day in a very practical sphere: the production, distribution, and consumption of food. How do Matthew and his people negotiate this sphere?

"For most people," in the Roman Empire, "life was a perpetual struggle for survival."[24] In the exploitative political-economic system of the Empire, the powerful and wealthy controlled food production, distribution, and consumption. The consumption of food expressed power, hierarchy, and injustice, with abundance for a few and deprivation for many. I will briefly summarize (and supplement) work concerning food availability, diet quality, and nutrition levels as the context in which Matthew's people live.

Two factors might suggest an adequate food supply in Rome's world. Famines were rare because both wealthy landowners and peasants employed strategies to prevent it. For example, peasants produced some surplus to trade, to store against crop failures, and to pay rents and taxes. Second, in theory, the "Mediterranean diet" was healthful.[25] Staples of cereals, olives, wine, and legumes (beans) supplied energy, protein, vitamins B and E, calcium, and iron.

The reality, however, was quite different. Food shortages were frequent as a result of bad harvests, unfavorable weather, distribution difficulties, speculation by traders (see Philostratus, *Life of Apollonius* 1.8), wars, taxes, and so forth. Shortages meant endemic undernourishment or chronic malnutrition, especially for the poor. Poor nutrition diminished capacity for work, reducing the earnings of laborers and capacity for manual labor among peasants. Other factors reduced the diet's actual healthfulness: availability due to harvests, distribution control, location (urbanites, about 10 percent of the Empire, relied largely on the surrounding *chora* or *territorium* or lands), seasonal variations, high prices, storage limitations, limited range of foods (resulting in deficiencies in vitamins), varying qualities of wine and cereals, and low social status.

The poor food supply is reflected in pervasive diseases of deficiency and contagion. Widespread malnutrition among nonelites[26] was evident in deficiency diseases such as painful bladder stones (linked to limited animal products), eye diseases (vitamin A deficiency, diets low in animal-derived products and green vegetables), and rickets (limb deformity, deficiency in vitamin D, difficulty absorbing nutrients like calcium and iron). Early weaning of infants and the denial of protein-rich, infection-fighting colostrum to newborns meant early experience of nutritionally inadequate foods. Skeletal remains evidence considerable malnutrition.

Malnutrition rendered people vulnerable to infectious diseases such as malaria, diarrhea, dysentery, cholera, typhus, and the plague bacillus meningitis. High population densities in cities, inadequate sewage and garbage disposal, limited sanitation with restricted water supply, inadequate water distribution and unhygienic storage, public baths, animal feces, flies, mosquitoes and other insects, and so on ensured widespread infection. Swollen eyes, skin rashes, lost limbs, measles, mumps, scarlet fever, and smallpox affected many.

Matthew's Gospel and the experience of Matthew's people clearly resonate with important aspects of the above discussion.

Food production, distribution and trade, and consumption and diet figure prominently in the Gospel. Matthew depicts the imperial world's land-based economy and reliance on agriculture for food with references to sowing seed (13:3-9, 18-24), harvesting (12:1), vineyards (20:1-16; 21: 28-32, 33-45), day laborers (20:1-16), and fieldwork (24:40-41), as well as to fishing (4:18-22; 13:47-50), trading (13:45-46), and marketplaces (11:16). Various food products such as fish (7:9-10), bread (15:9-10), and wine (26: 26-29) are mentioned. It recognizes that people "labor and are burdened" in attempts to supply daily necessities (11:28-30), and it acknowledges that the food supply is precarious. Disciples pray for daily bread (6:11). People worry about what they will eat and drink (6:25-34). A householder's enemy (competitor) sabotages the food supply by sowing weeds or poisonous darnel among the crop (13:24-30). Famine threatens (24:7), beggars abound (9:27-31; 20:29-34), and acts of relief are necessary (5:42; 6:2-4).

But while those with little power lack food, the powerful such as Herod

Antipas feast lavishly (14:1-12). The powerful have landholdings, slaves, and day laborers (13:24-30; 20:1-16; 21:33-43, and so forth). Food divides the powerful and the powerless of this hierarchical society. The Gospel depicts the struggles of Matthew's people in procuring their daily food.

The Gospel also depicts the consequences of this precarious and nutritionally inadequate food supply. Numerous summary passages (4:23-25; 9: 35; 11:4-5; among others), and individual healing scenes (chapters 8–9; 12:9-14, 22; 15:21-28; 17:14-20; 20:29-34), reflect the pervasiveness of diseases of contagion and deficiency in the world of Matthew's people. Specified diseases include contagious leprosy (8:1-4; 11:5), blindness (9:27-31; 11:5 12:22; 15:30-31; 20:30; 21:14), pains (4:24), and deformities and paralysis (4:24; 8:6; 9:2; 11:5; 12:9-14; 15:30; 21:14). Jesus' healings transform the destructive impact of Rome's imperial structures.

The Gospel makes clear to Matthew's people that this devilish political-economic system that results in inadequate food and malnutrition for the majority is contrary to God's purposes. In chapter 3 John the Baptist's clothing evokes Elijah's confrontation with King Ahab and Baal's prophets (2 Kings 1:8). It aligns John with the prophetic tradition and God's purposes against the ruling elite. His stark diet (3:4b; 11:18) contrasts with and opposes the powerful. While John eats sparsely, Herod feasts extravagantly, in which context he executes John, God's agent (14:1-12).

Matthew's people are not to accept this situation of deprivation as normative. Jesus challenges it and instructs his followers in doing the same thing. Their prayer for God's empire and will to be done on earth includes prayer for their daily bread. The petition critiques the elite-controlled system that does not supply adequate food (6:11).

Jesus' critique of the Jerusalem leaders in 9:36 as illegitimate shepherds involves their depriving people of food. With God as shepherd, people will "not want" (Ps. 23:1), but the Roman client priestly rulers do not enact God's purposes. Jesus echoes Ezekiel 34's condemnation of leaders. Ezekiel's "bad" shepherds deprive the sheep of adequate food and rule with "force and harshness" (Ezek. 34:4), eat plentifully (34:2-3, 8), devour the sheep (34:10), and render them weak and sick (34:4). Ezekiel 34 envisages the replacement of these exploitative, self-serving leaders and their societal order with God's agent and a new creation order that supplies bountiful food and heals and strengthens the sheep (34:13-31).

In 12:1-8 Jesus conflicts with the Pharisaic representatives of the high priestly rulers over Sabbath observance. The Pharisees attack Jesus' disciples for harvesting on the Sabbath (12:2). Jesus argues that procuring food is a merciful act consistent with God's will (12:7). In the tradition of Sabbath and Jubilee years, he rejects Sabbath observance that prevents access to food. They respond to his threat to their power and societal order by plotting his death (12:14). Supplying food is one way in which Matthew's people honor the Sabbath.

Further condemnations of the leader's food-depriving actions follow. In 15:1-20, Jesus condemns the Temple-based rulers for encouraging contributions that enrich the elite, while depriving parents, the vulnerable elderly, of resources necessary to procure food and sustain life (15:5-6). With an image drawn from agricultural food production (15:13), Jesus condemns such leadership as contrary to God's purposes.

In 23:23-24 Jesus condemns their extending the food-tithing laws from flocks, wine, grain, and oil (Lev. 27:30-33; Num. 18:21-32; Deut. 14:22-29; 26:12-15; Mal. 3:8-12), a means of supplying the Temple, to herbs such as mint, dill, and cumin. Jesus' objection is not to tithing; rather, their practice has neglected "weightier matters of the law: justice and mercy and faith." Instead of ensuring access to adequate resources for all, they have enacted a social structure that harms the poor.

Such is the way of the world for Matthew's people until the final establishment of God's purposes. Jesus speaks of and performs actions that point to God's eschatological purposes for a world under God's rule in which all have abundant food and health. Two mass-feeding scenes (14:13-21; 15:32-39) contrast God's abundant provision (14:19; large numbers; leftovers) with limited human supply (desert; large numbers; few resources). Healings accompany both feedings (14:35-36; 15:29-31). The feeding and healing scenes recall prophetic traditions that depict God's empire as a feast of abundant, good-quality food and physical wholeness. Isaiah envisions a feast "for all peoples" on Zion ("the mountain," Matt. 15:29) "of rich food, a feast of well-aged wines" (Isa. 25:6-10; Ezek. 34:25-31). Establishing God's reign means the death of death (Isa. 25:8) and healing all diseases—the blind, deaf, lame, mute (Isa. 35:5-6). Apocalyptic writers also envisage God establishing a world of abundant fertility and health. "The tree of life is planted, the age to come is prepared, plenty is provided, rest is appointed" (4 Ezra 8:52-54). There is no more sinful excess (4 Ezra 7:112-115), evil, illness, death, hell, corruption, or sorrow (4 Ezra 8:52-54). 2 Baruch's new world also comprises nourishment, abundant fertility, no hunger, the dew of health (29:5-8), the end of imperial rule (72:5-6), peace, joy, rest, health, no social contentions and evil (73; also *Apocalypse of Abraham* 21). These visions, like Matthew's, reveal as false Rome's claims to have created such a world.[27]

Matthew's people live in anticipation of the final establishment of these purposes. The Gospel assures them that establishing God's empire in a new heaven and earth (Matt. 19:28; 24:35) also means access to land necessary for adequate food supply. Jesus promises the suffering poor ("the meek") that they will inherit the land (Matt. 5:5, evoking Psalm 37). This justice (5:6), God's saving presence or reign (4:17), is the "rest," the life free from oppression, the salvation from imperial powers that Jesus promises to those who labor. They are "heavy laden" not with the burden of sin (the usual argument) but with the economic and sociopolitical sin of the elite who deprive them of resources (11:28-30).[28] Jesus depicts this world in the parable of the householder, in which all are equally rewarded by God's purposes (20:1-16). Matthew's people are to anticipate God's eschatological victory that establishes God's justice and transforms malnutrition and inadequate food supply into abundant food and good health.

In the meantime, in contrast to the hierarchical distribution of food in the Roman imperial order, Matthew's people in Antioch are to embody an alternative social experience that participates in and anticipates God's purposes. Jesus represents this order in the meal scene in 9:10-13. As Mary Douglas has argued, meals reflect and reinforce patters of societal interaction.[29] For the elite, meals enact social hierarchy, privilege, and the subordination of the nonelite through ranked seating order, different qualities of food, and tableware. Lower-ranked guests in client relationships reciprocated the host's favor by enhancing his honor and status (Juvenal, *Satires* 5).

Jesus' meal depicts an alternative social experience by involving tax collectors, "sinners," and disciples (9:10). Tax collectors were agents of elite control, despised for transferring wealth and food from the nonelite (Cicero, *On Duties* 1.150). As retainers they had some political power and wealth but little social status. "Sinners" denotes those considered to be outsiders in God's purposes and societal interaction. Jesus' opponents evaluate his low-status dinner companions negatively (9:11). Jesus' guests cross lines of occupation (tax collectors), gender ("sinners" often denoted women prostitutes), socioeconomic status, and religious (non)observance. In 26:20-29, Jesus' companions include Judas, his betrayer and collaborator with the Jerusalem and Roman elite (26:14-16, 47-56). Thus Matthew's people are to participate in meals not to emphasize hierarchical power (contrast 14:1-12) but to experience God's merciful purposes that constitute an alternative societal experience.

Matthew's people are to continue Jesus' agenda of sharing food with the hungry and healing the sick (10:8). This agenda has four key aspects: (1) Food and hospitality shared with the missioner indicates receptiveness to their mission preaching (10:10-15, 40-42). (2) They are to do "acts of mercy" (almsgiving, 6:2-4) that involve providing food to the hungry (Prov. 25:21; Tobit 1:16-17). (3) Jesus also instructs them to fast (6:16-18). In the tradition, Isaiah defines "true fasting" as requiring providing food to the hungry (Isa. 58:6-7, 10). (4) A criterion for judgment comprises supplying food to the hungry, the "least of these" (25:35, 37, 42, 44). Disciples who undertake such work comprise those who are blessed as hungering and thirsting for justice (5:6). With these actions, Matthew's people distinguish themselves as a community of disciples with alternative political and economic interactions.

AN ALTERNATIVE SOCIETY

The Gospel addresses Matthew's people as they negotiate the attempts of Rome and a local synagogue to define and subordinate them. They are to respond to attempts by the ruling elite to subordinate them with neither (violent) fight nor flight. Rather, they are to employ calculated collaboration and self-protective dissent shaped by an alternative worldview of God's empire and expressed in practices that differentiate and embody an alternative societal experience. Matthew's people are to live out a fundamental conceptual (theological) and societal challenge to elite cultural formation. A people's history approach identifies these struggles of the powerless against the powerful as central to the historical inquiry.

FOR FURTHER READING

Carter, Warren. *Matthew and Empire: Initial Explorations.* Harrisburg: Trinity, 2001.
———. *Matthew and the Margins: A Socio-religious Reading.* Maryknoll: Orbis, 2000.
Riches, John, and David Sim, eds. *The Gospel of Matthew in Its Roman Imperial Context.* London: Sheffield University Press/Continuum, 2005.

THE GOSPEL OF JOHN
AS PEOPLE'S HISTORY

ALLEN DWIGHT CALLAHAN

CHAPTER SEVEN

It is "the spiritual Gospel," as Clement of Alexandria dubbed it in the middle of the second century of the Common Era. Seventeen centuries later, the German theologian Friedrich Schleiermacher asserted that the Gospel of John is not only the most spiritual but also the most historical of the four Gospels. Though historical-critical scholars of the New Testament might take issue with Schleiermacher's characterization, most would agree that the narrative of the Gospel of John is a literary site of embedded historical memory. In telling the story of Jesus, the Gospel gives many telling indications of the history and concerns of the Johannine community in which the memories of Jesus' mission were shaped. Read with a discerning critical eye, it is a resource for reconstructing a people's history of the Jesus movement. In its unique dramatis personae and dramatic itinerary through the various regions of Galilee, Samaria, Judea, and the Transjordan, the Gospel of John presents Jesus as an agent of restoration of the ancient kingdom of Israel.[1]

TO RESTORE THE SURVIVORS OF ISRAEL

The narrative of the Gospel of John traces a crimson thread that runs through the Law and the Prophets of Israel: the ingathering of all Israel's far-flung children. The division of Israel into two kingdoms—the kingdom of Israel in the north and the kingdom of Judah in the south—and the kingdoms' subsequent history as the victims of Levantine imperialism were damage almost a millennium old that God would nevertheless undo in the fullness of time. The prophet Ezekiel looked forward to a monarch who would rule over a unified kingdom as David had. In the fullness of time the Israelite homeland would gather outcasts from the ends of the world. The "Servant of the Lord" in the Book of Isaiah proclaimed, "The Lord . . .

formed me in the womb...to raise up the tribes of Jacob and to restore the survivors of Israel" (Isa. 49:5-6).

The northern kingdom of Israel came under a combination of imperial and local rule that variously affected the people of the districts of Galilee, Samaria, Judea, and the Transjordan. In the capital city of Samaria, the Assyrian conquerors deported the Israelite monarchy and imported a new ruling class of foreigners. After the fall of the Assyrian Empire the region by turns fell under the dominion of the Babylonians, the Persians, Alexander the Great, and the regime of Alexander's Seleucid successors. In the south, the Babylonian conquest of the kingdom of Judah and destruction of the Jerusalem Temple were followed by the Persian imperial regime.

Fig. 7.1. Both in Judea and throughout the Mediterranean world, Jews sought to live out the ancient traditions of Israel in the complex environment of Roman cities. Stone capital showing a menorah, carved in relief, from a synagogue at Caesarea, Israel. Photo: Erich Lessing / Art Resource, NY.

The Persians sponsored the restoration of the ruling class that had been deported by the Babylonians as the instrument of imperial rule. They rebuilt the Temple in Jerusalem, from which the temple-state's high priesthood controlled the surrounding area of Judea. Thus, for several centuries rival regimes in Jerusalem and Samaria controlled the Judean and Samaritan people, respectively, under the Persian and, later, the Hellenistic empires. While the cultural traditions of Jerusalem and Samaria developed separately, both claimed to be exclusive heir and guardian of the Israelite heritage.

The Romans took over the whole of Syria and Palestine in 63 BCE and installed an indigenous military strongman, Herod, as "king of the Judeans." Herod crushed dissent in his new realm as an oppressive, totalitarian sovereign. He retained the temple-state as an instrument of his rule and gradually recruited from the Judean diaspora a whole new high priestly aristocracy. After Herod's death in 4 BCE, the Romans continued to support these same high priestly families in Judea under the authority of a Roman governor and granted parcels of Herod's realm to his sons as client rulers. Thus Galileans, Samaritans, and Judeans eked out their existence under the treble rule and treble tax burden: they were simultaneously beholden to the Roman imperium, the Herodian monarchy and its heirs, and the high priestly aristocracy in Jerusalem. This sad state of affairs continued from 40 BCE until the great Judean revolt against Rome in 66 CE.

And so at the time of Jesus, the land of Israel was a geopolitical patchwork of layered, oppressive rule. But the new political realities did not efface the old traditions of Israel's tribal solidarity. Gabinius, who ruled Palestine just after Pompey's conquest, divided the land into five *synedria* (districts) with seats in Sepphoris (Galilee), Ammathus (Perea), Jericho (Samaria), Jerusalem (Judea), and Adora (Idumea). Josephus says that this artificial administrative division proved unworkable because of "the unity of the people," and the *synedria* were dissolved (*Ant.* 14:74–76; *War* 1:156–66, 169–70).

TO RESTORE THE TRIBES OF JACOB

The depth of historical divisions in Palestine was matched by the height of Israelite hopes for a restored national unity. Elijah was expected to return "to restore the tribes of Jacob" (Sir 36:13; 48:10). It was Elijah who, rallying the ten northern tribes against the oppressive rule of King Ahab, had built an altar of twelve stones symbolizing all twelve tribes of Israel as a whole (1 Kings 18:31-32). The Judean historian Josephus portrays the imminent restoration of the Babylonian exiles to Judea as a "recovery and rebirth" of the people. And even though that restoration was only of the two tribes of Judah and Benjamin, it was celebrated with the sacrifice of twelve he-goats, "one for each tribe" (*Ant.* 11.64–70, 107). Acting in anticipation of imminent fulfillment of the restoration of Israel, the community at Qumran structured its leadership as twelve symbolic representatives of the twelve tribes of Israel (1QM 2:2-3; 5:1-3; 1QS 8:1-3). We can see in the scribal Psalms of Solomon 17, where the anointed son of David will "destroy the nations with the word of his mouth." Then "he will gather a holy people whom he will lead in righteousness; and he will judge the tribes of the people that have been made holy by the Lord their God. . . . He will distribute them upon the land according to their tribes" (17:26-28).

The Israelites in the various regions of Palestine yearned for an anointed deliverer, and Jesus was born into a moment when claimants came forward in force.[2] Josephus reports that when Herod died, movements erupted in every major district, in which the people acclaimed a leader as king. The Galilean Judas, son of the famous brigand-chieftain Hezekiah, and the Transjordanian rebel Simon both led their followers in attacks against Herodian fortresses to reclaim goods that had been taken from the people. In Judea the shepherd Athronges led his followers in raids on Roman baggage trains. These movements established a de facto regional independence from Rome for some years until the Romans finally suppressed them with massive and brutal military force.

Later, around the middle of the first century, signs and wonders supplanted warfare in mass movements of Israelite renewal. Several prophets styled as Moses or Joshua led ill-fated mass movements of renewal. Other regions saw pretenders to the ancestral Israelite kingdom. Josephus reports that a Samaritan prophet led people to the holy Mount Gerazim, claiming that he would lead them to the place on the mount where Moses had buried sacred vessels. As Josephus goes on to report, "Pilate was quick to prevent their ascent with a contingent of cavalry and armed infantry. They attacked those who had assembled beforehand at the village, killed some, routed others, and took many into captivity." As the prophet Theudas and his Judean followers marched to the Jordan River for a new exodus, they were slaughtered by a surprise attack of Roman cavalry. Another prophet, returned from Egypt, led a mass of Judeans up to the Mount of Olives, claiming that God would cause the walls of Jerusalem to fall down, overpower the Roman garrison there, and return control of the city to the people. Before God effected these miracles, Roman troops viciously attacked the expectant crowd. The prophet escaped with his life; most of his followers did not.

All these movements were regional. According to the Gospel of John, however, they all were anticipated by the movement of an Israelite messiah who attracted followers among Israelites in Galilee, Samaria, the Transjordan, and Judea: that messiah was Jesus of Nazareth. In his peregrinations through the ancestral lands of Israel and his direct contact with Galileans, Samaritans, the Pereans, and Judeans, Jesus sought to overcome the historically rooted hatreds that had caused Israel to fracture along the fault lines of region, ethnicity, and class.

BEYOND JORDAN, IN GALILEE

The narrative of the Gospel of John begins in Perea on the eastern shore of the Jordan River, the first territory of the Promised Land claimed by the ancient Israelites under Joshua.[3] With a few newly minted disciples in tow, Jesus heads north and west to the northernmost region of the northern kingdom of Israel, the Galilee. In the Gospel of John, Galilee is the region of miracles: every time Jesus is there something miraculous happens. The first of these miraculous interventions in the narrative, which the narrator calls a "sign," is the wine that Jesus supplies for the wedding feast in Cana of Galilee. The traditional northern Israelite wedding feast lasted seven days, and by the time Jesus and his entourage arrive, the party has exhausted its reserves of wine. Jesus transforms into wine the water in six stone jars used in Judean ritual ablutions, saving the wedding party from social disaster in a feat of miraculous sacrilege by turning consecrated vessels into an open bar. This "sign" is the first of several acts in which Jesus shows flagrant disregard for Judean ritual.

Classical Israelite prophecy looked forward to an abundance of wine in the time of Israel's restoration: "The time is surely coming, says the LORD, / when . . . the mountains shall drip sweet wine, / and all the hills shall flow with it. / I will restore the fortunes of my people Israel" (Amos 9:13-14). In Judean apocalyptic literature, wine is a symbol of the coming messianic age of peace and righteousness. *First Enoch* 10:19 looks forward to the vine yielding wine in abundance, and in 2 Bar. 29:5, each vine shall have one thousand branches and each branch one thousand clusters. The abundant wine suddenly flowing at the wedding feast in Cana is a "sign" that the "day surely coming" has now arrived.

Later in the narrative, Jesus performs a second sign after "coming from Judea to Galilee." The Galileans receive him with a warm welcome. When he comes again to Cana, Jesus is accosted by a "royal official" *(basilikos)* from Capernaum. The official demands that Jesus "go down" to heal his son. Jesus rebuffs the official's importunate requests and sends him away with an assurance that his son is well. As the official returns home, his son is healed by remote control, as it were. This is "the second sign" Jesus performs after coming to Galilee from Judea. In the prophetic tradition of Isaiah, healing is a root metaphor for communal restoration (Isa. 29:18-21; 35:5-6; 42:18-20; 43:8). In the Gospel of John, the restoration of infirm persons to health is a sign of God's restoration of Israel.

After attending a festival in Jerusalem, Jesus is again in Galilee. When he goes to the other side of the Sea of Galilee, a large crowd follows him because of the miraculous cures he has performed. At the time, anyone intending to observe the Passover in Jerusalem should have been en route to the holy city. But when Jesus withdraws to the mountains with his disciples, the large crowd continues to follow, despite the fact that "the Passover of the Judeans was near." The Galilean masses here effectively boycott the Judeans' feast to be with Jesus. He proceeds to provide a great meal for them out of meager resources, a pointed contrast to the Passover of the Judeans celebrated in the Temple and the city of Jerusalem. At this feast in the Galilean hills, no money changes hands, no animals are sacrificed: the meat of the feast is the flesh of a ritually clean animal never sacrificed—fish. The feast in Galilee

Fig. 7.2. Remains of the entrance to the synagogue in Capernaum in Galilee. Late second or early third century CE. Photo: Erich Lessing / Art Resource, NY.

is a counter-Passover: without shekels, without sacral slaughter, and without the Jerusalem priesthood that oversees the exchange of the one for the other. And the twelve baskets of leftovers gathered signify that this superabundant feast, though it takes place in the Galilee, is for all of Israel, with more than enough for all.

"HE MUST NEEDS GO THROUGH SAMARIA"

Though the Book of Acts includes Samaria in its schematic restoration of the kingdom to Israel, it is only after persecution in Jerusalem scatters the apostles into the countryside that Philip finally proclaims the Messiah to the Samaritans. After the Samaritans have responded to Philip's preaching, Peter and John bring them under the authority of the apostles in Jerusalem. But according to the Gospel of John, Samaritan believers were integral participants in a movement of pan-Israelite renewal that was not under apostolic control from Jerusalem. Jesus is "a prophet like unto Moses" according to traditional Samaritan expectations, which were especially fervent in the middle of the first century CE. It was only a few years after he executed Jesus that Pontius Pilate massacred the Samaritan prophet and his mass of followers at the foot of Mount Gerazim.

According to the narrative of the Gospel of John, when Jesus becomes aware of the menacing surveillance of the Pharisees, he moves north. En route to Galilee, he crosses into Samaria. Though Samaria lay between Galilee and Judea on the western bank of the Jordan, Galilean Israelites coming from or heading to Jerusalem often crossed the Jordan twice to do an end run around hated Samaritan territory. In the Gospel narrative, however, Jesus takes the direct route.

After centuries of parallel development with the Judeans as peoples under rival temple-states, the Samaritans had been conquered and subjected by the Jerusalem high priestly rulers, who then destroyed the Samaritan temple on Mount Gerazim in Sychar. The setting for the encounter between Jesus and the Samaritan woman, Sychar is thus freighted with the troubled history that the Judeans and Samaritans share. Nestled in the valley below the seven-hundred-foot shadow of Mount Gerazim, Sychar is the ancient Shechem, where all Israel had gathered for covenant renewal. Less than a half mile from the northwestern side of Mount Gerazim lay Jacob's Well. In the traditions of Israel's ancestors, Jacob was associated with all regions of the people, Judea, the Transjordan, Samaria, and Galilee. This made him a suitable eponymous ancestor of all Israel, as father of the twelve eponymous ancestors of the twelve tribes.

It is at this well that Jesus makes his bold request to the Samaritan woman to "Give me a drink." Assuming that he is a Judean and so despises her, the woman is surprised by his request. Only here in the narrative is Jesus ever identified by anyone as a Judean—an identification that Jesus neither confirms nor denies. But from the woman's point of view, anyone on his way from Jerusalem was presumed to be Judean and so an enemy. Yet despite the assumed hostility between Jesus and the Samaritan woman, the romantic innuendo of the scene is unavoidable to anyone familiar with the narratives of the ancestors of Israel. The well was where a man found his mate: Isaac (Gen. 24:11), Moses (Exod. 2:15), and, especially important for this narrative, Jacob (Genesis 29). The whole scene plays upon the traditional lore of betrothal and is reminiscent of Jacob's meeting of his future wife, Rachel.[4] Jesus' command to the woman to go get her husband is the rhetorical equivalent to the question, "Are you married?"

And here the conversation takes an abrupt, bizarre turn. The woman answers that she is not married, and Jesus replies that she has had five husbands and is now with a man to whom she is not betrothed. As in his conversation with Nathaniel at the beginning of the story, Jesus seems to make a clairvoyant pronouncement; once again the language of the pronouncement makes it more of a double entendre than a parlor trick. In ancient Aramaic as in modern Hebrew, "five husbands" translates as "five lords *(ba'alim)*." Sources produced by the Judean elite, in an attempt to undermine the legitimacy of Samaritan ruling circles, insisted that the local rulers of the Samaritans had been foreigners, people from Babylon, Cuthah, Avra, Hamath, and Sepharvaim (2 Kings 17:24; Josephus, *Ant.* 9.14.3). "Five lords" also suggests the series of regimes that had ruled Samaria: the Assyrian, Babylonian, Persian, Greek, and Jerusalem-based Hasmonean. Jesus speaks of the five *ba'alim* of the Samaritans, and the sixth *ba'al*, which is not a "husband" but which has nevertheless reduced Samaria to political concubinage to Rome, ruling from Jerusalem through Herodians and high priestly stooges.

The woman catches the political double entendre of Jesus' rejoinder and continues the conversation in a chauvinistic key: Jesus, after all, is on her turf. She speaks of the holy mountain of her people, the sacred tradi-

> Jesus said to her, "Go, call your lord, and come here." The woman answered, "I have no lord." Jesus said to her, "You are right in saying, 'I have no lord'; for you have had five lords, and he whom you now have is not your lord; this you said truly." The woman said to him, "Sir, I perceive that you are a prophet. Our fathers worshiped on this mountain; and you say that in Jerusalem is the place where people ought to worship." Jesus said to her, "Woman, believe me, the hour is coming when neither on this mountain nor in Jerusalem will you worship the Father. You worship what you do not know; we worship what we know, for salvation is from the Judeans. But the hour is coming, and now is, when the true worshipers will worship the Father in spirit and truth, for such the Father seeks to worship him. God is spirit, and those who worship him must worship in spirit and truth." The woman said to him, "I know that the Messiah is coming (he who is called Christ); when he comes, he will show us all things." Jesus said to her, "I who speak to you am he."
> —John 4:16-26

tions of her people, and of Jacob, the great ancestor of her people. Jesus meets the woman's Samaritan chauvinism with what has been erroneously interpreted as Judean chauvinism of his own, claiming that "salvation is from the Judeans." But the phrase makes more sense rendered, "For it is salvation from the Judeans." What Jesus offers is deliverance from the Judeans—from their disdain, animosity, and oppression.

At the enthusiastic invitation of the townspeople of Sychar, Jesus remains there two more days: "And many more believed because of his word." The "word" *(logos)* that the Samaritans hear for themselves and receive so enthusiastically is liberation from the enormous ideological and political pressure that Judea had exerted on the Samaritans for centuries. For the Samaritans, the *logos* of Jesus is "salvation from the Judeans."

THE FEAST OF THE JUDEANS

Though Jesus is seen flouting Judean observances in Galilee, it is in Jerusalem that the Gospel most dramatically portrays Jesus' opposition to the Judean temple-state. There he launches an attack on the Temple itself. In the Gospel of John, Jesus' attack on the Temple is the main event of Jesus' first swing through Judean territory. Like the separatists at Qumran on the northern shore of the Dead Sea, Jesus deplored Jerusalem and prophetically anticipated the Temple's destruction. The Qumranites went so far as to establish an alternative priesthood; they intensified concern for Israelite purity and solidarity and carried on a vitriolic campaign against the Jerusalem priesthood. But nothing in their tattered literary legacy calls into question ritual purity or priestcraft as such: priesthood and ritual purification were avidly and abstemiously pursued at Qumran. According to the Gospel account, Jesus was interested in neither priesthood nor ritual purification. In his attack on the Temple, he incites the Jerusalem crowd to do away with both.

The Gospel of John depicts the so-called Temple cleansing early in the public ministry of Jesus. Jesus attempts to incite his interlocutors to destroy the Temple, commanding the masses in the Jerusalem Temple to tear it down, but the silence of the text suggests that his efforts did not carry the day. In Synoptic traditions Jesus is merely accused of anti-Temple propaganda: neither Jesus' words nor his actions substantiate these charges, and the Gospel of Matthew characterizes as perjurers those who level such accusations against Jesus under oath.[5] In all of Gospel tradition, only the Gospel of John places these words in the mouth of Jesus in a failed attempt to rally pilgrims to violence against the Jerusalem cult.

The antagonism between Jesus and the Jerusalem elite is vitriolic—and mutual. In his penultimate visit to Jerusalem, followers from the Galilee are among those who accompany Jesus. The pilgrims are circumspect because of the hostility of the Judean leaders. The leaders as a group are distinguished from the Jerusalemite masses (7:26). Mentioned specifically are the chief priests and the Pharisees (7:45-48), who act as a police force that unsuccessfully attempts to apprehend Jesus (7:32-36). Nicodemus is a dissenting voice among them (50). As verse 26 and subsequent notices in 9:22 and 19:38 make clear, these hostile Judeans are the Jerusalemite rulers, whom commoners, including Judean commoners, fear. Jesus is speaking to those Judeans "who had had confidence in him" (8:31). The perfect participle indicates that these Judeans had put their trust in Jesus at an earlier time as a consequence of his prior activities in Jerusalem.

What follows is a knot of nasty accusations against Jesus. The text in 8:41 is reminiscent of early questions about Jesus' parentage. Doctrines of pneumatic, "immaculate" conception are revenge against early anti-Christian polemic claiming that Jesus was a bastard. The Gospel of John is aware of this accusation but does not answer it: there are no accounts of his birth and childhood, and only one brief mention of his father, Joseph (1:45; 6:42). Jesus contests the charge of being possessed (8:48-49) but passes over in silence the accusation of being a Samaritan—a slur in Jerusalem. The Gospel is punctuated with accusations against Jesus. He is evil (7:12; 9:16, 24; 10:21, 33) possessed (see 7.20), or deranged (2:17; 6:42; 7:20; 8:48, 52; 10:20).

BEFORE THE PASSOVER

Though the Gospel of John shows Jesus drawing followers from communities of Israelite heritage all over Palestine, the orientation of the narrative is nevertheless southern; that is, the narrative point of view is Judean. Judea is the locale of most of the second half of the narrative. That locale encompasses Jerusalem, of course, along with the suburbs of Ephraim and Arimathea receiving honorable mention. The geographical fulcrum of the narrative, however, is Bethany. Bethany, home of Martha, Mary, Lazarus, and their Judean friends, is the setting for the crisis of love and death that turns the narrative toward the catastrophe of the cross.

When Jesus arrives in Jerusalem a week before what is to be his last Passover, pilgrims greet him with palm branches that they wave aloft in celebration of his entry into the city. To wave palm fronds in Israel was to commit a political act. The palm frond was an ancient symbol of Israel's liberation. The Israelites had waved palms two centuries before as victorious

Israelite troops, having repelled their Syrian enemies, entered Jerusalem in triumph and purified the Temple that had been desecrated by the Syrians. In both revolts against Rome, the first a generation after the crucifixion of Jesus and the second a century after his crucifixion, the Judean rebels would mint coins with the image of palm fronds and the legend reading, "The Liberation of Israel."

According to the narrative of the Gospel of John and in contrast to the other three Gospels, this is the fourth time in the course of his public career that Jesus enters Jerusalem. This time, however, he receives, quite literally, a royal welcome. After he causes the lame to walk, the blind to see, and the dead to escape the grave, the people are convinced that God is working out the salvation of the dispersed children of Israel through Jesus. Only now does Jesus mount a young donkey in fulfillment of traditional Israelite oracles of the restored monarchy.

Jesus is a king who comes to bind up the broken patrimony of Israel. And, in accordance with ancient Israelite prophecy, he is a king who comes in peace. Instead of a war chariot, the customary vehicle of imperial kings, Jesus rides on a donkey, a peasant mode of transportation (Zech. 9:9-13). With a tumultuous reception, the crowds in Jerusalem on the eve of the Passover exalt Jesus as a king of peace. He is "lifted up," *nasa*, the Aramaic verb signifying exaltation, especially the exaltation of one who is humble or humiliated. One so exalted is a *nasi*, often translated as "prince." Jesus, as one who is lifted up, is Israel's *nasi*. Earlier in the story, the Samaritans enthusiastically received Jesus as the Messiah. The Galileans acclaimed him king in the northern Israelite tradition of charismatic deliverers recorded in the Book of Judges. Now the Judeans receive Jesus as a king in "the city of the great king," Jerusalem.

THE KING IS DEAD

The plot to kill Jesus is hatched in reaction to the groundswell of Jesus' Judean acclaim following the resurrection of Lazarus, whereas in Synoptic tradition the plot is inaugurated with Jesus' entry into Jerusalem. Both traditions agree, however, that it is precisely the acclamation of the masses that attends Jesus' arrest. The Jerusalem Pharisees are accessories to the conspiracy against Jesus. They bring their hostile influence to bear in the deliberations of the Jerusalem leaders, putting pressure on those who might be positively disposed toward Jesus. But throughout the Gospel of John, the Pharisees are distinguished from the real decision-makers in Jerusalem, the priestly establishment. The chief priests—and they alone—plot

Fig. 7.3. The raising of Lazarus is a climactic turning point in the plot of the Fourth Gospel, serving both to antagonize the Judean leadership and to propel Jesus toward confrontation with the Temple establishment (John 11). Early Christian fresco of the Raising of Lazarus, late third century CE. Catacomb of the Giordani, Rome. Photo: Scala / Art Resource, NY.

Jesus' death. The Pharisees are in fact divided in their assessment of Jesus; the priests, however, are of one mind that Jesus must die. The high priests' statements to the Roman governor Pilate dramatize the collaboration of the Judean high priesthood and the Roman imperial order. Pilate, as a "friend of the emperor," must execute Jesus, they insist, because "everyone who claims to be a king sets himself against the emperor" (19:12). And when Pilate asks, "Shall I crucify your king?" the high priests answer, "We have no king but the emperor" (19:15).

The Johannine Passion narrative makes reference to Jesus as king or Jesus' kingdom ten times in two chapters—18:33, 36 (twice), 37; 19:3, 12, 14, 15, and 21. Though the high priests quibble about Jesus' royal pretensions, the people recognized Jesus' claims, and so did Pilate, who inflicted upon him an execution worthy of a rebel king. Pilate condemns Jesus only after the Jerusalem authorities make it clear that Jesus has popular support and is accused of a crime that is not merely an offense against arcane Judean sensibilities but a violation of the Roman order. Pilate presents the condemned Jesus to the Judeans as "your king" (19:14), and over the protests of the chief priests insists that Jesus be crucified beneath the titulus "Jesus of Nazareth, the King of the Judeans" (19:19-22).

"GOD'S CHILD"

It is not only as king that the Johannine Jesus dies. The Gospel tells a distinctive version of the suffering and death of Jesus; nevertheless, it concurs with other Gospel traditions independently informed by the understanding of Jesus as a murdered prophet of Wisdom and a rejected son sent from God.

The oldest literature of the early Jesus movement reflected an interpretation of Jesus' death as an obedient son and rejected prophet of Wisdom. The accounts of conflict and evasive maneuvers, coupled with the Passion and resurrection of Jesus, together comprised a complex "wisdom tale" similar to those found in the literature of ancient Israel. Much older than the Jesus traditions, the genre of "wisdom tale" represents "a story in which the protagonist is threatened with trial or ordeal but later is rescued, vindicated, and restored to power, while his or her opponents are made to suffer for their wrongdoing."[6] Earlier versions of the "wisdom tale" treated the problem of the protagonist's senseless, untimely death.[7] The wisdom tale thus came to include stories of the wrongful death of a righteous person, a "child of wisdom."

Early Jesus traditions also drew on the portrayal of the suffering righteous one in Israelite scriptures in order to make sense of Jesus' death. Jesus' body has been pierced because this was the scriptural characteristic of an innocent victim (Zech. 12:10). His bones had not been broken because this "fulfilled" the biblical commandment regarding the Passover meal (Exod. 12:46; Num. 9:12); but the allusion is not to sacrifice. That Jesus should be offered as a sacrifice for Israel is the final solution of the high priest Caiaphas (John 11:49-53), and we are reminded of his murderous prophecy in the Passion Narrative. It is those who conspire against Jesus who propose to understand his death as a sacrifice, an interpretation that the evangelist puts on the lips of the arch-villain in the narrative.

The Gospel of John uses the language of the beloved, "firstborn" son to describe the sufferings of Jesus. It is not the language of divine sacrifice but metaphor of righteous innocence. The *Wisdom of Solomon* describes this innocence and the wrath and violence it provokes:

> Let us lie in wait for the righteous man, because he is inconvenient to us and opposes our actions. He reproaches us for sins against the law, and accuses us of sins against our training. He professes to have a knowledge of God, and calls himself a child of the Lord. . . . Let us see if his words are true, and let us test what will happen at the end of his life; for if the righteous man is God's child, he will help him, and will deliver him from the hand of his adversaries. Let us treat him with insult and torture, so that we may find out how gentle he is, and make trial of his forbearance. Let us condemn him to a shameful death, for, according to what he says, he will be protected. (2:12-13, 17-20)

Jesus is just such a "righteous man." He disputes with legal authorities about his healing on the Sabbath, and defends his actions by claiming God as his father (5:2-18). It is in the context of this dispute that the Judeans resolve to kill Jesus (5:18). The Sabbath controversy is revisited in 7:21-24, where Jesus invokes the authority of Moses against the Law of Moses. The chief priests and the Pharisees respond with an abortive attempt to arrest Jesus (7:32). Divine paternity is the focus of the vituperative argument between Jesus and his Judean interlocutors in chapter 8. Jesus performs another healing on the Sabbath in chapter 9, provoking more legal debate. In chapter 10 Jesus claims unity with the Father, a claim that provokes yet another attempt to destroy him (10:30-31). Thus the first half of the narrative of the Gospel of John is punctuated by acrimonious conflicts over the law and claims of divine paternity. Jesus bases his defense on the proverbial relation of father and son: the father disclosed his "works" to the son, and the son, in imitation of the father, performs those works. Jesus invites his interlocutors to put their confidence in him exclusively on the basis of his deeds. As *Wisdom of Solomon* puts it, "the righteous man is God's child" (2: 12-24). This is the core of the argument of the Gospel of John—not that Jesus was God's son and thus righteous, but that Jesus was righteous and thus God's son.

DISCIPLE OF THE BELOVED COMMUNITY

John's narrative focuses on the conflict in Judea between Jesus and the Judean authorities. Jesus himself has clearly come from Nazareth in Galilee, but repeatedly evokes the loyalty of Judeans. Some of these Judeans presumably provided the testimony upon which the written narrative of the Gospel of John depends. A member of Jesus' inner circle, "the beloved disciple" or "the other disciple" (13:23; 20:1-10), becomes an important supporting character in the latter half of the story and so is associated with Jerusalem and its environs. The Gospel concludes with a notice that it is he who has testified to the events that the narrative reports. He was the authoritative figure of the community but remained anonymous until later ecclesiastical tradition came to insist on calling him John.

The beloved disciple and his collaborators offer only their testimony: they do not put forward their names and their claims to authority, and implicitly disparage those who do. The Twelve are hardly distinguished from the rest of the disciples, and Peter is hardly distinguished among the Twelve. There is no apostolic hierarchy, no chain of command, no designated succession. To lead, according to the words and deeds of Jesus, is to serve: Jesus exhorts the disciples to wash one another's feet as he has washed theirs (13:1-20). This humble act of love is dirty work, customarily rendered by a slave. But the Gospel of John avoids the language of slavery to describe discipleship, and Jesus explicitly rejects slavery as a metaphor. All the proverbial sayings about slaves in the Gospel of John are pejorative.

> The slave does not remain in the house forever, but the son does. (8:35)
> The slave is not greater than his master, and the messenger is not greater than the one who has sent him. (13:16)
> The slave does not know what his master does. (15:15)
> The slave is not greater than his master. (15:20)

Jesus is not an obedient slave; he is an obedient son. His followers are not his slaves; they are his "little children." There is no basis for a new temple cult or a new priesthood: indeed, Jesus' movement, according the Gospel of John, sought to put an end to those very things. The community at Qumran had learned to make do without the Jerusalem Temple; after the war with the Romans, the Rabbis would learn to make do without the Jerusalem priesthood. John the Baptist, with his one-note apocalyptic piety of ritual ablution, had gotten along quite well without both.

And so the narrative of the beloved community places Jesus' debut in Perea at the site of John's riverside appeal to all Israel. Jesus' appeal would be just as grandiose in scope. But it would be more aggressive: whereas Israel came to John in the Jordan Valley, Jesus would go to Israel in all its disparate territories.

In the Gospel of John, Jesus never travels beyond the borders of ancestral Israel. This apparently was not true for the literary testimony about him: some early version of the story appears to have traveled even farther abroad than its protagonist did. The Gospel comes to us with editorial interventions to make the story more user-friendly for readers and hearers beyond the communities that were familiar with the events the Gospel purports to portray. The narrator glosses Hebrew and Aramaic words (1:38, 41, 42; 4:25; 5:2; 9:7; 11:16; 19:13, 17; 20:16, 24; 21:2), and local practices (2:6; 4:9; 18:28; 19:40). Embedded in the Gospel along with the words and deeds of Jesus is discourse in which the narrator's voice elides with the words of Jesus, comments in parentheses, and glosses upon his deeds.[8]

IN MEMORY OF HER

Perhaps because of the influence of women in the Johannine community, the Gospel's account of the life of Jesus features women at several critical moments.[9] It is in Cana of Galilee, the site of Jesus' first miracle, that Jesus' anonymous mother speaks to him not as God's son but as her son. It is at her behest, his own hesitation notwithstanding, that he refreshes the depleted wine at a wedding party (2:1-11). As we saw above, in Samaria Jesus' interlocutor is a woman who tacitly engages the bitter schism between the Samaritans and the Judeans, a schism that could be expressed in terms of sexual contempt (as when a Judean synod declared that "the daughters of Samaritans are menstruants from their cradle," and so perpetually impure: *Mishnah Niddah* 4.1). The Samaritan woman is one of several women who recognize Jesus as the promised deliverer of Israel. Though the evidence of ancient manuscripts casts doubt that the story of Jesus offering absolution to a woman taken in adultery (sometimes printed as John 7:53—8:11) was a genuine part of the Gospel from the beginning, the association of the story with this Gospel may reflect an early awareness of the important role women played in the Johannine account.

Later in the Gospel, Mary anoints Jesus in the suburb of Bethany just before his triumphal entry into Jerusalem. The narrative context highlights the political tenor of this act. The Jerusalem priests have plotted to kill Jesus because of his project to reunify all Israel, in Palestine and beyond. Suspecting their designs, Jesus has left Jerusalem and remains in the village of Bethany, where the community throws a party in his honor. Martha is the party's hostess, and her brother Lazarus was among those reclining at table with Jesus. The other member of Jesus' beloved family in Bethany, Mary, anoints Jesus at the party. It is after his anointing—and the brief report that the priests have decided that Lazarus, too, should be murdered—that Jesus enters Jerusalem to public acclaim.

This sequence shows Mary's anointing of Jesus to be what it had been in Israel for more than a millennium—a political act. Unlike the respective accounts of this event in Matthew and Mark, in the Gospel of John a woman anoints Jesus before, not after, his triumphal entry into Jerusalem. Just as anointing was the ancient Israelite ritual that marked a king, so in Bethany Mary presides over the coronation of Jesus: at her hand, he becomes Messiah. Although as Matthew and Mark recount their versions of this scene they affirm that the woman's expensive gesture will be remembered wherever the gospel is preached, neither Gospel remembers her name. It is the Gospel of John that records Mary's name, as well as her act, for posterity.

Fig. 7.4. In contrast to the Synoptics, the Fourth Gospel names the woman who pours out the contents of a jar of ointment upon Jesus: she is Mary, sister of Lazarus, and her action is described as "anointing" (John 12:1-8). Terracotta jug, Roman period, first to third century BCE. Israel. Photo: Erich Lessing / Art Resource, NY.

Who were the original authors of the Johannine account? The "editorial board" that brought together the testimonies of the beloved disciple put forward neither his persona nor their own personae: the writers of the Gospel of John all but disappear behind their words. They appeal to the Jesus of popular memory, recalling his prophetic actions to bring Israel together. They bear testimony to him in words that were likely written soon after the dream of a restored Israel had become the nightmare of a failed revolt.

FOR FURTHER READING

Brown, Raymond E., and Francis J. Moloney. *An Introduction to the Gospel of John.* Anchor Bible Reference Library. New York: Doubleday, 2003.

Callahan, Allen Dwight. *A Love Supreme: A History of the Johannine Tradition.* Minneapolis: Fortress, 2005.

Culpepper, R. Alan. *The Gospel and Letters of John.* Interpreting Biblical Texts. Nashville: Abingdon, 1998.

DISCIPLINING THE HOPE OF THE POOR IN ANCIENT ROME

NEIL ELLIOTT

Not long after Paul wrote his letter to Rome, the emperor Nero's adviser Seneca complained bitterly about the Judean population of the city. "The customs of this accursed race have gained such influence that they are now received throughout all the world. The vanquished have given laws to the victors" (*On Superstition,* as quoted by Augustine, *City of God* 6:10). The customs Seneca names are the lighting of household lamps on the Sabbath and the increasingly popular idea—among how many of the capital's laborers, we cannot say—of refraining from work on the seventh day. No doubt Seneca, one of the Roman world's richest men, was more alarmed by the second practice than by the first!

Note the terms in which Seneca phrases his complaint. It had been more than a century since the Roman general Pompey subjugated distant Judea and introduced thousands of his captives as slaves in Rome, causing his contemporary Cicero to characterize the whole people as "born to slavery" (*Of the Consular Provinces* 5:10). Seneca could still think of the remote descendants of those captives as *victi,* "the vanquished." Even before the disastrous Roman war against Judea (in 66–73 CE), Seneca the Roman could look down upon his Judean neighbors as one of their conquerors, *victores.*

While his comments might suggest that the Judean population of the city was getting along well enough in his day, a people's history must ask at what cost they purchased their survival in a city where those in power regarded them as subjects, and noxious subjects at that. A people's history must ask to what extent the conquerors circumscribed the possibilities for living out the ancestral practices and hopes of Israel. And because in Seneca's time another community, the *Christiani,* began to attract similar suspicion and contempt as a "barbarous superstition," we must ask to what extent the power of the self-styled conquerors served to limit the horizon of their vision as well. As we shall see, the history of the Judean and Christian communities in Rome was shaped by imperial pressures to discipline the hopes of the poor.

THE TASK

A people's history of early Judean and Christian assemblies[1] in ancient Rome faces two fundamental problems.

First, the bulk of the literary material at our disposal comes from the hands of elite authors and naturally reflects upper-class sensibilities. These writings often express frank contempt toward the poor and powerless, as when Cicero referred to the common people of Rome as the "dirt and shit of the city," *sordes urbis et faecum* (*Letters to Atticus* 1:16:11). The rich and powerful occasionally deigned to devote some part of their leisure (a luxury the poor rarely enjoyed) to complaining about the actions and motivations of their inferiors. We must therefore read their literary productions "against the grain" if we want to catch glimpses of the actual experience and attitudes of the masses. A people's history does more than simply give an account of the poor in a particular place and time. It also provides a critical account of the way the powerful have propagated self-serving characterizations and stereotypes that echo in "gentlemen's history" down to the present (on which, see the invaluable works by Michael Parenti and G. E. M. de Ste. Croix cited in n. 10).

Second, much previous history writing about Jewish and Christian communities in Rome has been implicitly but decisively shaped by the presuppositions of a Christian theological program. The resulting story line has ancient roots. In the second and third century CE the contrast between two *religions,* Judaism and Christianity, served to describe the superiority of the second to the first and the (divine) inevitability of Judaism's supersession by Christianity. Much later, a similar contrast fueled Protestant polemics against Catholicism. In the nineteenth century, the "orientalizing" strategy of European imperial civilization sought to describe the superiority of enlightened European intellectual culture to the primitive peoples of Asia, Africa, and the Americas, in part through the supposedly scientific insights into fundamental differences between "races." Not coincidentally, this was also the formative period for modern New Testament studies, in which F. C. Baur's distinction between the tribalism, nationalism, and exclusivism of Judaism and the spiritual "universalism" of Christianity still holds tremendous sway.[2]

These two factors—the acceptance of the elite perspective of the Roman aristocracy and the controlling paradigm of universal Christianity's supersession of ethnocentric Judaism—play out consistently in conventional accounts of ancient Rome. The spotlight customarily falls not only on the Judean population as an ethnic community, which it certainly was, but on Judaism as a religion characterized by the principle of ethnocentrism or ethnic exclusivism. Some scholars describe the Judean community as separatist, restive, and troublesome, speaking of "the problems presented by the Jewish people," "the rigidity of the Jewish faith," "the inflexible temper of Judaism," "the Jewish tendency to disturb the public order," their "inability to compromise," and their "sense of their own self-importance."[3] The primary evidence they offer includes Cicero's heated rhetorical blasts at Judean clannishness and avarice (*For Flaccus* 28:66–69), taken at face value; Suetonius's apparent reference to the emperor's suppression of Judean "disturbances" (*Divine Claudius* 25:4), a difficult text to which we must return below; and, of course, Paul's letter to the Romans, which (in a curious circular argument) they take as evidence for the ethnocentric Judaism that they have first postulated as the letter's rhetorical target.

Paul's letter plays a pivotal role in this story. Many scholars read it as the apostle's defense of the "law-free" Gentile church against supposed pressures from Jewish or Judaizing elements, either outside (that is, the synagogue) or within the church (that is, Jewish-Christian apostles). In this view, the challenge to the interpreter is simply to locate the center of this Jewish or Judaizing opposition, whether in Rome, in Jerusalem, or in Paul's previous experience. From this point on, many historians turn to focus on the emerging Christian movement, portraying them as a brave little band, publicly distinguishable as *Christiani,* by the time of the notorious fire of 64 CE, and on subsequent stages of development, in the *Shepherd of Hermas* and *1 Clement,* toward the religious practice and ecclesiastical preeminence of the third-century Roman church.

A people's history requires a different story of ancient Rome. Rather than serving as "background" to the emerging Christian church, we must give an account of the Judean population's experience under imperial rule in its own right. But we must also set that experience in the wider context of the enduring struggle between the powerful few and the masses who thronged the streets and shops of the capital. However uncomfortable we may be speaking in terms of class struggle, the ancient elite acknowledged it quite candidly among themselves, even while their public pronouncements emphasized themes of cooperation and harmony. The relative silence from the Roman Judean community after the war of 66–70 is a consequence of the fiercely anti-Judean propaganda campaign of the Flavian dynasty; the ensuing history of Christian communities, marked by the relinquishment of messianic fervor and a growing acceptance of Roman power relations within the church, reveals a corresponding lesson about the power of coercion.

READING AGAINST THE GRAIN: AN IDEOLOGY OF EMPIRE

Gentlemen's history—ancient as well as modern—echoes the ideology of empire. It regards the prosperity of the ruling class as theirs by right of virtue. The exploitation of conquered lands is evidence not of the rapacity of the conquerors but of their wise stewardship of resources that the natives would have squandered if abandoned to their own devices. Subjection and enslavement reveal the benevolence of a superior people, who nobly accept the responsibility of caring for the wretched, who clearly cannot govern themselves. The poor and vanquished, on the other hand, show by their indolence and ingratitude that they are unworthy of equality with free citizens; their preoccupation with the means of material sustenance reveals their spiritual inferiority. These well-rehearsed themes are the foundations of an ideology of benefaction by which rulers, ancient and modern, represent to themselves the fundamental justice of their position and attempt to present to the ruled the inevitability of their lot.

A very different understanding emerges when we attend to the strong currents of class and class struggle in the Roman world: to the "sheer rapacity" that drove Rome's almost constant warfare against other peoples or the "regular war" between the rural poor and the urban centers that preyed upon them through taxation. These realities were sore enough to those who bore the brunt of them. We must take account of the inexorable process through which a tiny but powerful elite expropriated much of the arable land surrounding Rome, forcing people off the land and into the increasingly choked streets and tenements of the city, where their concentrated misery presented a constant offense to their social superiors. Because the accidental survival of papyri allows us to hear cries of protest against the violent exactions of taxes, we must read against the grain of elite texts that lionize the powerful as simply serving the common good.

We must observe the unrestrained ferocity with which the self-styled best men who dominated the Senate, the *optimates,* met even the most modest attempts at land reform on the part of their populist rivals, the *populares,* with assassination, massacre, and treachery: from the murders of Tiberius, Gaius Gracchus, and hundreds of their followers (second century BCE), to the brutal suppression of Spartacus's rebellion (73–71 BCE), to the assassination of the *popularis* Julius Caesar (44 BCE), to the violent suppression of tax protests in Nero's day, and beyond.

The ruling class felt constantly threatened by the very slave population they themselves sought to maintain through terror—and for good reason. Beyond the accounts of actual slave uprisings, we must take note of the frequency with which elite sources expressed alarm at riots and disturbances in the streets or allow ourselves to hear, through the filter of their condescension and contempt, the constant murmur of resentment, the echoes of a "permanent current of hostility to senatorial misrule and exploitation" on the part of the ruled, as, for example, when they passed along the cleverer bits of hostile graffiti.[4]

Their fear of the masses led the aristocracy to the consistent and systematic application of violence, on the one hand, but also to "condescending patronage," on the other, to maintain control over a restive population. Patronage worked to cement the loyalty of the lower class to the rich. Wealthier *populares* could always bind their hungrier neighbors to themselves in loyalty, for example, through the inadequate but flamboyant distributions of free grain. Whether a *popularis* like Julius Caesar provided benefits out of genuine sympathy for the needy or from an ambition to mobilize the political power of a crowd in the streets was a matter of vivid debate and partisan accusation in his own day (and in our own). Those controlling the greatest wealth channeled it strategically to serve their own interests, "giving and taking away as they please, oppressing the innocent, and raising their partisans to honor": that protest came, not from the masses of the vanquished, but from a low-ranking newcomer to the Senate. "What appears desirable, they seize and render their own, and transform their will and pleasure into their law, as arbitrarily as victors in a conquered city" (Sallust, *Epistles to Caesar* 1:3).

The fabulously rich were evidently outraged only by those forms of patronage that allowed some benefit to the poor. The policies of a *popularis* like Julius Caesar, himself a man of tremendous political ambition, were generous enough to provoke concern and hostility among the upper class. His willingness to provide food and debt relief to the masses may well have sealed his fate.

How does this social context help us to understand the situation of Judean communities in ancient Rome?

THE JUDEAN POPULATION

I do not intend here to provide a comprehensive account of Judean communities in ancient Rome. I want rather to resituate the experience of the Judean population within the outlines of the Roman class struggle sketched above.

Origins

Judeans first appeared in Rome, according to our sources, as a delegation from the Hasmonean Judah around 161 BCE, seeking the intervention of the imperial power against his opponents in Jerusalem (1 Macc. 8:1-32). Rome was only too happy to extend its military reach in order to shape circumstances in Judea. But it was not until the next century, when the Roman general Pompey subjugated Judea and brought thousands of captives back to Rome as slaves, that a distinct Judean population began to take root in the city, settling in poorer neighborhoods across the Tiber (Philo, *Embassy to Gaius* 155). Philo's point is that through the process of manumission, slaves became the ancestors of a significant population of freeborn Judeans and citizens of Rome. Nevertheless, Pompey's later contemporary Cicero no doubt gave voice to a segment of the Roman aristocracy when he declared the whole people "born to slavery" (*On the Consular Provinces* 5:10).

Fig. 8.1. Literary and archaeological evidence bears witness to the presence of a Jewish population in Rome from the second century BCE. This tombstone, decorated with the menorah and other Jewish symbols, reads, "Here rest Primitiva and her grandson Euphrenon. May their sleep be in peace." Catacomb of Monteverde, Rome. Photo: Erich Lessing / Art Resource, NY.

We know nothing at this early stage of individual Judeans in Rome, aside from the mute testimony of funerary inscriptions. Otherwise they appear only in caricature, as the menacing "crowd of Judeans" against which Cicero railed in his defense of a corrupt Roman governor, Flaccus, who had expropriated money Judeans had set aside for the Temple in their homeland (*For Flaccus* 28:66–69). Cicero's speech suggests that Judeans were a visible and cohesive community, capable of mobilizing in support of their self-interest, and that they perceived their self-interest as one with the interest of Judean communities in other Roman cities.

Cicero's speech also offers us a glimpse into the notoriety in Rome of disturbances in distant Judea. The stiff resistance Pompey had faced from Aristobulus's partisans in the Temple revealed to Cicero the incompatibility of Judean rites "with the glory of the Roman Empire." Their eventual defeat at Pompey's hands revealed the will of the gods (*For Flaccus* 28:69). We can see, in the aristocrat's facile identification of political success with divine approval, a key ideological element informing Roman policy toward Judeans: military victories offered self-evident proof of the superiority of Roman religion and piety.

Under the Caesars

To the likes of Cicero, the eccentricity of the Judeans and their "barbarous superstition" may have provided only a particularly obnoxious example of the general offensiveness of the Roman "herd." In contrast, an ambitious champion of the masses like Julius Caesar could find in the Judeans an indispensable part of a power base in his struggle against the *optimates* in Rome and their man, Pompey, in the east.

Pompey and Caesar struggled against each other, through their surrogates in Judea, until Pompey's death in 48 BCE left Caesar even more firmly in a position of power (Josephus, *Ant.* 14: 123–39). Caesar's strategy in other cities he had conquered was to champion somewhat more democratic policies, seeking to thwart the entrenched aristocracies who more often sided with his enemies in the Senate. His recognition of "friends and allies" in Judea went hand in hand with benefits to diaspora Judean communities as well, as attested by the civic decrees that Josephus so carefully collected in Books 14 and 16 of his *Antiquities*. Caesar favored the Judeans of Rome as he sought to present himself as a champion of the Roman people, gaining for himself the support of a population held in suspicion by the *optimates*. Upon his assassination in 44 BCE, the Judean community expressed genuine grief (Suetonius, *Divine Julius* 84:5), but they were not alone: multitudes of the lower classes perceived a senatorial coup d'état and responded with days of rioting.

Fig. 8.2. "Chrestus caused Claudius to expel from Rome the continuously rebelling Judeans" (Suetonius, *Claudius* 25:4, author's translation). According to Acts 18:2, Paul's companions Prisca and Aquila had been part of this expulsion (in 49 CE). Portrait bust of the emperor Claudius, first century CE. Museo Arquelogico, Tarragona, Spain. Photo: Vanni / Art Resource, NY.

Once Caesar's avenger and successor, Octavius, had defeated the assassins in open warfare and come to power in Rome as Augustus, he continued Caesar's favorable policy toward the Judeans. He even extended it, for example, by allowing those who were citizens to collect their share of grain on the following day when the distribution fell on the Sabbath. Beyond whatever personal sympathy might have been involved, this policy and the donations Augustus made to the Jerusalem Temple were undoubtedly shaped by his role (with Anthony, then later with Marcus Agrippa) as political patron of Herod the Great (Philo, *Embassy to Gaius* 158). The Judeans of Rome were grateful and no doubt wary as well. Four of the Roman synagogues known to us bore the names "of the Augustans" (or "Augustesians"); "of the Agrippans" (or "Agrippesians"), probably for Augustus's right-hand man Marcus Agrippa; "of the Herodians"; and "of the

Volumnians," perhaps honoring the procurator of Syria who gave Herod support against the Nabateans and, at last, against his own treacherous sons. The fact that the Judeans of Rome so carefully honored three Romans seen as supporting Judean interests and the king whom Augustus had installed in Judea might reflect their acculturation in Rome; on the other hand, it might represent an anxious response to their political vulnerability as a relatively powerless minority population. Marcus Agrippa's scarcely veiled warning to the Judean community—that their rights would be honored so long as they did not undermine the Roman order—shows clearly enough that the imperial authorities felt no compunction about applying coercive force whenever they found Judean activities detrimental to state interests.

From the time of Augustus, the civic status of the Judean community in Rome remained precarious. They consequently exercised vigilance and caution, only occasionally offering public gestures of courage (as when, on Josephus's report, some eight thousand Judeans massed in 4 BCE to protest Archelaus's claim to succeed Herod). They were nonetheless subject to peremptory acts of suppression. Despite Josephus's best efforts to present a case for generally recognized Judean civic rights, in fact Judean communities had to fight for these concessions anew in crisis after crisis, especially in the early first century CE. No generally recognized rights protected them from Tiberius's decision to expel Judeans from the city in 19 CE, or to conscript four thousand Judean males to do military service in Sardinia. Possibly there were economic (and thus political) factors as well: a disruption of the corn supply had brought protesters into the streets, and it was not unusual for the Roman authorities to target easily identifiable groups— like the Judeans—in political crises.

The outrages that Tiberius's successor, Gaius (Caligula), planned against the Temple (39 CE) are notorious, as are the public contempt he showed the astonishingly patient delegation sent to Rome in protest and the viciously anti-Judean propaganda that rival Alexandrian delegations introduced into the Roman court in this episode. No doubt the Judean population of Rome was driven to share in the despair Philo attributes to the delegates themselves (*Embassy* 184ff.).

Alas, Caligula's death and the accession of Claudius brought only momentary reprieve. The dreadful violence in Alexandria in 38–41 CE resulted from a failed Roman policy of imposing a poll tax from which citizens were exempted. Compounding the brutality with which taxes were exacted against Judean farmers, the efforts of some Judeans to seek citizenship (and thus escape taxation) provoked a vicious backlash against them and accusations of anti-Romanism. Under intense political pressure from the aristocracy, the Roman governor declared the Judeans "aliens and strangers" in the city, seized their synagogues, and turned a blind eye

Claudius's edict to the Alexandrians (41 CE): Josephus's more sympathetic version, *Ant.* 19:278–85 (LCL):

Tiberius Claudius Caesar Augustus Germanicus, holding the tribunician power, speaks. Having from the first known that the Jews in Alexandria called Alexandrians were fellow colonizers from the very earliest times jointly with the Alexandrians and received equal civic rights from the kings, as is manifest from the documents in their possession and from the edicts, and that after Alexandria was made subject to our empire by Augustus their rights were preserved by the prefects sent from time to time, and that these rights of theirs have never been disputed; moreover, that at the time when Aquila was at Alexandria, on the death of the ethnarch of the Jews, Augustus did not prevent the continued appointment of ethnarchs, desiring that the several subject nations should abide by their own customs and not be compelled to violate the religion of their fathers; and learning that the Alexandrians rose up in insurrection against the Jews in their midst in the time of Gaius [Caligula] Caesar, who through his great folly and madness humiliated the Jews because they refused to transgress the religion of their fathers by addressing him as a god; I desire that none of their rights should be lost to the Jews on account of the madness of Gaius, but that their former privileges also be preserved to them, while they abide by their own customs; and I enjoin upon both parties to take the greatest precaution to prevent any disturbance arising after the posting of my edict.

Claudius's edict to the Alexandrians (41 CE), as recorded on papyrus (*CPJ*, no. 153):

Tiberius Claudius Caesar Augustus Germanicus, imperator, pontifex maximus, holder of the tribunician power, consul designate, to the city of the Alexandrians, greeting....

With regard to the responsibility for the disturbances and rioting, or rather, to speak the truth, the war, against the Jews...I have not wished to make an exact inquiry, but I harbor within me a store of immutable indignation against those who renewed the conflict. I merely say that, unless you stop this destructive and obstinate mutual enmity, I shall be forced to show what a benevolent ruler can be when he is turned to righteous indignation. Even now, therefore, I conjure the Alexandrians to behave gently and kindly toward the Jews who have inhabited the same city for many years, and not to dishonor any of their customs in their worship of their god, but to allow them to keep their own ways, as they did in the time of the god Augustus and as I too, having heard both sides, have confirmed. The Jews, on the other hand, I order not to aim at more than they have previously had and not in the future to send two embassies as if they lived in two cities, a thing which has never been done before, and not to intrude themselves into the games presided over by the *gymnasiarchoi* and the *kosmetai*, since they enjoy what is their own, and in a city which is not their own they possess an abundance of all good things. Nor are they to bring in or invite Jews coming from Syria or Egypt, or I shall be forced to conceive graver suspicions. If they disobey, I shall proceed against them in every way as fomenting a common plague for the whole world....

as mobs began a brutal campaign of wanton violence against them. When—at long last—Claudius intervened, he made a point of refusing to investigate the sources of the violence. He nevertheless held the Judeans primarily responsible, forbade them to aspire to citizenship or to equal participation in public life "in a city which is not their own," and warned them not to agitate for their own rights separately from their Alexandrian neighbors nor to accept visitors from Judea or Syria, lest he "proceed against them as fomenting a common plague for the whole world."[5]

Expulsion under Claudius

The events in Alexandria provide a crucial point of reference for interpreting Suetonius's report of events in the year 49 CE: "*Iudaeos impulsore Chresto assidue tumultuantes Roma expulit*" (*Divine Claudius* 25:4).

Much hangs on the interpretation of this terse statement, which is routinely translated "Since the Jews constantly made disturbances at the instigation of Chrestus, he [Claudius] expelled them from Rome" (LCL). Luke's statement (in Acts 18:2) that Prisca and Aquila, later Paul's apostolic co-workers, were among the *Ioudaioi* expelled by Claudius has led many interpreters to suppose that Suetonius has mistakenly written "Chrestus" for "*Christus*," that is, the Messiah of Israel's scripture. That supposition quickly leads to others: (a) that the phrase "the instigation of Chrestus" is Suetonius's confused reference to the proclamation in Rome of *Jesus* Christ; (b) that this proclamation, itself politically innocuous, was nevertheless the cause of public disturbances, of sufficient ferocity to provoke the emperor's harsh reaction; and (c) that the disturbances therefore must reflect the intolerance within the Judean community for the proclamation of Jesus as Messiah, or for the allegedly characteristic Christian practice of including Gentiles in community life (for example, common meals).

This reading is popular, not least because it provides an important link in the dominant story of Christianity's emergence within the Roman Judean context. Unfortunately, that theological usefulness is one reason we should regard this reading as historically dubious. In effect, this Christianizing interpretation removes the Claudian expulsion from Judean history and appropriates it as an important episode in the emergence of Roman Christianity, implying for example that it was as Jewish Christians, rather than as members of the Judean community in Rome, that Prisca and Aquila were caught up in the expulsion. Further, it relies on the presupposition of a stereotyped picture of Judean intolerance and exclusivism that has precious little basis in the historical evidence.[6]

This Christian-centric interpretation also relies upon several dubious exegetical moves. First, Suetonius was unlikely here to have mistaken a reference to *Christiani*, a group he elsewhere identified clearly and just as clearly held in contempt ("a sect professing a new and mischievous religious belief," *Nero* 16). More likely he expected his readers to recognize in "Chrestus" a prominent Roman figure, perhaps one close to the emperor's inner circle. Further, syntactically the phrase *impulsore Chresto* more likely modifies Claudius's action: that is, it was the emperor, not the Judeans, who acted "at Chrestus's instigation"—just as Tiberius had earlier moved against the Judeans of Rome at the instigation of Sejanus, and Gaius had suppressed the Judeans of Alexandria at the instigation of Helicon. Finally, the phrase *assidue tumultuantes* tells us not about the character and causes of a specific disturbance on the part of Judeans in Rome but about the stereotyped way Suetonius looks upon the Judeans in general as perennially troublesome, on the apparent assumption that if the emperor had expelled them, they must have deserved it.

These observations lead to a dramatically different translation of Suetonius's report: "Chrestus caused Claudius to expel from Rome the continuously rebelling [Judeans]."[7] But if the report is not about Christians, then we have no evidence for distinctly Christian propaganda or practices under Claudius, let alone for Judean intolerance and hostility directed against them. This means we must regard the widely held proposition that Jews and Christians were being distinguished this early in Rome as anachronistic.[8]

Instead, this episode shows us that the Judean population in Rome was the target of imperial suppression, especially vulnerable by virtue of the Judeans' perceived distinctiveness. But this is hardly a surprise; the Roman authorities were always primarily concerned with maintaining order. Especially during moments of civic unrest they found the Judeans (and others) to be convenient targets to the extent that their rituals and practices could be represented as un-Roman and anti-Roman, threats to the values and security of Roman society.[9]

"HIDDEN TRANSCRIPTS" OF DEFIANCE

Far from presenting a hotbed of anti-imperial agitation, then, the Judean community in Rome appears to have represented a more vulnerable subpopulation of the city's lower classes. There is no reason to presume that they were, as such, more frequently involved in civic disturbances than the broader collection of "starving, contemptible rabble" that Cicero held in contempt (*Philippics* 2:116).

The Roman "mob"—as much the object of vilification from modern "gentlemen historians" as from ancient aristocrats—was nevertheless capable of sufficient historical memory and critical judgment to recognize the common interest they held with one another and with the city's slave population. Admittedly, we have only limited evidence of a class consciousness among the poor that might correspond to the abundantly documented class consciousness of the Roman elite. We find only occasional references to a solidarity strike, for example, or fragments of a populist's speech calling the masses to feel the strength of their own numbers, or (reading against the grain) the rare acknowledgment on the part of the *optimates* that the most dreaded radical was not a solitary individual but one who could depend upon the mobilization of the masses. Missing are forthright and articulate declarations of an anti-imperial ideology.[10]

Given the situation of the Judean population in Rome, it is not surprising that we hear only rare expressions of dissatisfaction or defiance on their part: they had every reason to exercise caution. A people's history must tease out subtler clues, partially hidden forms of evidence, bearing in mind James C. Scott's observation, in his work on "everyday forms of class struggle," that "the hidden transcript of many historically important subordinate groups is irrecoverable for all practical purposes."[11] Scott alerts us to the "strategies of indirection" used by the ruled to resist their rulers under the cover of anonymity or political disguise.

From the early first century CE, we have several specimens of the (partially) hidden transcript of Judean defiance from other parts of the Roman world. Significantly, these often accompany clear exhortations to political caution and patience. Fourth Maccabees, for example, discusses Judean invincibility and the eventual overthrow of all tyranny under the disguise of a philosophical treatise on "knowledge," "wisdom," and "self-control" (*enkrateia*). Philo's treatise *On Dreams* presents a veiled indictment of the recklessness and violence of Roman tyranny under the guise of biblical commentary on Joseph's dreams; his stated theme is "caution" (*eulabeia*). The *Psalms of Solomon* and the *Book of Biblical Antiquities* provide critiques of Roman arrogance, exhortations to the innocent poor to endure in the hope of eschatological vindication, and deliberations on strategy, all cloaked in the pious garb of prayer or biblical recital. All of these reveal, to the attentive eye, glimpses of hidden transcripts in which an oppressed minority on the landscape of the Roman city assess their situation and consider their options.[12]

Our best evidence for a hidden transcript of defiance in Rome itself appears in a surprising source. Despite a long history of being regarded as a "compendium of Christian doctrine" or theological last will and testament, Paul's letter to the Romans actually sounds the tones of a particularly defiant anti-imperial transcript, not only echoing Israel's scriptural tradition but clashing discordantly with the vaunted claims of Roman imperial ideology.

Paul's rhetoric reaches its climax in his expression of anguish on behalf of his people who have "stumbled," and the stern warning to Gentiles not to "boast" over an Israel that appears—but only appears—to have fallen (Romans 9–11). Indeed, the whole of the letter is directed against the danger of a smug self-satisfaction on the part of the Gentiles, rooted in the latent, toxic, anti-Judaic propaganda current in Rome, sentiments surely exacerbated in the wake of the Claudian expulsion. The tensions in the Roman situation cannot be reduced to ethnic conflicts alone. We must recognize the decisive role of a Roman ethnocentrism promoted by imperial propaganda and by the more traditional contempt the Roman elite expressed toward the poor and powerless, who would naturally have included indigent Judeans. Paul's exhortations to the "powerful" to make up the deficiencies of the "powerless" (15:1), to welcome the "weak" (14:3, 10) and associate with the "lowly" (12:16), directly contravened the powerful social codes of patronage; in their place he urged a community standard of mutual esteem and the sharing of resources (12:11-16).

We can be even more specific. Not long before Romans was written, popular protests over taxes in nearby Puteoli provoked the immediate dispatch of Roman troops, who secured "peace" through "a few executions" (Tacitus, *Annals* 13:48). The threat of similar unrest in Rome (*Annals* 13:50), and of the "collateral" risk to the Judean community, on the precedent discussed above, may have prompted Paul's warning in Romans 13 to "be subject to the governing authorities" and "pay your taxes." He casts that exhortation in terms of praise for the authorities so "blatantly implausible" that an urban audience would immediately have recognized his use of irony.[13] His larger goal, however, may well have been to encourage solidarity with the vulnerable Judean population, who were most likely to suffer an imperial backlash in the event of civic unrest. That is, Paul strives in Romans to protect the interests of the Judean community in the same sort of volatile environment, and against the same threat of disenfranchisement and abuse, that Judeans had already faced in Alexandria and Rome itself.

Significantly, Paul does not ground his exhortation in a general ethic of concord or fellow feeling, despite the availability and popularity of such themes in Augustan culture. Rather, he evokes the messianic transcript of Israel's scriptures, asking his hearers to fulfill the "prophecies" of Isaiah and the Psalms that Israel and "the nations" should together honor the Lord (15:1-13). By their positive response they will guarantee what he calls his "priestly service" (15:16; see also 1:9). This is a service

> Let every person be subject to the ruling authorities. For there is no authority except from God, and those that presently exist have been set in order by God. Therefore one who resists the authorities resists the order God has set in place, and those who resist will incur judgment. For rulers are not a cause of fear [*phobos*] to good conduct, but to bad. Would you have no fear of the one in authority? Then do what is good, and you will receive his approval, for he is God's servant for your good. But if you do wrong, have fear [*phobou*], for he does not wield the sword as an empty threat; he is God's servant as an agent executing wrath on the wrongdoer. Therefore subjection is an obligation, not only on account of wrath but also on account of conscience. For the same reason you also pay taxes, for they [the authorities] are ministers of God as they devote themselves to this very matter. Hand over to each what is owed: taxes to whom taxes are due, tribute to whom tribute is due, fear [*phobos*] to whom fear is due, honor to whom honor is due.
>
> —Rom. 13:1-7, author's translation

without precedent in Israel's cult, however. It more closely resembles—or parodies—the "priestly" self-presentation of Augustus, for Paul's "service" is to present "the offering of the nations" (15:16), their "faithful obedience" (1:5).

This language coheres within a more comprehensive apocalyptic transcript that Paul evokes—intentionally, though so obliquely as to be cryptic—as "the hour," "the time to wake from sleep," "the day" (13:11-12). Romans evokes this apocalyptic transcript in critical counterpoint to the ideology of empire from its very first lines. The announcement of a victory proclamation *(euangelion)* concerning a "son of God" and "lord" would surely have struck a note discordant with the language on the emperor's coins regarding his status as "Son of God" *(divi filius)* and the ubiquitous declarations of the inscriptions that Caesar is "lord" *(kyrios)*. Written not long after Nero had officially declared the deceased Claudius "deified," assuring the world of his own filial piety (and providing some thin cover against allegations that he was himself a conspirator in Claudius's murder), Romans declares that *another* "Son of God" stands in the physical lineage from an ancient king, confirmed in his status by no less a demonstration than resurrection from the dead "in power" by "the spirit of holiness" (Rom. 1:1-4). The rhetorical barrage that follows is meant to illustrate an apocalyptic reality, the current "revelation" of God's justice in the execution of divine wrath against the wicked and impious (1:16-18). Paul's indictment of "those who in their injustice suppress the truth" (1:18-32) fits no target so well as the emperors themselves. What Paul offers in the letter is far more powerful than an exhortation to "self-mastery" amid a decadent age; it is a repudiation of the claim at the heart of imperial propaganda, that a "golden age" has arrived in the person of the emperor himself.[14]

We may reasonably suppose that the hopes given cryptic expression in Romans were rehearsed regularly and enthusiastically, though offstage; the pragmatic strategy for the public transcript was "subjection" (13:1-7; compare Philo's counsel of "caution"). There is little evidence, however, to indicate that such offstage rehearsals survived the traumatic events of the following years.

NERO AND THE WAR AGAINST JUDEA

Nero's court propaganda emphasized his having come to power peacefully, in contrast to his ancestor Augustus.[15] He postured as a champion of the people against the overweening power of the Senate. For example, he answered calls for tax relief by offering to cancel indirect taxes, though he knew well the Senate would countermand the action as irresponsible (they did: Tacitus, *Annals* 13:50–51). The primary beneficiaries of his policies were, of course, the fabulously rich. He was ready enough to use force to suppress tax riots, in Puteoli and in Rome itself, and called out troops to put down protests when the Senate ordered the mass execution of four hundred slaves in retaliation for the murder of their master. Nero found a new target of convenience—the *Christiani*—on which to exact a horrible and sadistic punishment after the "great fire" destroyed hundreds of homes in a slum neighborhood (64 CE). That the fire coincidentally provided space for the construction of Nero's long-planned sacred complex aroused open suspicion: Tacitus doubted the Christians were responsible (though he still accused them indiscriminately of "hatred of the human race," *Annals* 15: 44). The apostles Paul and Peter were victims of Nero's violence at about this time.

Such spectacular brutality must have had an educative effect on the Roman crowds. The position of the Judean community in Rome remained precarious. There were isolated exceptions: a few celebrities, like the actor "of Judean origin" whom Nero favored; his mistress and later wife, Poppaea Sabina, gave patronage to Judean priests on trial in Rome, at the request of the aristocrat Josephus (*Life* 16). But general hostility to the Judean people and their customs was more the rule in the imperial court, to judge at least from Nero's adviser, Seneca. He decried them as an "utterly heinous nation" and complained of the prevalence of their practices *(On Superstition)*.

We can only imagine how the majority of the Judean population in Rome fared during the war against their homeland (66–70 CE) and in the years immediately afterward. The Roman general in charge of the war,

Fig. 8.3. The vicissitudes of Jewish populations in other parts of the Roman world were keenly felt by the Jews in Rome. Philo of Alexandria led an embassy to the emperor Gaius (Caligula) to protest the Roman governor's encouragement of riots against the Jews in Alexandria (37–38 CE). The Arch of Titus, erected on the Forum in Rome, depicted Judean captives and worship symbols being looted from Jerusalem by Roman soldiers. Arch of Titus, Rome. Photo: Erich Lessing / Art Resource, NY.

Flavius Vespasianus, returned to Rome to claim the principate, leaving his son, Titus, to carry out the siege of Jerusalem. Upon his return at the head of a victorious army, Titus celebrated a massive triumph, making a spectacular display (represented on the Arch of Titus) of prominent Judean captives and the property of the destroyed Temple (Josephus, *War* 7:123–62). He struck new coinage depicting "vanquished Judea," *Iudaea capta*, as a disconsolate woman sitting beneath a palm tree. Unable to claim continuity with the Julio-Claudian dynasty and unwilling to stake their legitimacy on naked military power, Vespasian and Titus struck upon a novel strategy. In contrast to previous Roman practice, in which the holy places of a defeated enemy were left sacrosanct, Titus presented himself in iconography as the pious defender of Roman religion against the hostile and sacrilegious cult of the Judeans, whose impious Temple had perforce to be destroyed. The "*fiscus Iudaicus*" added insult to injury, replacing the earlier collection of funds for the Temple in Jerusalem with a Roman tax, imposed only on Judeans, to fund a temple in Rome to Jupiter Capitolinus—no doubt especially painful for Judeans in the capital, who had to watch its construction.

The fates of the few Judean aristocrats who became postwar celebrities suggests the range of restricted options available to the rest. Titus brought Berenice, sister of Agrippa II, to Rome as his mistress and might have married her but for the unanticipated popular outcry; he dismissed her (Tacitus, *History* 2:2:1; Dio, *History* 66:15:3–4). On the other hand, the erstwhile rebel-turned-apologist, Josephus, had guaranteed his survival after being captured at the siege of Jotapata by hailing Vespasian as a future emperor (*War* 3:399–408). After the war, he continued a similar strategy, settling into an estate provided by Vespasian. He provided the emperor, in turn, a fawning history of the war, expounding the themes that God was on the side of the Romans and that at any rate "thralldom is hereditary" for the Judeans (see *War* 2:345–401). That "Flavius" Josephus could present these echoes of imperial ideology as the authentic teaching of Israel's scriptures, even representing messianic prophecy as pointing to Vespasian's rise, says much about the range of possibilities for the Judean community in Rome in the wake of the first revolt.[16]

In subsequent decades, the introduction of a large population of prisoners of war and the burden of the *fiscus Iudaicus* contributed to increased destitution within the Judean community. Domitian's aggressive enforcement of the *fiscus Iudaicus* against the Judean people reportedly gave rise to an "atmosphere of terror." It also promoted a distinction between Judaism as a way of life and a Judean ethnic identity, as some individuals hoped to escape taxes by quietly practicing the first but disguising the second (Suetonius, *Domitian* 12:2). The anxiety of a conservative Roman elite about foreign influences among the lower classes contributed to an atmosphere of scorn and contempt, which was fueled by writers like Tacitus and Juvenal, for whom Judaism was un-Roman and anti-Roman.[17] Rome's suppression of a second revolt in Judea (132–35 CE) was even more disastrous.

EMERGENT ROMAN CHRISTIANITY

In the mid-first century CE, the apostle Paul had addressed gatherings in private homes of Christ-worshippers, including Judeans and non-Judeans alike, seeking to reorient their common life within a constraining vision of the obedience of the nations to Israel's God. We do not know how the letter to the Romans was received; we know only that Paul's hopes for the importance of his delegation to Jerusalem (Rom. 15:25-33) were disastrously disappointed (Acts 21:27-36). The subsequent rise of a Pauline school, most likely in Asia Minor, took place within a decidedly Gentile-Christian environment, so that the summary of Pauline theology in Ephesians, for example, reduces the complexity of the apostle's thought to a charter of equality for Jew and Gentile based in the abrogation of the law (Eph. 2:13-15; contrast Rom. 3:31).

A scattering of writings often attributed to first- and early second-century Rome offers possible glimpses into the emergence of Christian communities in the decades following Paul's death and the great fire of 64. These writings exhibit, first, the development of a Christian symbolic repertoire that appropriates Jewish symbols and themes and reinterprets them, often quite freely, in the apparent absence of Jewish interlocutors, and second, the development of an internal organizational structure and community discipline that increasingly reflected the norms of patronage and the Roman household.

Fig. 8.4. For decades after the defeat of Judea, Jews and Christians in Rome, and elsewhere, contested the symbolic heritage of Israel. Here Abraham is depicted in an early Christian fresco, Cubiculum of the Velatio, Catacomb of Priscilla, Rome. Photo: Scala / Art Resource, NY.

The misnamed "letter" to the Hebrews, which (though it lacks other epistolary characteristics) includes a greeting from "those from Italy" (13: 24), gives few clues to its actual date or provenance. The document addresses a community that has undergone harassment and persecution (10:32-34) and exhorts them to persevere, evoking the example, first, of God's sustenance of the wandering people of God (3:1—4:13)—though, significantly, the question of how the addressees relate to historical Israel does not arise. Christ's perseverance in the face of temptation, threat, and death is then presented as an example (4:14—7:27), and his complete, adequate, and permanent sacrifice is contrasted to the partial and temporary sacrifices of the Temple (8:1—10:18). This argument relies on allegorical reading of the Septuagint; it reveals no awareness of actual practices in the Jerusalem Temple in the first century. The point is to establish the hearers as a covenanted community; the possibility that other communities, for example, the Jewish synagogue, might make similar claims does not arise. Actual Judeans who might read their own scriptures differently and relate to (or remember) their Temple in different terms do not appear on the text's symbolic landscape. If this document comes from Rome, it reflects a Christianity that avails itself of Israel's scripture for its own paraenetic purposes but has no connection with the actual experience of Judean communities.[18]

In contrast, *1 Clement* is clearly a genuine letter, written in the last decade of the first century from the Roman church to the church in Corinth. Clement situates his audience within living memory of the apostles (5:1—6:1) and mentions "misfortunes" that might be identified with persecution under Domitian. The letter is written to admonish a Corinthian faction that has deposed its leaders, whom Clement would see reinstated. He quotes, throughout the document, from Jewish scripture and from the examples of Christ and the apostles, in which he finds precedents both for the present uprising of "the worthless" against the honorable and for the "humility and obedient submission" he now counsels (19:1). As does the letter to the Hebrews, *1 Clement* appeals to the example of Temple sacrifices offered by priests, but only as a type for Christian worship; the point is that "offerings and liturgies" may only be offered by those duly appointed, "bishops and deacons," as the precedent set by the apostles also requires (44:1-2).

The letter probably addresses the assertion of rights—or, from Clement's viewpoint, the usurpation of authority—by the well-off householders who are hosts and understand themselves to be the patrons of the Corinthian house churches, over against the leadership of bishops and presbyters. While Clement's rhetoric relies on terms derived from scripture, his vocabulary also mirrors Roman class ideology: his talk of "people," "rank," and "eminent" and "worthless persons" is readily translated into the Roman vocabulary of class.[19]

The *Shepherd of Hermas* comes from a predominantly oral culture, indicating a relatively lower-class context in turn-of-the-century Rome. Its revelations borrow heavily but imprecisely from Jewish wisdom and apocalyptic traditions, as well as pagan myths, reflecting the syncretistic and practical nature of turn-of-the-century Roman Christianity. Hermas himself holds no formal church office but couches his admonitions in the rhetoric of prophecy, a role presumed in his community. He nevertheless bears responsibility for the conduct of the members of his "household" (*Visions* 2:2:2; 2:3:1), apparently meaning the subgroup of his freedmen peers, a responsibility laid upon him by the female figure, the church, who addresses him (2:4:3).

This authorizing female personification of the church resembles the figure of Rhoda, the woman whom he once served as slave before she emancipated him. The book begins with Hermas recounting an episode in which, years after his emancipation, he came upon Rhoda bathing in the Tiber and helped her out of the river, noticing her beauty. Not long after they part, Hermas kneels to confess his sins and is startled by a vision of Rhoda, now in heaven, appearing to him to "convict" him of his sins. The *Visions* thus rely upon a symmetry of obligation: the obligation Hermas bears to secure the holiness and obedience of his "household" is fueled by the potent mix of shame and obligation owed by any freedman to his former owner. Hermas appears to exhort his peers—a class of moderately successful freedmen—to renounce their newfound possibilities for individual prosperity and to serve the interests of the church with the same sense of obligation they would feel toward their patrons.[20]

These three writings from the late first and turn of the second century show tendencies that would continue to be decisive for later Christianity. One is the increasing distance from contact with Judean communities and the appropriation of Jewish scripture as a resource for (Gentile-)Christian paraenesis. By the early second century, Ignatius, the bishop of Smyrna, who wrote to the Roman church in anticipation of his martyrdom in the imperial capital, wrote to other churches that "it is utterly absurd to profess Jesus Christ and to practice Judaism" (Ignatius, *To the Magnesians* 10:3); "if anyone expounds Judaism to you, do not listen to him" (*To the Philadelphians* 6:1). By the mid-second century, the diversity of Roman Christianity included a number of Gentile-Christian theologies that presumed the inferiority and irrelevance of Israel's scripture: not just Gnostics like Marcion or Valentinus but even orthodox opponents like Justin Martyr or Tertullian shared a fundamental theological hostility to Judaism. A fundamental theological anti-Judaism became the basis for Christian appropriation of Jewish scripture.[21]

These writings also show tensions within early Roman Christianity, as church leaders promoted a code of authority resembling the codes of obligation and deference operative in the Roman class system. Clement sought to suppress the self-assertion of Corinthian householders by shaming them into submission to the clergy as the church's true "worthy men." Hermas, for his part, sought to promote a sense of obligation to church-as-patron among freedmen tempted to exercise power and independence in their own interests. Later in the second century, the *Apostolic Constitutions* of Hippolytus would seek to ease tensions between bishop and householder by encouraging an ethic of reciprocal obligation between them; more specifically, the bishop was encouraged to honor his patron, the householder, to whom he apparently stood in an inferior position.[22]

And what of "the hope of the poor"? The writings just discussed show that the role played by eschatological hope was shifting in the early second century CE. After the first, and especially the second Judean revolt (132–35 CE), Jewish communities de-emphasized the eschatological themes of their traditions. Apocalypses like *4 Ezra* and *2 Baruch* functioned more to explain the catastrophe of Jerusalem's destruction and to promote piety than to offer a vision of the future that would rival Rome's imperial eschatology. Although currents of millennial thought persisted in Roman Christianity, they became the exception in a religious movement more concerned with personal afterlife as the reward for performing one's duty—as that duty was increasingly defined along lines borrowed from Roman society.[23]

The Christianity that emerged in second-century Rome had only tenuous claims to contact with the anti-imperial apocalyptic vision of Paul and a practical indifference, if not actual hostility, to the fate of the Judean community for whose safety Paul had struggled. A people's history of Judean and non-Judean messianic communities in Rome allows us to recognize not just the distressed circumstances of the poor and powerless through the first century of Roman Empire but the declining relevance of the messianic and apocalyptic traditions as expressions of the hope of the poor.

FOR FURTHER READING

Barclay, John M. G. *Jews in the Mediterranean Diaspora from Alexander to Trajan (323 B.C.E.—117 C.E.* Edinburgh: T. & T. Clark, 1996.

Cohen, Shaye J. D. *The Beginnings of Jewishness: Boundaries, Varieties, Uncertainties.* Berkeley: University of California Press, 1999.

Garnsey, Peter, and C. R. Whittaker, eds. *Imperialism in the Ancient World.* Cambridge: Cambridge University Press, 1978.

Lampe, Peter. *From Paul to Valentinus: Christians at Rome in the First Two Centuries.* Trans. Michael Steinhauser. Minneapolis: Fortress, 2003.

Leon, H. J. *The Jews of Ancient Rome.* Updated ed. Peabody, Mass.: Hendrickson, 1995.

MacMullen, Ramsay. *Enemies of the Roman Social Order.* Cambridge: Cambridge University Press, 1966.

———. *Roman Social Relations 50 B.C. to A.D. 284.* New Haven: Yale University Press, 1974.

Parenti, Michael. *The Assassination of Julius Caesar: A People's History of Ancient Rome.* New York: New Press, 2003.

Schäfer, Peter. *Judeophobia: Attitudes toward the Jews in the Ancient World.* Cambridge: Harvard University Press, 1997.

Schürer, E. *The History of the Jewish People in the Age of Jesus Christ.* New English ed. by Geza Vermes, Fergus Millar, and Martin Goodman. 3 vols. Edinburgh: T. & T. Clark, 1973–87.

SOCIAL PATTERNS AND PRACTICES

Part 3

FAMILY MATTERS

CAROLYN OSIEK

CHAPTER NINE

The task of tracing a people's history of the family, or social history from below, in the first decades of the Christian movements poses some particular methodological problems. There is almost no material evidence for Christian life during the first two centuries, and literary evidence is scant, notably the New Testament and other documents of early Christian literature. Meanwhile, there is an abundance of both material and literary evidence for social and family life in the surrounding environment. The majority of it comes from the city of Rome and the nearby sites of Ostia, Pompeii, and Herculaneum, though substantial evidence has also been found at a few other sites around the Mediterranean, such as Jerusalem, Ephesus, and Carthage, and the distant site of Vindolanda on the British frontier. One of the interpretative questions is: to what extent is what happened in these locations typical of life elsewhere in the Empire at the same time?

FINDING THE PEOPLE

In a people's history of the first decades of Christianity, who are "the people"? The elite families in these societies are fairly easy to identify, and they are a small minority. In the early Empire they consist of three classes: the senatorial order, the equestrian order just below them, and the decurionate or local aristocracy in the provinces. Together they probably did not compose even as much as 5 percent of the population. Do we then exclude these power wielders and shapers of politics and assume that everyone else belongs to the people? This raises the much-debated question of how class and status operated. Class was determined by birth, and status relatively so, though it could change under certain circumstances. Wealth was expected of the upper classes, though, if impoverished, they did not lose their class

Fig. 9.1. Foundations and first-floor walls of simple four-room apartments at Ostia, second–third centuries CE. Each building contained four such units on the ground floor, all of similar design. A staircase indicates at least a second floor, and there were probably more. Photo: Carolyn Osiek.

membership. Status was more heavily dependent on relationships, social networks, and family reputation.

Naming the status of early followers of Jesus is not easy. The one thing agreed upon by scholars is that there is little evidence of elites in the movement until the late second century.[1] That leaves, among others, the rural poor, of whom, outside Galilee, probably few belonged to the Jesus movement, for there is not much evidence—aside from the Gospels, possibly the *Didache*, and Pliny's Letter to Trajan—for a rural mission movement in the early years. Even Philip's mission to Samaria has him sticking to cities and towns (Acts 8:1, 40). The church surely drew from the ranks of the freeborn urban poor and lower classes of the cities, the tradespeople, and the craftspeople. Slaves and freedpersons depended on the households with whom they were associated. Family life of some kind existed in all of these social groupings that were intricately interrelated with one another.

Early followers of Jesus lived not just in their own world but the larger world of the Roman Empire. Part of the process of retrieval, therefore, is an effort to reconstruct a picture of the lives of ordinary people in cities of the Empire. Only in this way can we see early Christians in their own context and make some informed judgments about their lives based on what their contemporaries were doing and not doing. At the same time, we must take into account the differences that their own writers claimed character-ized the members of their movement. Apologists of the second century give the impression that Christians were just like any of their neighbors. Yet early members of the Jesus movement from Paul onwards claimed that they did not do certain things that others did commonly, such as practice divorce or abortion or abandon newborns (1 Cor. 7:10-11; *Didache* 2.2; 5.2; *Diognetus* 6; Tertullian *Apology* 6–7, 9). But one wonders why in internal discussion they sometimes needed to place such emphasis on these differ-ences; perhaps it was to convince not-so-convinced followers that these differences needed to be observed.

GLIMPSES OF EVERYDAY LIFE

We can learn a great deal from the remains of housing, especially what little is preserved of the lower classes and poorer inhabitants of the cities. The dark, cramped quarters of one- and two-room apartments like those of some multiple-residence buildings of Her-culaneum, Pompeii, and Ostia, or the small back and upper rooms of shops in places like the main street in Eph-esus, are examples of the crowded, poorly ventilated, and generally un-healthy conditions in which most of the urban population lived. If such people cooked for themselves at all, it would have to have been on some makeshift portable apparatus in a nearby outside space. More likely, they bought fresh bread, fruit, and vegeta-bles at local markets and got most of their cooked food from neighbor-hood vendors and *thermopolia*—the equivalent of fast-food restaurants. They ate meat rarely if at all, typically only when present at feasts given by wealthy city patrons. If they bathed, it was in the public baths, apparently open to both men and women. They used public latrines. They birthed their children at home with the possible help of a midwife. They were raised in an environment of intimate social relationships and no privacy.

Fig. 9.2. Courtyard and only common space of a crowded multi-resident, multi-storied apartment building, known as the *Casa a Graticcio* in Her-culaneum, first century CE, so called because of its use of a common low-standard method of construction using cemented rubble in wood frames. Such apart-ment houses were notorious for danger of fire and col-lapse. Photo: Carolyn Osiek.

Material remains, of course, cannot tell the whole story. When they are combined with select literary evidence, a picture of everyday life emerges. We know little about the family life of the lower classes in the Roman Empire: it is not at all certain how much legislation affected them, and the letters that yield valuable information about how life was really lived come largely from the elites. Even inscriptions, which in the Roman era often give extensive social information, come mostly from those with sufficient wealth to be able to afford them. Sometimes, however, the most imposing monuments are not those of the elite but of people of humbler origins who have acquired enough property to be able to proclaim to the world their success and prosperity. One thinks, for instance, of the garishly imposing monument of the baker Marcus Virgilius Eurysaces and his wife, Atistia, at Porta Maggiore in Rome or the double commemoration of the freedwoman Naevoleia Tyche, who erected an imposing monument for herself and her freedman husband,

Fig. 9.3. Single-room apartment with remains of wooden bedstead on the second floor of the same apartment building (Fig. 9.2 above) in Herculaneum, first century CE. Remnants of a painting adorn the back wall. A whole family may have lived in such a room, cooking on a brazier outside. Photo: Carolyn Osiek.

Gaius Munatius Faustus, and their *familia* of freedmen and freedwomen outside the Herculaneum Gate at Pompeii, but whose remains were found, with those of her husband, in a simple tomb in a different cemetery area.[2]

The poor inhumation and incineration burials of the open field at Isola Sacra near Ostia probably once had such family information painted on their clay tiles, now disappeared. And beyond these, there was the feared common public burial ground. To avoid that unacceptable alternative, burial societies of *tenuiores,* or little people, were common. Members would meet regularly, usually once a month, and make a modest contribution into a common chest. These gatherings functioned as social clubs as well, but one of their main purposes was to provide a decent burial for their members, who otherwise feared not to be able to afford it. The late-second-century theologian/apologist Tertullian describes the monthly contribution of Christians toward burials and other charitable works in very similar terms (*Apology* 39.6). Guilds and social clubs of those who had a common trade were also readily formed. Patronage of these burial societies and workers' associations was part of the honorable behavior of the elite, both men and women. It earned them statues, inscriptions, and glory from the grateful members.

Whether for upper or lower classes, standards of sanitation and safety left much to be desired. Disease was rampant and life expectancy low. With no knowledge of how diseases spread, inhabitants were defenseless against it, especially in the large cities. Most methods of prevention and healing were folk remedies or magical incantations with very mixed success. Garments made of wool, the standard material for most clothing, were bleached with urine, both human and animal, before being treated with other chemicals, including sulphur, and washed. Most hygiene arrangements were primitive. Apartment buildings and larger houses had their own common latrines, but no centralized plumbing for waste removal. Public latrines were accessible to all, seemingly for both sexes. Defecation and urination were not considered private functions.

The cities had public baths, accessible to everyone, and these promoted cleanliness and hygiene but could also be a way of spreading disease. Diseases like malaria and tuberculosis were indigenous in many areas; no one had knowledge of how they were spread. The use of lead piping to bring in the city water supply was common, with no one aware of the health hazards involved in the use of lead. Lacking knowledge of bacteria or how to kill them, people had no way except visual and olfactory inspection to know whether water was drinkable or not. Though there were famous medical schools in existence by this time and scholarly medical manuals being written, actual knowledge of diseases and how to prevent and treat them

was very primitive. Generally, if the body could not heal itself of disease and illness, the person simply died. Illnesses like influenza, pneumonia, or appendicitis were surely fatal.[3]

Fig. 9.4. House of Lucius Caecilius Jucundus, son of a freedman, at Pompeii, first century CE. This simple *domus* illustrates the relative wealth possible for a freedman and his immediate descendants. The owner was involved in a number of business ventures, as witnessed by the records he left behind. Photo: Carolyn Osiek.

Child mortality was extremely high. If one survived the first year or so, life expectancy rose considerably, but never beyond about forty years. By the time a child reached the age of ten, half of his or her birth cohort were dead. Few children grew to adulthood with both parents surviving. The customary age disparity at first marriage, in which the husband was as many as ten to fifteen years older than the bride, resulted years later in many marriageable widows. In times of war, the imbalance may have evened out as male mortality mounted. But even in times of peace, the high incidence of women's death in childbirth also contributed to balancing out the population. Probably more among the elites than ordinary people, girls were often married by the age of twelve and sometime pregnant even before their first menstruation. Early and constant childbearing took a terrible toll on their health.

The health of most inhabitants must have been rather miserable most of the time. With the possible exception of the pampered wealthy, people were old, with rotting teeth and poor eyesight, by about the age of thirty. Diseases associated with malnutrition must have been abundant, especially among the poorer segments of the population. A few survived into their seventies, eighties, and perhaps even nineties. Those who were still alive at these advanced ages, however, represented 1 percent or less of their birth cohort. Skill in counting years of age varied. Roman epitaphs sometimes record age at death not only by years, but by months and days. Yet in other cases, age is estimated or guessed at, sometimes with the approximation symbol ±, "plus minus," "more or less."

Another factor to take into account when trying to get some sense of the world in which the first followers of Jesus lived is the level of violence and overt sexuality to which they were constantly exposed. First of all, artistic representations in everything from official civic art to the paintings on the walls of private houses graphically portrayed violent scenes: battles between armies, fights between two individuals, gladiatorial shows, mythological battles and conflicts, mythological stories depicting torture, and animals fighting and devouring one another, the last usually a lion attacking a bull, deer, or other defenseless animal. These artistic representations must have created a level of desensitization that enabled the inhabitants to view the real thing. Public executions were carried out in the most brutal way possible, and public games featured varying forms of violent entertainment: animal against animal, animal against gladiator, gladiator against gladiator, and execution of criminals by animal attack and whatever other ingenious ways could be thought up, often the enactment of the same mythological stories of torture and death depicted in sculpture and painting.[4] In a culture in which the thirst for blood is mostly satisfied vicariously in competitive sports and artificial representation in film and television, it is very difficult to imagine what life was like when surrounded constantly by such a level of actual violence in public adornment and entertainment.

Fig. 9.5. Four servants assist in a lady's toilet. Roman relief, second or third century CE. Rheinisches Landesmuseum, Trier, Germany. Photo: Erich Lessing / Art Resource, NY.

Nor was violence limited to civic uses. Slavery was an institution maintained by the threat and use of violence. Slaves were punished by beatings, torture, and executions. Every slave knew the consequences of breaking the rules or of just being in the wrong place at the wrong time. For example, four hundred household slaves of Lucius Pedanius Secundus were executed under Nero, according to ancient custom, in spite of pleas for mercy both in the Senate and from the public. This was because their master had been murdered in his urban house; the assumption was that someone in the household was guilty and that if someone wanted to, he or she could have prevented it (Tacitus *Annals* 14.42–45). This underlying violence maintained the social system. Those who benefited from it taught their children to perpetuate it.

The schoolmasters and tutors, afforded only by the wealthy elite, assumed that children were recalcitrant and must be forced to learn by threat of punishment, which the teacher did not hesitate to carry out when necessary. Boys were raised with strict rules and expectations to form them into strong and courageous men who could be self-disciplined and resist pain.[5] In Roman discussions of child rearing, severe corporal punishment of sons was considered bad form and discouraged, though some beating of male children was condoned. Yet a clear distinction was made between the loving discipline of a father for his son and the harsh discipline with which slaves were treated. Only under Christian influence did the difference recede somewhat. Along the lines of the Stoic argument that virtue is freedom and vice is the real slavery, later Christian authors like Lactantius and Augustine lessened the rhetorical difference between slaves and sons, the result of which was the principle that, since both sons and slaves are sinners saved by Christ, so both should be equally punished for their own good![6]

Sexuality, too, was inescapable from an early age. Nudity in public art and sculpture was quite common, as it was in the garden sculpture and paintings that adorned the walls of houses and other places where children might see them.[7] The close quarters in which most poorer people lived made any kind of privacy impossible. Even in most well-to-do houses, young slaves attended their master or mistress for the most intimate of functions and activities. We would suspect that no one grew up innocent of sex, except the daughters of wealthy families who were brought up in sufficiently spacious houses and deliberately shielded from public display to make them acceptable elite brides. But even in this case, there was still the household art.

An ancient Mediterranean history from below is not confined to the lives of independent poorer people. The advanced agrarian society of the first-century Roman Empire had no middle class as it is known today in capitalist societies, an independently wealthy middle sector of the society that is dominant in numbers. The majority were rather the peasants working the land and villages, along with the urban poor. There were certainly varying levels of poverty and wealth, however. In this noncapitalist, advanced agrarian society, prestige was not judged primarily by wealth but by status. Those who belonged to the underside of society did not have and would never have the status they envied in the small number of elites who possessed their high status from birth. They could observe these elites during public functions, and they must have been quite aware of how the entire social system was controlled by them and oriented to their opulent lifestyle. Others aimed to emulate them in whatever ways they could. There is evidence that some fortunate few who began in slavery could achieve a relatively comfortable and affluent way of life, though without the social recognition and access to public honors that they envied. Petronius's Trimalchio in his *Satyricon* set in first-century Rome, like Molière's *Bourgeois Gentilhomme* in seventeenth-century France, is the parody of someone, in this case a very wealthy freedman, who aspires to live as the elites live. As a result, he is brilliantly satirized and made to appear as a fool. While wildly exaggerated for the sake of satire, the figure of Trimalchio represents the elite's resentment for such people.

FAMILIES IN SOCIAL NETWORKS

Many of what we would classify as lower-class people did not live independently of their social betters. Family systems included people of many social levels, so that the houses of the wealthy were also the residences and workplaces of slaves, freedmen and freedwomen, and others who were attached to wealthy houses for a variety of reasons. It is important to realize that the different social strata in first-century Mediterranean societies were not as segregated as they are in a modern industrial city.

Older ways of classifying members of Roman society were by the first century giving way to a new division between elites, or *honestiores,* and nonelites, or *humiliores.* This twofold categorization was fully in place by the second century and was primarily a legal distinction that applied to legal penalties: *honestiores* would be exiled or decapitated, while *humiliores* were subject to more degrading forms of execution, including crucifixion and execution in the amphitheater. Nevertheless, this status-conscious society created distinctions of honor and status wherever it could.

Social Status and Slavery

Slavery remained an inhumane but widespread system in which slaves were totally vulnerable to the whims of owners. It is not possible to think of slaves together as a social class or even status. Their position derived solely from that of their owners. Imperial slaves and freedmen may have performed menial jobs but still carried imperial status. On the contrary, many imperial slaves and freedmen had responsible and sometimes powerful positions in which they had authority over high-status persons, with all the resentment that entailed. Paul's reference in Phil. 4:22 to believers in the household of Caesar is to persons of that group. Dale Martin has shown that being a slave was not necessarily degrading if one were the slave-agent of a high-status person, and even for a freeborn person to call oneself a slave of an important character, as Paul does, was not an act of humility but a claim to prestige.[8] By the time Christian thinking became the norm, the believer's status as slave of God and Christ was a corollary claim to status.

Slaves belonged to the family, yet did not. Slaves and freedpersons were usually buried with the natal family as dependents. They were present in Greco-Roman households for the morning ritual devotion to the household gods, and represented in household religious celebrations.[9] Yet their status in the household, their welfare, and their very existence depended on the goodwill of their owners. They could be bought, sold, punished, and, within some legal restraints, executed at will. We cannot forget the basic brutality of the system, in which human persons were deprived of a past and a future, unable to claim natal family or legitimate offspring, and answerable with their bodies in a brutally exploitative system that early Christians did little to alleviate.[10]

We will never know the numbers of slaves who were members of communities of Jesus-followers, but texts like 1 Cor. 7:21-24, Gal. 3:28, Paul's Letter to Philemon, Eph. 6:5-9, Col. 3:22—4:1, 1 Tim. 6:1-2, and 1 Peter 2:18-25 indicate that their numbers were not few and that Christian communities continued to have slave members who were not freed by virtue of baptism. Slaves were members of the household who sometimes converted with the owning family, sometimes on their own, and sometimes not at all. Household slaves were sometimes trusted and sometimes seen as the strangers in the house whose betrayal was not unreasonably feared, especially since slaves could only be interrogated by the authorities under torture and thus, understandably, were highly likely to give incriminating testimony, whether true or not.[11] In *Martyrdom of Polycarp* 6.1, it is a young male slave who, under torture, gives away Polycarp's hiding place.

Yet the stories that have come down to us also contain not only amazing accounts of slaves loyal to their owners but examples of strength and courage to all their companions. Blandina, a slave arrested with a group of Christians in Lugdunum in Gaul in 177, has a mistress also under arrest, who fears lest Blandina through weakness will not hold up under torture but recant. Instead, to everyone's amazement, Blandina turns out to be the most courageous and most enduring of all, the one who rallies the whole group, gives them courage, and is configured by the author of the account to Christ himself as she is hung on a stake (Eusebius, *Ecclesiastical History* 5.1.17–19, 40–42). A few years later in Carthage, North Africa, in 203, the slave Felicitas, also arrested with a group of catechumens, but with no mention of her owner (pace the frequent misconception that the highborn Perpetua is her mistress), is also a center of strength in the group, as she delivers her child in prison and prepares to die in the amphitheater with the others.

Slave marriages and slave families existed de facto but with no legal acknowledgment, and they could be broken up at any time. The papyrus deeds of sale preserved from Egypt indicate that many slaves were minor children when sold. Many slave owners encouraged marital unions between slaves for the stability of the household and the increase of slaves. Perhaps Christian slave owners would have been less likely to separate slave families,[12] yet there is no evidence of this. Though their marriages were not legally recognized, there appears to have been some social recognition, for the burial evidence that remains of them often uses the terminology of legal marriages, terminology denied to them under the law.[13] Mixed marriages between slaves and freed, between slaves and freeborn, and between individuals of different clearly defined social levels existed everywhere—and were headaches for Roman legislators. We mostly know of the possibility and frequency of such marriages through their discussions. While the marriage of a free male with his female slave freed *matrimonii causa* (freed in order to marry him) was not unusual, marriage of a freeborn or even higher-status woman with a slave or former slave was harshly condemned—but still practiced widely. Various penalties were intermittently applied, including reduction of the free woman to slavery by her husband's owner, a penalty enacted by the *Senatus Consultum Claudianum* under Claudius. Marriage of a free woman to her own slave was considered a particularly heinous role reversal between superior and inferior, incurring various social and legal penalties and culminating in the extreme of threatened capital punishment for such a woman in the fourth-century Christian legislation of Constantine.[14]

By the fourth century, Christians were still keeping slaves, as is attested from many sources. A testimony of somewhat equal treatment by this time is that they were sometimes singled out for religious leadership. Already in the early second century, Pliny the Younger, governor of Bithynia and Pontus, had reported in his famous account of Christian activity there that he had tortured two *ancillae* (female slaves) who bore the title of *ministrae* in their Christian community.[15] Scholars continue to debate whether this Latin title is the equivalent of "deacon," given to women both earlier (Phoebe in Rom. 16:1) and later. Whether it is an equivalent, it must certainly be some kind of official leadership position.

The *Apostolic Canons* (*Apostolic Constitutions* 8.47.82) of the late fourth century specify that a slave is not to be ordained to the clergy without his master's or mistress's consent, because this would upset the household. But if the owner allows it, the slave must be manumitted and dismissed from the house and can then be ordained. Similarly, Gregory Nazianzen tells a lady to whom he is writing that she must manumit a slave who has been consecrated bishop against his will (*Epistle* 79)! Still in the middle of the sixth century, Justinian's legislation decrees that anyone chosen to be bishop must be manumitted from slavery (*Novellae* 123.4). All of this is confirmation of two things: slaves could become clergy, but there is still no question of Christians abandoning the institution of slavery.

Marriage

Marriage between followers of Jesus and others is already reflected in 1 Cor. 7:12-16 and 1 Peter 3:1. Nothing is said there about disparity of status, but this problem is voiced later in Tertullian, *To His Wife* 2.8.4, and Hippolytus, *Refutations* 9.12.24-25, because of both defiance of law and social disapproval. Tertullian notes that poverty and lowliness are not so bad for a wife to consider in her husband, in view of Christ's love of poverty. Hippolytus maintains "family values" by excoriating his rival Callistus for allowing upper-class women to marry beneath themselves in order to find Christian husbands. Both situations reflect what we know from other sources. Christian communities, like Judean synagogues and some of the other unofficial cults, were very appealing to women, who often joined such groups independently of their husbands and families. Moreover, the Christian inversion of the social values of honor and status also led at least some Christian theorists to encourage such flaunting of custom, presumably for the sake of women's finding good marriage partners among believers.

Fully legal marriages in Roman law *(conubium, matrimonium iustum)* existed only between Roman citizens or Junian Latins (a category of former slaves freed informally or under the age of thirty, except a female for marriage). All other unions were concubinage *(contubernium, concubinatus)*. It is important, however, to realize that the unfavorable connotations attached to terms like "concubinage" today did not apply. Concubinage was simply a marital union not fully recognized under the restrictive marriage legislation of Rome.[16] While perhaps a good number of believers in Jesus in colony cities like Philippi or Corinth may have been Roman citizens, probably the majority overall were not.[17] While the marriages of those who were not Roman citizens (certainly the vast majority in the early Empire) were recognized by local law and by community custom, they were not recognized in Roman law. By the early third century, Roman citizenship seems to have increased exponentially, so that by the time of

Caracalla's declaration of universal citizenship in 212, the legal situation with regard to marriages would have changed.

Women

All cultures and subcultures of the ancient Mediterranean world were publicly androcentric and patriarchal. At every level of society, men were publicly more powerful and considered superior to women. Yet this male dominance must be qualified in a number of ways. While women could not serve in elective office, there is intriguing evidence, especially from Asia Minor, of elite women holding certain civic offices. In the Roman world, status was always more important than gender; that is, higher social status always took preeminence over the sex of the persons involved. Thus, in the highly developed system of patronage and benefaction, women were actively engaged at every level. They not only held property but ran businesses and exercised personal, financial, and political patronage. Though excluded from elective office, they were able to influence politics in many direct and indirect ways.[18]

Under the influence of interpretations of Mediterranean anthropological studies brought into biblical scholarship, students of early Christianity are now accustomed to thinking of ancient Mediterranean societies as honor-shame cultures, in which women embody family honor, sensitivity to honor, and the possibility of shame in their conduct. In this view, women are potentially dangerous to their families as those who can easily bring shame by sexual conduct inappropriate to their state of life.

One can see this, for example, in the way the second-century BCE scribe Ben Sira frets over the troubles that a daughter brings (Sir. 42:9-14). He loses sleep over worrying whether he will be able to get her a good marriage, whether she will be seduced beforehand, whether she will please her husband, and whether she will bear children. Her father is to keep careful guard over her while she is in his house to be sure there is no secret way into her room. She should not spend time with married women. He concludes that it is a woman who brings shame into the house.

This pessimistic meditation reflects a pattern that in its larger lines is generally accurate, yet it must be nuanced by consideration of other factors that contribute to the social dynamic: the way in which the kinship and hierarchy structures work in any given situation. Crucial here is the degree of women's economic control of resources, for where women have greater economic power, they also have greater social power. Another mitigating factor is the ability to form social networks. Where women live in close proximity to each other and have the social mechanism in place for quick and trustworthy communication, they have wide unofficial power to determine the direction of life in their families and communities.

Some Mediterranean societies were probably in fact more matrifocal and functionally (though not theoretically) egalitarian than we suspect. When a woman's name occurs before that of her husband, it is usually because she is of higher social status than he.[19] The task here is the attempt to read between the lines of public theory, whether that be Roman law or the New Testament household codes, to ascertain how life was really lived.

The idea can be found among male writers all over the Mediterranean world that the public forum and the world of politics is male, whereas the house and the indoor life belong to women. Select passages from authors like Philo are often quoted to suggest that the women of these cultures were kept as secluded as possible. This was manifestly not the case in much of the Mediterranean world. First of all, where such a (male) ideal existed, it was an elite picture of the family for those who had the luxury to keep (freeborn, elite) women indoors. Lower-class families could not do it. We can be sure that in spite of public ideology of the all-male forum, slave and lower-class women were there in abundance, conducting business and shopping in the market. Even classical Athens, where the ideology of seclusion appears most clearly, was not so decidedly segregated by gender in public. By the first century CE Roman women were running businesses, exercising patronage, attending public dinners, and administering their own property, in spite of formal ideology that continued to deny to them what they were actually doing. Some nonelite examples are Julia Felix, who operated a large rental entertainment complex at Pompeii; Naevoleia Tyche, wealthy patron at Pompeii; among believers in Jesus, Lydia at Philippi (Acts 16) and Phoebe at Cenchrae (Rom. 16:1-2).

Children

Children of a Roman citizen father and a free mother normally became citizens. In the case of noncitizen parents, the child usually took the status of the mother. Differences of legal status had severe effects on inheritance laws. A slave freed by a citizen in the correct way before a magistrate or by will normally received citizenship. From the *Lex Aelia Sentia* in 4 CE to Justinian in 531, informal manumission of slaves *inter amicos* or "among friends," or of a slave under thirty except of a female slave for marriage, inserted the newly freed slave into the category of Junian Latin, with freedom but not citizenship and no right to make a will. Their marriage was legal, *iustum conubium,* their children free, but unable to inherit. These restrictions often led persons to pretend to higher status than they actually possessed. There are, for instance, legal discussions about women marrying men they thought were free but turned out to be slaves. Apparently the law did not intervene unless someone who stood to suffer from the situation pressed charges. Given the widespread custom of manumitting slaves in midlife, this must have meant great numbers of children who suffered, being freeborn but with no right of inheritance from their parents.[20] This would have affected Christians as well who had been slaves of Roman citizens, and their children.

Childhood was short. Children of slaves and poorer free families joined in the labor force as soon as they were able. Wealthier and upper-class children were sent to school or privately tutored on a rigorous schedule. The prevailing attitude toward children was that they were inherently resistant to civilizing, so harsh discipline was imposed to make them conform to societal expectations. The available evidence indicates that lower-class children married later than upper-class children, probably because the labor of the former was needed as long as possible, while in the case of the latter, the sooner an advantageous marriage match could be made, the better. Generally, first marriages were arranged by families with the best interests of both children and their families in view. Girls were as much as ten years younger than their future husbands, sometimes more in elite situations where politics was involved. But the age disparity created many widows—one reason for the frequent mention of widows in the social-care literature of early Christianity. In second and further marriages, women seem to have exercised more choice, with husbands closer to their own age.

The Roman ideal of the once-married woman, the *univira*, did not hinder the practice of multiple marriages. Beginning already with 1 Corinthians 7 and 1 Tim. 3:2, 12, we see Christian sources disparaging second marriages, which then placed on the community the burden of support of poorer widows who followed church leaders' advice.

The meeting of the Christian house church consisted of people like those described above. In some cases, a household was large enough and there were sufficient church members to constitute an *ekklesia* composed entirely of household members. This seems to be what is envisioned in the household of Cornelius at Caesarea (Acts 10) or that of the jailer in Philippi (Acts 16). But these are idealized narratives. The more complicated reality is reflected in the letters of Paul, where there are marriages between believers and others, and there are believing slaves in nonbelieving households and vice versa. In spite of the patriarchal ideology of the dominance of a male head of household, as given in Hellenistic and Roman treatises on marriage and in the household codes of the Pauline letters derived from them, the real-time discussions of family life tell a different story.

AN ACTUAL EARLY CHRISTIAN FAMILY

Into this complex and difficult world the challenge of the Jesus movement came. How it was received and how believers adapted what they already knew and were living to what they were now learning is revealed in glimpses of their writings. We have some information about the family life of one particular Christian social unit in early second-century Rome: that of Hermas as revealed in the biographical details of his narrative of the *Shepherd*.[21] Hermas was raised as a *threptos*, an abandoned baby picked up and raised by someone else, probably, as in most cases, in slavery. At some point he was manumitted, after having been sold at least once. How and when he came into the Christian community is not known. At the time of writing, he is a freedman householder with an *oikos*, that is, a familial establishment, probably a modest *domus* of the kind to be seen at Pompeii or Herculaneum. Nothing is said of slave ownership, but probably slaves are present in the household. He has a wife and children, and they do appear briefly in the narrative.

Hermas is engaged in various financial ventures, and his household seems to be a rather typical Roman family of humble status but comfortable means. His wife, never named, is criticized for having too loose a tongue, a typical misogynist complaint. His children may in fact be adult children, still under his *potestas*, who have been behaving irresponsibly, disrespectful of his parental authority. Details are not given, except to say that they have acted lawlessly, and that Hermas, because of his affection for them, has not exercised appropriate discipline. A Roman citizen householder of any rank had legal power over all in his *familia*, even adult sons and daughters. He was expected to act with authority to control them. If his children were indeed adults, it would determine Hermas's age to be rather advanced as the survival norms went. Hermas is the one upon whom the blame falls for the misbehavior of both wife and children; as paternal authority, he is legally and socially responsible for the conduct of everyone under his power. Hermas is not a leader but a member of a Christian community (*Vision* 1.2–3). When, however, he receives his special revelation, he is instructed to read it "with the presbyters (or elders) who preside over the church" (*Vision* 2.4.3).

These details about the family life of Hermas are woven into the revelatory narrative of the text in such a way that it is difficult to extract them.

All is not well in either household or church of Hermas. This is perhaps a mirror of what family life in the early church was like, caught, as it always is, between ideal and reality.

PRO-FAMILY PROPAGANDA

Followers of the Jesus movement reading their own literature in the last decades of the first century CE must have thought they were receiving a confusing message. On the one hand, the household codes of Colossians and Ephesians and the domestic policies of the Pastoral Epistles and 1 Peter reinforced the family values of domestic order in a hierarchical universe (Col. 3:18—4:1; Eph. 5:21—6:8; 1 Tim. 2:8-15; 5:11-16; 6:1-2; Titus 2:2-10; 1 Peter 2:18—3:7). As reflected in treatises on household management that had been in vogue since Aristotle, the authority of husband, father, and male slave owner is confirmed, though not without differences. However little emphasized, there is an articulated ideal of mutual submission (Eph. 5:21). The role description for the dominant male is one of benevolence, not merely out of enlightened self-interest but because of his identity in Christ along with that of all involved. He is to love his wife, not provoke his children, and treat his slaves fairly, remembering that he too has a master in heaven.[22]

There are other differences as well. The subordinate members of the household—wives, children, and slaves—also have a significant role to play. They are addressed, and addressed first, as persons in their own right endowed with dignity. Wives become the image of the church (Eph. 5:23-24), slaves of the suffering Christ (1 Peter 2:21-24). Through these passages, believers in Jesus must have gotten the same message as was communicated in civic politics and official religion: the well-run household is the foundation of society, and well-run means maintaining the hierar-

---

Ephesians 5

[21]Be subject to one another out of reverence for Christ.

[22]Wives, be subject to your husbands as you are to the Lord. [23]For the husband is the head of the wife just as Christ is the head of the church, the body of which he is the Savior. [24]Just as the church is subject to Christ, so also wives ought to be, in everything, to their husbands.

[25]Husbands, love your wives, just as Christ loved the church and gave himself up for her, [26]in order to make her holy by cleansing her with the washing of water by the word, [27]so as to present the church to himself in splendor, without a spot or wrinkle or anything of the kind—yes, so that she may be holy and without blemish. [28]In the same way, husbands should love their wives as they do their own bodies. He who loves his wife loves himself. [29]For no one ever hates his own body, but he nourishes and tenderly cares for it, just as Christ does for the church, [30]because we are members of his body. [31]For this reason a man will leave his father and mother and be joined to his wife, and the two will become one flesh. [32]This is a great mystery, and I am applying it to Christ and the church. [33]Each of you, however, should love his wife as himself, and a wife should respect her husband.

chical structure that had always been the philosophical and political ideal.

Throughout all this domestic propaganda, the idealization of the structures does not change, whatever the reality. Marriage remains ideally the hierarchical relationship of benevolent monarch to his loving and submissive wife. The obedience of adult children owed by law to their paternal head is not compromised. Most important, the structures of slavery remain in place. In spite of Paul's Letter to Philemon, the practice of slavery continues, even if there is strong teaching that slaves are not to be mistreated. Certainly followers of Jesus were not in a political or social position to abrogate slavery, but they could have freed their own slaves. There is ample evidence that they did not. Slaves and freedmen/women continue to be incorporated into the family structure as always. They are to continue to serve wholeheartedly, not taking it upon themselves to think more of themselves or less of their masters since both are members of the assembly, but to treat their masters as they would the Lord (Eph. 6:5-8; Titus 6:1-2). They are to continue to be answerable with their bodies (1 Peter 2:24). Being slave or free is proclaimed as a matter of indifference, though the opportunity for freedom is to be taken if available (Gal. 3:27-28; 1 Cor. 7: 21-24). Slaves should not expect that funds from the assembly will be appropriated to purchase their freedom—although that must have been done in some cases, or there would have been no such expectation (Ignatius, *To Polycarp* 4.3). On the other hand, some take the heroic measure of selling themselves into slavery to ransom others or to secure food for the hungry (*1 Clem.* 55.2).

Ephesians 6

Children, obey your parents in the Lord, for this is right. Honor your father and mother—this is the first commandment with a promise: so that it may be well with you and you may live long on the earth.

And, fathers, do not provoke *your children to anger, but bring them up in the discipline and instruction of the Lord.*

Slaves, obey your earthly masters with fear and trembling, in singleness of heart, as you obey Christ; not only while being watched, and in order to please them, but as slaves of Christ, doing the will of God from the heart. Render service with enthusiasm, as to the Lord and not to men and women, knowing that whatever good we do, we will receive the same again from the Lord, whether we are slaves.

THE FAMILIAL COST OF DISCIPLESHIP

While from some of their own writings the first generations of believers in Jesus were receiving a message of domestic harmony as fulfillment of the will of God, a different message, standing in some tension with the former, was coming through from another part of their tradition. The Synoptic Gospels and some of their sources conveyed the hard message of the cost of discipleship. Part of that message was the preferment of discipleship over family ties, of community cohesion over family integrity. In case of conflict, the newly constituted community was to take precedence. The tone is struck early in Mark (not the most popular early Gospel, but one surely circulating by the 80s of the first century) when Jesus' family comes to take him home from his more and more popular ministry in Capernaum because they thought he was out of his mind (Mark 3:21).[23] Jesus retaliates at 3:31-35 by rejecting their visit and declaring that the disciples around him are family to him. No one from Jesus' family appears again in Mark's Gospel. Matthew and Luke pick up the same story, which Luke softens considerably (Matt. 12:46-50; Luke 8:19-21).

The Q tradition heightens the tension by having Jesus declare that one inevitable result of his preaching, in the words of Micah 7:6, is that family members will be set against each other, son against father, daughter against mother, daughter-in-law against mother-in-law, making one's enemies those of one's own household (Matt. 10:34-35; Luke 12:51-53). Matthew goes on to say (and Luke echoes in a less determined way) that anyone who loves a family member, father, mother, son, or daughter more than Jesus is not worthy of him (Matt. 10:37; Luke 14:26). Discipleship takes precedence over all family ties, even the solemn obligation of a son to bury his father (Matt. 8:22; Luke 9:60). Luke softens the impact of the story of Jesus' preference for disciples over family (Luke 8:19-21), rehabilitates the mother of Jesus as prophet in the infancy narrative (Luke 1:46-55), makes John the Baptist into a relative, and suggests continuity with the family by the presence of the mother of Jesus at Pentecost and James, the brother of the Lord, as ongoing leader in the Jerusalem community. Matthew and Mark do not engage in such reconciliation. Even the Gospel of John, which does not reflect this tension about family, remarks that "even his brothers [that is, family] did not believe in him" (John 7:5), although he was moving about with them in Galilee.

These and sayings like them must have created confusion among families in the late first century that included a large number of followers of Jesus. It is interesting that no positive sayings about the goodness of family life were preserved and attributed to Jesus. In one sense, we could say that the strong position attributed to him with regard to prohibition of divorce (especially the extended discussion in Mark 10:2-12; Matt. 19:1-9) was in fact a counterpoint affirmation of the marriage bond as core of the family and household. But these passages hardly offset the impact of others that foretell disruption, and it is noticeable that none of those passages (discussed above) speak of separation of husband and wife. Given what we know about kinship structures in antiquity and in traditional societies, especially the leading role played by parents in the arrangement of marriages and the close ties among siblings, it is unlikely that they would have said that the core of family life resided in the nuclear family (for which, by the way, they had no name). Rather, it is disruption of parent-child and sibling relationships that would have seemed more severe.

The point here is not to assess whatever historicity there may be in this Gospel tradition that relativizes family ties, though such a difficult thematic undoubtedly originated with Jesus. The point is that when the "memoirs of the apostles," as Justin calls them, were read at worship, these sayings must have been part of the readings, counteracting to some extent the domestic agenda of the Epistles cited above.

It is not a case of elite versus nonelite ideals: both visions, in fact, could be understood as elite ideals that influenced other social levels. The long tradition of structured household management based on hierarchy and submission certainly came from elite circles. At the same time, the radical philosophical teachings of some schools advocated a rupture with family ties similar to that attributed to Jesus, to enable the philosopher to transcend the pulls of family loyalty and transfer that loyalty to a new circle of like-minded people. The ideal of the hierarchical family certainly was reinforced by elites and was perhaps more difficult to maintain in other situations with more poverty and less education. But there is no reason to assume that lower-class families were any less devoted to each other and to preserving family unity. The lack of leisure and need for everyone to be involved in family business and labor among the lower classes may well have contributed, however, to less patriarchal and more egalitarian structures, not so much so that everyone had the same rights as that everyone had the same obligation to join in the common labor.

The power of the family over its members could not have remained absolute through this process of competing tensions. It was relativized in favor of discipleship, the new absolute loyalty to the death. Thus, while family ties were to be respected and even strengthened when possible, they were always to be seen as secondary to the formation of a new family of believers, where old men were to be revered as one's new fathers, old women as mothers, younger men as brothers, younger women as sisters (1 Tim. 5: 1-2). The family ideal was not abandoned, but it was significantly altered by creating a new substitute family to whom the same loyalty was owed.

Nor did the tension with the natal family end with the New Testament. As different understandings proliferated in early Christianity, readers began to encounter slightly later and considerably more romanticized versions of apostolic adventures in what we now know as the Apocryphal Acts. Here great apostolic figures like Peter, Paul, John, and Thomas set out on their own adventurous journeys, confronting evil and conquering it. Despite some differences of theology, all of these early Christian romances have one thing in common: they all advocate celibacy as the only way of

Fig. 9.6. Inhumation and incineration burials of the poor, first–third centuries CE, at Isola Sacra, the cemetery of Portus, port of Rome. While wealthier people chose family mausolea (visible in background), these represent those of more modest means, who could yet afford a decent burial rather than deposition in the common pits with the poorest people. Photo taken in 1973; these burials are no longer in place. Photo: Carolyn Osiek.

Christian existence, even if it means the breakup of marriages and espousals to accomplish it. A major difference from the Synoptic Gospels is that these stories focus on women, notably women of the upper classes. The stories in these works are full of women of leading families in their city who abandon husbands and fiancés in favor of an ascetic lifestyle in imitation of and companionship with the apostle. By doing this, these tales continued the deep suspicion of the claims of the natal family and contributed to its relativization in Christian circles. The upper-class values of domestic harmony under firm male control were now under direct attack in these depictions.[24]

This tension between the traditional patriarchal family and the radical denial of family claims on the believer was to continue throughout early Christianity not only through official teachings but also in the cult of martyrdom and the ascetic life. In both cases, the person who resisted the claims of family with its earthly obligations in favor of renunciation of a normal family life and the embrace of death or a prolonged life of asceticism conformed to the type of heroic sanctity approved of by the same church that continued to preach the hierarchical authority of the family. The vast majority of early Christians were neither martyrs nor ascetics. They lived lives of quiet virtue and vice. As always with the silent majority, their stories go mostly untold.

FOR FURTHER READING

Balch, David L., and Carolyn Osiek, eds. *Early Christian Families in Context: An Interdisciplinary Dialogue.* Grand Rapids: Eerdmans, 2003.

Osiek, Carolyn, and David L. Balch. *Families in the New Testament World: Households and House Churches.* Louisville, Ky.: Westminster John Knox, 1997.

Osiek, Carolyn, Margaret Y. MacDonald, with Janet H. Tulloch. *A Woman's Place: House Churches in Earliest Christianity.* Minneapolis: Fortress Press, 2006.

THE EYES HAVE IT: SLAVES IN THE COMMUNITIES OF CHRIST-BELIEVERS

CLARICE J. MARTIN

Slaves, obey your earthly masters in everything, not only while being watched and in order to please them, but wholeheartedly, fearing the Lord.

—Colossians 3:22

Slaves, obey your earthly masters with fear and trembling, in singleness of heart, as you obey Christ; not only while being watched, and in order to please them, but as slaves of Christ, doing the will of God from the heart.

—Ephesians 6:5-6

> We wear the mask that grins and lies,
> It hides our cheeks and shades our eyes—
> This debt we pay to human guile;
> With torn and bleeding hearts we smile,
> And mouth with myriad subtleties.
>
> Why should the world be over-wise,
> In counting all our tears and sighs?
> Nay, let them only see us, while
>   We wear the mask.
>   —Paul Laurence Dunbar (1872–1906)[1]

To focus on slaves in a history book may appear as a contradiction in terms. History presumably focuses on human beings. The very humanity of slaves, however, was contested in ancient philosophical circles, in which slaves were viewed as "speaking tools" *(instrumentum vocale)*. Yet many slaves were among those who formed new communities of Christ-believers, communities that significantly affected the course of history in late antiquity. So a people's history not only involves but requires the investigation of the lived experiences of enslaved believers.

Knowledge about slaves and slavery in Greek antiquity and Roman imperial society was long obscured and mystified by classicists. In search of the sources of classical humanism, historians and literary interpreters idealized antiquity as a golden age, a mythical utopia. They nostalgically prized the ancient Greeks and Romans as the noble and heroic generators of Western culture, progenitors of science, philosophy, and democracy. Until recently, German, British, and American classical scholarship portrayed slavery in ancient Greek cities and in the Roman Empire as relatively benign for the enslaved, offering them ample opportunities for social mobility and bright prospects for manumission by the age of thirty. Some even argued that the lot of slaves was so decidedly improved in the first century that there was negligible difference between a slave and a son in the Roman household. Eager to downplay its severity, classical historians had little interest in exploring the extent, the brutality, or the dehumanization involved in slavery in Western antiquity. New Testament interpreters, moreover, in their dependence on classical scholarship, tended merely to replicate this uncritically benign view of ancient slavery.[2]

Only following the sharp criticism by classicist M. I. Finley and the monumental comparative historical study by Orlando Patterson in the early 1980s did classical historians pursue more critical investigations of the complexities and contradictions of one of the most repressive, dehumanizing, violent, and exploitative social arrangements in history.[3] And only slowly have studies of Christian origins adjusted toward the more critical approach. Even the more critical recent studies of ancient slavery, however, focus only on the "public transcripts," the extant literature of the wealthy and powerful slaveholding elite and the inscriptions by those who could afford them, with little or no attention to the "hidden transcripts"[4] of the dissident subcultures of the subordinated. Slaves were, after all, mere props, the unseen scaffolding of the landscape of life.

We must proceed with caution, however, in reconstructing the experiences of slaves in the Roman Empire. In Roman imperial society the experience of enslaved men, women, and children remained in the shadows and is known only through those with greater status and voice. The sources are thus usually indirect as well as meager and disparate. The documentation for Greek and Roman social history includes little that corresponds to the voluminous first-person African American slave narratives and oral histories of the antebellum South. The sources of antiquity yield only indirect evidence, available, for example, in selected ancient tales *(fabulae)* written in the tradition of Aesop's *Fables,* which provide intriguing satires and parables of the master-slave relationship. Such satires and parables offer at least some intriguing vignettes of life in which the major players reflect the minutely graded hierarchies of power and powerlessness.

Letters, bills of sale, business contracts, farming manuals, iconographical and inscriptional evidence, papyri, and other literary and material evidence bear witness to the ubiquity of slaves as a presence that often evoked curiosity, anxiety, suspicion, and fear. The anxiety surrounding the interactions of masters and slaves in households *(domus, familia)* was evident on a broad continuum of sometimes bewildering and tension-filled displays and practices of domination and subordination, authority and conformity, and farce or subversion. The proverb repeated by Seneca the Younger (4 BCE–65 CE), that "all slaves are enemies," should have alerted idealist historiographers to the cloud of suspicion, fear, and tension that surrounded the tie binding master and slave together in Roman society. Hostility of Roman slave owners to their slaves and of slaves to their owners simmered just below the surface of Roman civilization like an unexploded volcano.[5] Slaves had to pay endless and vigilant attention to their own cultural performance in the presence of those exercising oversight.

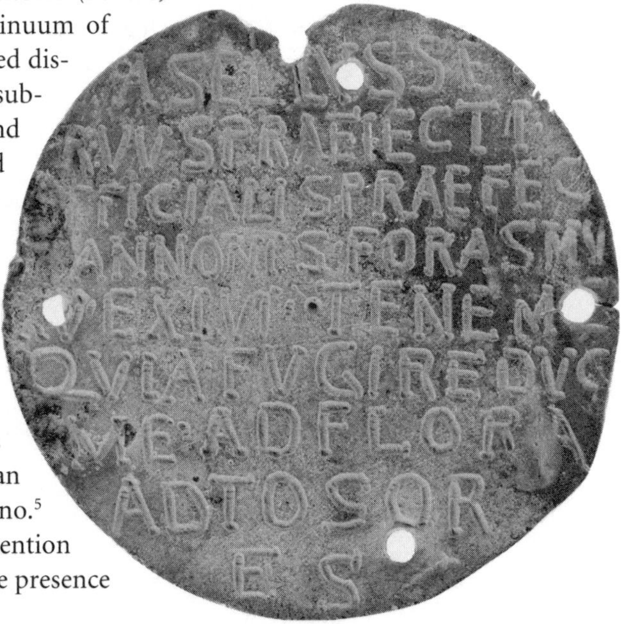

Fig. 10.1. A notice of a runaway slave. Musee du Petit Palais, Paris, France. Photo: Réunion des Musées Nationaux / Art Resource, NY.

Substantively, the task at present is neither a full-scale review of the evidence for slavery in Roman imperial society nor a complete documentation of the imprints of slave life in the various *ekklesiai* attested in the literature of the Christian Testament. It is not possible to fully document the imprints of slave life in antiquity, nor can we know with certainty what slaves thought or how slaves felt. I will avoid positivist and scientific models of historical inquiry that claim definitive and transparent access to the past while failing to address issues of rhetoric, the instability of historical paradigms, and the political engagement of the interpreter.[6]

Instead I will explore textual and material evidence for clues about ways in which slaves strategically used their bodies—particularly their eyes—in performance relative to the slave master to serve the political and survivalist interests of deference, desire, and resistance. I will examine aspects of what may have occurred in the intimate and strategically freighted power relations of slaves in communities of Christ-believers with their masters and mistresses, whether believers or unbelievers. The contexts of these power relations ranged from the domestic household *(domus)* to the community of Christ-believers and the urban areas in which they were located, even to the emperor's household *(familia Caesaris)*. The presumption that slaves necessarily required such a repertoire of survival skills in the nuanced politics of master-slave relations is amply documented, as we shall see, in ancient novels, fables, drama, historical narratives, and epigraphical records. Such negotiations and sometimes outright warfare are implicit in the kyriarchal (hierarchical) rhetoric of the tables of household duties addressed to slave believers in Eph. 5:22—6:9, Col. 3:18—4:1, and 1 Peter 2:18—3:7.

SLAVE EXPERIENCE IN THE ROMAN EMPIRE

> *I have exempted from work the slave-women who deserve reward for producing a certain number of children. Occasionally, I have even granted them their freedom when they have brought up a lot of children.*
>
> —Columella, *On Agriculture* 1.8.19, circa 60 CE[7]

The invisibility and marginalization of slaves in the reconstruction of Greek and Roman social history, in which their presence was pervasive, is a paradox par excellence. As in many other slaveholding societies throughout human history, free Greeks and Romans were often not actively conscious of the particular, more intimate experiences of slaves, including the hidden transcript of the dissident subculture of slave life. Slaves were props, the background, the furnishings of the household of life, who existed to make daily affairs go smoothly for the free. At the beginnings of Western civilization some human beings were always deemed much more human than others. And further, contemporary students of history tend to identify with and claim as their ancient ancestors the more visible, freeborn, propertied, and powerful historical winners, and not the masses of people whom they conquered and enslaved to serve them.

The apostle Paul compared the Corinthians' imperfect knowledge of divine reality with seeing in a mirror dimly (1 Cor. 13:12). This is a fitting analogy for the present task. The dim, ad hoc flashes of the lives of slaves in the assemblies of Christ remain shrouded in the concealed world of shadows on offer in standard scholarly reconstructions. In contrast to the amply visible dramas of their masters and mistresses, glimpses of slave life are like the dim, dull, and distorted reflection of images in the polished bronze or silver mirror of antiquity. We seek rather a fuller clarity and recognition, closer to a face-to-face knowledge, of slave life in those nascent communities.

M. I. Finley's apt admonition attests to the ubiquity of slaves as pervasive unpaid labor in every aspect of ancient social, political, and economic life: "I should say that there was no action or belief or institution in Greco-Roman antiquity that was not one way or another affected by the possibility that someone involved *might* be a slave."[8]

Slaves were visible in every facet of Roman imperial society. Of the population of the city of Rome alone, 30 percent were slaves. Historians have extensively documented that the wealthy aristocracy that presided over the Empire had created a dependence on slave labor for the major portion of basic production. In fact, Rome's ambitious empire-building aspirations from the third century BCE well into the first century CE led to enslavement of conquered peoples on a grand scale. The corollary of the enslavement of millions of conquered peoples in Rome's military campaigns, moreover, was the impoverishment and devastation of the peasantry, who were displaced from their ancestral lands in the formation of *latifundia*, the huge landed estates of the Roman elite. Large gangs of carefully supervised slaves worked the expansive agrarian landscapes of the Roman Empire. In his *Natural History* Pliny the Elder (23–79 CE) describes bounteous harvests "tilled by slaves whose legs are in chains, by the hands of malefactors and men with branded countenances" (18:4).[9] Similarly, the second-century CE Roman historian Appian describes the rise of the *latifundia* in Rome as dependent on thousands of enslaved agricultural laborers:

Fig. 10.2. Fundamental to Roman slavery was the erasure of the human identity of the slave and the treatment of the slave as property. Slave collar bearing Latin inscription. Roman bronze. Museo Nazionale Romano, Terme di Diocleziano, Rome. Photo: Scale / Art Resource, NY.

> The Romans, as they subdued the Italian peoples successively in war, used to seize a part of their lands and build towns there . . . for the rich, taking possession of the greatest part of the undistributed lands and being emboldened by the lapse of time to believe that they would never be dispossessed, absorbing any adjacent strips and their poor neighbors' allotments partly by purchase under persuasion and partly by force, came to cultivate vast tracts instead of single estates, using purchased slaves as agricultural laborers and herdsmen, since free laborers could be drawn from agriculture into the army. At the same time the ownership of slaves brought them great gain from the multitude of their progeny, who increased free from danger because they were exempt from military service. Thus certain powerful men became extremely rich and the class of slaves multiplied throughout the country, while the Italian people dwindled in numbers and strength, oppressed by

penury, taxes and military service. If they had any respite from these evils, they passed their time in idleness, because the land was held by the rich, who employed slaves instead of freemen as cultivators. (*Civil Wars* 1.1.7)

It would be impossible to delineate the extent of slavery and the ways it affected family and community life in the Roman imperial order. Important for the subject of this volume, hundreds of thousands of conquered people were enslaved from Galilee, Judea, Syria, and Asia Minor, the very areas in which the movements of Christ-believers originated and expanded. Rome's initial conquests of Judea and Galilee flooded the Roman slave markets with tens of thousands of new slaves. The historian Josephus recounts the enslavement of thousands of men, women, and children in villages and towns such as Japha, Jotapata, Tarichaeae, and Tiberias. Judeans and Syrians were deemed good for little other than enslavement, like "equally inferior beings" from Galatia, Cappadocia, and Phrygia. Asia Minor was thus a "great source of slaves."[10]

A lower panel of a stele (an upright stone or slab with an inscribed or sculpted surface, used as a commemorative tablet in the face of a building) commissioned by the freedman M. Publilius Satyr from Capua graphically illustrates the then familiar and routine sale of a slave during this age when Rome ruthlessly exploited its control of the Mediterranean world (see fig. 10.3). The image dates from the late Republic or early Principate period (133–27 BCE). Facing the viewer, the slave occupies the

Fig. 10.3. Publilius Satyr, a freedman, chose to honor his patron—his former master—by depicting their first encounter, on the auction block, in his own funerary stele. Museo Campano, Capua, Italy.

center of the scene. Dressed only in a loincloth, he stands on the auction block, the object of a transaction between two figures on either side of him, the seller to the left, in Greek dress, and the purchaser on the right, in a Roman toga. Slaves could be purchased from private individuals or slave dealers. Slaves would be examined carefully to ensure their bodies were in good health; sellers would vouch that the slave was neither a runaway nor guilty of a crime. The sale of slaves as commodities served the larger interests of Roman pragmatism and fostered the integration of conquered people—slave and free—in service of the growth and consolidation of the Empire demographically, militarily, and economically.

Thus, even more than classical Athens, touted as the birthplace of democracy, the Roman Empire has aptly been characterized as a slave society. The most menial labor of every kind was performed by human beings who were the property, the possessions of their masters. Huge gangs of slaves worked the mines and the vast agricultural estates of the Roman patricians. Slaves also were deployed across the continuum of manual labor, in flour mills, local and regional transport, the construction of roads, aqueducts, and city buildings, and the maintenance of the public baths and temples. They also regularly replenished the supply of gladiators, *pornai* (prostitutes), and *hetairai* (high-end prostitutes or courtesans). In addition to the masses of slaves engaged in manual labor, large numbers of slaves worked in the domestic sphere as business managers, secretaries, merchants, domestics, nurses, tutors, pedagogues (male slaves who looked after young children, sometimes as teachers), litter bearers (of sedan chairs), or barbers, butlers, laundrywomen, seamstresses, bath attendants, and wet nurses. Even dancers or actors were usually slaves, owned property.

The operation of the Roman imperial order at every level thus depended on the labor of these dishonored and inferior beings, these "speaking tools." When Sosia, slave of Amphityron in Plautus's Roman comedy *Amphityron* (2 BCE), rushes about at night doing the bidding of his master while trying not to admit his fear of the dark, he dolefully laments his status as a slave, even the slave of a rich man. There is no mistaking his pained intonations of regret for his status as a commodified object required to be perennially available for another's use:

> Why else would I be here, against my will,
> Rushing from harbor into town? why not
> By daylight? Couldn't I do his errands then?
> > The wealthy make bad masters;
> > Don't envy a rich man's slaves—
> "Do that!" "Say this!"—never a bit of rest.
> And that spoiled master who never worked a day
> Thinks you must satisfy his lightest whim—
> This he expects, and who cares how you work?
> Oh, slavery's the mother of injustice:
> *Take up your load and carry it*—that's life.
> > (*Amphityron* 154–64)

In the words of sociologist Orlando Patterson, the system of power reproduced by force and violence, slavery's constitutive internal elements, produced a form of "social death," which can be summarized in three principal features. First, the perpetual threat of coercion and violence ensured obedience and continued mastership. Slaves bore *with* their bodies and *in* their bodies the visible and invisible imprints of their masters' *patria potestas,* the legal and absolute despotic power of the male, master, ruler, husband, and father in the patriarchally constituted homes of Roman imperial society.

Second, enslavement gave rise to "natal alienation." Slaves were forcibly uprooted from family and community and taken into utterly strange new situations in which they were forced to learn new language and culture. This was a particularly devastating and disempowering experience for those accustomed to the supporting relationships of transgenerational kinship and the solidarity of local community.

Fig. 10.4. The careful control of the eyes, the face, and of bodily gestures was required of slaves to conceal their resentment or defiance of their masters. Comical theater mask of a slave, second century BCE. National Archaeological Museum, Athens. Photo: Vanni / Art Resource, NY.

Third, there was an utter and profound loss of honor as slaves had no fully independent social existence: they were the absolute property of their masters with no legal rights; they were inferior beings. Unlike contemporary labor dynamics between employer and employee, wherein an employee has a right of appeal in conflictive labor relations, the slave as mere "speaking implement" was governed fully by the master's will and whim and was thus a fully disposable, subhuman commodity. Slaves were deemed to be inferior by nature and largely distasteful by association. An adult male slave was usually called "little one" or "boy" *(pais, puer),* which underscored his utter lack of dignity. Whereas the freeborn male citizens in elite Roman households were favored with the honorable *tria nomina* (or three names, such as Gaius Julius Caesar), slaves bore only one name, often one that mocked his status (for example, Felix, meaning "Lucky"). The funerary description of the freedman Titius Primus included an epitaph of his concubine, also a freed slave, named Lucania Benigna. Lucania held a baby girl named Chloe in her arms. The single name designated the child as a slave—perhaps born when her mother was a serving woman or slave to the father.[11] Slaves, in the words of the nineteenth-century African American poet Paul Laurence Dunbar (a son of ex-slaves), "wore the mask" of those with dishonored status, who of necessity sought to perfect the art of good service and obedient behavior so characteristic of social subordinates.

SLAVERY IN THE COMMUNITIES OF CHRIST-BELIEVERS

We cannot exaggerate how integral and pervasive a feature slavery had become in the Greco-Roman world that provided the context for the formation of *ekklesiai* of Christ-believers. In the early decades of the first century the Jesus movement comprised a network of poor people, peasants, and marginal communities scattered across the Roman Empire. Located in both rural areas and cities, the movement would eventually include some members of the artisan and propertied classes and some members of the aristocracy. Begun as a renewal movement in Judean society and diaspora Jewish communities, the composition of the Jesus movement would eventually reflect the vivid patchwork of ethnic groups, regions, and peoples across the Roman Empire. But, as social historians of the Jesus movement have amply demonstrated, the social and political climate of this movement was anything but stable. Those who embraced the person and teachings of Jesus of Nazareth held views that often stood in stark contrast to Roman imperial ideology and "family values."[12] A vivid illustration is the apparent baptismal formula used in Asia Minor in the first two decades of the Jesus movement, a formula that Paul quotes in Gal. 3:26-28:[13] "For in Christ Jesus you are all children of God through faith. As many of you as were baptized into Christ have clothed yourselves with Christ. There is no longer Jew or Greek, there is no longer slave or free, there is no longer male and female; for all of you are one in Christ Jesus." Insofar as this baptismal formula reflected and directed the actual practices of the early communities of Christ-believers with regard to Greek and Jew and male and female, we may ask to what degree this was also the case with regard to slave and free. Hearing such language pronounced in the baptismal ritual, slaves may well have imagined they were being incorporated into a community in which they would no longer be treated as slaves, in which they would be released from the master-slave relationship. Such slaves would have been able to eye the goods of freedom, daring to believe they, too, had been called into a new society of wholeness and renewal as equals.

The writings produced by nascent Christian communities, in particular some of the letters of Paul and some letters written later in his name, are our only direct sources for information regarding slaves within these communities. Unfortunately, they offer precious little evidence for how the ideal articulated in that baptismal formula was implemented. On the basis of that limited evidence, however, some have discerned two lines of development with regard to slaves in the communities of Christ-believers: one that involved the emancipation of slaves, at least in some circumstances; the other, a general acceptance and reinforcement of slaveholding in the communities as well as in Roman imperial society.

The rhetoric appearing in Paul's own letters might well have intensified slaves' desire for eyeing the goods of freedom. Declarations that men and women—slaves in particular—had been set free by Christ's crucifixion and resurrection sound formulaic enough to indicate that they might have had broad currency in the movement: "For freedom Christ has set us free. Stand firm, therefore, and do not submit again to a yoke of slavery" (Gal. 5:1). "You were called to freedom" (Gal. 5:13). "You were bought with a price" (1 Cor. 6:20). "Where the Spirit of the Lord is, there is freedom" (2 Cor. 3:17). The significance and implications of two key references to slaves and slavery in Paul's letters, 1 Cor. 7:21 and the letter to Philemon, remain contested, however. A centuries-long interpretative tradition understood Paul as offering a tacit endorsement of slavery, attributed (when, in the modern period, an explanation was sought) to his own unreflective social position or to his theological conviction that the status of slaves, like other aspects of status in Roman society, was a matter of indifference. Some more recent interpretations of those key texts offer a dramatically different reading, however, suggesting that Paul actually encouraged slaves to choose freedom when presented with the opportunity to do so and exerted his influence in the Christ communities to encourage the release of slaves (through manumission, perhaps).

The letter to Philemon, read since the fourth century CE as concerning a runaway slave who had also stolen goods from his master, is currently being reappraised.[14] Nothing in this short letter suggests that Onesimus was a thief. The assumption that he was a runaway slave depends in part on the translation of the Greek particle *hōs* in verse 16. Did Paul encourage (or command) Philemon to welcome Onesimus back "as a slave" or "as if a slave," the latter translation remaining merely metaphorical? Does the next phrase, "but more than a slave, a beloved brother," exhort Philemon to set his slave free, in accordance with the ideal articulated in the baptismal formula cited in Gal. 3:28? In any case, it is increasingly difficult to assume on the basis of this letter that Paul intended slaves to remain slaves; the letter may have nothing to do with a runaway slave at all.

The notoriously ambiguous phrase in 1 Cor. 7:21 has proven equally fateful. Translated as a discouragement to slaves from seeking freedom ("even if you can gain your freedom, make use of your present condition now more than ever"), it has served as the basis for broad generalizations about the apostle's "social conservatism."[15] More recent studies, however, have argued for an alternative translation, printed in the Revised Standard Version (but relegated to a footnote in the New Revised Standard Version): "Were you a slave when called? Never mind. But if you can gain your freedom, avail yourself of the opportunity." This translation, others have argued, aligns better with the following declaration that "whoever was called in the

Lord as a slave is a freed person belonging to the Lord, just as whoever was free when called is a slave of Christ. You were bought with a price; do not become slaves of human masters" (1 Cor. 7:22-23). It is also regarded as making better sense of the larger argument in which Paul offers advice about marriage and sexual relations, repeatedly making exceptions to general rules (7:1-7, 8-9, 10-11, 12-16). The exhortation to "remain in the calling [*klēsis*] in which you were called" (7:17, 20, 24), Paul's "rule in all the assemblies," appears reminiscent of the baptismal formula. Throughout these verses Paul makes allowances for alternatives to his own preferences; whether men and women enter the community married or unmarried, they are not prohibited from changing their status (7:2-7, 9, 11, 15). The concession to slaves is even more forceful: slaves are not to consider themselves inferior within the assembly ("never mind," 7:21), and are encouraged "by all means" *(mallon)* to take advantage of any opportunity to gain their freedom.

Whether or not the Pauline assemblies actively practiced the release of slaves (through manumission, redemption, or some other mechanism), there is clear, albeit limited, evidence that into the early second century CE other communities of Christ-believers practiced "ecclesial manumission," that is, redeemed members from slavery from a community fund.[16] The practice apparently alarmed Ignatius of Antioch, who warned his fellow bishop Polycarp of Smyrna not to allow slaves to "desire to be made free from the common fund" (*Letter to Polycarp* 4:3). In contrast, similar practices are encouraged by the *Shepherd of Hermas,* written in Rome around 100 CE, wherein the faithful are exhorted "to minister to orphans and the destitute, . . . to redeem from distress the servants of God," and "instead of lands, to purchase afflicted souls and to look after widows and orphans" (*Mandate* 8:10; *Similitude* 1:8). Those redeemed "from distress" probably included slaves as well as prisoners, and these exhortations clearly concern use of economic resources. A later source relying on earlier material, the *Apostolic Constitutions* exhort Christian communities to gather resources in order to aid or rescue in difficult circumstances, including slaves: "Therefore maintain and clothe those who are in want. . . . And such sums of money as are collected . . . appoint to be laid out in the redemption of the saints, the deliverance of slaves and of captives, and of prisoners" (4.92.2). Christians were discouraged from attending public meetings, unless the purpose was "to purchase a slave and save a life" (2.62.4). Clearly, many nascent Christian communities, from Antioch and Syria in the east through Asia Minor to Rome in the west, maintained practices that embodied the ideal of the ancient baptismal formula.

Despite the efforts of such Christ-believing communities to emancipate at least some of their members from slavery, we may presume that some—perhaps most—enslaved members would have remained in slavery. If the principle "no longer slave" was actively pursued by some communities, it was actively opposed by others more concerned to maintain the long-established power relations of the Roman order. As in other slave-holding societies through the centuries, some communities were able to view strict maintenance of social boundaries and of the power of the dominant over the subordinate as compatible with Christian faith. As early as the late first century CE, letters written in Paul's name drew upon conventional codes of domestic behavior to insist that slaves remain obediently in their places. Even here, however, we should not read exhortations to subordination as uncomplicated evidence of the actual experience or attitudes of slaves in early Christ communities.

THE EYES IN BODY POLITICS

> *Nothing was so popular, nothing so fitting for our times as the*
> *opportunity we enjoyed of looking down at the informers at our feet,*
> *their heads forced back and faces upturned to meet our gaze.*
> —Pliny the Younger, *Panegyrics* 34.3[17]

The eyes are critical purveyors of meaning in the contested economy of body politics. In fact, body language in general, as a medium of nonverbal communication, has always functioned as an important signifying system in human societies. Decoding the semantics of bodily effects in life and literature from antiquity to the present has preoccupied philosophers and poets, politicians and humorists, for body language as a purveyor of communication and meaning plays a pivotal role in all human interaction. Posture, gesture (a nod of the head, a wave of the hand or finger), facial expressions (biting the lips, a trembling chin, a smile, or a frown), glances and eye contact (the use of the eyes in supplication or to convey threat or disdain), and touching behavior all function as powerful acts of communication, conveying myriad conscious and unconscious feelings and dispositions. Correctly apprehending and decoding the nuances of body language and nonverbal communication both within and across discrete cultural systems is essential in the dynamic politics of social interaction.

The distinctive role of the eyes in the economy of the human senses has long garnered notable attention. The Greek philosopher Heraclitus (500 BCE) concluded that "the eyes are more trustworthy witnesses than the ears" (*Allegories* 22B). Aristotle (384–322 BCE) declared that "we prefer sight, generally speaking, to all the other senses.... Sight best helps us to know things, and reveals many distinctions" (*Metaphysics* 980a 25). Even the rhetorician Quintillian (circa 23–90 CE) extolled the distinctive power of the eyes and the gaze in the repertoire of the nonverbal vocabulary, emphasizing their ability to convey a wide variety of feelings. Far from functioning as detached, mechanistic, and perfunctory organs that merely refract light from the external world, the eyes are beacons of the complexity of our interiority and subjectivity, mirroring our jealousies, insecurities, and inner turmoil or, alternatively, mirroring our hopes, aspirations, and dreams (*Inst.* 11.3.72–77). More than mere neurophysiologic instruments that aid us in navigating our world, our eyes are implicated in the drama of desire, power, deference, and survival.

The concept of the evil eye, for example, has long functioned as a familiar motif in ancient beliefs and folklore. The ancients thought that by casting an evil eye one could diminish another's good luck or fortune, as illustrated in Jesus' parable of the laborers in the vineyard (Matt. 20:1-15). When the laborers who have worked all day or part of the day complain at day's end that they have not received more pay than those who worked only a few hours, the wealthy landowner responds, "Am I not allowed to do what I choose with what belongs to me? Or are you envious because I am generous?" Literally, he asks, "is your eye evil?" *(ē ho ophthalmos sou ponēros estin?).* In an agrarian society in which day laborers dependent on wealthy landlords struggled for mere survival, the evil eye of resentment was serious business.

While the experience of slaves in Roman imperial society has been obscured and sanitized over the centuries, the enslaved in antiquity would not themselves have experienced the luxury of such veiled invisibility and anonymity. There was no way they could escape the uninhibited supervisory gaze of their owners and others who exercised dominion over them. We can hardly overestimate the controlling effect of the eyes of those with power to de-soul, shame, and dishonor those of lesser status.

In his *Agricola* Tacitus (55–117 CE) described the power of the imperial gaze as a kind of "visual assassination," when he observed the behavior of the emperors Nero and Domitian: "Even Nero averted his eyes and did not deign to watch the outrages that he ordered. The worst of our torments under Domitian was to see him with his eyes fixed upon us—with our every sigh being registered against us."[18] Similarly, according to Seutonius, Caligula would parade the wives of his dinner guests before his couch while he pointedly and leisurely assessed them—like a merchant inspecting goods—stretching out his hand to raise the chin of any woman who lowered her eyes from the shame of it all (*Caligula* 36.2). Experiencing the double violation of having to endure Caligula's rapacious inspection of their bodies, while also being forced to return his gaze by looking in his eyes, they became complicit in their own violation, sharing with their husbands their feeling of powerlessness to do anything but Caligula's bidding.[19]

As the lowest of the low, slaves were even subject to torture for the sadistic visual satisfaction of their masters and others of the imperial ruling class. Pliny the Elder (23–79 CE) writes that Vedius Pollio, a Roman equestrian (a member of the ruling class second only to the wealthier and more powerful senatorial order) and "friend of Caesar," a close associate and adviser of the emperor, "found that lamprey eels offered him an opportunity to display his cruelty. He used to toss slaves sentenced to death into ponds of lampreys, not because wild animals on land were not capable of killing a slave, but because with any other type of animal he was not able to enjoy the sight of a man being torn to pieces, completely, in one moment" (*Natural History* 9.39.77).

THE EYE SERVICE OF THE ENSLAVED:
RITUALS OF DEFERENCE AND RESISTANCE

> *It is plain enough . . . that the prudent subordinate will ordinarily conform by speech and gesture to what he knows is expected of him— even if that conformity masks a quite different offstage opinion. . . . Conformity in the face of domination is thus occasionally—and unforgettably—a question of suppressing a violent rage in the interest of oneself and loved ones.*
>
> —James C. Scott[20]

> *Each day in the store I watched the brutality with growing hate, yet trying to keep my feelings from registering in my face. When the boss looked at me, I would avoid his eyes.*
>
> —Richard Wright[21]

It is a commonplace that members of the Jesus movement or the *ekklesiai* of Christ-believers met in house churches, with the membership reflecting the social stratification of the larger Roman imperial society. The *familia* or household was the most fundamental institution in Roman society (see chapter 9 in this volume). The typical Roman household included the *paterfamilias,* the "father" of the household who functioned as the patriarchal head of the family unit and exercised legal power *(potestas)* over his wife, children, and domestic slaves. Hence, the father was at once husband, father of the children, property owner, slave master, and perhaps a patron to freedmen, freedwomen, and clients.

We should not presuppose a monolithic nuclear family structure as the only family model in which enslaved believers in the Jesus movement may have been situated.[22] Funerary inscriptions have documented the presence of slaves in extended families and mixed households with members both related and unrelated by birth. Believers who were slaves may have been in families under the authority of a *paterfamilias* who was also a believer, as appears to have been the case with Onesimus (if the latter was in fact a slave in the household of Philemon; see the discussion above). There were doubtless cases of enslaved believers who were members of domestic households of nonbelievers. This is implied in 1 Peter 2:18-25, part of a letter that stands in the deutero-Pauline tradition. The letter admonishes all slaves in the *ekklesia* to accept the authority of their masters "with all deference"—both the kind master and the harsh master, who may wrongly and unjustly beat them:

> Slaves, accept the authority of your masters with all deference, not only those who are kind and gentle but also those who are harsh. For it is a credit to you if, being aware of God, you endure pain while suffering unjustly. If you endure when you are beaten for doing wrong, what credit is that? But if you endure when you do right and suffer for it, you have God's approval. For to this you have been called, because Christ also suffered for you, leaving you an example, so that you should follow in his steps. (1 Peter 2:18-21)

In a society in which the slave body was always vulnerable and subject to being bound, beaten, and whipped with impunity by public and private masters, this injunction would have evoked familiar images. An allusion to the frequency and intensity of slave beatings in Plato's *Laws* recalls the familiar sight: "Some distrust the whole class and make their servants three-fold—nay, a hundredfold—slaves at heart by the scourge and the lash, as though they were dealing with so many wild beasts" (*Laws* 6.777a). Similarly, Roman laws dealing with slaves required the torture of their bodies *before* the slave gave evidence in a court case, for it was assumed the slave would not tell the truth unless first tortured. Or one can only pity the poor "whipping boy," the slave punished in place of the free. Plutarch records the interesting case of the scholar Ammonius, who used a slave as a whipping boy in an object lesson for his students. According to the anecdote, a frustrated Ammonius wanted to teach his students to be more frugal with their lunches, so he had a slave beaten during the afternoon lecture as a way to reinforce his message about the necessity of self-control. The students—subordinate by virtue of their youth but having free status—gained their new insight at the expense of the slave. The expendable slave's body thus provided the living pedagogical instrument for the free to advance ideological truth.[23]

While enslaved believers were encouraged to emulate the patience of Christ, who himself endured unjust suffering (1 Peter 2:19-25), they, like their pagan counterparts, endured with their bodies the travails and challenges of those with the lowest status of society. As we have seen, the pre-Pauline baptismal formula (cited in Gal. 3:28) that proclaimed that "in Christ," in the *ekklesia*, the standard social divisions had been overcome was a lively ideal among the assemblies. But it clearly failed to generate universal acceptance among believers, if Paul's ardent appeal to Philemon may be read as an attempt to secure the freedom of a slave still retained by a member of the Christ community. There is no evidence of a serious effort in the *ekklesiai* to abolish the institution of slavery. To the contrary, the literature of the nascent Christ communities shows that the household was the basic cell and site of the *ekklesia*, in which the ideals of *koinonia*, of unity and fictive kinship ties as brothers and sisters, were coterminous with strictly maintained boundaries and functioning hierarchies of social status. Paul's own ambiguous, possibly conservative stance toward slave emancipation (1 Cor. 7:17-24) may corroborate this observation.

Fig. 10.5. Elite depictions of luxury routinely included the service of slaves. Servant carrying a plate, mosaic fragment from "Preparation of a Banquet," Carthage, 180–90 CE. The Louvre, Paris. Photo: Erich Lessing / Art Resource, NY.

The tables of domestic duties in two deutero-Pauline letters (produced by "disciples" of Paul a generation or more after his mission) indicate that many enslaved believers were likely caught in the eye of a tempestuous storm swirling around mandates of strict conformity and unqualified obeisance to masters—whether believers or unbelievers:

Slaves, obey your earthly masters with fear and trembling, in singleness of heart, as you obey Christ; not only while being watched, and in order to please them [*ophthalmodoulian hōs anthrōpareskoi*], but as slaves of Christ, doing the will of God from the heart. (Eph. 6:5-6)

Slaves, obey your earthly masters in everything, not only while being watched [*ophthalmodoulia hōs anthropareskoi*] in order to please them, but wholeheartedly fearing the Lord. (Col. 3:22)

Such domestic codes developed from Stoic ethical instruction earlier in the Hellenistic world (see 1 Peter 2:13—3:7). Intended to stress mutual obligations and responsibilities of those within the household—husband and wife, parents and children, master and slave—the codes mirrored prevailing philosophical assumptions about patriarchy, gender, power, and status in Roman imperial society. Slaves in particular received very specific instructions about the use of their eyes as signifiers of their motives for service while performing their duties for those in power over them.

The Greek term *ophthalmodouleia*, "eye service," a term virtually confined to these letters, has traditionally been interpreted to mean "a service performed for the sole purpose of attracting attention," in contradistinction to service "from the heart," ungrudging service, or service with a motive to please God or one's conscience. In this traditional reading, these codes of behavior in Colossians and Ephesians thus required the enslaved to avoid insincere behavior as "people-pleasers" in favor of serving masters and mistresses with "singleness of heart." The codes prohibit service out of false or ulterior motives, such as to gain the praise of others, and insist upon disposition and action rooted in service to God.

These codes, presented as a model of behavior for slaves involved in the assemblies of Christ, in fact clearly reflect and defend the interests of the dominant free males and females of the ruling and propertied class. The command of service "from the heart, with a smile" expected of slaves—especially when further reinforced by the commands to mirror the model of Christ and to perform "unto the Lord"—made no concession whatever to the enslaved. The ideal of the abolition of distinctions between slave and free, as well as Jew and Greek and male and female, which was articulated in the baptismal formula cited by Paul, seems to have been simply ignored or forgotten. Unmitigated in such codes, the slave's experience of domination and dishonor as a deracinated outsider continued in full force.

Interpreters of these letters, however, have not yet begun to appreciate the implications of these commands about "eye service" and "people-pleasers." Four aspects stand out in particular.

First, the male-master rhetoric of the domestic codes in Colossians and Ephesians, enjoining slaves in the Jesus movement to perform labor with sincerity for the men and women in power over them, recalls the function of the popular *exemplum* literature in Roman society. Such "loyalty tales" were a subgenre in Roman literature constructed and maintained by husbands and masters to advance a particular cultural value: the absolute loyalty and devotion of wives and slaves. These self-contained short stories reiterated popular ideals about wives and slaves as potentially dangerous, subversive, and disloyal, while also providing exemplary models for wives and slaves to emulate in service to husbands and masters. In many *exempla*, slaves perform their services (*ministeria*) from a motive of love for the master—a love that takes precedence over the slave's own well-being, safety, and life. In fact, the "good slave" would willingly suffer and die for his or her master. "Eye service" truly "from the heart" in these instances functions to comfort and honor the master and provides a powerful model for other slaves to emulate.[24]

Second, in Roman imperial society being noticed was a route for personal gain and advancement; therefore, eye service as men-pleasers was, understandably, a sage strategy for advancement. Eye service as serving the interests of a "politics of desire" that could manipulate or alter the social order in one's favor, either in finely graded increments or on a much grander scale, was a tempting procedure for both free and slave. This dynamic is abundantly illustrated by slaves at Roman banquets, at which slaves performed table service for the propertied elite, with ample opportunity for eye service. Surely, enslaved persons in the communities of Christ-believers would have found opportunity for similar or parallel behavior.[25]

Third, as the citations from James C. Scott and Richard Wright attest, eye service as men-pleasers is often a mask of conformity, a masquerade of deferential obeisance, that functions strategically and effectively to conceal the slave's dissent from the master's will and desire for greater autonomy. Farcical eye service thus conceals the authentic personality, dreams, and aspirations of the social subordinate in the interest of survival and self-preservation, further impeaching the master's or mistress's deeply cherished presumptions of the absoluteness of their masterly authority.

Finally, an aspect especially deserving of further analysis is eye service and the construction of gender, particularly in the wide-ranging experiences of enslaved women relative to their masters and mistresses. What continuum of experiences might enslaved women have undergone as they demonstrated deference and obeisance to those in power over them—whether believers or unbelievers—in a society in which enslaved women had no right to protect their bodies from rape and abuse? Enslaved women would have frequently found themselves squarely in the eye of the storm relative to issues of domination and subjection in master/mistress and slave relations and the fate of their own bodies.[26]

The Roman satirist Juvenal (60–128 CE) is known for writing acerbically critical satires detailing the corruptions in Roman imperial society. Despairing of ever notably improving or reforming Roman moral laxity, he brilliantly painted searing images of Roman depravity, cruelty, and hypocrisy. Juvenal's indignant speaker in Book 1 of the *Satires* condemns the decadence of the Roman elite, in particular, as paradigms of moral corruption. An episode in his sixth *Satire* provides a glimpse of domestic power relations in the ancient slave system that would be repeated centuries later in the antebellum slave system of America. A suspicious wife, ignored by her husband in bed, immediately assumes he is in a sexual liaison with the household secretary (a slave) and has her repeatedly whipped. The punishment does not forestall the enslaved woman's responsibilities to immediately tend to her mistress' hair:

> If her husband turns his back on her in bed at night, his secretary suffers! . . . Some women hire a torturer on a yearly salary. He whips, while she puts on her makeup,

talks to her friends, and examines the gold thread of an embroidered dress. He lashes, while she looks over the columns of the account book. He lashes, and is exhausted by lashing—until she bellows out, "Go away." Poor Psecas, whose own hair has been torn out by her mistress, and whose clothing has been ripped from her shoulders and breasts by her mistress, combs and styles her mistress' hair. "Why is this curl so high?" the mistress screams, and at once a whipping punishes Psecas for this crime of the curling iron and a sin of a hairstyle. (Juvenal, *Satire* 6.474–511)[27]

In a social context in which such capricious brutality could be a matter of daily routine for the enslaved, in which slaves could raise no claim for security from physical and sexual abuse, constant vigilance over the eyes, the gaze, the whole repertoire of gesture and demeanor was a requisite strategy of survival through the careful concealment of dissent or defiance. Certainly, we can no longer read exhortations within the early *ekklesia* to "single-hearted service" without keeping our own eyes open to the sometimes delicate, sometimes violent, but always precarious conditions that characterized the intimate power relations of the household in Roman slave society.

FOR FURTHER READING

DuBois, Page. *Slaves and Other Objects.* Chicago: University of Chicago Press, 2003.

Garnsey, Peter. *Ideas of Slavery from Aristotle to Augustine.* Cambridge: Cambridge University Press, 1996.

Glancy, Jennifer A. *Slavery in Early Christianity.* New York: Oxford University Press, 2002.

Joshel, Sandra R., and Sheila Murnaghan, eds. *Women and Slaves in Greco-Roman Culture.* New York: Routledge, 2001.

Patterson, Orlando. *Slavery and Social Death: A Comparative Study.* Cambridge: Harvard University Press, 1982.

INJUSTICE OR GOD'S WILL: EXPLANATIONS OF POVERTY IN PROTO-CHRISTIAN COMMUNITIES

STEVEN J. FRIESEN

CHAPTER ELEVEN

Poverty is one of the great religious issues of all time. At least at the grass-roots level, religious groups and individuals throughout history have had to deal with perennial questions related to poverty. What is the meaning of poverty and wealth? Why are economic resources distributed unequally among humans? How does one meet one's obligations in the condition of deprivation and in the condition of abundance? Why are the poor often considered to be more pious while the rich are often given more status? Such themes should be part and parcel of the story of Christianity, but they rarely play an important role in the official histories.

This suppression of poverty in church history is fairly easy to explain. One important factor is that the poor rarely have the opportunity to leave lasting records of their experiences, and so later historians have little data for examination. Another important factor is that most people who write history are not poor and their work is not paid for by poor folks, so the official histories dwell on a limited set of experiences from a limited, well-to-do sector of the population.

A people's history of Christianity cannot ignore issues related to the uneven distribution of economic resources, for economic inequality has characterized churches and societies throughout Christianity's existence. In this chapter I explore these issues for the earliest period by examining the early literature of the movements that later came to be known as Christianity. My two main questions are the following: (1) Did the literature of the saints suggest theories about why economies are unjust? (2) Did the texts recommend any actions in response to the fundamental inequity of the Roman imperial economy?

Most of the texts do not address these questions directly. The unequal distribution of goods and resources is not a topic in Hebrews, 1 and 2 Peter, 1, 2, and 3 John, Jude, *1 Clement*, or the letters of Ignatius (I leave the Gospels and Pauline literature to others in this volume). I am left with only four texts around which to organize my investigation: the Letter of James, who is more accurately called "Jacob"; the Revelation of John; the Acts of the Apostles; and the *Shepherd of Hermas*. Together, these four proto-Christian texts provide us with four distinct ways of explaining the causes of poverty and four calls to action regarding one of the most intractable human problems. They do not demonstrate a linear evolution in the economic thinking and practices of the early assemblies, for the texts come from several communities over the course of decades. Rather, the texts illustrate four models for analysis and for action. Before we examine the texts, however, we need a framework for understanding economic inequality in the Roman imperial world.

ECONOMIC INEQUALITY IN THE ROMAN EMPIRE

In their analysis of Roman imperial society, Peter Garnsey and Richard Saller employ the poignant phrase "the Roman system of inequality."[1] With this phrase Garnsey and Saller call our attention to the fact that the Roman Empire maintained its hegemony through judicial institutions, legislative systems, property ownership, control of labor, and brute force. Like all societies, the Empire developed mechanisms for maintaining multifaceted inequality, and like all "civilized" societies the Empire promoted justifications that made the inequity seem normal, or at least inevitable.

As we turn our attention specifically to the economic facets of the Roman system of inequality, we should keep in mind three fundamental ideas. First, as economic historians point out, the Roman imperial economy was preindustrial. The vast majority of people lived in rural areas or in small towns, with only about 10 to 15 percent of the population living in cities of ten thousand or more people. This means that most of the population (80 to 90 percent) worked in agriculture and that there was relatively little large-scale commercial or manufacturing activity. The level of commerce and manufacturing would have varied from region to region and especially among urban centers, but the Empire as a whole had an advanced agricultural economy rather than an industrial economy.

Second, there was no middle class in the Roman Empire. Because the economy was primarily agricultural, wealth was based on the ownership of land. Most land was controlled by a small number of wealthy elite families. These families earned rent and produce from the subsistence farmers or slaves who actually worked the land. With their wealth and status these families were able to control local and regional governance, which allowed them to profit also from taxation and from governmental policies. These same families also controlled public religion.

This economic system enforced the dominance of a few and the impoverishment of the majority. In between these extremes there was no middle category of people whose economic relationships allowed them to gather capital or to move up the economic hierarchy. There were, of course, some families whose economic situations improved above the level of subsistence but this was usually due to exceptional circumstances (adoption, found treasure, fortunate patronage relationships, and so forth). They did not form a class of people whose similar economic relationships formed an integral part of the economic system. Thus, we say that the Roman economy had no middle class.[2]

Third, poverty (defined as living at or below the level of subsistence) was widespread in both rural and urban areas. Interpreters of the New Testament and related Christian literature tend to underestimate the overwhelming poverty that characterized the Roman Empire. To make matters worse, we tend to use undefined binary categories of "rich" and "poor" in our descriptions. In order to promote clarity, I use instead the following poverty scale, which provides seven categories for economic resources. Detailed arguments for the scale can be found elsewhere.[3] The percentages are based on data from urban centers of ten thousand inhabitants or more, but we need to remember that in rural areas poverty was even worse: while super-wealthy elites (categories 1–3) made up about 3 percent of an urban population, they were only about 1 percent of the total imperial population. The focus on urban centers is necessary because this type of city is where the communities who received these four texts were located.

It is difficult to put monetary values on these categories because prices varied greatly in rural and urban areas. The following chart provides some rough guidelines.

Poverty is, of course, a more complicated phenomenon than the mere possession of financial resources. In the twenty-first century poverty is affected by many factors, and we should expect no fewer complications in ancient societies. In the early Roman Empire financial resources were probably the single most influential factor in determining one's place in the social economy, but they were not the only factor. Others would have included at least gender, ethnicity, family lineage (common or noble), legal status (slave, freed, or freeborn person), occupation, and education. Patronage relationships were especially important in one's economic survival, for a patron gave one restricted access to resources that were otherwise unavailable. In times of crisis a patron could mean the difference between life and death. Financial resources provide us with a way to open the discussions and also have the virtue of sometimes being quantifiable in ways that other factors are not.[4]

Fig. 11.1: Poverty Scale for a Large City in the Roman Empire[5]

Percent of Population	Poverty Scale Categories
0.04%	1. *Imperial elites:* imperial dynasty, Roman senatorial families, a few retainers, local royalty, a few freedpersons.
1%	2. *Regional or provincial elites:* equestrian families, provincial officials, some retainers, some decurial families, some freedpersons, some retired military officers.
1.76%	3. *Municipal elites:* most decurial families, wealthy men and women who do not hold office, some freedpersons, some retainers, some veterans, some merchants.
(7%?)	4. *Moderate surplus resources:* some merchants, some traders, some freedpersons, some artisans (especially those who employ others), and military veterans.
(22%?)	5. *Stable near subsistence level* (with reasonable hope of remaining above the minimum level to sustain life): many merchants and traders, regular wage earners, artisans, large shop owners, freedpersons, some farm families.
40%	6. *At subsistence level* and often below minimum level to sustain life: small farm families, laborers (skilled and unskilled), artisans (especially those employed by others), wage earners, most merchants and traders, small shop/tavern owners.
28%	7. *Below subsistence level:* some farm families, unattached widows, orphans, beggars, disabled people, unskilled day laborers, prisoners.

Fig. 11.2: Annual Income Needed by Family of Four.[6]
Categories from the poverty scale are found in parentheses.

For wealth in Rome (PS3)	25,000–150,000 *denarii*
For modest prosperity in Rome (PS4)	5,000 *denarii*
For subsistence in Rome (PS5–6)	900–1,000 *denarii*
For subsistence in a city (PS5–6)	600–00 *denarii*
For subsistence in the country (PS5–6)	250–300 *denarii*

When we discuss the explanations of economic inequality found in proto-Christian texts, then, we must fight the tendency to impose the categories of modern industrial economies on the Roman Empire. Most of the recipients of these four texts lived in large urban areas with a preindustrial economy. Unless there is evidence to the contrary, we should assume that most or all of the recipients of a particular text lived near the level of subsistence. Even in a city many inhabitants would have had rural connections, and few of them would have had significant financial resources beyond basic survival needs.

PROPHETIC CRITIQUE IN THE LETTER OF JACOB

We do not know exactly when this letter was written, but it probably comes from the last half of the first century CE. Some scholars think the text reflects the ideas of Jacob, the brother of Jesus, which would make it one of the earliest documents in the New Testament, while other scholars consider it to be a document of the late first century. Those who take a late date tend to consider the author to be an anonymous writer claiming the authority of Jacob.

One reason it is so hard to pin down the author or date is that the letter is very general. In fact, the content is so general that some specialists would not even call this a proper letter. The author does not say where he or she writes from, and the recipients are named as "the twelve tribes of the diaspora." At first glance this phrase would suggest that the document is directed to diaspora Jews (those living outside the Jewish homeland). The phrase, however, should probably be taken metaphorically, referring to the assemblies as connected to Israel in some way.

We do not need to settle the questions of date and authorship in this chapter. For the purpose of charting proto-Christian explanations of poverty, it is enough to recognize that this is a text from the last half of the first century CE that was intended for wide circulation among assemblies. The text probably claims the authority of Jacob, brother of Jesus and leader of the Jerusalem assemblies, whether he is responsible for the content or not. The content focuses on the theme of proper living in ways that echo the prophetic traditions of Israel: one should trust God completely and act accordingly, keeping one's life pure and taking care of those who suffer.

This Letter of Jacob provides a relatively simple explanation for economic inequality. Jacob blames local elites for economic injustice but also criticizes the general population for complicity. In this sense it is reminiscent of the Israelite prophets who denounced the ruling class for their exploitation of the poor and called the people to repentance. I call the model "relatively simple" because it reflects primarily on local conditions. It does not address larger issues of empire or social discourse, locating the problems instead in personal desire and temptation. I elaborate by looking at three sections of the letter.

In Jacob 2:1-6 the author opposes two features of the Roman system of economic inequality: social status based on wealth and manipulation of the judicial system against the poor. With great rhetorical energy, Jacob describes a hypothetical situation in which his readers' assembly *(synagōgē)* is visited by two men. One wears fine clothes and a gold ring, placing him in category 4 or higher on the poverty scale (PS).[7] The other is filthy and desperately poor, a *ptōchos* (PS7). According to Jacob, if the assembly operates according to the normal standards of social status by showing honor to the wealthy and disrespect or neglect to the poor, then they are contradicting the faith of their Lord Jesus Christ.

The author's rhetorical purpose here is to distance his fellow synagogue members from this status system. The author asserts that in the synagogue all should be treated with compassion. The wealth-based social system that characterized normal social interaction was wrong. If the saints take part in this aspect of the dominant social system of their time, they perpetuate inequality and become accomplices in the victimization of the poor.

As the author works to convince his audience to abstain from showing honor based on wealth, he poses a rhetorical question that implies a condemnation of a second characteristic of the Roman imperial system of inequality: "Listen, my beloved brothers and sisters. Has not God chosen the poor in the world to be rich in faith and to be heirs of the kingdom that he has promised to those who love him? But you have dishonored the poor. Is it not the rich who oppress you? Is it not they who drag you into court? Is it not they who blaspheme the excellent name that was invoked over you?" (Jacob 2:5-7).

Along with complicity in the status system, another reason for the inequitable distribution of resources is that the rich manipulate the judicial system for their own gain. The rhetoric of this section follows up the idea of participation in the dominant status system with the assertion that there are two alternative systems available to the audiences, the system of the world and the system of God's kingdom. In the synagogues of God's kingdom the materially poor are rich in faith, and so they should not be dishonored by brothers and sisters who are financially better off. In this context the author then seals the argument with a bit of irony: how can they honor the rich of the world who use the court system to oppress them but dishonor those who are rich in God's kingdom? So, in the course of discussing the gap between society's system of honor and God's system of honor, Jacob cites a second reason for economic inequality: the courts are not for justice but rather for injustice.

A second passage, Jacob 4:13-16, criticizes another aspect of the dominant system—opportunistic economic planning that recognizes neither God's sovereignty nor the frailty of human life.

Come now, you who say, "Today or tomorrow we will go to such and such a town and spend a year there, doing business and making money." Yet you do not even know what tomorrow will bring. What is your life? For you are a mist that appears for a little while and then vanishes. Instead you ought to say, "If the Lord wishes, we will live and do this or that." As it is, you boast in your arrogance; all such boasting is evil.

In this argument, wealthy merchants (PS4 or even PS3) are criticized for conducting economic activities without considering the divine and without a proper understanding of the transience of life. With the rise of capitalism, of course, what Jacob called arrogant and evil became codified as standard economic practice.

In a third passage, Jacob 5:1-6, we see the author's most caustic critique of the Roman system. Here Jacob criticizes a fundamental feature of the Roman system of economic inequality: wealthy landowners (mainly PS1–3, and occasionally PS4) exploiting the laborers who worked their fields. As noted above, land ownership was the primary means by which the elite minority generated and maintained their wealth. Poor laborers, sharecroppers, and slaves did most of the production in exchange for subsistence wages or provisions. Most of the value of their labor was taken by the elite families who paid them low wages, charged them rent, appropriated their crops, and demanded payment of taxes from them.[8] According to Jacob, this economic practice of the rich was equivalent to murder.

Fig. 11.1. The working poor? Roman relief with two slaves turning an olive press. Museo Archaeologico Nazionale, Aquileia, Italy. Photo: Scala / Art Resource, NY.

There are two aspects to Jacob's critique of rich landowners, both of which draw on the traditions of the Israelite prophets. First, Jacob condemns the accumulation of capital using the imagery of corrosion (compare Isaiah 51, especially vv. 8-16). The corrosion building up on their stored gold and silver is a testimony against the wealthy, but also more than evidence. The imagery takes a surprising turn so that the corrosion consumes not simply the riches but also the very flesh of the wealthy ones. Second, Jacob accuses the wealthy of squandering the surplus production that is generated by the unpaid labor of the workers (5:1-3). Because the rich use the surplus for their own satisfaction, the divine warrior of Israel, *kurios sabaōth*, will avenge those who oppress the poor (5:4-6; drawing explicitly on Isaiah 5, Jer. 12:9, and other biblical texts).

Can we locate Jacob's audience on the poverty scale? Since we only have Jacob's letter, we must work with the author's description of the audience rather than with outside evidence about the audience. The author assumes that there are no wealthy landowners in the congregations to which he writes, since 5:1-6 speaks of them as outsiders. The rhetoric of 2:1-6 locates the audiences mostly between the desperate poor (PS7) and the man with extravagant clothes (PS4). The case of the arrogant merchants (PS4 or maybe 3) is harder to evaluate: does the author speak of them as outsiders or insiders (4:14-16)? They are perhaps insiders because they are told that they should have recognized God's prerogative, but sorting out rhetoric from reality is even harder here than elsewhere.[9] In general, however, the author implies that the audiences live near subsistence level (PS5–6), probably with some destitute (PS7) and some with moderate surplus resources (PS4), but no one from the wealthy elites (PS1–3).

In light of this economic injustice, what call to action does Jacob give to his audience? Jacob recommends participation in the community of faith and works. This community should be characterized by at least four features: renunciation of the system of prestige based on wealth; an ethos of mercy for those who suffer (2:13); compassion for those within the assembly (5:13-20); compassion for widows and orphans (the most desperately poor, 1:27); and eschatological patience until the Lord of Hosts, the Divine Judge, acts on their behalf (5:7-11).

To sum up what we know of the Jacobean perspective, then, resources are distributed unequally in society because landowners exploit workers, because the rich manipulate the justice system, because entrepreneurs make arrogant decisions without considering the power of God or the brevity of human existence, and because the rich squander their immoral gains on self-indulgence. In addition, the system survives because those who are exploited participate in the system: they maintain the system of honor for the wealthy few and dishonor for those who are financially disadvantaged.

In terms of its economic analysis, this perspective draws on the conceptual world and public protests of the prophets of Israel. There is a special concern for the poor and disadvantaged and strident criticism of wealthy elites. The context of the prophetic critique, however, has been relocated from the earlier struggle of Israelites with their own ruling elites to the struggle of small urban assemblies with Roman imperialism. This relocation results in less discussion of the responsibilities of the ruler and greater focus on the abuses of those who are rich. Jacob denounces injustice and advises the community to share what resources they have until the Lord of Hosts avenges the cries of the exploited workers.

CONDEMNATION IN REVELATION

In the Revelation of John we encounter a very different kind of literature. Whereas Jacob wrote a general letter to unspecified assemblies throughout the Roman Empire, John wrote an apocalypse to seven specific assemblies in one province of the Roman Empire. Since the text is an apocalypse, it is a visionary text with spectacular imagery. It makes its case not so much through argumentation as through symbols. The symbols are steeped in the traditions of Israel but the author seldom quotes those traditions. Instead, John narrates visions that mix elements of biblical traditions with clear allusions to the sociohistorical settings of the assemblies. The result is an apocalypse that portrays the Roman Empire as Satan's tool, opposed to the God of Israel and destined for destruction.

The assemblies to whom John wrote were all located in large cities in the Roman province of Asia (the western section of modern Turkey). Scholars are currently debating the extent to which these seven assemblies agreed with John about the dangers of participation in Roman imperial society.

Fig. 11.2. In the Roman economy, tremendous wealth was produced by the labor of millions—and controlled by a much smaller elite. Grain mills in the bakery of Popidius Priscus. Pompeii. Photo: Erich Lessing / Art Resource, NY.

The specialists mostly agree, however, that John circulated his Revelation in the late first century CE, after the fall of Jerusalem in 70 and probably before the year 100.

In Revelation we encounter a more dramatic explanation of the causes of poverty. It moves beyond the localized perspective of the Letter of Jacob, attempting an overview of international commerce and politics in the idiom of apocalyptic symbolism. Revelation portrays local oppression as part of a larger system: the Roman Empire authorizes local aristocracies to exploit commercial interactions and to dominate their regions. This is a much broader analysis than the one found in the Letter of Jacob. Jacob's prophetic model described wealthy individuals exploiting their own laborers. Revelation, however, ties that local exploitation into international systems of oppression.

This broader condemnation is seen especially in Revelation 13. In this chapter, the regional elite (mostly PS2-3 but also some members who are PS1) is portrayed with apocalyptic symbolism as the beast from the earth (Rev. 13:11-18).[10] This beast—the wealthy elite minority that controlled governmental and religious institutions—is presented as the entity that enforces economic injustice, for no one can engage in commercial activity without its stamp of approval on the hand and head. In addition, this beast from the earth also forces everyone to worship the Empire (portrayed as the beast from the sea). Thus, it defines the character of dominant society, specifically linking it to illicit worship and Roman economics. The aristocracy ensures the participation of the masses through deception (13:14) and through brute force (13:16-17).

Revelation 13 does not limit itself simply to a condemnation of these local oppressors. The success of the regional and local aristocracy is made possible by Roman imperial domination, portrayed in this chapter as a blasphemous, seven-headed, ten-horned monster that arises from the sea to conquer the earth (Rev. 13:1-4). The regional and local aristocracy (mostly PS2–3) receives its authority from the imperial elite (mostly PS1), whose control is based on its unprecedented brute force and its blasphemous arrogance. No one can oppose it, and none can successfully wage war against it. Even the saints of God are defeated. The regional and local elites are thus portrayed as a privileged class within the broader Roman system of inequality.

But John goes further still. The Seer begins Revelation 13 by noting that the beast from the sea—the Roman Empire—receives its authority directly from Satan (13:2). With this final piece in place the vision presents us with a wide-ranging and remarkably cynical appraisal of Roman politics and economy: Satan empowers the Empire, the Empire authorizes local aristocracies to manipulate the economy, and everyone—"both small and great, both rich and poor, both free and slave" (13:16)—will comply or be killed.

Revelation supplements this critique of the dominant discourse with a trenchant description of international commerce. In Revelation 17 Roman imperial power appears once again in a more complicated apocalyptic image—a seven-headed, ten-horned beast bearing the great prostitute Babylon, who is drunk on the blood of the saints. John learns from an angel that the image represents the imperial center Rome (17:9, 18).

Then in Revelation 18 the author takes the reader through a series of proclamations and laments that portray how international commerce and politics figure into the Roman system of inequality. Four sets of players are mentioned: Babylon the queen (mostly PS1), the kings of the earth (PS1–2), merchants and shippers (considered together here; PS2–3), and the general population ("the peoples of the earth"; mostly PS4–7). Babylon the queen is the central figure in the system, manipulating each of the other figures in different ways. Her relationship with the kings of the earth is called prostitution (*porneia*, 18:9), for theirs is a game of power and payment. With the merchants and shippers, however, the issue is only payment. When the queen is destroyed, their laments are only for the lost profits (18:16-19). According to the Seer, the general population is also complicit in this system of commercial and political exploitation, but their motives are different. They were drunk on the queen's wine (18:3), deceived by her potions and spells (18:23).

The Seer's call to action is also broader than that of Jacob. While Jacob urged his audience not to reproduce society's wealth-based system of honors,

John calls for a complete break with dominant society. Revelation advocates a total withdrawal from the machinations of Empire in the interests of purity until the Lamb intervenes in history. In the words of the angel of Revelation 18, "Come out of her, my people, so that you do not take part in her sins, and so that you do not share in her plagues" (18:4). In the words of the risen Christ, "only hold fast to what you have until I come" (2:25). John's denunciations of injustice are also more extreme, with attacks on the entire imperial system (government, economy, religion, and enforcement) and threats of divine eternal judgment.

The Seer's model for understanding economic inequality, then, is that Satan controls this world through Empire. The Empire suppresses all opposition to its hegemony. This domination is a form of blasphemy because the emperor claims to be the king of kings, the ruler of history, the lord of the destinies of all peoples. According to the apocalyptic model, alliances between kings and rulers provide the political context for the economic exploitation of the people. The regional and local aristocracies implement the exploitation and ensure that commerce benefits the wealthy. These alliances allow the wealthy elites to move goods and capital around the Empire to the place where it will most benefit the oppressors. This system would collapse without the participation of the people, who are deceived or awed or intimidated into compliance. John's admonition to the people is that they remove themselves from this system even if it requires martyrdom, for their blood will be avenged by God in the end.

CHARITY IN ACTS

Our third text represents yet another form of literature. We have already examined a general letter and an apocalypse, but in Acts we encounter a theological form of historical writing. The author first composed the Gospel of Luke and then followed it with a second volume that we now know as the Acts of the Apostles. Scholars conclude that Acts was written in either the late first century or the early second century CE.

All history writing is done with certain goals in mind. In the case of Acts, the author used travel narratives and the sequence of events to portray the early decades of the assemblies as a trajectory away from the movement's Jewish roots. The narrative starts in Jerusalem but moves out into Judea, then Samaria, and finally to Rome. Jews tend to oppose the assemblies, whether in the homeland or in the diaspora. Gentiles tend to be more receptive to the gospel, and they need not conform to the requirements of Torah (circumcision, Sabbath observance, and so forth). Thus, as the nar-

rative moves from the periphery of the Empire to the imperial capital, the
author moves the readers away from Judaism and toward imperial culture.

With the Acts of the Apostles we encounter an important problem: the
first known attempt to write a history of the first-century assemblies is
not a people's history. It focuses on leaders of the movement and is silent
on the issue of economic injustice. Rather than deal with the root causes of
inequality, the author restricts economic redistribution among believers to
an idealized past in Palestine and focuses his economic policy on alms and
charity rather than on injustice. Four observations support this conclusion.[11]

First, the author of Acts does not criticize any facets of the Roman
system of inequality and makes no attempt to explain the huge gap between
the wealthy imperial elites and everyone else. Rather than call attention to
exploitation as Jacob and John do, the author of Acts presents Roman military officers—the enforcers of imperialism—as sympathetic characters,
and he portrays Roman governors mostly as disinterested protectors of the
fledgling assemblies.

Second, the author of Acts organizes his narrative to avoid the topic of
economic injustice. Even though the author is aware of poverty in assemblies and knows of assemblies that have implemented economic redistribution, he portrays systematic economic sharing as a quaint artifact of an
idealized past (Acts 2:42-45; 4:32-37). Economic redistribution is limited in
time and space to the original Jerusalem assemblies. Since Acts was written
after the Roman destruction of Jerusalem, the effect is to present redistribution of goods as restricted to an earlier period of history that has ended.

The author's effort to suppress criticism of economic inequality can be
seen especially in three important examples in the narrative. One example
is the renunciation of private property in the early Jerusalem assemblies
(Acts 2:42-45; 4:32-37). The author's summaries of this practice are idealized rather than pragmatic, and he concludes discussion of the practice
with a story that undercuts the utopian ethos: two saints—Ananias and
Sapphira—abuse the practice and are struck dead (5:1-11) in an extreme
"one strike and you're out" sentencing policy. A second example is the care
for widows in the Jerusalem assemblies (6:1-7), which heightens the author's
subtle criticism of communal property. The author records complaints that
arose within the assemblies that blamed economic inequality inside the
group on ethnic or cultural favoritism. Again, the author does not deal with
the root causes but treats it as an administrative problem, solved by the
appointment of more administrators.

The third example of the author's attempt to restrict references to economic inequality in the narrative is more drastic: the author suppresses
the story of Paul's collection for the destitute in the Jerusalem assemblies.

While some argue that the author did not know about Paul's collection, it seems clear that Paul's final trip to Jerusalem in Acts 20–26 reflects an account of the ill-fated attempt to deliver the collection. Even though the author attempts to recast the trip as an effort to end Paul's mission journey in Jerusalem on Pentecost, the original purpose of the journey (delivery of the collection to Jerusalem) shows through the cracks: the use of some of the money to pay a vow (21:24) and a speech that mentions Paul's gift (24:17).[12]

His own letters, however, show that Paul himself undertook the collection as a crucial part of his ministry. The collection was a dramatic initiative by Paul, designed to accomplish several goals: to provide for the needy saints in Jerusalem, to build bridges between Jewish and Gentile saints, and to give tangible expression to his proclamation of the gospel (Rom. 15:25-27; 2 Cor. 9:13). Instead of relying on the exploitative vertical flow of resources that characterized the imperial system, Paul's gospel called for a network of horizontal sharing among the Mediterranean assemblies (2 Cor. 8:13-15). This collection entailed a renunciation of the ideals of patronage, in which large occasional benefactions would come from a patron whose wealth was built on the daily exploitation of the masses. The collection, rather, would be built with many gifts from many moderately poor saints in order to provide for brothers and sisters who were desperately poor (1 Cor. 16:1-4; 2 Cor. 8:10-12).

In spite of the collection's importance for Paul, the author of Acts suppressed it, and the reason for the suppression is my third observation about the economic model proposed by Acts: the author presents personal gifts and household hospitality (rather than redistribution) as the normal method of economic sharing for the assemblies after the early period.[13] As the narrative moves out of Jerusalem the economic references begin to shift. In chapter 8 the Samaritan magician Simon Magus wants to dispense the Holy Spirit and offers a goodly sum for the local franchise. Peter rebukes him for trying to commodify the free gift of the Spirit, but there is no hint of communal property or redistribution as the proper alternative. In chapter 9 Peter goes down to the coast and raises Tabitha from the dead; she is known for her assistance to widows. Her deeds are presented as acts of charity, not as assembly policy. In chapter 10 Peter goes up the coast to Caesarea, where he converts Cornelius the Gentile centurion. Cornelius is described as a man whose piety is manifested in the giving of alms (10:4, 31). His household is saved, but the narrative does not record any further economic developments.

Once the narrative moves beyond Judea and Samaria, the shift from community property to faith-based initiatives is almost complete.[14] Beyond

Palestine, the normal model for assemblies is hospitality and charity. Lydia offers hospitality for Paul and his companions in Philippi (Acts 16), Jason provides housing in Thessalonica (17:7-8), and so on.[15] Thus, the unfolding of the narrative suggests that the early period of systematic redistribution in Jerusalem is over; for the long haul, the standard economic practices will be individual charity and household hospitality.

This policy of the author may be related to my fourth observation: the author of Acts portrays the assemblies as much wealthier than the portrait gleaned from Paul's undisputed letters. The following chart (fig. 11.3) constructs an economic profile of Paul's assemblies based on references to economic resources in his undisputed letters.[16] The numbers in the left column come from the poverty scale outlined earlier.[17]

The results can be summarized as follows. In Paul's undisputed letters only two people can certainly be categorized in the "moderate surplus resources" category (PS4), and one of them (Chloe) was perhaps not a

*Fig. 11.3: Economic Profile of Paul's Assemblies
Based on the Undisputed Letters*

PS	Name	Reference	Location
[4]	[Chloe?][18]	1 Cor. 1:11	Corinth
4	Gaius	Rom. 16:23	Corinth
4–5	Erastus	Rom. 16:23	Corinth
4–5	Philemon	Philemon 4–22	Colossae?
4–5	Phoebe	Rom. 16:1-2	Cenchraea, Rome
4–5	Aquila	Rom. 16:3-5	Rome (or Ephesus?)
4–5	Prisca	Rom. 16:3-5	Rome (or Ephesus?)
5	Chloe's people	1 Cor. 1:11	Ephesus
5–6	Stephanas	1 Cor. 16:17-18	Ephesus
5–6	The household of Stephanas	1 Cor. 16:15-16	Corinth
5–6	(Many) saints in Corinth	1 Cor. 16:1-2	Corinth
5–6	Churches in Galatia	1 Cor. 16:1-2	Galatia
5–7	(Many) brothers (and sisters)	1 Thess. 4:11	Thessalonica
6	(Many) saints in Corinth	2 Cor. 8:12-15	Corinth
6	The assemblies of Macedonia	2 Cor. 8:1-6	Macedonia
6	Paul	2 Cor. 11:1-21	Corinth
6	Paul	1 Thess. 2:1-12	Thessalonica
6	Paul	Phil. 4:12-13	Rome? Ephesus? Caesarea?
6–7	Onesimus	Philemon 10–19	Ephesus? Rome?
6–7	Those who do not have food for the Lord's Supper	1 Cor. 11:22	Corinth
7	Paul	Phil. 2:25-30	Rome? Ephesus? Caesarea?

Fig. 11.4: Economic Profile of Paul's Assemblies Based on Acts of the Apostles

PS	Name	Reference	Location
[1]	[Proconsul Sergius Paulus?][19]	13:6-12	Paphos, Cyprus
2–3	Dionysios the Areopagite	17:34	Athens
2–3	Not a few of the Greek men of high standing	17:12	Beroea
2–3	Not a few of the Greek women of high standing	17:12	Beroea
2–3	Women of high standing (in the city)	17:4	Thessalonica
4	Crispus	18:8	Corinth
4?	(Jailer, unnamed)	18:22-36	Philippi
4?	Lydia	16:13-15	Philippi
4	Titius Justus	18:7	Corinth
4–5	Jason	17:5-9	Thessalonica
5–6	Paul	18:3-8; 20:34	Corinth; Ephesus

participant in the assemblies. Another five individuals were either above subsistence level or had moderate surplus resources. Beyond that, we have three references to individuals (including Paul) and eight references to groups or assemblies that were near subsistence level or below. According to Paul's undisputed letters, then, the overwhelming majority of saints in Paul's assemblies were poor, very poor, or desperately poor (PS5–7).

We can contrast this with an economic profile constructed from the references in Acts to Paul's assemblies.[20]

The economic profile based on Acts is radically different from the one based on Paul's letters. According to Acts, it is possible that Paul was the only believer near the subsistence level! Everyone else about whom we are given some economic information in the narrative could be in the top 10 percent of the poverty scale (PS1–4). The contrast is even clearer if we note that while there are no references in Paul's undisputed letters to any members from the super-wealthy elites (PS1–3), in Acts there are members of the elites at least in Thessalonica, Beroea, and Athens, and perhaps on Cyprus as well. The figure of Paul himself is interesting in this regard. In both profiles he is listed at the bottom of the poverty scale, and in the undisputed letters Paul records no positive contact with any of the super-wealthy elites; rather, Paul records that the elites beat him and threw him in prison. In Acts, however, Paul is portrayed as interacting easily with people in the top 1 percent of the poverty scale: Sergius Paulus, Asiarchs in Ephesus, the unnamed chiliarch who arrests Paul in Jerusalem, King Agrippa II, the procurator Felix, his wife, Drusilla (who was also a sister of Agrippa II), Festus (procurator after Felix), the chiliarch Lysias, and

Bernice (sister of Drusilla, sister and consort of Agrippa II, later consort of Titus until he became emperor). Whether these interactions took place in this manner is beside the point; the crucial observation is that the author of Acts portrays Paul not simply as a poor man but as a man of the highest social skills who commands respect from some of the wealthiest and most powerful Roman imperialists.

The model that informs Acts is clear. There is no explanation of unequal distribution of goods, no critique of systemic causes of poverty, no denunciation of exploitation. The text recognizes that the earliest assemblies in Jerusalem experimented in communal property but gives no explanation why they did this. Instead, the author restricts such efforts in time (the early years of the movement) and in space (in Jerusalem). Beyond that earliest period, the text recognizes some cases of economic need, but these can be handled through hospitality and charity. In contrast to the Letter of Jacob and the Apocalypse of John, this text envisions that the earliest assemblies included some of the wealthiest inhabitants of the Empire.

WEALTH AS BLESSING IN *THE SHEPHERD OF HERMAS*

The Shepherd of Hermas is an apocalypse, but it has some literary features that distinguish it from the Revelation of John. *Hermas* is much longer than Revelation, and the character of the visions is also quite different. While Revelation is full of fantastic apocalyptic symbols, *Hermas* tends to report more sedate visions that function as allegories. Revelation rarely explains its symbols, but in *Hermas* the meanings of the visions are almost always stated clearly. In contrast to Revelation, in which the visions tend to deal with politics, religion, and economy, the visionary allegories in *Hermas* often deal with issues of theology and personal morality.

The Shepherd of Hermas was probably written a few decades later than the other three texts under consideration. The visions in the text appear to come from a single author during the first half of the second century CE, with the final form of the text taking shape by the mid-second century. Moreover, the text comes from the city of Rome, so it is also distinct in its provenance.[21] As I mentioned above, in the course of this chapter we are dealing with several different decades and locations in the first century of the Christian movement, and we should not think of these four texts as points along one line of development. In some ways *The Shepherd of Hermas* is similar to the Acts of Apostles on economic questions. Neither of these two texts attempts a systematic analysis of the causes of poverty; economic inequality is simply a fact. This absence of analysis is made possible by a lack of attention to the machinations of imperial power. Both texts occasionally allude to imperial pressure on the assemblies, with *Hermas* mentioning persecutions (*Vision* 3.6.5–7) and Acts recording various trials. Acts, however, presents most imperial officials in a positive light, while Hermas is silent about officials.

We saw also that Acts presents a positive view of wealthy believers in the assemblies. In this regard *Hermas* goes further by describing wealth as a divine gift. Even though *Hermas* does not explain the origins of poverty, wealth is said to come from God (*Similitude* 1.9; 2.10; *Mandate* 2.4-5). The gift of wealth is not seen as a pure blessing, however, and we need to be aware of the complexity of the theme in *Hermas*. Wealth can also bring difficulties such as renunciation of the faith (*Similitude* 1:4–5), distraction leading to spiritual weakness (*Similitude* 2.5; *Mandate* 10.1.4), and temptation to avoid persecution (*Vision* 3.6.5–7). Thus wealth is an ambiguous blessing according to *Hermas* and must be properly used.[22]

Some of these themes can be seen in the extended parable and discussion known as *Similitude* 1. In this section a heavenly messenger who looks like a shepherd tells Hermas a parable. In the parable the life of a believer in the world is compared to the life of a slave of God who lives in a foreign city. In the foreign city (life in this world) the slave (a believer) should not rely on possessions or wealth, for the slave could be expelled at any time, and these goods would be left behind. A proper course of action is a frugal self-sufficiency (*autarkeia*). This simple lifestyle allows one to use the remaining foreign wealth to help widows and orphans; in the logic of the parable this action is equivalent to buying goods in one's native city (heaven) that cannot be confiscated.

Fig. 11.3. People at work: a shoemaker. Relief on a sarcophagus. Museo Nazionale Romano (Terme di Diocleziano), Rome. Photo: Erich Lessing / Art Resource, NY.

> Instead of fields, then, purchase souls that have been afflicted, insofar as you can, and take care of widows and orphans and do not neglect them; spend your wealth and all your furnishings for such fields and houses as you have received from God. For this is why the Master made you rich, that you may carry out these ministries for him. It is much better to purchase the fields, goods, and houses you find in your own city when you return to it. This kind of extravagance is good and makes one glad; it has no grief or fear, but joy instead. And so, do not participate in the extravagance sought by outsiders; for it is of no profit for you who are slaves of God. (*Similitude* 1:8-10)

The interpretation of the parable repeats the idea that wealth comes from God but also indicates that wealth can lead one into tendentious and ultimately fruitless endeavors because wealth is transient, like life itself. Note also that the city is not described as an evil location, as would be the case in John's Revelation. Urban life is not necessarily bad, according to Hermas, only foreign and temporary. The implied audience of the parable is clearly those in the assemblies who have disposable resources, the rich (probably PS4 or higher in this case), and not widows and orphans (PS7). In the instructions for these rich folks, the shepherd indicates that charity is the proper use of wealth. God has given them wealth precisely for this reason.

Similitude 2 works out in more detail the proper use of wealth and its role in the life of the assemblies. *Similitude* 2 takes the agricultural practice of using young elm trees to support grapevines and compares this to relations of rich and poor in the assemblies. According to the shepherd's interpretation, the elm tree (symbolizing the rich) only appears to be fruitless. If the elm supports the vine (the poor), the vine is able to grow fruit because it is off the ground and it is able to draw moisture from the elm in times of drought.[23] "And so, when the vine attaches to the elm, it bears fruit both of itself and because of the elm. And so you see that the elm also gives much fruit—no less than the vine, but rather more" (*Similitude* 2:3b–4a). This model, then, is quite at odds with Revelation and James, which portrayed the wealthy as oppressors, and it is more extreme than Acts, which states that the wealthy also have a place in the assemblies. Here the wealthy are credited with producing more fruit, even though the poor actually do all the production.

The call to action in *Hermas* is significantly different from that of Acts. Both texts call for charity and not for justice. The difference is that while Acts advocates hospitality and charity in the service of community, charity in *Hermas* is portrayed as an individual act that helps the poor in material terms and helps the rich at the final judgment. For example, *Vision* 3.9.2–6 discusses the way in which some in the assemblies are injured by overeating (PS4 or higher), and some are injured by not eating enough (PS6–7). The advice given to the wealthy is that they should practice moderation and share, thus gaining a place in heaven.

Fig. 11.4. People at work: an artisan. Roman pavement mosaic. Piazzale delle Corporazioni, Ostia, Italy. Photo: SEF / Art Resource, NY.

This perspective that focuses on the rich and marginalizes the poor is seen throughout the text's admonitions. The advice in *Similitude* 5.3 tells the wealthy who are fasting to give the money they save on groceries to the poor, but it says nothing about those for whom fasting is a daily economic necessity. The advice in *Mandate* 2.4–6 absolves the wealthy of trying to decide whether the poor truly deserve help and places the burden on those who receive the charity. This is one of the only places in the text where the poor are addressed directly; the reason is that the rich have suspicions about whether the poor are opportunists who live off welfare.[24]

Thus, in *Hermas* we find an explanation of poverty that is useful for a people's history as an example of a perspective that disenfranchises the poor. As a model for action, it holds little promise. Poverty and wealth are not simply recognized as facts of social life; they are rationalized as important components of the life of the assembly. *Hermas* suggests that the poor need wealthy people in order to meet their daily needs for material survival and that the rich need the poor so that they have objects for charity that will eventually get the rich into heaven. It is a codependent model that is individualistic and ultimately antithetical to the goal of ending economic inequality.

A CONTINUUM OF PERSPECTIVES AND ACTIONS

This paper deals with a phenomenon found in all human societies: the economic deprivation of many to the advantage of a wealthy few. Every society promotes the unequal distribution of resources and provides justifications for economic inequality. And always, somewhere in the populace, there is criticism of economic exploitation. The critiques are often suppressed by the official histories and hidden from view in public culture, but they exist. Sometimes the critiques are related to religious considerations, and other times they are not. A people's history of Christianity must be attentive to the reconstruction of these perspectives and arguments.

An examination of these four particular proto-Christian texts evokes four early responses by the saints to economic inequality. In terms of their evaluations of the origins of poverty, the responses can be placed along a continuum with Revelation at one extreme and the Shepherd of Hermas at the other. At one extreme, Revelation argues that poverty is the result of imperialism and international exploitation and that wealth is the accumulation of ill-gotten gains. Emperors, kings, commercial institutions, and shippers are all engaged in a network of exploitation that deceives and conquers the world. At the other end, *Hermas* ignores the causes of poverty, focusing instead on how people should act given the fact of economic inequity. For *Hermas*, wealth comes not from injustice but from God. In between these two extremes are Jacob and Acts. Jacob is closer to Revelation in its condemnation of injustice, but its perspectives are more localized and its analysis less systematic. Acts is closer to *Hermas* in that the Roman imperial system of inequality is not critiqued and wealth is considered mostly benign.

If we create another continuum to organize the actions proposed by these texts, the order of texts looks much the same. At one extreme, Revelation argues for complete separation from imperial society in the interests of faithfulness and purity, for all commercial activity requires the mark of the beast. Jacob is the text closest to Revelation because it focuses on the renunciation of certain aspects of the imperial system, such as status based on wealth, manipulation of judicial institutions, secular commercial planning, and the exploitation of workers by landowners. When we consider the actions advocated by Acts of the Apostles, we have crossed over to the other side of the continuum. Rather than withdrawal, Acts seeks a place for the assemblies in the Roman world. Some members of the assemblies are described as very wealthy and are called to practice charity in order to cover needs in the community. *Hermas* is also on this side of the continuum but at the far end, for the text calls for charity as a personalized endeavor. Alms are described not as a community endeavor but rather as a personal good deed for which the giver will be rewarded in the afterlife.

These four models for understanding poverty and for acting are not foreign to us today. They have all played a role in the official histories of Christianity, and they have been a part of the people's histories of Christianity as well. Church history is full of narratives of radical resistance to economic exploitation similar to the position of Revelation, narratives of practical compassion exercised in spite of exploitation similar to the position of Jacob, narratives of accommodation to exploitation as in Acts, and narratives of Christian benefactors who use a portion of their wealth to help alleviate individual cases of misery and crisis that reflect the advice in *The Shepherd of Hermas.*

But what about a people's future of Christianity? Which models might guide us into the coming decades? Which models might help us shape a more equitable future, in which unpaid labor and unquenched hunger are found only in the history books? Should the pious poor denounce the wealthy (Revelation), tolerate the wealthy (Jacob), embrace the wealthy (Acts), or become dependent on the wealthy *(Hermas)*? Should the wealthy seek the purity of divestment (Revelation), should they attempt to end exploitation (Jacob), should they support the community of faith with charity and hospitality (Acts), or should they give alms to earn personal salvation *(Hermas)*? Such questions cannot entirely be answered with paper and ink. They can only be fully answered with flesh and blood.

FOR FURTHER READING

Bauckham, Richard. *James: Wisdom of James, Disciple of Jesus the Sage.* New York: Routledge, 1999.

CARE. Web site: http://www.careusa.org.

Ehrman, Bart D., trans. "The Shepherd of Hermas." In *The Apostolic Fathers,* vol. 2, 162–473. LCL. Cambridge: Harvard University Press, 2003.

Garnsey, Peter, and Richard Saller. *The Roman Empire: Economy, Society, and Culture.* Berkeley: University of California Press, 1987.

Howard-Brook, Wes, and Anthony Gwyther. *Unveiling Empire: Reading Revelation Then and Now.* Maryknoll, N.Y.: Orbis, 1999.

Maier, Harry O. *Apocalypse Recalled: The Book of Revelation after Christendom.* Minneapolis: Fortress, 2002.

Osiek, Carolyn. *Shepherd of Hermas: A Commentary.* Hermeneia. Minneapolis: Fortress, 1999.

Pleket, Henri Willy. "Wirtschaft." In Friedrich Vittinghoff, ed., *Europäische Wirtschafts- und Sozialgeschichte in der römischen Kaiserzeit,* 25–160. Handbuch der europäischen Wirtschafts- und Sozialgeschichte, vol. 1. Stuttgart: Klett-Cotta, 1990.

Tamez, Elsa. *The Scandalous Message of James: Faith without Works Is Dead.* Rev. ed. New York: Crossroad, 2002.

PROPHETS, PROPHETIC MOVEMENTS, AND THE VOICES OF WOMEN

BARBARA R. ROSSING

CHAPTER TWELVE

Spirit possession, prophetic oracles, and prophetic movements were prominent and widespread phenomena in the various movements of Christ-believers. The early communities esteemed prophets and their prophecies highly, believing them to be the continuing voice of God or of their exalted Lord to guide them in their struggles. In the Book of Acts, for example, the apostle Peter declared the community's experience at Pentecost to be the manifestation of the living presence of God's Spirit. The apostle Paul esteemed prophecy among the most revered gifts of the Spirit (1 Corinthians 12), and the Apocalypse, or Book of Revelation, calls the voice of prophecy "the spirit of Jesus" (Rev. 19:10).

Prophecy is an important aspect of the study of early movements of Christ-believers in three principal respects. First, prophecy was a prominent form taken by popular resistance to the Roman imperial order. The Roman Empire, of course, had its own prophets who helped legitimate the consolidation of imperial power.[1] Most of the prophecy among communities of Christ-believers, however, belonged among the widespread populist strand of anti-imperial critique of institutionalized injustice. In fact, in this regard, many manifestations of prophecy in early Christ-believers parallel the outbursts of various forms of prophecy among recently conquered peoples in the Americas and Africa.[2]

Second, prophecy represented a charismatic model of leadership and authority within the early Jesus movements and communities of Christ-believers. Prophets ultimately lost out to the threefold offices of deacon, presbyter, and bishop in the process of the institutionalization of leadership. But the move toward consolidation of episcopal authority in the second century was not without opposition. At the same time that Bishop Ignatius was seeking to consolidate his own episcopal authority in the assemblies of western Asia Minor and Rome, for example, prophets continued as leaders in other communities. Prophecy was one of the principal alternatives to the emerging hierarchical authority in nascent Christianity.

Third, prophecy provided perhaps the most prominent mode in which women exercised leadership, from the outset of the movements and continuing well into the second century. Numerous women prophets appear in our sources. The four daughters of Philip gave prophetic leadership to the community in Caesarea (Acts 21:9) and later in Hierapolis. Many if not most of the prophets in the Corinthian assembly were women (1 Corinthians 12–14). The woman labeled "Jezebel" served as a prophetic leader in the assembly in Thyatira (in western Asia Minor; Rev. 2:20). That women continued in their roles as prophets for several generations is evident in the appearance of Ammia of Philadelphia and the leaders of the New Prophecy movement, Maximilla, Priscilla, and Quintilla.[3] Mary Magdalene was revered by some communities as the model of prophetic authority. And in general the prophetic speech of women was highly valued and contributed significantly to emerging Christian teaching and practice.

Fig. 12.1. Women's religious experience was often regarded with suspicion in the writings of elite males-when it was acknowledged at all. Young woman making an offering, Herculaneum, Italy. Museo Archeologico Nazionale, Naples. Photo: Erich Lessing / Art Resource, NY.

Prophecy in the communities of Christ-believers was largely a community phenomenon that emerged in the gatherings of the assemblies. In New Testament and related literature, the word for prophets generally occurs in the plural. Prophets and their prophecy, however, varied in both form and function.[4] Some received intelligible messages as "the word of the Lord" to deliver to their communities. In addressing the Thessalonians' concern about those who had died before the return of the Lord, the apostle Paul delivered a prophetic message of reassurance that he "declared by the word of the Lord" (1 Thess. 4:13-18). In some cases the prophecy was understood as a "revelation" *(apokalypsis)* received in a transcendent ecstatic experience of being transposed into the heavens (Revelation 1; see also 2 Cor. 12:1-5). Others focused mainly on ecstatic experiences themselves, experiences that sometimes involved unintelligible speech *(glōssa,* 1 Corinthians 14). Some strands emphasized the formation and solidarity of the assemblies as alternative communities in the midst of the Roman imperial order. Others emphasized personal spiritual transcendence. The relationship of these strands is difficult to reconstruct. Prophecy may have offered an avenue for popular resistance both against Rome and against nascent Christian institutional and patriarchal leadership. But if we investigate how these forces interact, we find at least one ironic phenomenon: some of the first-century prophetic voices viewed as the most anti-imperial in resisting accommodation to the Roman imperial order (for example, the apostle Paul, John of Patmos) were later invoked in efforts to silence women prophets and prophetic leaders.

Prophecy also became a source of confusion and conflict. The prophets themselves and their communities did not always agree about the voice of prophecy or about who had the prophetic authority to mediate God's word to new situations. How were communities to adjudicate competing claims to prophetic authority and inspiration? What was the role of prophetic experiences and prophets in the cultivation and regulation of community life? Communities differed over matters such as the interpretation of ecstatic speech, the role of the spirit (or Paraclete of John's Gospel), the role of women, the criteria for authentic prophecy, and the necessity of martyrdom and anti-imperial witness against Rome.

The very plethora of prophecy and prophets posed particular problems of authenticity. In the *Shepherd of Hermas,* a document specially concerned with prophets located in Rome in the late first century, the principal criterion of authenticity was their behavior vis-à-vis the rest of the community, including requests for money:

> "How, sir," I said, "is anyone supposed to know which of them is a prophet and which a false prophet?" "Listen," he said, "about both of the prophets, and what I am about to tell you is how you will discern the prophet from the false prophet. You can tell the one who has the spirit of God by the way of life.... The person who pretends to have a spirit exalts oneself and wants to take precedence ... and accepts payment for prophecy." (Hermas, *Mandate* 11.7–12)[5]

Many prophets and apostles became itinerants traveling from community to community. Given the extreme poverty of most participants in the local assemblies, however, their expectation of economic support posed a burden to the locals' subsistence. The late-first-century handbook called *The Teachings of the Twelve Apostles,* or *Didache,* offered guidance to communities in Syria on how to evaluate such itinerant prophets: "Let every apostle who comes to you be received as the Lord. He shall stay only one day, or, if need be, another day too. If he stays three days, he is a false prophet. When the apostle leaves, let him receive nothing but enough bread to see him through until he finds lodging. If he asks for money, he is a false prophet" (*Didache* 11.4–6). Yet despite such warnings about false prophets and their requests for money, communities held both itinerant and resident community prophets in high esteem. A newly arrived prophet who desires to remain with the community is to be welcomed as the equivalent of high priests: "Every true prophet who wants to settle in with you deserves his food.... So when you take any firstfruits of what is produced by the winepress and the threshing floor, by cows and by sheep, you shall give the firstfruits to the prophets, for they are your high priests. If you do not have a prophet, then give it to the poor" (*Didache* 13.3–4).

In the sections below we will examine some of the different forms and functions of prophecy and the competing claims to the prophetic spirit and leadership in the early communities of Christ-believers. We will pay particular attention to the role of prophets in relation both to the Roman imperial order and to the emerging institutionalization of leadership in nascent Christianity. We will look specifically at the role of polemics against women prophets in prophetic debates and how these relate to competing views of how Christ-believers should relate to the Empire. Finally, we can look specifically into the suppression of the movement known as New Prophecy, a movement noteworthy for its highly visible women leaders. It was this second-century movement that finally led the nascent orthodox church to attempt to rein in prophecy.

ISRAELITE PROPHETIC TRADITIONS OF RESISTANCE

The earliest Jesus movements emerged from Israelite culture in Galilee and Judea, and from there other movements spread to Syria, Egypt, Asia Minor, Greece, and Rome and across the Empire. The standard view in the elite scribal circles of Jerusalem was that prophecy had ceased after Haggai, Zechariah, and Malachi—and would be revived only at the time of history's fulfillment (1 Macc. 9:27; Josephus, *Against Apion* 1.37–41; *t. Sota* 13.2). Yet, as the Judean historian Josephus tells us, numerous prophetic figures were active among the people right around the time of Jesus. Richard Horsley suggests that those prophets, moreover, were of two distinctively Israelite forms, both deeply rooted in Israelite tradition.[6] Much of the prophecy in the early Jesus movements and communities of Christ-believers can be viewed as continuations of these Israelite forms of prophecy.

Best known from the prophetic books of the Hebrew Bible are oracular prophets. They received "the word of the Lord" addressed to a particular situation and declared it to the people, to rulers and their officers, or to all of these groups. A few passages in the Hebrew Bible provide windows onto the way these prophets received the oracles they then declared. They were caught up, in an ecstatic experience, into the divine heavenly court, where they overheard what God was saying with regard to a particular historical circumstance and felt compelled to proclaim "the word of the Lord" to the rulers or the people or both. In the most elaborate descriptions of such ecstatic experiences, the prophet Micaiah ben Imlah (a contemporary of Elijah in northern Israel; 1 Kings 22) and the prophet who produced Isaiah 40–55 claim that they heard God's and other voices in the heavenly court, even that they had seen the proceedings of the divine council. Most of the fragments collected in books such as Amos, Hosea, Micah, the early chapters of Isaiah, and Jeremiah are from oracles of judgment against the rulers and their representatives for their oppressive practices against the people. In circumstances of distress for the people, on the other hand, some prophets declared oracles of comfort or deliverance.

Judean and Galilean peasants apparently paid no attention to the official view that prophecy had ceased. Since popular prophets were written up in the history books only when they made serious trouble for the literate ruling elite, we know of only a handful of them. Prophets who pronounced oracles of deliverance appeared, not surprisingly, during the widespread revolt against the Roman and Jerusalem rulers in 66–70 CE, particularly when the Roman armies pressed their brutal reconquest (Josephus, *War* 6.286–87, 290–95). Particularly interesting is the prophet of doom, Jesus son of Hananiah, a "crude peasant" who repeatedly pronounced God's judgment in the Temple courtyard and the alleyways of Jerusalem during the last four years before the great revolt:

> A voice from the east, a voice from the west,
> a voice from the four winds.
> A voice against Jerusalem and the temple,
> A voice against the bridegrooms and brides,
> A voice against the whole people.
> (*War* 6.300–309)

The other principal type of Israelite prophet, besides delivering oracles, led movements of resistance or liberation. Moses' leading the exodus of Israel from bondage under the Egyptian Pharaoh provided the prototype. The long line of prophets leading movements continued with Joshua, remembered most for the fantastic battle of Jericho, and the "judges" or "liberators" *(shophetim)* such as Deborah, who was remembered explicitly as a "prophet" (Judg. 4:4-5). Having received "the word of the Lord" that deliverance was at hand, they inspired their followers to resist or struggle against oppressive foreign rulers. Sometimes the prophetic frenzy brought about by the people's possession by the divine Spirit was a group phenomenon expressed with music and dance. When Saul was anointed as chieftain by the prophet Samuel he met "a band of prophets coming down from the shrine [at Bethel] with harp, tambourine, flute, and lyre playing in front of them . . . in a prophetic frenzy"—leading to the proverb, "Is Saul also among the prophets?" (1 Sam. 9:1-13). That this occurred under the very shadow, as it were, of a garrison of the Philistines indicates that such collective prophecy and prophetic movements were responses to social dislocation and economic distress resulting from raids and attacks by foreign rulers. Elijah was remembered as the most prominent prophet who led a renewal of Israel, with works of healing as well as oracles of judgment against unjust rulers. The memory of Elijah included also his commissioning of his protégé Elisha to continue his work of renewal and his working with a larger group of (the sons of the) prophets in a widespread resistance to the oppressive rule of King Ahab and Jezebel. These prophets were leaders of movements among the people in resistance to their foreign or domestic rulers.

This tradition of prophets leading movements of deliverance must have remained alive among villagers of Israelite heritage, for it clearly informed several popular movements in mid-first-century CE Palestine (as they appear in the hostile accounts of Josephus). In the role of a new Moses, a Samaritan prophet led a crowd of followers to Mount Gerizim, where he promised they would recover the tabernacle vessels Moses has left there. Pilate sent out the military to attack them and executed the leaders (Josephus, *Ant.* 18.85–87). Under the later Roman governor Fadus (45 CE), a prophet named Theudas, also in the role of a new Moses leading a new exodus, led "most of the common people" out to the Jordan River, where "at his command the river would be divided and allow them an easy crossing." The cavalry sent out by Fadus to attack them cut off his head and carried it off to Jerusalem (*Ant.* 20.97–98; also mentioned in Acts 5:36). About a decade later (56 CE), under the governor Felix, a prophet who had come from Egypt, assuming the role of a new Joshua at the battle of Jericho, inspired thousands of peasants to gather on the Mount of Olives opposite the Temple and Jerusalem "to show them that at his command the walls of Jerusalem would fall down and they could then make an entry into the city" (*Ant.* 20.169–71).

Early Jesus movements understood Jesus in similar terms, as a new prophet in the mold of Moses and Elijah. Like Theudas and other such leaders of popular prophetic movements, Jesus was leading a new exodus, as manifested in his sea crossings and wilderness feedings and even in his exorcisms (Mark 4:35-41; 6:30-44, 47-52; 8:1-9; Q/Luke 11:20: "if by the finger of God I cast out demons"). Like Elijah of old, Jesus performed healings and multiplication of food as features of his program for the renewal of Israel. Also in the mold of Elijah's commission of his protégé Elisha, Jesus commissioned disciples to carry out his project of renewal of the people (Mark 1:12-13, 16-20; 6:7-13; Q 9:57-62; 10:2-16).

Prophetic leaders of movements, of course, also pronounced oracles. Both the Gospel of Mark and the series of Jesus' speeches known as Q portray Jesus as declaring oracles of judgment against the Temple and Jerusalem rulers. It seems possible that behind the accusation in Mark and the report in John's Gospel that Jesus threatened to destroy the Temple was a declaration of the word of God that the Temple stood condemned for its exploitation of the people. In Mark's account of his prophetic demonstration against the Temple, Jesus reenacts and quotes the famous pronouncement by Jeremiah of God's judgment against the Temple (Mark 11:15-17; Jeremiah 7). And his prophetic lament that the Jerusalem ruling house already stands desolate (Q/Luke 13:34-35) is uncannily similar to the pronouncement of doom by the other Jesus a generation later.

It may not be surprising that the leaders of the Jesus movement that produced Q function as prophetic spokespersons who continue to speak the words of Jesus to the communities of his followers. These movement leaders, moreover, not only understand John the Baptist and Jesus as the greatest in the line of Israelite prophets (Q/Luke 11:49-51; 13:34-35) but also see themselves in the role of prophets ("blessed are you when people persecute you . . . for that is what their ancestors did to the prophets," Q/Luke 6:22-23. 26). One interpretation of the speeches in Q is that they constitute the prophetic words in which Jesus addressed his followers through the prophets who repeated his words of judgment against the rulers and with the encouragement of the people.

ACTS AND PAUL: ADAPTATIONS OF ISRAELITE PROPHECY

Considering how these two forms of popular prophecy deeply embedded in Israelite tradition influenced the very form and leadership of the early Jesus movements, we should look for how they may have been continued, adapted, or replaced in the movements of Christ-believers in Jerusalem as well as beyond Galilee and Judea. Accounts of the early decades of the assembly of believers in Jerusalem and others in contact with it have been heavily reshaped by the author of the Book of Acts (Luke). But they still provide significant windows onto the role of prophecy in those communities.

In the Acts of the Apostles the outpouring of the Spirit at the Pentecost festival enabled the handful of Galilean peasants to prophesy, speaking the many languages of Judeans long resident among other peoples, from Rome to Mesopotamia, from Greece and Asia Minor to North Africa. This was viewed as God's fulfillment of history spoken through the prophet Joel: "I will pour out my spirit upon all flesh, and your sons and your daughters shall prophesy" (Acts 2:5-21). And, significantly, some of the early recruits to the movement were diaspora Judeans who had come to Jerusalem on pilgrimage, "the Hellenists" (Acts 6:1-6). One of them in particular,

Stephen, "a man full of faith and the Holy Spirit," is presented as delivering a fundamentally prophetic interpretation of Israelite history before the ruling high priestly council that condemns Solomon for building the Temple and the Judean rulers for having killed the prophets (Acts 7; especially 7: 48-53). Although not labeled a prophet, Stephen is portrayed as one inspired by the Spirit, with his ecstatic vision of Jesus standing at the right hand of God in the heavenly court. He is then martyred as the latest in the line of those prophets. Stephen and others assume the role of oracular prophets who pronounce God's judgment against the rulers.

In the early decades of the Jesus movement, prophets mediated God's guidance of the movement and provided leadership in the assembly of believers in Jerusalem. The prophets in the Jerusalem assembly, moreover, like the apostles, took the lead in expansion of the movement and strengthening of new communities in other cities and towns, such as Antioch. "One of them named Agabus stood up and predicted by the Spirit that there would be a severe famine over all the world; and this took place during the reign of Claudius" (in about 46 CE; Acts 11:28). Acts presents the movement as the historical fulfillment of Israel, with prophets such as Agabus mediating prophecies from God that interpreted special historical circumstances and events. In this case the prophecy was evidently instrumental in organizing economic cooperation among the assemblies of Christ-believers, specifically a relief fund for the believers in Judea. Agabus again appeared as a prophet in Caesarea, indicating in a symbolic act that the apostle Paul would be arrested by the Jerusalem priestly rulers and handed over to the Romans. Multiple prophets also took leading roles in the assemblies that formed in other cities in the next decade or so. Prophets, along with teachers, are mentioned in Antioch, among whom were Judas and Silas, who later traveled with Paul (Acts 13:1; 15:32). And we find four daughters of the evangelist Philip as prophets in the assembly at Caesarea (21:7-14), who later become prophetic leaders in the assembly in Hierapolis (in Asia Minor), exercising the "gift of prophecy."

The apostle Paul and his coworkers also prophesied. As with the Acts descriptions of Judeans from the diaspora such as Stephen and the daughters of Philip assuming the traditional role of prophets in pronouncing God's judgment against rulers and mediating God's guidance of the communities, Paul's understanding of prophecy can be understood similarly. That is, his own practice of prophecy, the discussion of prophecy in his letters, and perhaps even the dramatic revelatory experience in which Paul received his special gospel were evidently adaptations of the Israelite tradition of prophecy. Indeed, descriptions of what happened in the assemblies sound much like what might be called Pentecostal meetings. "Our message of the gospel came to you not in word only, but in power and in the Holy Spirit," Paul and his colleagues Silas and Timothy wrote to the Thessalonians (1:5). "Do not quench the Spirit. Do not despise the words of the prophets," they urge (1 Thess. 5:19-20; see "be eager to prophesy," 1 Cor. 14:39). Paul reminds the Galatians how they experienced the Spirit and acts of power (Gal. 3:1-5). Although he understands his own role as primarily an apostle, he and his coworkers clearly operated also as prophets who delivered a "word of the Lord" on key occasions as guidance for the communities in various matters of concern, teaching others also to exercise prophetic gifts. In response to the Thessalonians' anxiety about those who had recently died before the return of the Lord, Paul and his coauthors deliver a "word of the Lord" about the resurrection of the dead at the coming of the Lord (1 Thess. 4:13-18). The practices of prophecy in the Pauline communities thus appear similar to and were likely a development of the role of the oracular prophet in earlier Israelite tradition as the mediator of the word of God to the people. This rootedness in Israelite prophetic tradition also informs Paul's discussion of prophecy in response to the Corinthians' emphasis on "spiritual gifts" (1 Corinthians 12–14), as we shall see below.

For Paul himself, this understanding of prophecy must have been the result of his own calling as an apostle, which he describes in fundamentally prophetic terms. "God set me apart before I was born and called me through his grace" (Gal. 1:15); that is, God called him to be an apostle to the nations, just as God had called Jeremiah from the womb and sent him as a prophet to the nations (Jer. 1:4-5). Paul received his gospel in a revelatory experience *(apokalypsis)* of the exalted Lord (1:11-12, 16). And he is clearly remembering his own ecstatic experience of transport to the heavens when he describes "vision and revelations" to the Corinthians, albeit in the third person: "I know a person in Christ who fourteen years ago was caught up to the third heaven—whether in the body or out of the body I do not know; God knows" (2 Cor. 12:2). Such an understanding of prophecy thus stands in the same tradition as Micaiah ben Imlah and the author of Isaiah 40–55 (also known as Second Isaiah), who received God's word in the heavenly court and then delivered it to their own historical situation. Paul's prophetic message, however, vastly expands the historical scope of God's action. Micaiah's prophecy pronounced judgment of the king of Israel in international conflict and Second Isaiah's prophecy declared the people's new exodus from their subjection to the Babylonian Empire. Paul's prophetic gospel pronounced both God's judgment of the Roman Empire and the fulfillment of God's blessings announced to Abraham, now available to all peoples subject to Roman rule through the crucifixion and resurrection of Christ (Gal. 1:11-16; 3:6—4:7).

PROPHETIC ECSTASY AND WOMEN PROPHETS IN CORINTH

Not all prophets in the early Jesus movements agreed with Paul's prophetic understanding or appealed to the same oracular Israelite prophetic traditions. A form of prophecy different from that favored by Paul emerged in the Corinthian assembly after Paul had left and gone to Ephesus, a form more associated with wisdom traditions and ecstatic personal transcendence. Unfortunately, we have no direct source for these "spiritual gifts" of the Corinthian prophets. We can only try to recover their voices by analyzing Paul's argument aimed at persuading the Corinthians to de-emphasize and control their prophetic gifts, primarily in 1 Corinthians 12–14.

In a close analysis of Paul's arguments concerning these prophets, Antoinette Clark Wire has argued convincingly that they were mostly women.[7] They were apparently drawn by God's Spirit into a deeper communion that moved beyond strictly intelligible speech into "tongues of angels," a form of prophetic speech by which they spoke with God and inspired one another. While this mode of prophecy is sometimes anachronistically called glossolalia, there is no such term in Paul's letters or in any other contemporary sources. It seems likely that members of the Corinthian assembly involved called their practice *pneumatika,* just as they referred to themselves as *pneumatikoi,* "the spiritual ones" (1 Cor. 2:10-15; 12:1; 14:1, 37). Paul's terminology of "the one who speaks in a tongue" (1 Cor. 14:2, 4, 13) may be his own formulation, not the Corinthian spirituals' or prophets' own phrase. Whatever it refers to, it is clearly not the same as the reference to tongues of fire at Pentecost that resulted in the rustic Galileans being able to speak other languages so that they were understood by Judeans from the diaspora (Acts 2:3-4, 11).

The Corinthians' experience of prophecy was evidently one in which they came into close relation to the divine while transcending the immediate contingencies of their situation. As Wire points out, the experience may have been intensely personal, yet it was also a community experience of spiritual transcendence that occurred in the assembly with others, some of whom were also experiencing a similar spiritual transcendence.

Women were active in Corinthian prophetic practices, as seen in Paul's affirmation of the rights of women to prophesy—although he admonishes the women prophets to cover their heads: "Any woman who prays or prophesies with her head uncovered dishonors her head" (1 Cor. 11:5). In 1 Corinthians 14, however, Paul constructs a distinction between prophecy and "tongues" (a distinction the Corinthians may or may not have agreed with), and he begins to rein in tongues for the sake of community upbuilding: "For those who speak in a tongue do not speak to other people but to God; for nobody understands them, since they are speaking mysteries in the Spirit. On the other hand, those who prophesy speak to other people for their upbuilding and encouragement and consolation. Those who speak in a tongue build up themselves, but those who prophesy build up the church" (1 Cor. 14:2-4). What bothers Paul about the particular form of speaking in a tongue in Corinth is that it is unintelligible to other people; in his view it has benefit only for the individual involved and not others or the whole community. While Paul also claims to "speak in tongues more than all of you" (1 Cor. 14:18), he insists that it is thus necessary to have someone "interpret" (14:27-28). His instruction that only two or three speak at once (14:27) suggests that in their practice several were speaking at once in the assembly. Paul is concerned about how outsiders will perceive this multiplicity of voices (14:22-25). His overriding concern, however, was that the prophetic utterance be intelligible to the people in order to have the effect of encouraging the group, thus "building up" the community (the thrust of the argument in 1 Corinthians 14). That concern was apparently rooted in his understanding of the standard function of prophecy in Israelite tradition as a mediation of divine spiritual comfort, encouragement, and guidance for the people. Moreover, such intelligible prophecy was from Paul's perspective part of God's guidance of the communities struggling to maintain their solidarity as alternative communities living in the hostile Roman Empire, which stood under God's judgment imminently to be enacted at the parousia of the Lord (1 Cor. 2:6-9; 15:24-28; 1 Thess. 1:2-10; 2:13-20; 5:1-11).

Fig. 12.2. Women with tambourines. Reddish-brown earthenware, with residue of pink paint on a light green base. From Salamiya near Hama, Syria, first or second century CE. National Museum, Damascus. Photo: Erich Lessing / Art Resource, NY.

The Corinthian prophets saw things differently, however. We may gain a fuller sense of their understanding of prophetic *pneumatika*, as contrasted with Paul's, both by examining how their arguments are related to other issues that Paul treats in the letter and by comparing their views with other Jewish understandings of prophecy and Wisdom. The Corinthian prophets' self-understanding regarding ecstatic speaking in "spiritual things" with the divine Spirit may be closely related to an intense focus on Wisdom *(Sophia)*, which Paul treats earlier in the letter (see especially 1 Cor. 1:17-30;

4:8-10). It may also be closely related to separation from one's spouse in order to embrace celibacy (1 Cor. 7:1-7) and a differing understanding of resurrection (1 Cor. 15:12), presumably because they understand themselves to have already gained immortality and resurrection in their relation with Wisdom (1 Cor. 15:12). The prophets' focus on Wisdom and spiritual status and gifts also seems to have some connection to Apollos, a Judean from Alexandria who had come to teach in the Corinthian assembly after Paul had left (1 Cor. 3:5-9; Acts 18:24).

That Apollos was a Jew originally from Alexandria leads to some suggestive comparisons of the Corinthian prophets with similar expressions in Alexandrian Jewish texts that may help us understand the Corinthians' prophecy. The Corinthian spirituals' focus on Wisdom and attaining immortality is strikingly similar to the pattern of religiosity in the Wisdom of Solomon and the treatises of the Jewish theologian Philo.[8] In fact, this was another standard way, at least in Alexandrian Jewish communities, of understanding prophecy and prophets: "There is in her (Sophia) a spirit. . . . And in every generation she passes into holy souls and makes them friends of God and prophets" (Wisd. of Sol. 7:22-27). Philo is even more suggestive about the person who becomes a prophet as well as wise through intimate relation with heavenly Sophia as his or her true love. He describes what "happens often to the prophetic class. Among us the mind is evicted at the arrival of the divine spirit, . . . [and produces] ecstasy and madness which is from divine possession" (*Heir* 265).

Even more fascinating are similarities that the Corinthian spirituals or prophets display with a group of Jewish ascetics, the "Therapeutai" or "Therapeutrides," as described by Philo. These people had formed a monastic community in the wilderness outside Alexandria in Egypt, where they meditated all day on the scriptures, understood allegorically as providing access to heavenly Sophia. Believing that their mortal life had ended (since they were gaining immortality through Sophia), they had abandoned all their property (*Contempl. Life* 13). They also left behind their spouses in their yearning to have Sophia as their true life mate, in devotion to whom they had become celibate (18, "elderly virgins," 68). And, says Philo, "carried away by a heaven-sent passion of love, [they] remain rapt and possessed like bacchanals or corybants until they see the object of their yearning" (*Contempl. Life* 12). The latter sounds very similar to the way Philo elsewhere describes ecstatic prophecy that comes in transcendent experience of Sophia or the divine Spirit.

From a socio-economic standpoint, such a comparison with the Corinthians' Wisdom-oriented prophecy may perhaps seem questionable. After all, the Therapeutrides as well as Philo and the author of the Wisdom of Solomon were all relatively well-off elite members of diaspora Jewish communities, whereas the Corinthians were largely poor. Apollos provides a bridge by which such teaching may have been brought to Corinth. But we need to ask why and how members of the Corinthian assembly—especially women—who were generally poor ordinary people, would be attracted to elite Wisdom teachings, aceticism, and spiritual things experienced in prophetic ecstasy.

The populace of Corinth, rebuilt as a Roman colony and a crossroads of commerce and travel, included large numbers of people who had been uprooted and displaced from their families and communities of origin. Many of those sent to populate the colony had been freed slaves and others of the urban mob in Rome. Thus many of the ordinary Corinthians from whom Christ-believers were recruited were both utterly deracinated, without family, ethnic, and cultural roots, and utterly without status and dignity, as slaves or descendants of slaves. In modern times it is just such rootless and marginal people who are sometimes attracted by Pentecostal religion. Thus it may well be that, however elite the origin of the terminology in Wisdom of Solomon and Philo that seems to parallel the Corinthians' religiosity, rootless ordinary people in Corinth were drawn to the prophetic/ascetic vision of authority over their own bodies and a transcendence of their mundane lives in the new assembly of Christ-believers. In his eighteen-month mission in Corinth, Paul had surely encouraged prophesying and must have spoken of the prophetic ecstasy in which he and others received the word of the Lord (giving credibility to his claim later in 1 Cor. 14:18 that "I speak in tongues more than all of you"). Apollos then may have led them into a deeper form of ecstatic prophecy that accompanied a devotion to divine Wisdom.

Women in particular may have been attracted to the prophetic practice that became a prominent feature in the assembly in Corinth. Besides sharing the poverty of the general populace that hovered around the subsistence level, women were subject to patriarchal customs and practices that made their life conditions unusually difficult. Usually married in their teens to men as much as twice their age, they were expected to bear children in subjection not only to the authority of their husbands but to the authority of the overall imperial society (the basic building block of which was the patriarchal family—see further chapter 9). As part of his program to restore the conservative traditional order of society, the emperor Augustus had launched a campaign to reinforce such "family values." When their husbands died or left them (life expectancy was about thirty to thirty-five years), women usually remarried and, again, were expected to bear children. The intense personal spiritual experience of the ecstatic prophecy practiced in the Corinthian assembly may have entailed withdrawal from marriage and sexual relations in devotion to the divine Spirit or Sophia. This meant not only a liberation from the oppressive role particularly of ordinary women, but a withdrawal from the imperial socioeconomic order to which they were subjected. Thus, the Corinthians' form of prophecy—although different from Paul's—was also in effect a powerful protest against and a form of resistance to the imperial order.

In reining in the prophets in 1 Corinthians, Paul was in effect also reining in the voices of women, since chapter 14 includes the command "let the women keep silent."[9] Paul seems to have been willing to trade off his own egalitarian teachings on gender (compare Gal. 3:28) for the sake of building up an alternative community movement to Roman imperial society, which in his view was not served by the prophetic ecstasy and withdrawal of the Corinthian women spirituals. Wire hypothesizes that the women's prophecy fostered "release from external authorities and communal expression of divine authority, not the ethics of self-discipline and community order."[10] Whereas community order may have been Paul's goal as a way of fostering an alternative to Roman imperial society, the women prophets emphasized a spiritual transcendence of the demeaning conditions of that society through the prophetic Spirit.

Paul's silencing of women prophets in Corinth may not have been fully embraced by the community, however. The second-century text *The Acts of Paul* provides evidence for a later generation of women's prophecy in Corinth. In an apocryphal correspondence between Paul and the Corinthians, two women, Theonoe and Myrta, exhibit prophetic powers. Knowing that Paul was about to be martyred, the Corinthians write words of assurance to Paul from Theonoe's prophetic vision: "We believe, namely—as was revealed to Theonoe—that the Lord has freed you from the hand of the lawless one." Similarly, they wrote, "the Spirit came over Myrta, so that she said, 'Brothers, why [are you frightened at seeing this sign]? Paul, the servant of the Lord will save many in Rome'" (*Acts of Paul* 8, 9). These prophecies of Theonoe and Myrta appear to take the form of oracular prophecy derived from the Palestinian Israelite tradition, although the way the women's prophecy is revealed in an ecstatic vision also recalls the earlier Corinthian women.

REVELATION

The Apocalypse of John provides the most elaborate and dramatic example of prophecy from any of the movements of Christ-believers, dating from the last decade of the first century CE. While presented as a "revelation of Jesus Christ" and focused on Jesus, the revelation contains little that we might yet identify as distinctively Christian. Rather, the revelation is a rich panoply of images and forms from Israelite prophetic tradition, written in highly idiomatic Greek.[11] This has led many interpreters to believe that the Book of Revelation is the work of a Judean prophet who may have been a refugee from Palestine after the Roman reconquest of 70 CE. John never calls himself a prophet, but he lays claim to the prophetic mantle by introducing his book as *propheteia*: "Blessed is the one who reads aloud the words of the prophecy" (*propheteia*, Rev. 1:3). He clearly stands in the tradition of Micaiah ben Imlah and the prophetic voice of Isaiah 40–55. John narrates experiences "in the spirit" (Rev 1:10; 4:2; 17:3; 21:10), and he ascends to the heavenly throne room to receive messages from God and from angelic intermediaries. In his prophetic prologue, modeled after that of the Hebrew prophets, John establishes the chain of revelatory prophetic authority: his prophecy comes from Jesus, who in turn received the revelation from God to give to "his servants" the prophets—via an angelic messenger. Just as the oracular prophets of Israel mediated the word of God, the words of John's prophecy are not his own words but the words of the exalted Jesus Christ.

John narrates two prophetic calls, the first call modeled largely after Daniel (Rev. 1:9-20) and the second after Ezekiel (Rev. 10:8-11), in which he is commanded to eat the scroll and then to prophesy. John employs an epistolary format to communicate his prophetic message, much like that of the apostle Paul. He also employs the genre of apocalypse or revelation, laying out his prophetic message not by logical proofs or arguments but by means of visionary journeys and apocalyptic symbolism.

John writes in order to persuade his audience of the evil of Rome and to exhort readers to faithfulness and to a praxis of resistance and hope in the face of imperial pressure.[12] While he draws on many apocalyptic conventions—vivid colors, mysterious numbers, multiheaded beasts, mythological battles, and stark dualisms of good and evil—his book is an "anti-apocalypse" in the sense that he does not hide behind a pseudonym of an ancient figure such as Daniel or Enoch or claim that his revelation comes from centuries before, as do the recipients of Judean apocalyptic literature produced in scribal circles. He addresses his prophecy to his own time and to his own communities, in his own name. He directs his words to be read aloud in their assemblies. He wants the audience to accept his urgent prophetic interpretation of their situation. The book closes with a warning addressed to "everyone who hears the words of the prophecy of this book" (Rev. 22:18).

Contrary to today's popular cultural understanding of "prophecy," John's primary purpose in writing prophecy is not to predict future events. He writes rather to exhort the communities of Asia Minor to faithfulness to God against Roman imperial pressure. His urgent message is that God—not the Roman emperor—rules the world and that God's people must follow the Lamb, Jesus, who has already won the victory. John signifies or "shows" (*esēmanen,* Rev. 1:1) to his communities what must soon take place—namely, the impending end of unjust Roman imperial power. To the question "How long?" (Rev. 6:10) he gives the answer "Just a little while longer." John's prophetic words in Rev. 22:10 underscore the eschatological nearness: "Do not seal up the words of the prophecy of this book, *for the time is near.*" The end that he proclaims is not some abstract end of the world, but the end of Rome.

John calls on God's people to make a choice between two contrasting cities or empires—Rome versus God's alternative city of justice and well-being. God's people must "come out" of Babylon (Rome) (Rev. 18:4) before its judgment, so that they can participate in the blessing of God's alternative realm, the New Jerusalem.[13]

As a prophetic letter, the book draws extensively on Hebrew prophets. The Exodus story offers the paradigmatic story for his entire book, with Jesus cast in the role of Moses and the community undertaking an exodus "not in Egypt but in the heart of empire."[14] Memories of Elijah and Elisha are invoked in the central section of the book, where the focus turns most strongly to prophesy. John tells the story of two witnesses or "prophets," cast in the role of Elijah and Moses, who are called to prophesy amid hostility (Rev. 11:3-6). These witnesses have the power to keep rain from falling on the earth, and by their prophetic word they can command fire to come down from heaven upon their enemies. While Elijah is not specifically named, the author clearly uses Elijah and Moses as prophetic models, as seen in the two witnesses' abilities to exercise the same powers regarding rain and fire that Elijah possessed (see 1 Kings 17). The two prophetic witnesses are brutally executed by Roman power, but then they are resurrected and taken up into heaven in the manner of the prophet Elijah. In the overall argument of Revelation, the two witnesses probably represent the Christian community as it is called to engage in "confronting the idolatry of Rome in prophetic conflict, like that of Moses with Pharaoh and his magicians or of Elijah with Jezebel and her prophets of Baal."[15] Elijah serves as a prophetic model for the community to undertake its own prophetic witness and testimony, even if it leads to martyrdom.

John's identity as a prophet and his prophetic revelation are thus deeply rooted in and draw extensively on Israelite prophetic tradition. He understands his call to be analogous to that of the Hebrew prophets, a call to proclaim the word of God for his own historical situation. John's imagery is steeped in prophetic lore, such as when he describes the Empire as the beast from Daniel, or when he portrays the judgment against the Empire in imagery that draws on Jeremiah and Ezekiel. As many as one thousand allusions to Israelite cultural tradition, as we know it from the Hebrew scriptures, have been discerned in the book. The net effect in fact is to suggest that the prophetic thrust of Israelite tradition was being fulfilled in the communities' situation.

Yet John's purpose was not to interpret the Hebrew scriptures but to address the communities' historical situation with prophetic proclamation and teaching. He locates himself in the concrete time and place of Asia Minor and addresses words of prophecy to his own local congregations, with the goal of encouraging and persuading them to resistance. He is called to swallow a scroll and then to "prophesy about many peoples, nations, tongues and kings" (Rev. 10:11). His prophetic denunciations of Rome as Babylon draw heavily on Israelite prophetic traditions. The primary purpose of Revelation as prophecy is to call God's people to steadfast resistance in their *own* situation, for which he draws on Israelite prophetic traditions as a template for his blistering critique of Rome.

CIRCLES OF PROPHETIC LEADERSHIP

John is not the only prophet mediating divine revelations to the communities of western Asia Minor. Formulaic listings of "prophets and saints" (Rev. 11:18; 16:5; 18:20, 24) throughout Revelation likely refer specifically to other prophets in a "circle of prophets" active throughout the assemblies of Christ-believers in western Asia Minor. Prophets, as well as apostles, seem to be distinct groups active in one or more local assemblies, singled out from other Christ-believers. John probably intends for these other prophets in his circle to mediate his prophetic teaching to the local assemblies by reciting or reading his revelation aloud and then expounding or expanding upon it in their communities. While John does not appear to have been an itinerant prophet like those described in the *Didache,* he certainly traveled a circuit of several assemblies, perhaps with some regularity.

In seeking the roots for such a "prophetic circle" in the seven churches of Asia Minor, Richard Bauckham makes the intriguing suggestion that the four prophesying daughters of Philip may have been the ones to transmit Judean apocalyptic prophecy to Asia Minor, when they moved to Hierapolis: "Philip the evangelist, whose four daughters were prophets (Acts 21:8-9), migrated to Asia, with at least three of the daughters. . . Since these prophets, like their father (Acts 6:5), must have been originally members of the Jerusalem church, they may well have brought Jewish and Jewish Christian apocalyptic traditions from Palestine into the circle of Christian prophets in Asia." Such a hypothesis could explain links between Revelation and the oracular prophetic strand from Palestine. It also underscores the importance of women prophets in the chain of early Christian prophetic succession.[16]

The *Ascension of Isaiah,* which is roughly contemporary with Revelation, offers further evidence for such prophetic circles with Judean apocalyptic leanings in Asia Minor. While *Ascension of Isaiah* purports to be set in the time of the prophet Isaiah, this apocalypse is the work of a late-first-century or second-century community of Christ-followers that valued corporate prophecy and prophetic leadership. This text lashes out against clerical officialdom, warning that "great discord will arise among them, between shepherds and elders" (3.29) who will be "lawless and violent shepherds to their sheep." The primary complaint against the office-holding elders is that they will "set aside the prophecies of the prophets" and will pay no attention to visions (3.31). In contrast to the low estimation of elders, the *Ascension of Isaiah* praises the ministry of a "circle of prophets" consisting of some forty "prophets and sons of prophets who had come from the neighboring districts, from the mountains and the plains," to exchange prophecies and mediate the principal prophet's ("Isaiah's") ecstatic visions to the people.

These multiple references to prophets and high regard for prophecy in the *Ascension of Isaiah* and Revelation enable us to reconstruct a submerged strand of leadership in some late-first-century and second-century Christian communities. The hierarchical leadership of the monarchical episcopate so prominent in the letters of Ignatius, written to some of the same communities in Asia Minor, is nowhere to be found in Revelation. Elders (presbyters) are named in Revelation, but only up in heaven, as counterparts to the faithful on earth. Bishops are not mentioned at all. Instead of the threefold deacon/presbyter/bishop model of leadership, Revelation indicates that for some communities in Asia Minor the leadership was primarily prophetic, not episcopal. Moreover, John envisions all believers as "priests."

We need to lift up this important submerged strand of leadership in constructing a people's history of early Christianity. Communities differed greatly in their theology as well as their structures of leadership and authority. Bishops ultimately became the self-proclaimed heirs to prophecy and to the prophetic tradition—a move that can be seen, for example, in the ways references to "prophet" in the *Didache,* an early-second-century text, were stricken and replaced with "bishop," "priest," or "deacon" when material from the *Didache* was incorporated into the later *Apostolic Constitutions.*[17] In his letter to the Philadelphians Bishop Ignatius claims the role of a prophet for himself, twice narrating how he "cried out with a loud voice," with God's own spirit speaking through him. The prophetic message he relays from the Spirit is a message commanding obedience to himself, as he exhorted his flock to "pay attention to the bishop and the presbytery and the deacons" and "do nothing apart from the bishop" (*To the Philadel-*

phians 7). Ignatius's insistence on episcopal authority was not a consensus shared by everyone, as we have seen in Revelation and the *Ascension of Isaiah*. Indeed, the very fact that bishops found it necessary to legitimate their authority by way of a word of prophecy suggests that prophets and prophecy had great authority in the Asian churches—perhaps more authority than bishops.[18] This tension between episcopal and prophetic authority continued for at least another century.

POLEMIC AGAINST A RIVAL WOMAN PROPHET

Like many other discussions of prophets and prophecy in early Christian literature, Revelation engages in polemic regarding false prophets and false prophecy. In his seven prophetic letters (Revelation 2–3) John repeatedly attacks fellow believers with whom he disagrees. In the letter to Thyatira he launches the most vitriolic attack of all, taking on a woman prophet (Rev. 2:18-29) who may have had a following also in Ephesus and Pergamum—if we can assume that the so-called Nicolaitians and followers of Balaam whom John attacks there represent the same group (see Rev. 2:6; 2: 14-15).

The conflict among prophets evident in Revelation focused on different understandings of the relationship of Christ-believers to Roman culture. In Thyatira a prophet and leader of a different prophetic circle who happened to be a woman clearly disagreed with John's sweeping rejection of eating meat that had been sacrificed to other gods. It may be that her followers were freedpersons or others who had gone into business and were intent on advancing in society both economically and socially.[19] She may have argued that a compromise could be worked out with Roman imperial cults of Asia Minor or that idols were nothing and therefore that eating meat was not a problem. As the polemic of Revelation shows, there was a range of views on such subjects. John's uncompromising voice represents one response among competing voices. Evidently other prophets did not perceive Roman culture as so oppressive or evil. Most members of these assemblies may have taken a position somewhere between the extremes of John and his rival.

John lashes out at this rival prophet in vitriolic terms, labeling her as "Jezebel" and threatening her followers with violence: "I have this against you: you tolerate that woman Jezebel, who calls herself a prophet and is teaching and beguiling my servants to practice fornication and to eat food sacrificed to idols....Beware, I am throwing her on a bed, and those who commit adultery with her I am throwing into great distress, unless they repent of her doings; and I will strike her children dead" (Rev. 2:20,

22-23). The fact that John invokes the label "Jezebel," the name of the powerful Phoenician princess married to King Ahab who had some 850 prophets of her own (1 Kings 16–18), suggests that John—like the beleaguered Elijah—may have been outnumbered in Thyatira. The woman's name is lost to us, but her prophetic circle may in fact have been more influential and her followers more numerous than those of John in Thyatira and perhaps in other communities. She clearly had followers—as seen in John's threat against "her children," which refers not to literal children but to her disciples.

John's dual use of Elijah traditions in the Book of Revelation shows how problematic the otherwise liberating prophetic memory of Elijah could be for women prophets. In Revelation 11 as elsewhere among Christ-believers, Elijah serves as a model for courageous witness in the face of Roman imperial power—Revelation's primary message. But in the letter to Thyatira John uses the memory of Elijah's prophetic battles with Jezebel not only as a slander against his rival, a woman prophet, but as a legitimation for divine violence against her.[20]

It is important to emphasize that John does not attack this rival prophet because she is a woman or because she claims prophetic authority and leadership as a woman. "Rather," notes Elisabeth Schüssler Fiorenza, John "calls her names because he does not agree with her teachings."[21] The subject on which they disagreed was the community's relationship to the Roman imperial order, not gender roles in the assemblies. But instead of criticizing her views, John slanders her as the dangerous and fearsome Jezebel—and thus becomes one of the more strident voices in the nascent Christian communities that attacked and condemned women prophets.

NEW PROPHECY ("MONTANISM")

In the mid-second century a prophetic renewal movement arose in Phrygia and swept through western and central Asia Minor. For a time the New Prophecy, as they called themselves, claimed nearly half of the churches in the provinces of Asia and Galatia and spread widely in North Africa and even to Rome. Whole cities such as Thyatira embraced the New Prophecy movement, believing that God's Spirit was being poured out anew through the ecstatic prophecy of Montanus, Priscilla, Quintilla, and Maximilla. Our sources for the movement come mainly from later opponents, such as the bishop and historian Eusebius and Epiphanius, who denounced it as dangerous and heretical, along with accounts by Tertullian, a church intellectual who became a proponent. Thus we must reconstruct its oracles and history through the hostile attacks of those who were beginning to define what became orthodox Christianity.[22]

The origins of the movement are impossible to reconstruct definitively. Like most grassroots popular movements, New Prophecy did not have a central organization, and its manifestations varied greatly over time and over geographical location. New Prophecy appears to have been partly a reaction to the emerging hierarchical institutionalization of the assemblies by building a grassroots alternative, a renewal movement along some of the same lines as earlier Judean prophetic move-ments. Its prophets claimed to stand in prophetic "succession" *(diadoche)* both with Israelite bibli-cal heritage and with earlier prophecy among Christ-believers (Eusebius, *Ecclesiastical History* 5.17). They invoked the Paraclete of John's Gospel as well as prophetic promises of Revela-tion, including the expectation of the descent of New Jerusalem.

Specifically, charges Hippolytus, followers had been "captivated by two wretched women whom they supposed to be prophetesses into whom the Paraclete Spirit" had descended (*Refu-tation of All Heresies* 8:12). Both in their reception of messages from the divine by way of ecstatic experiences inspired by the Spirit and in their understanding of those messages as the speech of Christ or "word of the Lord," the New Prophecy was a revival of the prophecy of the first genera-tions of Christ-believers such as Paul and John on Patmos. "Hear not me; rather, hear Christ [through me]," said Maxi-milla (Epiphanius, *Medicine Box* 49.12.4). Priscilla sounds like a new ver-sion of John of Patmos himself, both in a vision of Christ in which revelation was received and in the vision of the new Jerusalem: "Appearing in the form of a woman, radiantly robed, Christ came to me and implanted wisdom within me and revealed to me that this place [Pepuza] is holy, and that here Jerusalem is to come down from heaven" (Epiphanius, *Medicine Box* 49.1.3). The prophecies of these women, including the vision that the New Jerusalem was about to descend at Pepuza, in Phrygia, generated great excitement among ever-widening circles of believers.[23]

Fig. 12.3. Bust of Aqmat, daughter of Hairan, white limestone from the tomb of Shallamallat, western necropolis. Second half of the second century CE. National Museum, Palmyra, Syria. Photo: Erich Lessing / Art Resource, NY.

Phrygia, where the movement originated, was a rural backwater area of the Empire and the subject of ridicule by some detractors of New Prophecy. This area of central Asia Minor had not been taken over by Rome until the first century BCE, with eastern Phrygia becoming part of the Roman province of Galatia and the western part incorporated into the province of Asia. Understandably, some have speculated about the influence of local Phrygian religion in the emergence of New Prophecy. Yet to emphasize elements of amalgamation with local Phrygian cultic practices—whether the mother goddess Cybele or oracular prophetic tradition of Apollo and Leto in nearby Dionysopolis—may fall into the same kind of paganizing of the New Prophets that ancient heresiologists engaged in as part of their effort to discredit the prophetic movement.

The principal roots of the movement, however, lay in the broad landscape of Christian communities in Asia Minor. Prophecy had flourished before in some of the cities where the New Prophecy came to live. The same strand of prophecy had been active little more than two generations earlier in nearby cities of Philadelphia, one of the assemblies to which Revelation was addressed, and Hierapolis, where daughters of Philip the evangelist had settled (*Ecclesiastical History* 3.39.9) and were buried (5.24.2). Most of the movement's beliefs and practices were simply a continuation of those of earlier movements of Christ-believers. In fact, the beliefs of the new prophets were not significantly different from the later defenders of emergent orthodoxy who condemned them. The charges against the movement were never doctrinal. Church intellectuals such as Irenaeus and Hippolytus initially expressed sympathy with the movement, urging fellow Christians not to dismiss the spirit of prophecy.

The rise and rapid spread of New Prophecy was apparently the result of a constellation of factors that the prophets saw as "signs of the times."[24] The interior of Asia Minor, where the movement originated and spread, initially was relatively isolated from the coastal cities that had for centuries adjusted to the Roman imperial order. Having been brought under the rule of Rome only two centuries earlier, the people in particular still had a certain spirit of independence in which spiritual revival and prophecy that promised a new beginning could take root and flourish. The decade of the 160s, moreover, brought multiple hardships to this area, with earthquakes, a widespread plague that broke out in 166, tax increases, and other factors that exacerbated the stressed conditions. Continuing deterioration of events in the 170s led many more to respond eagerly to the prophets' revelations that God was about to act to overcome their suffering, even to send the New Jerusalem to earth. Finally, the reign of the emperor Marcus Aurelius, who is often thought of as a reclusive Stoic philosopher, brought an oppressive political environment to Asia Minor, with sporadic persecution and mob violence against Christ-believers.

As a grassroots movement, New Prophecy clashed with the increasingly institutionalized church and its emergent orthodoxy on a number of issues, although some of the criticism involved more personal vendetta and slander than theological substance. Points of contention included several interrelated issues: the role of prophecy, the growing power of bishops, interpretation of scripture, stance toward the Roman imperial order, and the role of women.

New Prophecy rose alongside the rise of the bishops to almost monarchical authority. As quickly became evident to the bishops—some of whom were also leading intellectuals who attacked the movement in their treatises—the New Prophecy was a threat to their own power. With its focus on ecstatic prophecy as the medium of divine guidance and its focus on the "little ones," the movement was a direct challenge to episcopal authority. The movement also criticized the institutionalized church as morally lax and promoted an ascetic way of life. In some cases they apparently paid no attention to bishops, while in others, if we can believe the accusation by Epiphanius (*Medicine Box* 49.2), women became elders and bishops of their assemblies.

While the bishops and intellectuals who vilified them did not attack their beliefs, they were adamant that Maximilla, Priscilla, Quintilla, and the other leaders were false prophets. They ordered that the written treatises produced by the movement be destroyed. The aspect that they latched onto as most objectionable was the prophets' loss of rationality in ecstatic speech, something they understood the apostle Paul to have also warned about in his First Epistle to the Corinthians when he mandated that all prophecy be given interpretation. Yet, as Irenaeus points out, the New Prophets cited scripture as authorization for their prophecy, the promised Paraclete of John's Gospel, the Israelite prophets who

> The Quintillians . . . and Priscillians say that [in Pepuza] either Quintilla or Priscilla . . . was sleeping in Pepuza when Christ came to her and lay beside her. . . . "In a vision," she said, "Christ came to me in the form of a woman in a bright garment, endowed me with wisdom, and revealed to me that this place is holy, and it is here that Jerusalem is to descend from heaven." . . . Some women working among them are called prophetesses. . . . They use both the Old and the New Testament and also speak in the same way of a resurrection of the dead. They consider Quintilla together with Priscilla as founder. . . . They acknowledge the sister of Moses [Miriam] as a prophetess as support for their practice of appointing women to the clergy. Also, they say, Philip had four daughters who prophesied. Often in their assembly seven virgins dressed in white enter carrying lamps, having come in to prophesy to the people. They deceive the people present by giving the appearance of ecstasy; they pretend to weep as if showing the grief of repentance by shedding tears and by their appearance lamenting human life. Women among them are bishops, presbyters, and the rest, as if there were no difference of nature. "For in Christ Jesus there is neither male nor female." They are called *"Artotyritai"* because in their mysteries they use bread and cheese and in this fashion they perform their rites.
>
> —Epiphanius, *Medicine Box* 49[25]

experienced visionary ecstasy, and perhaps most importantly the Apocalypse of John. Irenaeus criticized other intellectuals for rejecting the prophetic gift in the church. He argued that they were thus nullifying the apostle Paul, who had spoken in detail on the prophetic charismata in 1 Corinthians and knew many men and women who had prophesied in the assemblies (*Her.* 3.11.9).

As evident already, the prominent role of women as the inspired prophetic leaders of the movement was particularly threatening to the growing power of the authorities of the churches. In reaction, they sharply vilified the women prophets personally, for example, alleging that Maximilla was not a virgin, that the New Prophets encouraged women to leave their husbands, and that they accepted money for personal gain. They also ridiculed the New Prophets' rigorous discipline such as fasting, celibacy, and prohibition of remarriage for those were widowed.

Finally, the New Prophecy's opposition to the Roman imperial order set it clearly apart from the emerging institutionalized church that took a more accommodationist and apologetic stance toward the imperial authorities. New Prophecy insisted on rigorous personal and community ethical discipline and advocated uncompromising witnessing before imperial authorities and, if need be, martyrdom as the ultimate witness. At the very same time that the New Prophets were enthusiastically announcing their vision of the New Jerusalem established in Phrygia and urging martyrdom for God's cause, orthodox apologists were trying to persuade the Empire that Christianity posed no threat to the established imperial order.

WOMEN, PROPHECY, AND EMPIRE

As we have seen, prophecy took many forms in early communities of Jesus-followers. Prophecy provided a critical alternative vision to the claims of the Roman imperial order, as women and men became inspired by God's spirit to take up the liberating mantle of Jesus' prophetic voice. They situated their critique within the memory of Elijah and other Israelite prophets who had passed the prophetic mantle on to their successors.

Prophecy also provided a particularly powerful avenue for women's leadership. In many communities women seem to have shared the prophetic mantle equally with men, and in Corinth and perhaps in Thyatira they may have been the primary leaders. In the very process of critiquing Priscilla, Maximilla, and Quintilla, Eusebius cites a second-century list of women prophets in a line of prophetic succession:

> But they cannot show that any prophet, either of those in the Old Testament or of those in the New, was inspired in this way: they can boast neither of Agabus, nor of Judas, nor of Silas, nor of the daughters of Philip, nor of Ammia in Philadelphia, nor of Quadratus, nor of any others.... For if the Montanist women succeeded to Quadratus and Ammia in Philadelphia in the prophetic gift, let them show who among them succeeded the followers of Montanus and the women. (Eusebius, *Ecclesiastical History* 5.17)

Yet we have seen at least three very different situations in which women who were leaders of prophetic movements were censured, often with a gender-related critique. In Thyatira, a prophetic leader whose name we do not even know was condemned by John for compromising too much with Roman culture. In Corinth, Paul calls on women prophets to curtail ecstatic prophesying for the sake of building a united community movement as an alternative society to Rome. By contrast, in the New Prophecy movement, women prophets were the ones preaching an uncompromising ethical rigor and resistance to Rome in contrast to orthodoxy's more accommodationist tendencies. Yet they, too, were condemned. We must ask whether gender is simply incidental to the critiques of these various strands of prophecy or whether gender played a more decisive role.

Not all prominent women prophets were censured by orthodoxy, to be sure. Especially noteworthy are the four daughters of Philip of Caesarea (Acts 21:9-14), cited favorably in Acts and also in later sources. Eusebius ranks these prophesying women among the apostles and eyewitnesses whom the influential Bishop Papias of Hierapolis sought out for information and teaching (*Ecclesiastical History* 3.39.9). They are named along with another prophet, Quadratus, in a passage praising prophets as well as other disciples as continuing the apostolic legacy (*Ecclesiastical History* 3.37). As Ute Eisen suggests, "The history of reception allows us to conclude that these women were of great significance."[26]

Orthodoxy's curtailment of prophecy in the second and third centuries meant a curtailment of the critique of Empire. Indeed, the most antiimperial of first-century prophetic writings—the Book of Revelation—was barely accepted into the canon. New Prophecy had shown how susceptible this book was to apocalyptic end-times speculations, and orthodoxy was reluctant to encourage such prophetic outbursts. As the church settled into more institutionalized life, its prophetic critique was muted.

Even more problematic, the decline of prophetic succession in favor of episcopal succession and the appropriation of prophetic authority by bishops meant a demotion for women's leadership. As Karen King summarizes, "Insofar as women based their legitimacy on prophetic experience, the so-called 'dampening of the prophetic spirit' in the history of Christianity coincided with the exclusion of women from positions of leadership."[27]

Both a renewal of the prophetic critique of empire and the renewal of women's prophetic leadership are aspects of prophecy that await recovery by ecclesial communities today. As we have seen, marginalized Christbelievers often experienced the presence of the Spirit and claimed authority through ecstatic means—especially in the face of imperial oppression. We have also seen how the template of institutional suppression of such spirit-filled prophetic leaders, particularly women, has been a frequent and persistent dynamic throughout ecclesial history. The challenge for ecclesial communities today is to repudiate that template of institutional suppression and to find ways to recover again the lively prophetic trajectory—and thereby to honor the voice of the divine Spirit as it speaks through prophets.

FOR FURTHER READING

Horsley, Richard A., with John S. Hanson. *Bandits, Prophets, and Messiahs: Popular Movements at the Time of Jesus*. Harrisburg, Pa.: Trinity Press International, 1999 [1985].

King, Karen. "Prophetic Power and Women's Authority: The Case of the Gospel of Mary (Magdalene)." In *Women Preachers and Prophets through Two Millennia of Christianity*, edited by Beverly Mayne Kienzle and Pamela J. Walker. Berkeley: University of California Press, 1998.

Rossing, Barbara. *The Choice between Two Cities: Whore, Bride and Empire in the Apocalypse*. Harvard Theological Studies 48. Harrisburg, Pa.: Trinity Press International, 1999).

Schüssler Fiorenza, Elizabeth. *Revelation: Vision of a Just World*. Proclamation Commentary. Minneapolis: Fortress Press, 1991.

Trevett, Christine. *Montanism: Gender, Authority, and the New Prophecy*. Cambridge: Cambridge University Press, 1996.

Wire, Antoinette Clark. *Corinthian Women Prophets: A Reconstruction through Paul's Rhetoric*. Minneapolis: Fortress Press, 1990.

ABBREVIATIONS

1 Clem.	*1 Clement*
1 En.	*1 Enoch*
2 En.	*2 Enoch*
AAR	American Academy of Religion
Ant.	Josephus, *Jewish Antiquities*
Ap. Const.	*Apostolic Constitutions*
ARNW	*Aufstieg und Niedergang der Roemischen Welt*
b.	Babylonian Talmud
BAGD	W. Bauer, W. F. Arndt, F. W. Gingrich, and F. W. Danker, *Greek-English Lexicon of the New Testament and Other Early Christian Literature*, 2nd ed., Chicago, 1979
CBQ	*Catholic Biblical Quarterly*
CBQMS	Catholic Biblical Quarterly Monograph Series
CBR	*Currents in Biblical Research*
Contempl. Life	Philo, *On the Contemplative Life*
CPJ	*Corpus papyrorum judaicorum,* edited by V. Tcherikover, 3 vols., Cambridge, 1957–1987
Ep.	*Epistle*
Epig.	Martial, *Epigrams*
Heir	Philo, *Who Is the Heir of Divine Things?*
Her.	Irenaeus, *Against the Heresies*
ICC	International Critical Commentary
Inst.	Quintillian, *Institutio oratoria*

JBL	*Journal of Biblical Literature*
JITC	*Journal of the Interdenominational Theological Center*
JSNT	*Journal for the Study of the New Testament*
JSNTSup	Journal for the Study of the Old Testament: Supplement Series
Jub.	*Jubilees*
L.A.B.	*Biblical Antiquities (Pseudo-Philo)*
L.A.E.	*Life of Adam and Eve*
LCL	Loeb Classical Library
Liv. Pro.	*Lives of the Prophets*
Midr. Ele Ezkera	*Midrash on the Ten Martyrs*
NTS	*New Testament Studies*
SBL	Society of Biblical Literature
Sib. Or.	*The Sybilline Oracles*
SNTSMS	Society for New Testament Studies Monograph Series
t.	Tosefta
Tg. Neb.	*Targum Jonathan of the Former Prophets*
War	Josephus, *Jewish War*
Wisd. of Sol.	Wisdom of Solomon

NOTES

Introduction

1. As David Sabean concluded in his important study of seventeenth-century peasants, *Power in the Blood: Popular Culture and Village Discourse in Early Modern Germany* (Cambridge: Cambridge University Press, 1984), ordinary people were every bit as much involved as their landlords and rulers in the great issues of history: justice, responsibility, community, vision, faith, and political communication. They may have been exploited, but they were not supine. They engaged actively and creatively in the political dynamics that determined their lives.

2. Simon Swain, *Hellenism and Empire: Language, Classicism, and Power in the Greek World, A.D. 50–250* (Oxford: Clarendon, 1996).

3. Eric J. Hobsbawm, "History from Below—Some Reflections," in Frederick Krantz, ed., *History from Below: Studies in Popular Protest and Popular Ideology in Honour of George Rude* (Montreal: Concordia University Press, 1985), 72; Jim Sharpe, "History from Below," in Peter Burke, ed., *New Perspectives on Historical Writing* (University Park: University of Pennsylvania Press, 1992), 24–41.

4. Adapted from Peter Burke, "Overture: The New History, Its Past and Future," in *New Perspectives*, 1–23, especially 3.

5. Pioneers in the study of people's history and popular culture have recognized that, despite the many mediating social and cultural factors that developed during the dramatic transition from feudal medieval to capitalist modern political economic structures, "the polarities of elite and popular, dominant and subordinate, between powerful and powerless, us and them are so evident in the sources that we cannot ignore them" (Bob Scribner, "Is a History of Popular Culture Possible?" *History of European Ideas* 10/2 [1989]: 184). Those polarities were extreme in the Roman Empire, the context of Christian origins.

6. Scribner, "History of Popular Culture"; Peter Burke, *Popular Culture in Early Modern Europe* (New York: Harper & Row, 1981); and especially James C. Scott, *Domination and the Arts of Resistance* (New Haven: Yale University Press, 1990), which is applied to New Testament materials by the essays in Richard A. Horsley, ed., *Hidden Transcripts and the Arts of Resistance*, Semeia Studies 48 (Atlanta: Society of Biblical Literature, 2004).

7. William V. Harris, *Ancient Literacy* (Cambridge: Harvard University Press, 1989).

8. Catherine Hezser, *Jewish Literacy in Roman Palestine* (Tübingen: Mohr Siebeck, 2001).

9. Richard A. Horsley, *Jesus and the Spiral of Violence: Popular Jewish Resistance in Roman Palestine* (Minneapolis: Fortress, 1993 [1987]), 129–31.

10. Eugene C. Ulrich, *The Dead Sea Scrolls and the Origins of the Bible* (Grand Rapids: Eerdmans, 1999).

11. Hezser, *Jewish Literacy*. Martin S. Jaffee, *Torah in the Mouth: Writing and Oral Tradition in Palestinian Judaism, 200 BCE–400 CE* (Oxford: Oxford University Press, 2001), argues that even in scribal circles, the scriptural "texts" were inscribed in memory as much as on the scrolls deposited in the Temple or in the possession of the scribes themselves.

12. Richard A. Horsley, *Galilee: History, Politics, People* (Valley Forge, Pa.: Trinity Press International, 1995), chaps. 2 and 6.

13. Horsley, *Galilee,* 144–57.

14. Some otherwise illuminating recent studies of how the symbols and rituals of the Roman imperial cult virtually constituted power relations in certain Greek cities may be somewhat naive in imagining that merely to represent power makes it effective and compels assent. See the excerpts from Simon Price, "Rituals and Power," and Paul Zanker, "The Power of Images," in Richard A. Horsley, *Paul and Empire: Religion and Power in Roman Imperial Society* (Harrisburg, Pa.: Trinity Press International, 1997), 47–71, 72–86. A more appropriate approach would be to look for indications of popular cultural forms that operated among the mass of urban poor.

15. See Scott, *Domination.*

16. Horsley, *Jesus and the Spiral of Violence,* chapter 5; on particular differences, see Richard A. Horsley with Jonathan A. Draper, *Whoever Hears You Hears Me: Prophets, Performance, and Tradition in Q,* with Jonathan Draper (Harrisburg, Pa.: Trinity Press International, 1999), chap. 5.

17. As the extraordinary people's historian Eric Hobsbawm points out, "most sources for grassroots history have only been recognized because someone has asked a question and then prospected desperately around for some way of answering it. We cannot be positivists, believing that the questions and the answers arise naturally out of the study of the material. There is generally no material until our questions have revealed it" ("History from Below," 66).

18. Richard A. Horsley with John S. Hanson, *Bandits, Prophets, and Messiahs: Popular Movements at the Time of Jesus* (Harrisburg, Pa.: Trinity Press International, 1999 [1985]).

19. Antoinette Clark Wire, *Holy Lives, Holy Deaths: A Close Hearing of Early Jewish Storytellers* (Leiden: Brill, 2002), esp. chap. 3; Richard A. Horsley, *The Liberation of Christmas* (New York: Crossroad, 1989).

20. Elisabeth Schüssler Fiorenza, *In Memory of Her: A Feminist Theological Reconstruction of Christian Origins* (New York: Crossroad, 1983).

21. Still practiced in the standard sociological treatment by Wayne A. Meeks, *The First Urban Christians: The Social World of the Apostle Paul* (New Haven: Yale University Press, 1983); see now Antoinette Clark Wire, *The Corinthian Women Prophets: A Recon-*

struction through Paul's Rhetoric (Philadelphia: Fortress, 1990); Richard A. Horsley, *1 Corinthians*, Abingdon New Testament Commentaries (Nashville: Abingdon, 1999).

22. Scribner, "History of Popular Culture," 181.

23. Hence beyond Gerhard Lenski, *Power and Privilege: A Theory of Social Stratification* (New York: McGraw-Hill, 1966); to John H. Kautsky, *The Politics of Aristocratic Empires* (Chapel Hill: University of North Carolina Press, 1982); beyond Thomas F. Carney, *The Shape of the Past: Models and Antiquity* (Lawrence, Kans.: Coronado, 1975) to M. I. Finley, *The Ancient Economy*, 2nd ed. (Berkeley: University of California Press, 1985); Peter Garnsey and Richard Saller, *The Roman Empire: Economy, Society, Culture* (Berkeley: University of California Press, 1987); and G. E. M. de Ste. Croix, *The Class Struggle in the Ancient Greek World* (Ithaca: Cornell University Press, 1981); and beyond Gerd Theissen, *The Social Setting of Pauline Christianity* (Philadelphia: Fortress, 1982); and Meeks, *First Urban Christians;* to Justin J. Meggitt, *Paul, Poverty, and Survival*, Studies of the New Testament and Its World (Edinburgh: T. & T. Clark, 1998); and Steven J. Friesen, "Poverty in Pauline Studies: Beyond the So-Called New Consensus," *JSNT* 26 (323–59).

24. See many of the essays in Horsley, *Paul and Empire*.

25. On Greece, see Susan E. Alcock, *Graecia Capta: The Landscapes of Roman Greece* (Cambridge: Cambridge University Press, 1993); on Asia Minor, Stephen Mitchell, *Anatolia: Land, Men, and Gods in Asia Minor*, 2 vols. (Oxford: Clarendon, 1993); on Ephesus, Steven J. Friesen, *Imperial Cults and the Apocalypse of John* (Oxford: Oxford University Press, 2001); on Galilee, Horsley, *Galilee*.

Chapter One. Jesus Movements and the Renewal of Israel

1. Discussed more extensively in Richard A. Horsley, *Jesus and the Spiral of Violence: Popular Jewish Resistance in Roman Palestine* (Minneapolis: Fortress, 1993 [1987]), esp. chaps. 2 and 4.

2. Compared with studies of protests by modern urban crowds in ibid., 90–99.

3. Examined critically in Richard A. Horsley, "Popular Messianic Movements around the Time of Jesus," *CBQ* 46 (1984): 471–93; "'Like One of the Prophets of Old': Two Types of Popular Prophets at the Time of Jesus," *CBQ* 47 (1985): 435–63; "Popular Prophetic Movements at the Time of Jesus, Their Principal Features and Social Origins," *JSNT* 26 (1986): 3–27; and, more accessibly, in Richard A. Horsley with John S. Hanson, *Bandits, Prophets, and Messiahs: Popular Movements in the Time of Jesus* (Harrisburg, Pa.: Trinity Press International, 1999 [1985]).

4. See further my *Jesus and Empire: The Kingdom of God and the New World Disorder* (Minneapolis: Fortress, 2003), chap. 3.

5. The following discussion of Jesus movements draws heavily on my recent treatments of Q and Mark in *Whoever Hears You Hears Me: Prophets, Performance, and Tradition in Q*, with Jonathan Draper (Harrisburg, Pa.: Trinity Press International, 1999), and *Hearing the Whole Story: The Politics of Plot in Mark's Gospel* (Louisville: Westminster John Knox, 2001).

6. Fuller critical examination in Horsley, *Whoever Hears You Hears Me*, and Horsley, *Hearing the Whole Story*.

7. More fully analyzed and discussed in Richard A. Horsley, *Galilee: History, Politics, People* (Valley Forge, Pa.: Trinity Press International, 1995); and *Archaeology, History, and Society in Galilee* (Harrisburg, Pa.: Trinity Press International, 1996).

8. See especially James C. Scott, "Protest and Profanation: Agrarian Revolt and the Little Tradition," *Theory and Society* 4 (1977): 3–38, 211–45.

9. Horsley, *Galilee,* 147–57.

10. On the Herodian estates in western Judea, see David Fiensy, *The Social History of Palestine in the Herodian Period* (Lewiston, N.Y.: Mellen, 1991), 32–43; on the question of land tenure and royal estates in Judea and Galilee in historical political-economic context, see Horsley, *Galilee,* chap. 9.

11. Summary of evidence and analysis in Horsley, *Galilee,* chap. 10. Most of the buildings that archaeologists label as "synagogues" date to late antiquity. This suggests that village communities were not yet constructing such buildings at the time of Jesus and his movements.

12. Fuller analysis of the mission discourses in Horsley, *Whoever Hears You Hears Me,* chap. 10.

13. Building a movement by sending envoys to work in village communities sounds similar to the activities of at least two known organizations, Der Bundshuh and Der Arme Konrad, which sent delegates to towns up and down the Rhine Valley in the decade prior to the Peasant War of 1524–25 in southwest Germany. See Peter Blickle, *The Revolution of 1525: The German Peasants' War from a New Perspective* (Baltimore: Johns Hopkins University Press, 1977).

14. On the fishing enterprise under Herod Antipas, see K. C. Hanson, "The Galileans' Fishing Economy and the Jesus Tradition," *Biblical Theology Bulletin* 27 (1997): 99–111.

15. Horsley, *Galilee,* 147–57.

16. The following discussion draws upon the fuller analysis in Horsley, *Whoever Hears You Hears Me,* chap. 9, and Horsley, *Hearing the Whole Story,* chap. 8.

17. James C. Scott, *The Moral Economy of the Peasant: Rebellion and Subsistence in Southeast Asia* (New Haven: Yale University Press, 1976).

Chapter Two. Why Peasants Responded to Jesus

1. For a collection of essays on this theme, see Frederick Krantz, ed., *History from Below: Studies in Popular Protest and Popular Ideology* (Montreal: Concordia University Press, 1985). The essay by Eric Hobsbawm (63–73) is especially relevant for methodological issues.

2. See Richard A. Horsley, *Jesus and the Spiral of Violence: Popular Jewish Resistance in the Time of Jesus* (Minneapolis: Fortress, 1993 [1987]), 3–58, 90–129.

3. Cited in Richard A. Horsley with John S. Hanson, *Bandits, Prophets, and Messiahs: Popular Movements at the Time of Jesus* (Harrisburg, Pa.: Trinity Press International, 1999 [1985]), 42.

4. Marcus Borg, *Conflict, Holiness and Politics in the Teachings of Jesus,* new ed. (Harrisburg, Pa.: Trinity Press International, 1998), 47–49.

5. James C. Scott, *The Moral Economy of the Peasant: Rebellion and Subsistence in Southeast Asia* (New Haven: Yale University Press, 1976), 39, 40.

6. James C. Scott, *Weapons of the Weak: Everyday Forms of Peasant Resistance* (New Haven: Yale University Press, 1985), 29. Examples are "foot dragging, dissimulation, false compliance, pilfering, feigned ignorance, slander, arson, sabotage and so forth."

7. For a description of advanced agrarian societies, see Gerhard Lenski and Jean Lenski, *Human Societies: An Introduction to Macrosociology* (New York: McGraw-Hill, 1982), 169–217; Gerhard Lenski, *Power and Privilege: A Theory of Social Stratification* (New York: McGraw-Hill, 1966), 189–296. For an example of how to use knowledge of agrarian societies to understand early Christianity, see Ekkehard W. Stegemann and Wolfgang Stegemann, *The Jesus Movement: A Social History of Its First Century,* trans. O. C. Dean Jr. (Minneapolis: Fortress, 1999).

8. A fuller exploration in James C. Scott, "Protest and Profanation: Agrarian Revolt and the Little Tradition," *Theory and Society* 2 (1977): 1–38, 211–46. All quotations are from this two-part article.

9. The discussion of public transcripts and hidden transcripts is found in James C. Scott, *Domination and the Arts of Resistance: Hidden Transcripts* (New Haven: Yale University Press, 1990), 2.

10. Scott, *Weapons of the Weak,* xvii.

11. Scott, "Protest and Profanation," 20.

12. Scott, *Domination and the Arts of Resistance,* 18–19.

13. The basic text is Paulo Freire, *Pedagogy of the Oppressed,* trans. Myra Bergman Ramos (New York: Seabury, 1973). See page 36 for definition of *praxis.* Other important works by Paulo Freire are *Education for Critical Consciousness,* trans. Myra Bergman Ramos (New York: Seabury, 1973); *Pedagogy in Process: The Letters to Guinea-Bissau,* trans. Carman St. John Hunter (New York: Seabury, 1978); *The Politics of Education: Culture, Power and Liberation,* trans. Donaldo Macedo (South Hadley, Mass.: Bergin & Garvey, 1985); *A Pedagogy for Liberation: Dialogues on Transforming Education,* with Ira Shor (South Hadley, Mass.: Bergin & Garvey, 1987). It should be noted that Freire actually worked with two groups of illiterate people: peasant villagers and urban laborers. In order to keep the comparison between Jesus and Freire focused, I have used only his work with rural peasants.

14. For a discussion of Jesus as the leader of a faction, see Bruce J. Malina, "Social-Scientific Methods in Historical Jesus Research," in Wolfgang Stegemann, Bruce J. Malina, and Gerd Theissen, eds., *The Social Setting of Jesus and the Gospels* (Minneapolis: Fortress, 2002), 3–26.

15. The three elements of Freire's pedagogy employed here are those used to teach peasants how to read their world. These seem applicable to first-century Palestine as to twentieth-century Brazil. The fourth step in Freire's pedagogy, the formation of vocabulary cards used to teach literacy, has no counterpart among the nonliterate Galilean peasants. Jesus was, however, teaching peasants how to "read" their world.

16. For a discussion of the debt codes and purity codes of the Torah, see Fernando Belo, *A Materialistic Reading of the Gospel of Mark,* trans. Matthew J. O'Donnell (Maryknoll, N.Y.: Orbis, 1981), esp. chap. 1, "The Symbolic Order of Ancient Israel."

17. J. Duncan M. Derrett, "Fresh Light on St. Luke xvi:11: Dives and Lazarus and the Preceding Sayings," *NTS* 7 (1961): 364–80.

18. For a fuller description of an advanced agrarian society and the role of expendables, see Lenski, *Power and Privilege,* 189–296, esp. 281–84.

19. Malina, "Social-Scientific Methods in Historical Jesus Research," 11.

20. Bruce J. Malina, *The Social World of Jesus and the Gospels* (New York: Routledge, 1996), 123–42.

Chapter Three. Women's History from Birth-Prophecy Stories

1. Italics within the quoted stories highlight the words or phrases parallel to the corresponding biblical accounts.

2. For the full titles of all quoted sources, see the list of abbreviations. Unless otherwise noted, each story quoted here is my translation from an edition identified in my *Holy Lives, Holy Deaths: A Close Hearing of Early Jewish Storytellers,* Studies in Biblical Literature 1 (Atlanta: SBL, 2002), v–vi, 27–101. The commentary found there after each story includes textual decisions and an analysis of its text, texture, and apparent storytelling contexts.

3. Albert B. Lord, *The Singer of Tales,* 2nd ed., ed. Stephen Mitchell and Gregory Nagy (Cambridge: Harvard University Press, 2000); Dan Ben-Amos and Kenneth S. Goldstein, eds., *Folklore: Performance and Communication* (The Hague: Mouton, 1975); Richard Bauman, *Verbal Art as Performance* (Rowley, Mass.: Newbury, 1977), 3–58; John Miles Foley, *The Singer of Tales in Performance,* Voices in Performance and Text (Bloomington: Indiana University Press, 1995); Wire, *Holy Lives,* 1–26.

4. Bauman, *Verbal Art;* Dell Hymes, *"In Vain I Tried to Tell You": Essays in Native American Poetics* (Philadelphia: University of Pennsylvania Press, 1981), 223–51; Jill Brody, "Co-Construction in Tojolab'al Conversational Narratives: Translating Cycles, Quotes, Evaluations, Evidentials, and Emotions," in Kay Sammons and Joel Sherzer, eds., *Translating Native Latin American Verbal Art: Ethnopoetics and Ethnography of Speaking* (Washington, D.C.: Smithsonian Institution, 2000), 86–103; Foley, *Singer,* 93–94.

5. I have translated and commented on these stories in my *Holy Lives, Holy Deaths* (27–101). In this chapter I also discuss four other birth-prophecy stories from the same period found in Josephus, *Ant.* 5.276–85; Luke 2:8-20; Matt. 2:1-12; and Rev. 12:1-17.

6. Wire, *Holy Lives,* 183–396.

7. I follow here the reordering and numbering of this text suggested by Gottfried Reeg in his edition and German translation of *The Midrash on the Ten Martyrs,* which includes the Hebrew recensions in their order on pages 18*–21* and as reordered on 28*–31*, as well as a German translation on page 93: *Die Geschichte von den Zehn Märtyrern: Synoptische Edition mit Übersetzung und Einleitung* (Tübingen: Mohr Siebeck, 1985). Its earliest form is dated from the second century to many centuries later, but it shows how stories developed about figures thought to be from this period.

8. Wire, *Holy Lives,* 95–101.

9. This story was translated for me by Mary P. Coote from the Slavic shorter recension of *2 Enoch* as printed in A. Vaillant, *Le livre des secrets d'Hénoch: Texte slave et traduction français* (Paris: Institut d'Études Slaves, 1952), 74–82.

10. The Nestle/Aland Greek text refers to thirty-eight of the different biblical passages that parallel some phrase in Zechariah's song of Luke 1:68-79, cited here and above. See, for example, David's song in 2 Samuel 22 and the Greek text of Psalm 105. I have not tried to indicate this in italics.

11. For example, see Carlo Ginzburg, *The Cheese and the Worms: The Cosmos of a Sixteenth-Century Miller,* trans. John and Anne Tedeschi (New York: Penguin, 1982), and Ann Taves, ed., *Religion and Domestic Violence in Early New England: The Memoirs of Abigail Abbot Bailey* (Bloomington: Indiana University Press, 1989).

12. See Catherine Gallagher and Stephen Greenblatt, *Practicing New Historicism* (Chicago: University of Chicago Press, 2000), and Gina Hens-Piazza, *The New Historicism,* Guides to Biblical Scholarship (Minneapolis: Fortress, 2002). This is not to be confused with the very different understanding of historicism in recent American constructive theology as seen in Sheila Greeve Davaney's *Pragmatic Historicism: A Theology for the Twenty-first Century* (Albany: State University of New York Press, 2000).

13. See James Fentress and Chris Wickham, *Social Memory,* New Perspectives on the Past (Oxford: Blackwell, 1992), and Yael Zerubavel, *Recovered Roots: Collective Memory and the Making of Israeli National Tradition* (Chicago: University of Chicago Press, 1997). I have applied social memory theory to these stories in "Early Jewish Birth Prophecy Stories and Women's Social Memory," in Alan Kirk and Tom Thatcher, eds., *Memory, Tradition, and Text: Uses of the Past in Early Christanity* (Semeia Studies; Atlanta: SBL, 2005).

14. Peter Burke, "Overture: The New History, Its Past and Its Future," in Peter Burke, ed., *New Perspectives on Historical Writing* (University Park: Pennsylvania State University Press, 1992), 11–23. See an application of this in the chapter by Warren Carter in the present volume.

15. Musa W. Dube, *Postcolonial Feminist Interpretation of the Bible* (St. Louis: Chalice, 2000), 70–83, 142–55, 182–95; Hisako Kinukawa, "De-colonizing Ourselves as Readers: The Story of the Syro-Phoenician Woman as a Text," in Holly E. Hearon, ed., *Distant Voices Drawing Near: Essays in Honor of Antoinette Clark Wire* (Collegeville, Minn.: Liturgical, 2004), 131–44.

16. As with Zechariah's song, the Magnificat draws on too many biblical phrases to identify.

Chapter Four. Turning the Tables on Jesus: The Mandaean View

1. Ethel S. Drower, *Haran Gawaita and The Baptism of Hibil Ziwa,* Studi e Testi 176 (Vatican City: Vatican Library), 1953.

2. The translation of the passage is corrected from Ethel S. Drower, *Haran Gawaita.* See Rudolf Macuch, "Rez. von E. S. Drower, the Haran Gawaita and the Baptism of Hibil Ziwa," *Zeitschrift des Deutschen Morgenländischen Gesellschaft* 105 (1955): 359.

3. E. S. Drower, *The Canonical Prayerbook of the Mandaeans* (Leiden: Brill, 1959). Drower mistranslates the text at this spot; see the arguments in my *The Great Stem of Souls: Reconstructing Mandaean History* (Piscataway, N.J.: Gorgias, forthcoming), chap. 15.

4. See chapter 5 in my *The Mandaeans: Ancient Texts and Modern People,* AAR Religions (New York: Oxford University Press), 2002.

5. See Josef Wiesehöfer, *Das antike Persien: Von 550 v. Chr. bis 650 n. Chr.* (Munich: Artemis and Winkler, 1993), 406.

6. See Ulrich Kahrstedt, *Artabanos III und seine Erben* (Bern: Francke, 1950).

7. Against Edmondo Lupieri, *The Mandaeans: The Last Gnostics*, trans. Charles Hindley (Grand Rapids: Eerdmans, 2001), 157. I dispute the translation of this passage in *Haran Gawaita* and in E. S. Drower and Rudolf Macuch, *A Mandaic Dictionary* (Oxford; Clarendon, 1963), column 17a: AKL II.

8. M. Lidzbarski, *Das Johannesbuch der Mandäer* (Giessen: Töpelmann, 1915); idem, *Ginza: Der Schatz oder das grosse Buch der Mandäer* (Göttingen: Vandenhoeck & Ruprecht, 1925).

9. It is not clear what the word *qumba* means (see *A Mandaic Dictionary*, 408B). It is possibly a reference to the Dome of the Rock, which would put this text in a much later, Muslim stratum, but this is by no means a settled question.

10. For more detail here, see chapter 5 in my *The Mandaeans*. "Beni-Amin" is a man's name here, but it also literally means "son of the people" or "son of the Right."

11. Hermann Lichtenberger, "Täufergemeinden und frühchristliche Täuferproblematik im letzten Drittel des 1. Jahrhunderts," *Zeitschrift für Theologie und Kirche* 84 (1987): 47, 48, 56.

12. Edgar E. Hennecke, "Gospels Attributed to the Twelve as a Group" and "The Protevangelium of James," in W. Schneemelcher, ed., *The New Testament Apocrypha*, vol. 1 (Philadelphia: Westminster, 1959), 264–65, 378–80, and 387.

13. Shlomo Pines, *The Jewish Christians of the Early Centuries of Christianity according to a New Source*, Proceedings of the Israel Academy of Sciences and Humanities 2/13 (1966): 53, 58n232. See *Right Ginza* 1, 1, 30, and also 2, 1, 48, 5. (Pines does not give the second *Ginza* reference.) In Pines's Arabic text, Herod is viewed as Pilate's companion.

14. It is a peculiar feature of Mandaean mythology that one of their prominent Light-World figures is named "the great Nbat."

15. See especially Fergus Millar, "Empire, Community and Culture in the Roman Near East: Greeks, Syrians, Jews and Arabs," *Journal of Jewish Studies* 38/2 (1987): 146.

16. Shimon Gibson's *The Cave of John the Baptist* (New York: Doubleday, 2004) is much too facile in its summary dismissal of the Mandaeans as being of any possible relevance to the historical John (325–26). The idea that John was imported into Mandaeism in Islamic times is untenable.

Chapter Five. Conflicts at Corinth

1. On the history of Corinth and the province of Achaia, see J. Weisman, "Corinth and Rome," *ANRW* 7.1: 438–548; and Susan E. Alcock, *Graecia Capta: The Landscapes of Roman Greece* (Cambridge: Cambridge University Press, 1993); on the Roman Empire generally, see Peter Garnsey and Richard Saller, *The Roman Empire: Economy, Society and Culture* (Berkeley: University of California Press, 1987); on the emperor cult, see S. R. F. Price, *Rituals and Power: The Roman Imperial Cult in Asia Minor* (Cambridge: Cambridge University Press, 1984).

2. See the recent survey in Steven Friesen, "Poverty in Pauline Studies: Beyond the So-Called New Consensus," *JSNT* 26 (2004): 323–59. Compare Wayne A. Meeks,

The First Urban Christians: The Social World of the Apostle Paul (New Haven: Yale University Press, 1983), 43–44.

3. Orlando Patterson, *Slavery and Social Death: A Comparative Study* (Cambridge: Harvard University Press, 1982).

4. See Andrew Wallace-Hadrill, "*Domus* and *Insulae* in Rome: Families and Households," in David Balch and Carolyn Osiek, eds., *Early Christian Families in Context: An Interdisciplinary Dialogue* (Grand Rapids: Eerdmans, 2003), 4, who suggests the Roman *domus* was not a single-family unit so much as a big house inhabited by a "houseful" rather than a household, which might collapse the distinction between the *domus* and the *insulae.*

5. See especially E. A. Judge, *The Social Pattern of the Christian Groups in the First Century: Some Prolegomena to the Study of New Testament Ideas of Social Obligation,* Christ and Culture Collection (London: Tyndale, 1960); and Gerd Theissen, *The Social Setting of Pauline Christianity: Essays on Corinth* (Philadelphia: Fortress, 1982); compare Meeks, *The First Urban Christians,* 43–44.

6. Justin J. Meggitt, *Paul, Poverty and Survival,* Studies of the New Testament and Its World (Edinburgh: T. & T. Clark, 1998), 97–153; and Friesen, "Poverty in Pauline Studies," 323–59.

7. Allen D. Callahan, "A Note on 1 Corinthians 7:21," *JITC* 17 (1989–90): 110–14.

8. Peter Berger and Thomas Luckmann, *The Social Construction of Reality: A Treatise in the Sociology of Knowledge* (Garden City, N.Y.: Doubleday, 1966).

9. Recent treatments of the issues addressed in 1 Corinthians are David Horrell, *The Social Ethos of the Corinthian Correspondence* (Edinburgh: T. & T. Clark, 1996); and Richard A. Horsley, *1 Corinthians,* Abingdon New Testament Commentaries (Nashville: Abingdon, 1997).

10. Ray Pickett, *The Cross at Corinth: The Social Significance of the Death of Jesus* (Sheffield: Sheffield Academic, 1997), 39–58.

11. Antoinette Clark Wire, *The Corinthian Women Prophets: A Reconstruction through Paul's Rhetoric* (Minneapolis: Fortress, 1990).

12. See Richard A. Horsley, ed., *Paul and Empire: Religion and Power in Roman Imperial Society* (Harrisburg, Pa.: Trinity Press International, 1997), 1–24, 242–52.

13. See Stanley Stowers, "Greeks Who Sacrifice and Those Who Do Not: Toward an Anthropology of Greek Religion," in L. Michael White and O. Larry Yarbrough, eds., *The Social World of the First Christians: Essays in Honor of Wayne A. Meeks* (Minneapolis: Fortress, 1995), 293–33.

14. See further Horrell, *Ethos,* 238–80.

Chapter Six. Matthew's People

1. Warren Carter, *Matthew and the Margins: A Sociopolitical and Religious Reading* (Maryknoll, N.Y.: Orbis, 2000), 9–49; idem, *Matthew and Empire: Initial Explorations* (Harrisburg, Pa.: Trinity Press International, 2001), 9–53; Anthony J. Saldarini, *Matthew's Christian-Jewish Community* (Chicago: University of Chicago Press, 1994).

2. Peter Burke, "Overture: The New History, Its Past and Its Future," in Peter Burke, ed., *New Perspectives on Historical Writing* (University Park: Pennsylvania State

University Press, 1992), 1–23, esp. 3; Robert Scribner, "Is a History of Popular Culture Possible?" *History of European Ideas* 10 (1989): 175–91.

3. Glanville Downey, *A History of Antioch in Syria: From Seleucus to the Arab Conquest* (Princeton: Princeton University Press, 1961); Rodney Stark, "Antioch as the Social Situation for Matthew's Gospel," in David Balch, ed., *Social History of the Matthean Community* (Minneapolis: Fortress, 1991), 189–210; Christine Kondoleon, ed., *Antioch: The Lost Ancient City* (Princeton: Princeton University Press, 2000).

4. Raymond Brown and John P. Meier, *Antioch and Rome: New Testament Cradles of Catholic Christianity* (New York: Paulist, 1983), 12–86; D. Sim, *The Gospel of Matthew and Christian Judaism: The History and Social Setting of the Matthean Community* (Edinburgh: T. & T. Clark, 1998).

5. For example, Gerhard Lenski, *Power and Privilege: A Theory of Social Stratification* (Chapel Hill: University of North Carolina Press, 1984), 189–296; Peter Garnsey and Richard Saller, *The Roman Empire: Economy, Society, and Culture* (Berkeley: University of California Press, 1987); Janet Huskinson, ed., *Experiencing Rome: Culture, Identity and Power in the Roman Empire* (London: Routledge, 2000); for resistance, Klaus Wengst, *Pax Romana and the Peace of Jesus Christ* (Philadelphia: Fortress, 1987); James C. Scott, *Domination and the Arts of Resistance: Hidden Transcripts* (New Haven: Yale University Press, 1990); idem, *Weapons of the Weak: Everyday Forms of Peasant Resistance* (New Haven: Yale University Press, 1985); Warren Carter, "Vulnerable Power: The Roman Empire Challenged by the Early Christians," in Anthony J. Blasi, Jean Duhaime, and Paul-André Turcotte, eds.), *Handbook of Early Christianity: Social Science Approaches* (Walnut Creek, Calif.: AltaMira, 2002), 453–88.

6. C. R. Whittaker, "The Consumer City Revisited: The *Vicus* and the City," and "Do Theories of the Ancient City Matter?" in C. R. Whittaker, *Land, City, and Trade in the Roman Empire,* Collected Studies 408 (Aldershot, England: Variorum, 1993), 110–17, 1–20; Tim Cornell and Kathryn Lomas, eds., *Urban Society in Roman Italy* (New York: St. Martin's, 1995); Neville Morley, "Cities in Context: Urban Systems in Roman Italy," in Helen M. Parkins, ed., *Roman Urbanism: Beyond the Consumer City* (London: Routledge, 1997), 42–58.

7. Peter Garnsey and C. R. Whittaker, eds., *Trade and Famine in Classical Antiquity* (Cambridge: Cambridge Philological Society, 1983); John Rich and Andrew Wallace-Hadrill, *City and Country in the Ancient World* (London: Routledge, 1991); Helen M. Parkins, "The Consumer City Domesticated? The Roman City in Elite Economic Strategies," in Parkins, *Roman Urbanism,* 83–111.

8. Kenneth Scott, *The Imperial Cult under the Flavians* (New York: Arno, 1975 [1936]); Simon R. F. Price, *Rituals and Power: The Roman Imperial Cult in Asia Minor* (Cambridge: Cambridge University Press, 1984).

9. Donald D. Binder, *Into the Temple Courts: The Place of the Synagogues in the Second Temple Period,* SBL Dissertation Series 169 (Atlanta: SBL, 1999), 343–71; Tessa Rajak and D. Noy, "Archisynagogoi: Office, Title, and Social Status in the Greco-Jewish Synagogue," *Journal of Roman Studies* 83 (1993): 75–93.

10. C. R. Whittaker, "The Poor," in Andrea Giardina, ed., *The Romans,* trans. Lydia G. Cochrane (Chicago: University of Chicago Press, 1993), 272–99; Peter Garnsey, *Cities, Peasants and Food in Classical Antiquity* (Cambridge: Cambridge University Press, 1988),

28–44, 91–106, 134–50; Ramsay MacMullen, *Roman Social Relations* (New Haven: Yale University Press, 1974).

11. A. Scobie, "Slums, Sanitation, and Mortality in the Roman World," *Klio* 68 (1986): 399–433; Whittaker, "Poor," 288.

12. Ramsay MacMullen, *Enemies of the Roman Order: Treason, Unrest, and Alienation in the Empire* (Cambridge: Harvard University Press, 1966); Carter, "Vulnerable Power;" Scott, *Domination;* idem, *Weapons.*

13. Frantz Fanon, *The Wretched of the Earth,* trans. Constance Farrington (New York: Grove, 1968), esp. 45, 53, 289–93; Paul W. Hollenbach, "Jesus, Demoniacs, and Public Authorities: A Socio-Historical Study," *Journal of the American Academy of Religion* 49 (1981): 567–88; D. Amos, "The Littlest Victims," *ABC News,* April 13, 1999.

14. Warren Carter, "Evoking Isaiah: Matthean Soteriology and an Intertextual Reading of Isaiah 7–9 in Matthew 1:23 and 4:15-16," *JBL* 119 (2000): 503–20; also Carter, *Matthew and Empire,* 93–108.

15. P. Brunt, *Roman Imperial Themes* (Oxford: Clarendon, 1990), 53–95, 163–87, 215–54; Warren Carter, *Pontius Pilate: Portraits of a Roman Governor* (Collegeville, Minn.: Liturgical, 2003), 35–54.

16. Anthony J. Saldarini, *Pharisees, Scribes and Sadducees in Palestinian Society: A Sociological Approach* (Wilmington, Del.: Michael Glazier, 1988), 35–49; Lenski, *Power and Privilege,* 231–66.

17. K. C. Hanson and Douglas E. Oakman, *Palestine in the Time of Jesus: Social Structures and Social Conflicts* (Minneapolis: Fortress, 1998), 131–59.

18. Carter, "Paying the Tax," in *Matthew and Empire,* 130–44, also *JSNT* 76 (1999): 3–31; Brent Shaw, "Taxation," in Michael Grant and Rachel Kitzinger, eds., *Civilization of the Ancient Mediterranean,* 3 vols. (New York: Scribner's, 1988), 2:809–27, esp. 810. Suetonius, *Gaius Caligula,* 40–41, *Vespasian,* 23.

19. William Herzog, "OnStage and OffStage with Jesus of Nazareth: Public Transcripts, Hidden Transcripts, and Gospel Texts," in Richard A. Horsley, ed., *Hidden Transcripts and the Arts of Resistance,* Semeia Studies 48 (Atlanta: SBL, 2004), 41–60.

20. Warren Carter, "Evoking Isaiah," in *Matthew and Empire,* 93–107.

21. Warren Carter, "Are There Imperial Texts in the Class? Intertextual Eagles and Matthean Eschatology as 'Lights Out' Time for Imperial Rome (Matthew 24:27-31)," *JBL* 122 (2003): 467–87.

22. Homi Bhabha, "Of Mimicry and Man: The Ambivalence of Colonial Discourse," in *The Location of Culture* (London: Routledge, 1994), 85–92.

23. Walter Wink, "Beyond Just War and Pacifism: Jesus' Nonviolent Way," *Review and Expositor* 89 (1992): 197–214; Naphtali Lewis, "Domitian's Order on Requisitioned Transport and Lodgings," *Revue internationale des droits de l'antiquité* 15 (1968): 135–42.

24. Peter Garnsey, *Food and Society in Classical Antiquity* (Cambridge: Cambridge University Press, 1999), xi; Peter Garnsey, *Famine and Food Supply in the Graeco-Roman World* (Cambridge: Cambridge University Press, 1988), 3–39; for Rome, G. S. Aldrete and D. J. Mattingly, "Feeding the City: The Organization, Operation, and Scale of the Supply System for Rome," in D. S. Potter and D. J. Mattingly, eds., *Life, Death, and Entertainment in the Roman Empire* (Ann Arbor: University of Michigan Press, 1999), 171–204.

25. L. Foxhall and H. Forbes, "*Sitometreia:* The Role of Grain as a Staple Food in Classical Antiquity," *Chiron* 12 (1982): 41–90; D. J. Mattingly, "First Fruit? The Olive in the Roman World," in Graham Shipley and John Salmon, eds., *Human Landscapes in Classical Antiquity: Environment and Culture* (London: Routledge, 1996), 213–53; Garnsey, "The Bean: Substance and Symbol," in *Cities, Peasants*, 214–25.

26. Garnsey, *Food and Society*, 34–61; D. V. Sippel, "Dietary Deficiency among the Lower Classes of Late Republican and Early Imperial Rome," *Ancient World* 16 (1987): 47–54; Robert Garland, *The Eye of the Beholder: Deformity and Disability in the Graeco-Roman World* (Ithaca: Cornell University Press, 1995), 11–27.

27. Virgil, Fourth Eclogue; *Aeneid* 1.257–96; 6.791–807; Horace, *Carmen saeculare* (Secular Hymn) 29–68; Philo, *Embassy*, 8–13, Statius, *Silvae* (Forests) 1.6.39–42; Martial, *Epig.* 5.19.1–6. D. Castriota, *The Ara Pacis Augustae and the Imagery of Abundance in Later Greek and Early Imperial Art* (Princeton: Princeton University Press, 1995).

28. Carter, "Take My Yoke," in *Matthew and Empire*, 108–29.

29. Mary Douglas, "Deciphering a Meal," in Clifford Geertz, ed., *Myth, Symbol, and Culture* (New York: Norton, 1971), 61–81.

Chapter Seven. The Gospel of John as People's History

1. The presentation here will draw heavily on the fuller reading in Allen Dwight Callahan, *A Love Supreme: A History of the Johannine Tradition* (Minneapolis: Fortress, 2005).

2. References in Josephus for the popular "kings" and prophets in the next two paragraphs in Richard A. Horsley with John S. Hanson, *Bandits, Prophets, and Messiahs: Popular Movements at the Time of Jesus* (Harrisburg, Pa.: Trinity Press International, 1999 [1985]).

3. We are coming to recognize that the Gospels are narratives—sustained stories about the mission of Jesus of Nazareth. To be appreciated, therefore, they should be read as sustained narratives, as complete stories, and not divided up into chapter and verse. Readers are encouraged to become acquainted with the Gospel of John by reading it all the way through (without distraction by chapter and verse and editorial subheadings) before reading the presentation in this chapter. The reading presented here will assume familiarity with the Gospel as narrative and accordingly will generally avoid interruptive references to chapter and verse—although at points such may be made.

4. Ellen Aitken, "At the Well of Living Water: Jacob Traditions in John 4," in Craig A. Evans, ed., *The Interpretation of Scripture in Early Judaism and Christianity*, Studies in Scripture in Early Judaism and Christianity 7 (Sheffield: Sheffield Academic, 2000), 345.

5. The lacunae of the parallel text in Thomas, in addition to the absence of narrative context, render it useless for comparative analysis. The Gospel of John places this scene at the beginning of Jesus' public activity, thus at variance with the Synoptic narrative that suggests that the Temple incident incited the priests to arrest Jesus. In the light of the analysis offered here, the Johannine narrative is the more plausible.

6. Catherine Cory, "Wisdom's Rescue: A New Reading of the Tabernacle Discourse," *JBL* 116/1 (1997): 95–116. Catherine Cory has described the Tabernacles

discourse (John 7:1—8:59) as "a unique Johannine innovation, a story about Wisdom's 'rescue' from the enemies' hands" (95).

7. Ibid., 107.

8. Gilbert van Belle, *Les parenthèses dans l'Évangile de Jean: Aperçu historique et classification texte grec de Jean* (Leuven: Leuven University Press, 1985), 106–12.

9. Elizabeth Schüssler Fiorenza, *In Memory of Her: A Feminist Theological Reconstruction of Christian Origins* (New York: Crossroads, 1983), 323–34.

Chapter Eight. Disciplining the Hope of the Poor in Ancient Rome

1. Some recent scholars argue convincingly that translating the Greek *Ioudaios* and Latin *Iudaeus* with "Jew," referring to a *religious* identity, is anachronistic through the early first century CE. They prefer the properly *ethnic* designation "Judean," which I use here. See the discussions by Shaye J. D. Cohen, *The Beginnings of Jewishness: Boundaries, Varieties, Uncertainties* (Berkeley: University of California Press, 1999); Philip F. Esler, *Conflict and Identity in Romans: The Social Setting of Paul's Letter* (Minneapolis: Fortress, 2003); and Dale Martin, "Paul and the Judaism/Hellenism Dichotomy: Toward a Social History of the Question," in Troels Engberg-Pederson, ed., *Paul Beyond the Judaism/Hellenism Divide* (Louisville: Westminster John Knox, 2001), 29–61. The matter is delicate, because *Ioudaioi* clearly shared religious practices as well; the term cannot reasonably be reduced to a geographic designation that effectively breaks the connection between first-century *Ioudaioi* and modern Jews (as, for example, happens in Bruce J. Malina and Ricahrd L. Rohnbaugh, *Social Science Commentary on the Gospel of John* [Minneapolis: Fortress Press, 1998], 44–46).

On the term "Christian," see note 8, below.

2. On the influence of modern racial and imperial discourse in biblical studies, especially the study of Paul, see *On the Prominence of Hegelian Categories in the Legacy of F. C. Bank,* see Richard A. Horsley, ed., *Paul and Empire: Religion and Power in Roman Imperial Society* (Philadelphia: Trinity Press International, 1997); Shawn Kelley, *Racializing Jesus: Race, Ideology, and the Formation of Modern Biblical Scholarship* (London: Routledge, 2002); and Martin, "Paul."

3. H. Dixon Slingerland protests these prejudicial characterizations in *Claudian Policymaking and the Early Imperial Repression of Judaism at Rome* (Atlanta: Scholars, 1997), 27–31.

4. For example, Plutarch reports that a wealth of graffiti supported the agrarian reform campaign of Tiberius Gracchus (*Tiberius Gracchus* 21:2–3). Tacitus and Suetonius pepper their accounts with amusing graffiti hostile to one or another emperor. On the importance of graffiti for people's history, see Justin J. Meggitt, *Paul, Poverty, and Survival,* Studies of the New Testament and Its World (Edinburgh: T. & T. Clark, 1998), 30–35; James C. Scott, *Domination and the Arts of Resistance: Hidden Transcripts* (New Haven: Yale University Press, 1990), 36, 150–51.

5. On the violence of tax gatherers: Philo, *On the Special Laws* 2:92–95; 3:159–63; on Claudius's response to the "war," John G. Gager, *The Origins of Anti-Semitism* (New York: Oxford University Press, 1985), 48; Peter Schäfer, *Judeophobia: Attitudes toward the Jews in the Ancient World* (Cambridge: Harvard University Press, 1997), 147–52.

6. Some scholars understand the Claudian expulsion as the occasion, even the cause, of the emergence of a distinctive Roman Christian community (Peter Lampe, *From Paul to Valentinus: Christians at Rome in the First Two Centuries,* trans. Michael Steinhauser [Minneapolis: Fortress, 2003], 11; Rudolf Brändle and Ekkehard Stegemann, "The Formation of the First 'Christian Congregations' in Rome," in Karl P. Donfried and Peter Richardson, eds., *Judaism and Christianity in First-Century Rome* [Grand Rapids: Eerdmans, 1998], 125). Others consider the expulsion a reaction to disturbances arising from the practice, already well established, of including Gentiles in common Christian meals (James Walters, "The Impact of the Romans on Jewish/Christian Relations," in Donfried and Richardson, *Judaism and Christianity,* 175-95). I find Paula Fredriksen's arguments regarding Judea telling for Rome as well: "mixed table fellowship itself could not have been the issue" provoking Judean opposition to "Christian" assemblies (*From Jesus to Christ: The Origins of the New Testament Images of Jesus,* 2nd ed. [New Haven: Yale University Press, 2000], 149–53).

7. I rely here on Slingerland's meticulous and convincing study, *Claudian Policymaking.* (I've substituted "Judeans" for "Jews" in his translation.) Slingerland proposes several candidates for the Roman Chrestus, most likely a Gaius Iulius Chrestus, who stood "only a single person away from the innermost circles of the imperial family" (179–201).

8. On the anachronism of the term apart from Suetonius's report, see Brändle and Stegemann, "Formation," 117–18. According to Acts 11:26, the followers of Jesus "were first called *Christianoi* in Antioch"; presumably Luke means some time in the 40s. Even if that is not an anachronism on Luke's part, it is clearly not a self-designation of the community. No text written before Luke-Acts or Ignatius (early second century CE) uses the term; with regard to Rome, outsiders use it only in the early second century CE. See also Esler, *Conflict,* 12–13; Donald Harman Akenson, *Saint Saul: A Skeleton Key to the Historical Jesus* (Oxford: Oxford University Press, 2000), 62–67.

9. The persuasive argument of Leonard V. Rutgers, "Roman Policy toward the Jews," in Donfried and Richardson, *Judaism and Christianity,* 98–103; also Slingerland, *Claudian Policymaking.*

10. Michael Parenti observes that "as with just about every ruling class in history, the Roman nobility reacted fiercely when their interests were infringed upon, especially their untrammeled 'right' to accumulate as much wealth as possible at the public's expense" (*The Assassination of Julius Caesar: A People's History of Ancient Rome* [New York: New Press, 2003], 82, 115–17). On acts of class solidarity: ibid., 204–22; G. E. M. de Ste. Croix, *The Class Struggle in the Ancient Greek World: From the Archaic Age to the Arab Conquests* (Ithaca: Cornell University Press, 1981), passim.

11. James C. Scott, *Weapons of the Weak: Everyday Forms of Peasant Resistance* (New Haven: Yale University Press, 1985), 138.

12. On Fourth Maccabees and the subversive "fourth philosophy," see Neil Elliott, *Liberating Paul: The Justice of God and the Politics of the Apostle,* Bible and Liberation (Maryknoll, N.Y.: Orbis, 1994), 151–56; on the *Psalms of Solomon* and the *Book of Biblical Antiquities,* ibid., 156–59. On Philo's *On Dreams,* see Erwin R. Goodenough, *An Introduction to Philo Judaeus,* 2nd ed. (Lanham, Md.: University Press of America, 1986 [1962]), 55–57; Neil Elliott, "The 'Patience of the Jews': Strategies of Resistance and

Accommodation to Imperial Cultures," in Janice Capel Anderson, Philip Sellew, and Claudia Setzer, eds., *Pauline Conversations in Context: Essays in Honor of Calvin J. Roetzel*, JSNTSup 221 (Sheffield: Sheffield Academic Press, 2002), 37–41.

13. T. L. Carter, "The Irony of Romans 13," *Novum Testamentum* 46:3 (2004): 209–49.

14. This interpretation of Romans relies in part on N. T. Wright, "Romans and the Theology of Paul," in David M. Hay and E. Elizabeth Johnson, eds., *Pauline Theology*, Vol. 3: *Romans* (Minneapolis: Fortress, 1995), 30–67; idem, "Paul's Gospel and Caesar's Empire," in Richard A. Horsley, ed., *Paul and Politics: Ekklesia, Israel, Imperium, Interpretation* (Harrisburg, Pa.: Trinity Press International, 2000), 160–183; W. S. Campbell, "The Rule of Faith in Romans 12:1–15:13," in Hay and Johnson, *Pauline Theology*, Vol. 3: *Romans*, 259-86; Neil Elliott, "Paul's Letter to the Romans," in F. Segovia and R. S. Sugirtharajah, *A Postcolonial Biblical Commentary* (Sheffield: Sheffield Academic Press, forthcoming); idem, *Liberating Paul*, 194–95. On the "weak" of Romans 14–15 as indicating social class rather than religious observance, see Mark Reasoner, *The Strong and the Weak: Romans 14:1—15:13 in Context*, SNTSMS 103 (Cambridge: Cambridge University Press, 1999), and Mark D. Nanos, *The Mystery of Romans: The Jewish Context of Paul's Letter* (Minneapolis: Fortress, 1996), 88–165. On mutualism as a survival strategy among the urban poor, see Meggitt, *Paul, Poverty, and Survival*, and Neil Elliott, "Strategies of Resistance and Hidden Transcripts in the Pauline Communities," in Richard A. Horsley, ed., *Hidden Transcripts and the Arts of Resistance: Applying the Work of James C. Scott to Jesus and Paul*, Semeia 48 (Atlanta: Scholars, 2004), 97–122. On the circumstances surrounding Rom. 13:1-7, see J. Friedrich, W. Pöhlmann, and P. Stuhlmacher, "Zur historischen Situation und Intention von Röm 13.1-7," *Zeitschrift für Theologie und Kirche* 73 (1976): 131–66; Neil Elliott, "Romans 13:1-7 in the Context of Neronian Propaganda," in Horsley, *Paul and Empire*, 184–204; and Carter, "The Irony of Romans 13." On echoes of the "Augustan imperial ideal" in Paul's rhetoric, see John L. White, *The Apostle of God: Paul and the Promise of Abraham* (Peabody, Mass.: Hendrickson, 1999), 110–38; Stanley K. Stowers, *A Rereading of Romans: Justice, Jews, Gentiles* (New Haven: Yale University Press, 1994); more polemically, Dieter Georgi, *Theocracy in Paul's Praxis and Theology*, trans. David E. Green (Minneapolis: Fortress, 1991), 79–104.

15. The chief sources are Calpurnius Siculus, Calpurnius Piso, and the "Einsiedeln Eclogues," available in J. Wight Duff and Arnold M. Duff, eds., *Minor Latin Poets*, vol. 1, LCL 234 (Cambridge: Harvard University Press, 1934); and the writings of Seneca.

16. On Flavian propaganda, see J. Andrew Overman, "The First Revolt and Flavian Politics," in Andrea Berlin and J. Andrew Overman, eds., *The Jewish Revolt: Archaeology, History, and Ideology* (London: Routledge, 2002), 213–20; on Josephus' "prediction" of Vespasian's rise, Steve Mason, *Josephus and the New Testament* (Peabody, Mass.: Hendrickson, 1992), 45–49.

17. John M. G. Barclay, *Jews in the Mediterranean Diaspora from Alexander to Trajan (323 B.C.E.–117 C.E.)* (Edinburgh: T. & T. Clark, 1996), 310–19; Gager observes that Tacitus is concerned to present "a rationale for the anti-Semitism of conservative senatorial groups of Rome," who were "troubled at least as much by the appeal of Judaism among Romans as they were by the war" (*Origins*, 64).

18. So Helmut Koester, *Introduction to the New Testament,* 2 vols., 2nd ed. (New York: de Gruyter, 2000), 2:272–76. William Lane's argument ("Roman Christianity during the Formative Years from Nero to Nerva," in Donfried and Richardson, *Judaism and Christianity,* 214–17) for a Roman provenance shortly after Nero's persecution in 64 CE is plausible, but not required by the evidence of the text.

19. Lane, "Roman Christianity," 224–37; David Rankin, "Class Distinction as a Way of Doing Church," *Vigiliae Christianae* 58 (2004): 298–315, here 300–301.

20. Carolyn Osiek's work on the *Shepherd* is decisive here: see "The Oral World of Early Christianity in Rome: The Case of Hermas," in Donfried and Richardson, *Judaism and Christianity,* 152; idem, *Rich and Poor in the Shepherd of Hermas: An Exegetical-Social Investigation,* CBQMS 15 (Washington, D.C.: Catholic Biblical Association of America, 1983); and idem, *Shepherd of Hermas: A Commentary,* Hermeneia (Minneapolis: Fortress, 1999).

21. See David Efroymsen, "The Patristic Connection," in Alan Davies, ed., *Anti-Semitism and the Foundations of Christianity* (New York: Paulist, 1979), 98–117; Gager, *Origins,* 160–73; Lampe, *From Paul to Valentinus,* chaps. 24 (on Marcion) and 27 (on Valentinians). Lampe rightly distinguishes the motives that would have attracted lower-class followers to these movements from the motives of the "intellectual class" that led them.

22. Rankin, "Class Distinction," 306–7.

23. On the history of these developments, see Brian E. Daley, *The Hope of the Early Church: A Handbook of Patristic Eschatology* (Peabody, Mass.: Hendrickson, 2003); Charles E. Hill, *Regnum Caelorum: Patterns of Future Hope in Early Christianity,* Oxford Early Christian Studies (New York: Oxford University Press, 1992).

Chapter Nine. Family Matters

1. See further on this topic: E. A. Judge, *The Social Pattern of the Christian Groups in the First Century: Some Prolegomena to the Study of the New Testament Ideas of Social Obligation,* Christ and Culture Collection (London: Tyndale, 1960); Richard L. Rohrbaugh, "Methodological Considerations in the Debate over the Social Class Status of Early Christians," *Journal of the American Academy of Religion* 52/3 (1983): 519–46; Bruce J. Malina, "Social Ranking, Morality, and Daily Life," in Philip F. Esler, ed., *The Early Christian World,* 2 vols. (London: Routledge, 2000), 1:369–400.

2. Discussion with photo in John R. Clarke, *Art in the Lives of Ordinary Romans: Visual Representations and the Non-Elite Viewers in Italy, 100 B.C.–A.D. 315* (Berkeley: University of California Press, 2003), 184–85.

3. See Alex Scobie, "Slums, Sanitation, and Mortality in the Roman World," *Klio* 68 (1986): 39–433, for further details on health and hygiene.

4. Cf. Donald G. Kyle, *Spectacles of Death in Ancient Rome* (London: Routledge, 1998); "Fatal Charades: Roman Executions Staged as Mythological Enactments," *Journal of Roman Studies* 80 (1990): 44–73.

5. The same idea is present in Jewish thinking about child raising; see John Pilch, " 'Beat His Ribs While He Is Young' (Sir 30:12): A Window on the Mediterranean World," *Biblical Theology Bulletin* 23 (1993): 101–13.

6. For example, Augustine *City of God* 19.16. For the background of this discussion, see Richard P. Saller, *Patriarchy, Property and Death in the Roman Family* (Cam-

bridge: Cambridge University Press, 1994), 144–50; Peter Garnsey, "Sons, Slaves—and Christians," in Beryl Rawson and Paul Weaver, eds., *The Roman Family in Italy: Status, Sentiment, Space* (London: Oxford University Press, 1999), 100–121.

7. Discussion and illustrations in John R. Clarke, *Looking at Lovemaking: Constructions of Sexuality in Roman Art 100 B.C.–A.D. 250* (Berkeley: University of California Press, 1998), esp. chaps. 6 and 7, pp. 145–240. The dust jacket and plate 1 show part of the silver Warren cup, which portrays a young boy peeking around a door to watch two men having sex.

8. Dale Martin, *Slavery as Salvation: The Metaphor of Salvation in Pauline Christianity* (New Haven: Yale University Press, 1990).

9. See Carolyn Osiek and David L. Balch, *Families in the New Testament World: Households and House Churches* (Louisville: Westminster John Knox, 1997), 81–87.

10. Orlando Patterson, *Slavery as Social Death: A Comparative Study* (Cambridge: Harvard University Press, 1982); Jennifer A. Glancy, *Slavery in Early Christianity* (Oxford: Oxford University Press, 2002). For a wider perspective on ancient slavery, see Allen D. Callahan, Richard A. Horsley, and Abraham Smith, eds., *Slavery in Text and Interpretation,* Semeia 83/84 (Atlanta: SBL, 1998).

11. J. Albert Harrill, "The Domestic Enemy: A Moral Polarity of Household Slaves in Early Christian Apologies and Martyrdoms," in David L. Balch and Carolyn Osiek, eds., *Early Christian Families in Context: An Interdisciplinary Dialogue* (Grand Rapids: Eerdmans, 2003), 231–54.

12. Suggested to me by Margaret MacDonald in conversation.

13. Dale B. Martin, "Slave Families and Slaves in Families," in Balch and Osiek, *Early Christian Families in Context,* 207–30.

14. Judith Evans-Grubbs, "'Marriage More Shameful Than Adultery': Slave-Mistress Relationships, 'Mixed Marriages,' and Late Roman Law," *Phoenix* 47 (1993): 125–54.

15. Pliny *Epistle* 10.96.8.

16. Beryl Rawson, "Roman Concubinage and Other *De Facto* Marriages," *Transactions of the American Philological Association* 104 (1974): 279–305.

17. A general consensus has been that, because Philippi was a Roman military colony, thus with a large number of Roman citizen inhabitants, most members of the Christian community there would have been Roman citizens. This consensus has recently been challenged by Peter S. Oakes (*Philippians: From People to Letter* [Cambridge: Cambridge University Press, 2001]), who argues that only the elites of the city were Roman citizens, and both the letter and the general pattern of first-generation members give no evidence of elite membership.

18. See, for example, Richard A. Bauman, *Women in Politics in Ancient Rome* (London: Routledge, 1992); Suzanne Dixon, *The Roman Mother* (London: Routledge, 1988), and *Reading Roman Women* (London: Duckworth, 2001).

19. Maureen Boudreau Flory, "Where Women Precede Men: Factors Influencing the Order of Names in Roman Epitaphs," *Classical Journal* 79/2 (1983–84): 216–24.

20. Jane Gardner, "Legal Stumbling-Blocks for Lower-Class Families in Rome," in Rawson and Weaver, *The Roman Family in Italy,* 35–53; Paul Weaver, "Children of Junian Latins," in *The Roman Family in Italy,* 55–72.

21. Carolyn Osiek, *The Shepherd of Hermas: A Commentary,* Hermeneia (Minneapolis: Fortress, 1999). Some have doubted the historicity of these family details, which is

irrelevant for these purposes. Whether historical or not, the story of the family is typical of its family's social location.

22. For discussion of the literary genre and social function of the household codes, see David L. Balch, "Household Codes," in David E. Aune, ed., *Greco-Roman Literature and the New Testament: Selected Forms and Genres* (Atlanta: Scholars, 1988), 25–50.

23. Some translations here say that it is other people, not the family, who think Jesus is out of his mind. But the Greek has an indefinite "they," and the nearest previous antecedent is *hoi par'autou*, those around Jesus.

24. Andrew S. Jacobs, "A Family Affair: Marriage, Class, and Ethics in the Apocryphal Acts of the Apostles," *Journal of Early Christian Studies* 7 (1999): 105–38.

Chapter Ten. The Eyes Have It:
Slaves in the Communities of Christ-Believers

1. Paul Lawrence Dunbar, "We Wear the Mask," in Ruth Miller, ed., *Black American Literature 1760–Present* (New York: Macmillan, 1971), 303.

2. Richard A. Horsley provides a helpful overview of the subject and scholarship in "The Slave Systems of Classical Antiquity and Their Reluctant Recognition by Modern Scholars," *Semeia* 83/84 (1998): 19–66.

3. M. I. Finley, *Ancient Slavery and Modern Ideology* (New York: Viking, 1980); Orlando Patterson, *Slavery and Social Death: A Comparative Study* (Cambridge: Harvard University Press, 1982); Keith R. Bradley, *Slaves and Masters in the Roman Empire: A Study in Social Control, Revue d'Étude Latines,* vol. 185 (Brussels: Latomus, 1984); M. I. Finley, ed., *Classical Slavery,* Studies in Slave and Post-Slave Societies and Cultures (London: Cass, 2003 [1987]); Keith Hopkins, *Conquerors and Slaves,* Sociological Studies in Roman History 1 (New York: Cambridge University Press, 1978); Page DuBois, *Slaves and Other Objects* (Chicago: University of Chicago Press, 2003).

4. "Public transcripts" and "hidden transcripts" are terms discussed in James C. Scott, *Domination and the Arts of Resistance: Hidden Transcripts* (New Haven: Yale University Press, 1990).

5. Keith Hopkins, "Novel Evidence for Roman Slavery," *Past and Present* 138 (1993): 5. For the proverb "All slaves are enemies," see Seneca, *Moral Letters* 47.5.

6. See the instructive discussion of critical approach in the introduction to DuBois, *Slaves.*

7. This and several other citations below are taken from Jo-Ann Shelton, *As the Romans Did: A Sourcebook on Roman Social History,* 2nd ed. (New York: Oxford University Press, 1998).

8. Finley, *Ancient Slavery and Modern,* 65. See also DuBois, *Slaves and Other Objects,* 4–18.

9. Slavery and *latifundia* are discussed in Naphtali Lewis and Meyer Reinhold, eds., *Roman Civilization: Selected Readings,* Vol. 1: *The Republic and the Augustan Age,* 3rd ed. (New York: Columbia University Press, 1990); and Hopkins, *Slaves and Conquerors.* See also C. P. Jones, "Stigmata: Tattooing and Branding in Greco-Roman Antiquity," *Journal of Roman Studies* 77 (1987): 139–55, and DuBois, "The Slave Body," in *Slaves,* 101–12.

10. Horsley, "The Slave Systems of Classical Antiquity," 36. See also William V. Harris, "Toward a Study of the Roman Slave Trade," in J. H. D'Arms and E. C. Kopff, eds., *The Seaborne Commerce of Ancient Rome: Studies in Archaeology and History* (Rome: American Academy in Rome, 1980), 117–40.

11. See Patterson, *Slavery and Social Death*, 1–38; Holt Parker, "Loyal Slaves and Loyal Wives: The Crisis of the Outsider Within and Roman Exemplum Literature," in Sandra R. Joshel and Sheila Murnagohn, eds., *Women and Slaves in Greco-Roman Culture* (London: Routledge, 2001), 152–73; on the funerary description and Chloe, see Paul Veyne, *The Roman Empire*, trans. Arthur Goldhammer (Cambridge: Harvard University Press, 1997), 85.

12. See the broad survey in Richard A. Horsley and Neil Asher Silberman, *The Message and the Kingdom: How Jesus and Paul Ignited a Revolution and Transformed the Ancient World* (Minneapolis: Fortress, 2002 [1997]).

13. See especially the reconstruction and discussion in Elisabeth Schüssler Fiorenza, *In Memory of Her: A Feminist Theological Reconstruction of Christian Origins* (New York: Crossroad, 1983), 205–18.

14. See especially John Knox, *Philemon among the Letters of Paul* (New York: Abingdon, 1935); Sara C Winter, "Paul's Letter to Philemon," *NTS* (1987): 1–15; Clarice J. Martin, "The Rhetorical Function of Commercial Language in Paul's Letter to Philemon (v. 18)," in Duane F. Watson, ed., *Persuasive Artistry: Studies in Honor of George A. Kennedy* (Sheffield: Sheffield Academic Press, 1991), 321–37; Allen Dwight Callahan, "Paul's Epistle to Philemon: Toward an Alternative Argumentum," *Harvard Theological Review* 86 (1993): 357–76; and idem, *Embassy to Onesimus: The Letter of Paul to Philemon*, The New Testament in Context (Valley Forge, Pa.: Trinity Press International, 1997).

15. See the summary of recent analyses and interpretation in Richard A. Horsley, "Paul and Slavery: A Critical Alternative to Recent Readings," *Semeia* 83/84 (1998): 182–90, and the references there.

16. See further Allen Dwight Callahan, "A Note on 1 Corinthians 7:21," *JITC* 17 (1989–90): 110–14; and the summary of recent discussion in Horsley, "Paul and Slavery," 190–94.

17. This and other texts on the eyes are cited and discussed in Carlin Barton, "Being in the Eyes: Shame and Sight in Ancient Rome," in David Frederick, ed., *The Roman Gaze: Vision, Power, and the Body* (Baltimore: Johns Hopkins University Press, 202), 223–24.

18. Ibid., 223.

19. Ibid.

20. Scott, *Domination*, 37.

21. Richard Wright, *Black Boy: A Record of Childhood and Youth* (New York: Harper & Brothers, 1937), 159; cited in Scott, *Domination*, 39.

22. Helpful here is Dale Martin, "Slave Families and Slaves in Families," in David L. Balch and Carolyn Osiek, eds., *Early Christian Families in Context: An Interdisciplinary Dialogue* (Grand Rapids: Eerdmans, 2003), 207–30.

23. See William Fitzgerald, *Slavery and the Roman Literary Imagination*, Roman Literature and Its Contexts (Cambridge: Cambridge University Press, 2000), 56–57. See also Plutarch, *Moralia* 70E.

24. See Parker, "Loyal Slaves and Loyal Wives."

25. For an illuminating review of how the eyes functioned personally and professionally, see John H. D'Arms, "Slaves at Roman *Convivia*," in William J. Slater, ed., *Dining in a Classical Context* (Ann Arbor: University of Michigan Press, 1991), 171–83; idem, "The Roman *Convivium* and the Idea of Equality," in Oswyn Murray, ed., *Sympotica: A Symposium on the* Symposium" (Oxford: Clarendon, 1990), 308–20.

26. On the distinctive issues enslaved women faced relative to their bodies, see the helpful discussion by Jennifer Glancy, *Slavery in Early Christianity* (New York: Oxford University Press, 2002), 16–24.

27. For a fuller discussion of the specific way in which the experience of enslaved women in Rome mirrors that of black women in the antebellum South, see my essay "Polishing the Unclouded Mirror: A Womanist Reading of *Revelation* 18:3," in David Rhoads, ed., *From Every People and Nation: The Book of Revelation in Intercultural Perspective* (Minneapolis: Fortress, 2005), 82–109.

Chapter Eleven. Injustice or God's Will: Explanations of Poverty in Proto-Christian Communities

1. Peter Garnsey and Richard Saller, *The Roman Empire: Economy, Society, and Culture* (Berkeley: University of California Press, 1987), 125.

2. For further discussions of these economic issues, see M. I. Finley, *The Ancient Economy,* updated ed. (Berkeley: University of California Press, 1999); Garnsey and Saller, *The Roman Empire,* 43–103; and Henri Willy Pleket, "Wirtschaft," in Friedrich Vittinghoff, ed., *Europäische Wirstchafts- und Sozialgeschichte in der römischen Kaiserzeit, Handbuch der europäischen Wirtschafts- und Sozialgeschichte,* vol. 1, 25–160 (Stuttgart: Klett-Cotta, 1990).

3. Steven J. Friesen, "Poverty in Pauline Studies: Beyond the So-called New Consensus," *JSNT* 26 (2004): 323–61.

4. For further discussions of these issues, a good starting point is Anthony J. Blasi, Jean Duhaime, and Paul-André Turcotte, eds., *Handbook of Early Christianity: Social Science Approaches* (New York: AltaMira, 2002).

5. The percentages for PS4 and 5 have question marks to indicate that these are only rough estimates.

6. Adapted from Ekkehard W. Stegemann and Wolfgang Stegemann, *The Jesus Movement: A Social History of Its First Century* (Minneapolis: Fortress, 1999), 81–85. The estimates are based on 2,500 calories per day for an adult male and include nonfood expenses such as housing, clothing, and taxes.

7. The gold ring could indicate an equestrian, but this is unlikely; Luke Timothy Johnson, *The Letter of James,* Anchor Bible 37A (New York: Doubleday, 1995), 221.

8. Garnsey and Saller, *Roman Economy,* 64–112.

9. Elsa Tamez (*The Scandalous Message of James: Faith without Works Is Dead,* rev. ed. [New York: Crossroad, 2002], 25) thinks they are members of the synagogue; David Hutchinson Edgar (*Has God Not Chosen the Poor? The Social Setting of the Epistle of James,* JSNTSup 206 [Sheffield: Sheffield Academic, 2001], 198–99) thinks they are not. For a good brief treatment of the audience's standing, see Richard Bauckham, *James: Wisdom of James, Disciple of Jesus the Sage* (New York: Routledge, 1999), 188–90.

10. See my chapter "The Beast from the Earth: Revelation 13:11-18 and Social Setting," in David Barr, ed., *Readings in the Book of Revelation: A Resource for Students* (Atlanta: Scholars, 2003), 49–64.

11. For an excellent summary of recent interpretation, see Thomas E. Phillips, "Reading Recent Readings of Issues of Wealth and Poverty in Luke and Acts," in *CBR* 1 (2003): 231–69.

12. Dieter Georgi suggests that the author of Acts did not know about the collection; *Remembering the Poor: The History of Paul's Collection for Jerusalem* (Abingdon: Nashville, 1992), 122. Joseph A. Fitzmyer, on the other hand, sees an awareness of the collection; *The Acts of the Apostles,* Anchor Bible 31 (New York: Doubleday, 1998), 692.

13. Here I reject the idea of K. F. Nickle that the author of Acts left out the collection because it might have been deemed illegal by readers; *The Collection: A Study in Paul's Strategy,* Studies in Biblical Theology 48 (London: SCM, 1966), 148–51; followed by C. K. Barrett, *A Critical and Exegetical Commentary on the Acts of the Apostles,* 2 vols. (Edinburgh: T. & T. Clark, 1994), 1:599. If that was the author's concern, he would have also expunged accounts of the community of goods in the Jerusalem assemblies.

14. There is one exception—the peculiar note in 11:27-30 that a prophecy about a worldwide famine caused the Antioch assembly to send a gift to Jerusalem, with Saul and Barnabas making the delivery. A hint of the collection seems to be behind this story, but the narrative in Acts 11 recounts a gift only from the assemblies of Antioch to alleviate hardship in anticipation of a crisis.

15. In Corinth Paul stays with Prisca and Aquila (18:3). In his farewell to the Ephesian elders he plays down sharing by pointing out that he supported himself and his coworkers and coveted no one's silver and gold. Paul presents this practice as a model for others based on the words of Jesus—they must support the weak and give rather than receive (20:33-35; a dominical word about sharing becomes the legitimation for self-sufficiency!). In Jerusalem Paul alludes to the collection as his alms and offerings for his nation (24:17). When he is shipwrecked on Malta, a prominent local family takes him in and gives him gifts when he leaves (28:7-10), and then finally the narrative ends with Paul paying his own keep under house arrest in Rome (28:30-31).

16. A defense of this information can be found in Friesen, "Poverty in Pauline Studies."

17. The information in figures 3–4 was worked out with the assistance of a database of the references to people in literature associated with Paul in the first century. I was able to build the database because of support in the form of a Society of Biblical Literature Technology Grant and a Research Council Grant from the University of Missouri–Columbia.

18. The text does not clearly state that Chloe was a participant in an assembly, but I think that is the most likely inference.

19. Sergius Paulus is in square brackets because the narrative does not clearly mark him as a participant in the assemblies. The text says that he believed and was amazed at the teaching of the Lord, but it does not record a baptism, reception of the Holy Spirit, or belief by his whole house.

20. This profile omits references to assemblies in Judea, Samaria, and Syria, because these were not Pauline assemblies.

21. Carolyn Osiek, *Shepherd of Hermas: A Commentary*, Hermeneia (Minneapolis: Fortress, 1999), 18–20.

22. Osiek mentions three texts in Hermas that talk about the removal of one's wealth; *Rich and Poor in the Shepherd of Hermas: An Exegetical-Social Investigation*, Catholic Biblical Quarterly Monograph Series 15 (Washington, D.C.: Catholic Biblical Association of America, 1983), 51–52. One of the texts deals primarily with the possibility that possessions will cause someone to give in to persecution of believers (*Vision* 3.6.5–7). The other two are enigmatic and do not agree with the general teaching in Hermas (*Similitude* 9.30.5; 9.31.2). These two might indicate that wealthy individuals whose riches are a temptation should remove their wealth, with the implication that those who are not tempted do not need to renounce riches.

23. Osiek, *Shepherd*, 162–64.

24. Osiek argues that Hermas was an upwardly mobile freedman from Rome; *Hermas*, 20–22. James Jeffers thinks that Hermas reflects a lower level of the social hierarchy; *Conflict at Rome: Social Order and Hierarchy in Early Christianity* (Minneapolis: Fortress, 1991), 116–20. For more about wealth in the congregations addressed by this text, see Harry O. Maier, *The Social Setting of the Ministry as Reflected in the Writings of Hermas, Clement and Ignatius*, Dissertations SR 1 (Waterloo, Ont.: Wilfrid Laurier University Press, 1991), 59–65.

Chapter Twelve. Prophets, Prophetic Movements, and the Voices of Women

1. Dieter Georgi, "Who Is the True Prophet?" *Harvard Theological Review* 79 (1986): 110–26.

2. See the classic studies by Vittorio Lanternari, *The Religions of the Oppressed: A Study of Modern Messianic Cults*, trans. Lisa Sergio (New York: Knopf, 1963); Anthony F. C. Wallace with Sheila C. Steen, *The Death and Rebirth of the Seneca* (New York: Knopf, 1969); and Bengt Sundkler, *Bantu Prophets in South Africa* (London: Oxford University Press, 1961).

3. Ammia of Philadelphia is listed as an authoritative prophet by the church historian Eusebius (*Ecclesiastical History* 5.17.3). Karen King includes Mary Magdalene as a prophet and prophetic revealer in "Prophetic Power and Women's Authority: The Case of the Gospel of Mary (Magdalene)," in Beverly Mayne Kienzle and Pamela J. Walker, eds., *Women Preachers and Prophets through Two Millennia of Christianity* (Berkeley: University of California Press, 1998).

4. See studies by David Aune, *Prophecy in Early Christianity and the Ancient Mediterranean World* (Grand Rapids: Eerdmans, 1983); Theodore Crone, *Early Christian Prophecy: A Study of Its Origin and Function* (Baltimore: St. Mary's University Press, 1973); Christopher Forbes, *Prophecy and Inspired Speech in Early Christianity and Its Hellenistic Environment* (Tübingen: Mohr Siebeck, 1995); Eugene Boring, "Prophecy (Early Christian)," in David Noel Freedman et al., eds., *Anchor Bible Dictionary*, 6 vols. (New York: Doubleday, 1992), 5:496.

5. Translation from Carolyn Osiek, *The Shepherd of Hermas: A Commentary*, Hermeneia (Minneapolis: Fortress, 1999). Other translations used are as follows: for

the *Didache,* Kurt Niederwimmer, *The Didache: A Commentary,* Hermeneia (Minneapolis: Fortress, 1998); Ignatius, Bart Ehrmann, trans., *The Apostolic Fathers,* vol. 1, LCL (Cambridge: Harvard University Press, 2003); *Acts of Paul* and the *Ascension of Isaiah* by R. McL. Wilson in E. Hennecke and W. Schneemelcher, eds., *New Testament Apocrypha,* vol. 2, rev. ed. (Louisville: Westminster John Knox, 1989); translation of "Montanist" Oracles by Ross S. Kraemer, *Maenads, Martyrs, Matrons, Monastics: A Sourcebook on Women's Religions in the Greco-Roman World* (Philadelphia: Fortress, 1988). Translations of Josephus texts by Hanson in *Bandits, Prophets, Messiahs.*

6. Richard Horsley develops this typology of two distinct forms of Israelite prophecy in "'Like One of the Prophets of Old': Two Types of Popular Prophets at the Time of Jesus," *CBQ* 47 (1985): 435–63; and Richard A. Horsley with John S. Hanson, *Bandits, Prophets, and Messiahs: Popular Movements at the Time of Jesus* (Harrisburg, Pa.: Trinity Press International, 1999 [1985]), chap 4. A different typology is proposed by Crone, *Early Christian Prophecy.*

7. So Antoinette Clark Wire, *The Corinthian Women Prophets: A Reconstruction through Paul's Rhetoric* (Minneapolis: Fortress, 1990). Her arguments for seeing most of the prophets as women include the silencing of women in 1 Cor. 14:33-35 as well as a sophisticated rhetorical criticism of Paul's argumentative strategy in 1 Corinthians 5–7, particularly in 7:1-7. Paul's seeming use of a "rhetoric of equality" in saying that women have rights over their husbands' bodies, just as the husbands have rights over their wives' bodies (1 Cor. 7:3-4), has the effect of curtailing women's authority. It seems highly likely that Paul is appealing to women who are withdrawing from marriage and sexual relations with his plea that they resume sexual relations in order to act as a buffer against men's uncontrollable sexual drives (sexual "immorality," a specter he had raised in the previous sections of his argument specifically related to men; see 1 Cor. 5:1-5, 6:12-18). See also Margaret Macdonald, "Women Holy in Body and Spirit: The Social Setting of 1 Corinthians 7," *New Testament Studies* 36 (1990) 161–81.

8. So Richard A. Horsley, *1 Corinthians,* Abingdon New Testament Commentaries (Nashville: Abingdon, 1998).

9. Because the declaration that "women should be silent in the assemblies" appears in some early manuscripts of 1 Corinthians as 1 Cor. 14:34-35, but in other manuscripts after 1 Cor. 14:40, some scholars suggest that this prohibition of women's prophesying does not go back to Paul himself but is an insertion into the letter by later Pauline writers using Paul as their authority to silence women.

10. So Wire, *Corinthian Women Prophets,* 184. On the inconsistency between the silencing of women prophets and Paul's overall anti-imperial critique, see Cynthia Briggs Kittredge, "Corinthian Women Prophets and Paul's Argumentation in 1 Corinthians," in Richard A. Horsley, ed., *Paul and Politics: Ekklesia, Israel, Imperium, Interpretation* (Harrisburg, Pa.: Trinity Press International, 2000), 103–9.

11. See Allan D. Callahan, "The Language of the Apocalypse," *Harvard Theological Review* 88 (1995): 453–70.

12. Elisabeth Schüssler Fiorenza, *Revelation: Vision of a Just World,* Proclamation Commentary (Minneapolis: Fortress, 1991) 36; and idem, "The Words of Prophecy: Reading the Apocalypse Theologically" in Steve Moyise, ed., *Studies in the Book of Revelation* (Edinburgh: T. & T. Clark, 2001), 1–19.

13. See Barbara R. Rossing, *The Choice between Two Cities: Whore, Bride and Empire in the Apocalypse*, Harvard Theological Studies 48 (Harrisburg, Pa.: Trinity Press International, 1999).

14. Pablo Richard, *Apocalypse: A People's Commentary on the Book of Revelation* (Maryknoll, N.Y.: Orbis, 1995), 77.

15. Richard Bauckham, *The Theology of the Book of Revelation* (Cambridge: Cambridge University Press, 1993), 120.

16. So Richard Bauckham, who also proposes the possible parallel of Revelation's circle of prophets to the model described in *The Ascension of Isaiah*. See his important discussion of these traditions in *The Climax of Prophecy: Studies on the Book of Revelation* (Edinburgh: T. & T. Clark, 1993), 86–88. For Papias's description, see Eusebius, *Ecclesiastical History* 3.39.9; for Polycrates, see Eusebius, *Ecclesiastical History* 5.24.2. Cf. also the links suggested between Revelation and earlier prophecy in Palestine by Crone, *Early Christian Prophecy*. For discussion of John's prophetic circle, see David Aune, "The Social Matrix of the Apocalypse of John," *Biblical Research* 26 (1981): 27.

17. So Anne Jensen, *God's Self-Confident Daughters: Early Christianity and the Liberation of Women* (Louisville: Westminster John Knox, 1996) 139. Jensen contrasts *Didache* 10.7, 13, 15 with *Ap. Const.* 7.26.6, 29, 31.

18. So Elisabeth Schüssler Fiorenza, *The Book of Revelation: Justice and Judgment* (Philadelphia: Fortress, 1985), 143.

19. Paul Duff, *Who Rides the Beast? Prophetic Rivalry and the Rhetoric of Crisis in the Churches of the Apocalypse* (Cambridge: Cambridge University Press, 2001), 127. Steven Friesen disputes the idea that there were wealthy people in the communities, as well as the claim that Jezebel's group is the same as the Nicolaitians. See his "Satan's Throne, Imperial Cults and the Social Settings of Revelation," *JSNT* 27 (March 2005): 351–73.

20. For this reason Tina Pippin (among others) warns that the Book of Revelation is dangerous for women, in *Death and Desire: The Rhetoric of Gender in the Apocalypse of John* (Louisville: Westminster John Knox, 1992).

21. Schüssler Fiorenza, *Revelation: Vision of a Just World*, 133.

22. Some labeled the movement according to geographical roots as "Cataphrygians" or "Phrygians." The name "Montanism" originated in the fourth century as a pejorative label given by Cyril of Alexandria. As a construct of ancient and modern heresiologists it should be avoided, as explained by Laura Nasrallah, *An Ecstasy of Folly: Prophecy and Authority in Early Christianity*, Harvard Theological Studies 52 (Cambridge: Harvard University Press, 2003).

23. Archaeological explorations have recently identified the probable sites of Pepuza and Timion, another town prominent in the New Prophecy movement, near Susuzoren in central Turkey. See William Tabernee, "Portals of the Montanist New Jerusalem: Discovery of Pepouza and Tymion," *Journal of Early Christian Studies* 11 (2003): 87–93.

24. Christine Trevett, *Montanism: Gender, Authority, and the New Prophecy* (Cambridge: Cambridge University Press, 1996), 42–45.

25. Translation in Kraemer, *Maenads*, 226.

26. Ute Eisen, *Women Officeholders in Early Christianity: Epigraphical and Literary Studies*, trans. Linda M. Maloney (Collegeville, Minn.: Liturgical, 2000), 69.

27. King, "Prophetic Power," 29.

INDEX